D1595325

The Rise of Charismatic Catholicism in Latin America

UNIVERSITY PRESS OF FLORIDA

Florida A&M University, Tallahassee
Florida Atlantic University, Boca Raton
Florida Gulf Coast University, Ft. Myers
Florida International University, Miami
Florida State University, Tallahassee
New College of Florida, Sarasota
University of Central Florida, Orlando
University of Florida, Gainesville
University of North Florida, Jacksonville
University of South Florida, Tampa
University of West Florida, Pensacola

THE RISE OF CHARISMATIC CATHOLICISM IN LATIN AMERICA

EDWARD L. CLEARY

University Press of Florida

Gainesville · Tallahassee · Tampa · Boca Raton

Pensacola · Orlando · Miami · Jacksonville · Ft. Myers · Sarasota

The publication of this book is made possible
in part by Providence College.

16 15 14 13 12 11   6 5 4 3 2 1

LIBRARY OF CONGRESS CATALOGING-IN-PUBLICATION DATA
Cleary, Edward L.
The rise of charismatic Catholicism in Latin America / Edward L. Cleary.
p. cm.
Includes bibliographical references and index.
ISBN 978-0-8130-3608-3 (alk. paper)
1. Pentecostalism—Catholic Church—History. 2. Catholic Church—Latin
America—History. 3. Pentecostalism—Latin America—History.
4. Latin America—Church history. I. Title.
BX1426.3.C55 2011
269.088'2828—dc22   2011000936

The University Press of Florida is the scholarly publishing agency for the
State University System of Florida, comprising Florida A&M University,
Florida Atlantic University, Florida Gulf Coast University, Florida Interna-
tional University, Florida State University, New College of Florida, Univer-
sity of Central Florida, University of Florida, University of North Florida,
University of South Florida, and University of West Florida.

University Press of Florida
15 Northwest 15th Street
Gainesville, FL 32611-2079
http://www.upf.com

In memory of James Colum Burke, leader, mentor, brother

CONTENTS

PREFACE

Pentecostalism and its Catholic counterpart, Charismatics, have become worldwide trends. This was confirmed by the Templeton Initiative, which made $3.5 million available to universities to research these movements. That initiative followed the groundbreaking study by the Pew Forum on Religion and Public Life, "Spirit and Power: A 10-Country Survey of Pentecostals," which included three Latin American countries.

Attention to global religious trends became necessary for informed citizens and foreign world diplomats when it became clear that Islam and other religions were thriving and were having both violent and subtle impacts on the developed world. World Christianity too has been growing at an amazing—and unpredicted—rate. Pentecostals and Charismatics form the center of growth, which has taken place in the global south and east, away from the ancient centers of Christendom in Europe.

Gilles Kepel described this phenomenon for European readers in his *Revanche de Dieu* [Revenge of God] and Philip Jenkins did so for North American readers in his *The Next Christendom: The Coming of Global Christianity*. His book received wide attention in the secular press and is held by most academic libraries in the United States. Jenkins noted that "the explosive southward expansion of Christianity in Africa, Asia, and Latin America has barely registered on western consciousness."[1]

While much of the attention of journalists and scholars in the last decade went to the Middle East, Africa, and Asia, Latin America has shown remarkable growth in numbers. Catholic Charismatics there, for example, are estimated to number 73 million of the some 200 million Catholic Charismatics in the world.

This book aims to impress upon readers with a Western consciousness that Latin America and its major Catholic renewal movement, the Charismatics, have grown dramatically in numbers and influence, changing to some unknown extent the face of Christianity there. The movement also has implications for the United States and Canada since migrants from Latin America have come in a widening stream to those countries.

Within Latin America, Catholic Charismatics dwarfed Protestant Pentecostals, being more than twice their numbers. But Catholic Charismatics in Latin America received far less attention than Protestant Pentecostals for reasons that have not been clear to me.

Scholars of Latin America who reside in the United States, for the most part, do not perceive Charismatics; they are invisible to all but a handful of North American scholars, despite forty years of high visibility. In Brazil, Father Marcelo Rossi is a celebrity seen by millions on television and in movies and he has been a top-selling singer. Other Brazilian priest-performers were featured in various media and they, too, sell impressive amounts of musical CDs and videos. In Colombia Minuto de Dios Charismatic efforts have been part of the national public consciousness for decades. In the Dominican Republic when Canadian Father Emiliano Tardif, the great Charismatic leader died, a national day of mourning was declared for him by the country's president. These personalities—and many others—have been prominent faces in secular newspapers and television. Yet North American scholars have overlooked them.

Scholars in Latin America have been much more attentive to the movement, but they tend to limit themselves to what they see within their own national boundaries. Brazilian scholars, especially anthropologists, not only study Catholic Charismatics but add significantly to information and theories about them. Mexican social scientists have investigated the Charismatic renewal not only in Mexico but also in the United States by looking into Mexican religious migrants who are Charismatic. Argentine social scientists also have joined in. These pathbreaking efforts are not a surprise since these large countries have well-developed social science enterprises. Brazil, for example, has the third largest organization of anthropologists in the world.

Moreover, the countries in which these researchers have worked have been zealous about making available on the Internet the findings of their investigations, including research in the field of religion. Brazil has been outstanding in posting its academic work on the Internet. Mexico and Argentina have been a bit less ambitious in making academic work accessible. But the fact remains that research on Latin American Charismatics is readily available in Spanish or Portuguese.

I grew up as a young professional, a priest, and a social scientist, alongside the birth and flowering of the Catholic Charismatic Renewal in Latin America. But I did not become a Charismatic. When an African scholar at a meeting of the Oxford Group on World Christianity asked me why I did not join the movement, I did not have a ready reply beyond citing cognitive dissonance: the movement seemed too far from my own values and preferences. I am an outsider who has lived alongside the movement, at first aware of uncommon growth and then fascinated by what grew into a giant living organism.

In the late 1960s I returned to Bolivia after completing the first segment of doctoral studies at the University of Chicago. From then until the present, I have interviewed major figures in the Charismatic renewal as well as countless participants. I have also observed at close hand the small prayer meetings, large conferences, and public worship of the movement in Latin America.

Francis MacNutt, one of the founders of the global movement, provided me with contacts for Charismatic leaders in many countries, including all twenty-one Latin American countries. Given the political chaos in Haiti, I relied on contacts in Florida and the mid-Atlantic states for information about the movement there. Francis MacNutt sent copies of original documents, which were especially valuable since there are few archives of the movement and, rarer still, records of the early periods.

In the early 1980s, I came to the realization that it was not helpful to write about the Catholic Church in Latin America without also having well-researched views on other religious groups in Latin America: Protestants, indigenous, African. The whole story of religion had to be told. Otherwise the picture would be distorted. One certainly cannot understand, say, Guatemala without Catholicism, Protestantism, and indigenous religion being part of the picture.

This decision cost me some years of study but repaid the efforts with fuller understanding of the religious impulse. I read some two hundred accounts of Protestant missionary history at Ivy League divinity school libraries and at the evangelical seminaries of San Jose, Costa Rica; Buenos Aires; and Rio Piedras, Puerto Rico. This in turn brought me to the study of Pentecostalism and opened a whole other chapter of academic life during the 1990s. The leap from Pentecostals to Charismatics was not great since they are family members. My participation in recent international congresses on global religion provided evidence that there was now a ready audience for works that look at Catholic Charismatics. The following then is an account based on uncommonly long acquaintance with the movement and key members.

ACKNOWLEDGMENTS

I have lived alongside the Charismatic movement, observing at first hand its beginnings in the Andean world, interviewing participants in all countries of Latin America and most regions of the United States, and listening to countless criticisms of the movement by Latin Americans and by U.S. theologians and social scientists.

In the process I acquired many debts to generous Charismatics, such as Francis MacNutt, Ralph Rogawski, Helen Raycraft, Patrick Rearden, and James Burke, who sent their written memoirs and documents of important meetings.

Social scientists and historians, such as Virginia Garrard-Burnett, Kenneth Serbin, Catherine LeGrand, Emelio Betances, Timothy Steigenga, Daniel Levine, Manuel Vasquez, Anna Petersen, Anthony Gill, Andrew Chesnut, and John Burdick, aided at various times by their comments. The Oxford Group on World Christianity, chaired by Lamin Sanneh, and the Yale-Edinburgh Group on World Christianity, both held at Yale Divinity School, allowed me to view more clearly the place of the Latin American movement within a global context. The members of the Center for Religion and Culture at the University of Southern California also provided a broad perspective on Pentecostalism.

The Day Missions Collection at the Yale Divinity Library and Martha Smalley provided a steady stream of published information on the movement. Early conversations with Cecília Mariz and Maria das Dores Machado in Brazil, Daniel Míguez in Argentina, and many others in Latin America were invaluable. The staff at the library of the Colegio Pio Latinoamericano and the International Catholic Charismatic Center in Rome aided me in many ways.

This book was written at the invitation of Amy Gorelick of the University Press of Florida and was supported substantially by Providence College and its academic vice-president, Hugh Lena.

INTRODUCTION

Latin America in the twenty-first century is not the region we thought we knew based on its long and slowly changing history. Nowhere are the changes more evident than in the field of religion. While large numbers of Latin Americans are now Protestant and many practice religion in soaring Pentecostal services and have done so for decades, the largest and most important shift has taken place within the Catholic Church.

To the surprise of many observers, the fastest growing movement in the Catholic Church in Latin America is the Catholic Charismatic Renewal (CCR). With estimates of some 73 million adherents, Latin America leads all Catholic regions of the world in this trend.[1] The numbers of this sector of Catholicism are greater than the 40 million or so Latin American evangelicals.[2] The movement is also changing the character of Catholicism in Latin America.[3]

Often called Catholic Pentecostals, Charismatics appear to be the Catholic Church's imitation of its stiffest challenger in the region, Protestant Pentecostals, who number some 25–35 million members, perhaps two-thirds of the Latin American evangelicals. Many Pentecostals are former indifferent Catholics who became active Christians they believe through the influence of the Holy Spirit.

Pentecostalization is said to be taking over the region, as well as becoming a major force in the world, with commonly accepted estimates of 500 million members, second to the Catholic Church's one billion members.[4] While the extent of Pentecostalization of Latin America is sometimes exaggerated, the continent is moving to a different style of worship and way of belonging than it had for the first five centuries of Christianity after 1492.

In the 1940s when he surveyed the Catholic Church in Latin America, John Considine, the influential Maryknoll priest, found a highly uneven situation.[5] Considine was assessing where American missionaries should go instead of China, which was then closing to Americans. He found strength in the churches of Mexico and Colombia and great weaknesses in vast areas of the Andes and Central America. The churches in Bolivia and Guatemala were dying. Few native priests could be found and seminaries were almost empty. Both countries will receive special attention in this volume.

In general he saw a dangerous situation: very large numbers of Catholics had only minimal ties to the church and weak knowledge of the faith. They were susceptible to being gathered up by evangelicals or Marxists. Considine sounded the alarm to the universal church. The alarm was answered by a crusade of missionaries to Latin America from North America and Europe in the 1960s and 1970s.[6]

In 2007 most media that covered Pope Benedict's first visit to Latin America found, according to their lights, that Latin America was a changed continent. Millions of marginal Catholics had become Pentecostals. The Catholic Church, they wrote, was no longer the only sizable church. While the losses were real, what the reporters missed was that the Catholic Church in Latin America was sharing in the religious revival that was sweeping through the region.[7] The Catholic Charismatic Renewal was a major element in this revival with a very large number of Catholics.

In a word, the religious landscape of Latin America changed drastically from the monolithic presence of the Catholic Church to a wide and diverse universe that includes African-based, indigenous, Mormon, Pentecostal, and Catholicisms of various tendencies. David Smilde has written to much approval that it is not useful to write about Catholicism when there are clearly (for many observers, at least) many Catholicisms.[8] There may be underlying unity beneath these various Catholic tendencies, but effort will be needed to see below the vibrant and confusing surface of contemporary religious practice.

Religion has not been everybody's deeply held commitment. Many men and women used to hide their true state of conscience by telling parents and poll-takers that they were still religious when, in fact, they did not assent to religious beliefs or practices. Increasingly, beginning in the 1990s in Latin America, respondents have tended less to hide their lack of religion. This openness is also part of the new face of religion in Latin America: there is greater freedom not to be religiously affiliated or practicing. The pool of respondents who say they have "no religion" has been growing year by year.[9] Pollsters don't know why. Many of these respondents may be ex-evangelicals, as suggested by Kurt Bowen.[10] Or, perhaps these respondents were persons who seldom or never attended Catholic or evangelical churches and felt free to respond "no religion" to poll-takers.

There is also a wide range of Latin American persons occupying the ground from no religion to highly religious: very large numbers of Latin Americans have been what David Martin has described as the religiously relaxed, the indifferent, many of whom attend Catholic or Pentecostal churches only on rare occasions, at least at birth and death.[11] Cuban Catholics, with their 2 percent of weekly church attenders under Castro and 4 percent under Batista, were only the best known of non-practicing groups among Latin Americans. In Chile, where Pentecostal churches have been established for about one hundred years, 38 percent of Pentecostals seldom or never attended church, according to a survey reported in 1991.[12]

Further the renewal itself was part of a global phenomenon. Pentecostalism, as a variant of Protestant Christianity, swept across the globe in the twentieth century and into the twenty-first. Catholic Charismatics are, in fact, Catholic Pentecostals, and are part of a later wave of this global expansion.[13] Pentecostalism is a religious innovation created in the United States with roots in the Holiness movement of the nineteenth century.

The Holiness movement and revival traditions grow out of a centuries-long impulse among ordinary Christians toward a deeper spiritual life, beyond mere church attendance to contact with God. In European Protestantism after the Reformation this impulse often was guided by Pietists. They accepted as foundations the seeking of personal experience of God, commencing with a new birth by the Holy Spirit; holding the conviction that experience leads to reforming lives; and living within a community, a community taking a stand against a corrupt world. Communities thus took on a *contra mundum* cast. To a remarkable degree the first wave of Pentecostals, called Classical Pentecostals, in the early twentieth century mirrored these characteristics.

The Pietist movement waxed and waned through the seventeenth, eighteenth, and nineteenth centuries. The impulse to "a higher life" took various forms in continental Europe. In England and the United States the Wesleyan tradition (that of John and Charles Wesley) gained special relevance. Those within the Pietist tradition fought not only against declining church attendance but also against a perceived loss of religious fervor in older churches. Revivals, camp meetings, retreats, full-throated hymn singing, and testimonies were employed.

In the United States in the nineteenth century, religious leaders were anxious about the spiritual condition of the partially de-Christianized Yankees (settled and godless) and frontier types (unsettled and godless). The Civil War was perceived as taking its moral toll, accentuating secularism, moral decline, and indifference to religion (if not to God). Through camp meetings and revivals, circuit riders, evangelists, and pastors led American Protestants to a fuller holiness.

Since, in the view of some participants, the older churches (older by one or two generations) from which they came, mostly Methodist or Baptist, had grown lifeless, innovators broke away to form new groups. After the Civil War a growing evolution of Holiness and revival teaching centered upon the Pentecost event. Holiness and revival participants used scriptures as their written guides. In their search they read the accounts of the early Christians in the Acts of the Apostles.

A number of scholars accept William Menzies's description: "The Pentecostal movement is that group of sects within the Christian church which is characterized by the belief that the occurrence mentioned in *Acts* 2 on the day of Pentecost not only signaled the birth of the church, but described an experience available to believers in all ages."[14]

In brief, Pentecostals are churches founded mostly in the early part of the twentieth century. They often are connected to foundational events, such as Charles Parham's spiritual revival in Topeka, Kansas (1901), and the subsequent revival at the Azusa Street Mission in Los Angeles (1906–1909). These are not arcane events in North American history but landmarks for many of the fastest growing churches in the United States and the world. Classical Pentecostal groups include the Assemblies of God, the Church of God (Cleveland, Tenn.), the Church of God in Christ, and the International Church of the Foursquare Gospel. These groups and their schools, such as Oral Roberts University or Lee College, may be unknown to many readers, yet Pentecostals are content to continue unnoticed in their counterculture, growing and changing to meet the times on their own terms.

Charismatics represent a later wave of religion attentive to the Holy Spirit and his work in individuals and churches. Charismatics, by a commonly accepted definition, are those congregations within established denominations that are open to Pentecostal influence, along with itinerant ministries and para-church organizations outside of these structures.[15] This movement came to national attention in the United States through a landmark Pentecostal-like event in Van Nuys, California, in 1960 and the work of Dennis Bennett, within the Episcopal Church. Individuals within Protestant, Roman Catholic, and Orthodox churches quickly spread a "Charismatic renewal" within their traditions. By 1972 the movement had affected key figures, such as Cardinal Léon-Joseph Suenens. Cardinal Suenens participated in the reform movement of Vatican Council II and acted as a mentor and integrator of international networks of leaders of the Catholic Charismatic Renewal. Many independent groups outside the classical Pentecostal tradition also grew up in the crazy quilt of religious changes taking place in the 1960s and 1970s.

Thus Charismatics are a later, "second-wave" development within Pentecostalism. They differ from Classical Pentecostals, such as the Assemblies of God, and from third-wave neo-Charismatics (the latter to be found especially between the independent and indigenous churches),[16] in ways that will be shown later. As noted, the Charismatic movement began in an Episcopal church in California where Dennis Bennett was its pastor, and then it spread quickly through Methodists and Presbyterians and Catholics in a matter of a few years in the 1960s. That history was commonly accepted by historians of the movement, but further research has shown multiple beginnings at various points in the world. Phenomena similar to Bennett's experience in California occurred in Brazil where Baptist pastors were preaching spirit-baptism in the late 1950s, as were black Anglicans in South Africa a decade earlier.

The Charismatic movement, again frequently called the second wave of Pentecostalism, gained many adherents in Latin America. The differences between Pentecostals and Charismatics are considerably less than their similarities, according to Peter Hocken, the theologian-historian of the Charismatic movement.[17] These shared characteristics include focus on Jesus, praise, love of the Bible, awareness of evil, spiritual gifts, and eschatological expectation. The Protestant wing of the Charismatic movement had a complex history in Latin America. In a general way, mainline Protestant churches in the region did not welcome the movement. The Protestant scholar Paul Freston noted that by 1975 in Brazil there were schisms caused by Charismatics in all historical Protestant denominations.[18] Protestant Charismatics thereby flowed into independent churches where impressive growth took place. In fact, spectacular growth in Argentina led by Carlos Annacondia, Omar Cabrera, and others brought banner-headline attention to Protestant Charismatic preachers for a few years. Eventually many of the historical Protestant churches allowed an opening to the movement and a number of congregations became more Pentecostalized in their worship style and preaching.

Jack Hayford and David Moore described what followed in this second wave as part of the "Charismatic [Twentieth] Century" in their book of the same name and showed an enduring impact of the Azuza Street revival. Despite close similarities between the two groups, observers believe that the distinction between Pentecostals and Charismatics, here meaning Protestants, is useful in Latin America. First, both pose strong challenges to Catholics and it is worth knowing why. Second, Protestant Charismatics, not Protestant Pentecostals, have been instrumental in fostering the Catholic Charismatic Renewal at various occasions. Third, the impetus for Christian unity—a spark that has barely flickered in Latin America—may come from the Charismatic sector, Catholics and Protestants alike. Hocken, a Catholic priest and a former executive secretary of the Society for Pentecostal Studies, sees clear evidence of movement in that direction.[19]

Charismatics place less emphasis on speaking in tongues, do not share Pentecostals' world-denying Holiness origins, typically belong to the middle and lower classes (although many are members of the upper class or the cultural elite), and have expressive lifestyles, as in music preferences. Charismatics, as Freston notes, retain their basic identities, with lifestyles frowned on by Pentecostals and older evangelicals.[20]

The Historical Place of the Catholic Charismatic Renewal

The Catholic Charismatic Renewal did not flow directly from the documents of Vatican Council II (the major milestone in the last four hundred years of the Catholic Church at least as it changed the church in Latin America).[21] Rather the renewal appeared in the church at roughly the same time and was able to enshroud itself in selected themes and emphases from the council (while apparently ignoring other themes). Because popes called the council "A New Pentecost" and Cardinal Suenens and others presented views during the council that called attention to the Holy Spirit, some Catholic Charismatic Web sites cite Vatican Council II as the starting point of the movement. But this is an exaggeration. After the council many observers remembered simply that the council brought greater attention in public worship to the Holy Spirit and that terminology within the Catholic Church changed from Holy Ghost to Holy Spirit.[22]

Looked at from the point of view of the papacy and the Vatican, probably the strongest statement of support for the renewal occurred at the Pentecost 1998 meeting in Rome of new movements in the Catholic Church when the impact of the renewal was clear in the numbers of participants and in Pope John Paul II's address to the group, which emphasized the importance of the Charismatic dimension that had been restored to the church. The long pontificate of John Paul II (1978–2005) brought a strong measure of affirmation for the movement and protection from the renewal's opponents inside and outside the Vatican. Among many signs of support for the renewal, John Paul issued an encyclical in 1986, *Dominum et Vivicantem: On the Holy Spirit in the Life of the Church and the World*. In 1993, after eight years of consultation, the Vatican officially recognized the central coordinating body and renamed it the International Catholic Charismatic Renewal Services. John Paul also named a famed Charismatic priest, Raniero Cantalamessa, as preacher to the papal household.

Conflict with Liberation Theology

Throughout much of its almost fifty years of history, the Catholic Charismatic Renewal has been seen by many Latin Americans, including many of its principal theologians and public intellectuals, as a direct challenge to liberation theology. The latter was thought by them to be the embodiment of the spirit of Vatican Council II and a treasured Latin American creation, one that men and women had died for, standing up to military dictators, Amazon land robbers, and rapacious global corporations.

The following pages will allow readers to judge whether a strong dichotomy exists between Charismaticism, portrayed by many as inward looking and deeply conservative, and liberationism, believed to be the embodiment of social justice and human rights. Craig Prentiss, a theologian at the Jesuit Rockhurst University who was trained at the University of Chicago, wrote in a major Pentecostal publication: "The Catholic Charismatic Renewal's conservative flavor has made the movement an effective tool in John Paul's struggle against liberation theology."[23]

Liberation theology and social justice seemed synonymous. To laypersons and priests in Latin America who were working to revitalize the

Catholic Church in the 1950s and 1960s, Vatican Council II (1962–65) and the Latin American Bishops Conference (CELAM) held at Medellín in 1968 seemed to place the church on the side of social justice and concern for the poor. But to Europeans using a geopolitical perspective that emphasis was seen as dangerous because of what seemed like a close affinity with Marxism.

David Martin, a member of the British Academy and a proponent of a general theory of secularization, saw liberation theology as part of "the openings to the Left" that secured "a qualified validation in the Catholic Church which at least for a time made good sense in terms of ecclesiastical geopolitics.... The Church needed to pre-empt the appeal of Pentecostalism or Marxism or both together."[24]

But, Martin said, the "problems of opening to the Left were several, in that the initial phases of liberation theology seemingly threatened the basis of hierarchical control," as in the case of the "People's Church" in Nicaragua.[25] Nicaragua became a battleground for just such conflict, one that pitted proponents of liberation theology against adherents of the Catholic Charismatic Renewal. Although the battleground in Nicaragua was, in fact, tiny and the crisis quickly passed from public view, so that references to it actually happening are difficult to locate, a great symbolic battle did take place.

The cast of characters involved in the Nicaraguan conflict could have come from a graphic novel and included the then Pizza King of the World, Tom Monaghan, the founder of Domino's Pizza. The conflict centered on what was called the "People's Church," a loose amalgam of Catholic and Protestant leftists and groups from Christian base communities, posed against conservative Catholics. Some of the conservatives were organized into Catholic Charismatic groups and were supported by Monaghan, who brought in, it was said, persons and educational programs from the Word of God Charismatic covenant community at Ann Arbor, Michigan (Monaghan's birthplace).

Cardinal Miguel Obando y Bravo of Managua supported initial efforts in the 1970s to overthrow the ruling dictatorial Somoza family by Sandinists and other rebels. But after the overthrow, Cardinal Obando soon opposed the course of the Nicaraguan revolutionary government (Frente Sandinista de Liberación Nacional, or FSLN), whose ideology was—by common agreement of scholars—nationalist, Marxist, and Christian.[26]

The Sandinists held the reins of power and were implementing a national educational program that looked like the imposition of Cuban-style socialism. The conflict for the church involved a few priests who held positions in the revolutionary government (contrary to the expressed wishes of Pope John Paul II, who scolded Father Ernesto Cardenal, the minister of culture, in public). The FSLN represented an unacceptable encroachment of Marxism, for the pope and many others, who were then greatly concerned about the domination of Russians in Eastern Europe and elsewhere.

The FSLN lost the presidency in the general elections of 1990. Violeta Barrios de Chamorro, the new president, brought into her government conservative Catholics to help govern the country during her term, which lasted until 1997. In the process of reforming the national educational curriculum, members of the Catholic Charismatic Renewal, again tutored by Catholic Charismatics from Ann Arbor, attempted, it was alleged, to impose a deeply conservative bent to the content of various courses for elementary and high school.[27]

The conflict was largely forgotten when the Soviet Union imploded in 1989 and the Nicaraguan economy collapsed under siege from the Reagan administration. But many Latin American observers and scholars were left with the strong impression that the Catholic Charismatic Renewal was the chosen instrument by the Vatican to oppose liberation theology and to close the opening to the Left that liberationists supported.

As the Charismatic renewal gained adherents all over Latin America in the 1980s, a few liberation theologians spoke out against Charismaticism. Leonardo Boff, one of the most prominent at the time, saw little in the movement to praise and spoke strongly against it. The other top tier liberation theologians—Gustavo Gutierrez, Juan Luis Segundo, Jon Sobrino—were mostly mute.

In general, many historians, whether religious or secular, have followed this lead of non-attention. However, Brazilian, Mexican, and Argentine researchers have devoted considerable attention to Catholic Charismatics since the 1990s, as noted in the preface.

In sum, then, in most countries of Latin America the Charismatic movement "was initially repulsed by historical Protestant churches" in the region but flowed into independent churches, according to Paul Freston, a Protestant scholar.[28] By contrast the Charismatic renewal flourished in the Catholic Church in Latin America. Indeed, it has flourished there more than in most other regions of the world, including Africa (for the time being).

Beginnings of the Catholic Charismatic Renewal

In treating the origins of the Catholic Charismatic movement, almost all institutional histories recount its beginning at an event at Duquesne University in Pittsburgh in March 1967. This is somewhat misleading in Latin America because a similar event was occurring in Bogotá, Colombia, at that time.[29] It is also misleading because a major figure in the United States and in initiating the movement in Latin America was Francis Mac-Nutt, who was not drawn into the movement by ties to the experience in Duquesne.[30]

At both Bogotá and Duquesne, participants said that they experienced baptism in the Holy Spirit and spoke in tongues. Baptism in the Spirit and speaking in tongues were at the time considered the threshold experiences for entry into the Charismatic movement. Some have described these as peak spiritual experiences; that is, a detachment from pedestrian concerns and a time of wonder and awe.[31]

Duquesne has been recognized by movement officials as the starting point for the movement because the first Catholic Charismatic prayer group was formed there in early March 1967. The key foundational event was what came to be known as the Duquesne Weekend, a faculty-student retreat during which various participants believed they experienced a baptism of the Holy Spirit.

Within a relatively short time, the principal centers of influence for the spread of the movement were established at the University of Notre Dame and at Ann Arbor, Michigan, where the Word of God lay community was formed under the leadership of Ralph Martin. (Martin and the Word of God community would have a strong impact in Latin America, even decades later.) While the first networks for the movement took shape largely through connections of persons from Catholic universities and Catholic campus centers at state universities, especially in the Midwest, the movement significantly expanded through social networks of families and friends who were anchored in small local prayer groups.

As important as the prayer groups were for the life of the movement, large national conferences provided wider visibility and fueled enthusiasm for the movement, especially among eighteen- to thirty-year-olds. Within nine years some thirty thousand people were attending annual meetings at Notre Dame. This concourse of people was too great to allow for personal interaction and spiritual counseling so in 1977 regional rather than national meetings were held. After a great expansion to several million Catholics in the 1960s and 1970s, the movement went into notable decline in the United States.[32] But a core of firm followers continued in the movement, notably at the Word of God community and at the Franciscan University at Steubenville, Ohio.

Meanwhile missionaries from the United States and Latin Americans who came in contact with the Charismatic movement in the United States were building the groundwork for the wide regional expansion of the movement in the church in Latin America. More, Latin America would reignite the movement in the United States in the 1990s and the following decade through the migration of seasoned and deeply convinced practitioners of Charismatism, especially from Colombia, Brazil, Haiti, and Guatemala. Returning American missionaries, such as Bishop Nicholas D'Antonio of New Orleans, also breathed new life into the faltering movement in the United States. Missionaries *from* Latin America would also come to evangelize Catholics of the United States as itinerant preachers or as residents.

Acceptance of the Catholic Charismatic Renewal

"Relations between CCR and Catholic church officials have not always been warm," wrote P. Thigpen in an authoritative volume on Pentecostals and Charismatics.[33] This bland statement obscures the active disdain of or polite distancing from the movement by many church leaders at that time. Francis MacNutt and other Catholic Charismatic pioneering leaders found a high degree of incredulity on the part of many progressives or centrist American bishops.[34] The bishops' criticisms and doubts centered on both practice and teachings. The spontaneity and exuberance of the movement's participants did not then fit well within the formality, even solemnity, of Catholic worship, especially its central celebration, the Mass. Then, too, Charismatic teachings about baptism in the Spirit, healing, and speaking in tongues appeared to be arcane, exaggerated, or unacceptable.

Fortunately for the movement in the United States (in contrast to many less developed countries), a number of key theologians were drawn into the movement from the very beginning. Edwin O'Connor at Notre Dame, Kilian McDonnell at St. John's University, and a number of other academic theologians took up active defense of the movement through carefully constructed apologias.[35] McNutt, who held a doctorate in theology, published a classic statement, *Healing*, that sold hundreds of thousands of copies.[36]

The theologians acted as intellectual mediators between the new movement and church authorities. The U.S. Catholic Conference of Bishops issued the first of several reports about the movement in 1969, just two years after the movement was founded, in which the movement was generally praised but reservations were expressed. A much fuller acceptance was expressed in later statements about the movement.[37]

The Catholic Charismatic movement was largely a U.S. innovation. The farther one went from the United States, the less likely the movement was to receive as ready an acceptance by the national body of bishops, as will be seen in Latin America. Relations with the Vatican deserve their own history with room for explanation about how much of the movement, such as the emphasis on healing, was actually understood by Vatican officials. The potential for conflict and misunderstandings was high because of the unusual practices of the movement, especially for Europeans used to classical liturgical celebrations.

The principal figure in the acceptance of the movement by Rome was Cardinal Léon Joseph Suenens, the archbishop of Brussels. He strongly promoted a more active role for laity in the Catholic Church and the recognition of charismatic gifts (talents received through the Holy Spirit)—two foundational themes of Charismatism—at Vatican Council II (1962–65). When he heard of the Charismatic renewal as it was occurring in the United States in the early 1970s he visited several Charismatic communities there. From then on, he acted as patron-sponsor for the movement, attending a national meeting at Notre Dame, hosting his own conferences, and introducing Pope Paul VI to the movement in 1975.[38] The pope, in turn, gave Suenens a special mandate to oversee the movement internationally.

Suenens created a CCR International Information Office at Brussels with two American laymen in charge. The office was moved by John Paul II to Rome in 1978 to become the International Coordinating Committee of the Catholic Charismatic Renewal Services (ICCCRS).

The Vatican also was conducting without fanfare a high-level dialogue with the older, "classical" Pentecostals, beginning in the 1970s.[39] This appeared to be early recognition that one cannot be active in global religion without understanding Pentecostals and Catholic Charismatics.

In sum, though, as the scholar-priest Peter Hocken noted, "It can be questioned whether any church or denomination has really acknowledged the significance, the importance, and the extent of the Charismatic Movement. . . . The Roman Catholic Church accepted the Catholic Charismatic Renewal and gave it space. . . . Despite this progress, it remains true that much church life continues as if the Charismatic Movement or Charismatic Renewal had never happened."[40] The following chapters will test that affirmation against a Latin American background. Catholic Charistmaticism[41] in itself is a remarkable story with strengths and deficiencies that need to be understood since it represents a major change in the Catholic Church, which was thought to be leaning left in the 1970s and now right.

Renewal Movements

To revitalize the Catholic Church in Latin America, beginning in the early twentieth century, several movements, most of them imported from Europe and the United States, were employed to help create an active and religiously educated laity. Some of these movements had a lasting effect on society as well as on the church.[42] Among a variety of revitalization movements, Catholic Action stands out. Using Brazil as an example, beginning in the 1930s Catholic Action groups formed hundreds of thousands of lay leaders. Catholic Action's greatest innovation was convincing laypeople that they had a role in the church and in society as members of the church. Members included the world famous educator Paulo Freire, and many others who influenced public spheres of Latin American life. Other lay movements in Brazil and elsewhere in Latin America added their own character to the mix of lay renewal. These included the Better World Movement, Cursillos de Cristiandad, and many others. A later generation of movements included Opus Dei, Focolare, and Schoenstat. Earlier movements had strong political implications through ties to political parties—such as the Christian Democrats in Latin America—unions, or human rights advocacy groups. Later movements tended toward spiritual renewal, typically without an activist orientation toward social justice.

Catholic Action in Mexico, Latin America's other large country, like-wise had hundreds of thousands of members and helped to lead sons of the movement to enter seminaries and daughters to enter convents in large numbers. The movement was one in which militant groups were formed to fight against an anticlerical state and against secularizing tendencies in society. Catholic Action and other initiatives brought the Mexican church an amazing vitality in terms of church attendance (the second best in Latin America in the 1980s) and enough seminarians to send missionaries to Japan and other countries.[43] The movement was also strong in Argentina and some other countries.

Catholic Action led to an equally important lay movement, Christian base communities (*comunidades eclesiâs de base; comunidades eclesiales de base*—CEBs). The progressive and centrist wings of the ranks of bishops frequently supported the movement. This was especially true in Brazil where the bishops' conference chose CEBs as the preferred policy at that time for extending the church's influence.

The CEBs brought perhaps two million laypeople into more intense church life through Bible study, prayer, and community action. Many priests and lay members of the CEBs were especially influenced by liberation theology. It should be noted that the Brazilian bishops said the communities began from *"conversions that involve the whole church . . . in which the Spirit is at work."*[44] The bishops and others viewed commitment to social justice as emphasized by communities as a second conversion after baptism; that is, a gospel demand requiring an internal arduous response. Emphasis on conversion is also central to understanding the high demands of the Charismatic movement, but it should be noted that this emphasis on conversion was already present within Catholic Action and older lay movements.

Enhancement of lay movements came with the great missionary influx to Latin America from Europe, Canada, and the United States in the mid-twentieth century. Nicholas D'Antonio, a U.S. Franciscan, was one of the missionaries. While bishop of Olancho, Honduras, he was thinking of joining the Catholic Charismatic movement but wondered if he would be betraying his commitment to change in the Catholic Church if he became Charismatic. He had painfully reshaped his own views on the church and society during the 1960s era of Vatican Council II and its Latin American follow-up, the meeting of CELAM in Medellín in 1968. During this period, he changed his view of the church from being hierarchical to participatory, from concentrating on devotions and rituals to encouraging activity to make better the world in which the people of Olancho lived.

For Bishop D'Antonio to be drawn into a social justice orientation meant a conversion, a commitment to standing up for justice issues that was demanding and would cost him considerable sacrifice, even possibly threats to his life. His justice orientation was closely linked to the Christian base community movement. In neighboring El Salvador Archbishop Oscar Romero had been gunned down for his commitment to human rights. The later step of becoming Charismatic in the 1980s also involved a conversion, in this case a deepening of a commitment to living a life in the Spirit.

Bishop D'Antonio was caught up in the confluence of these renewal movements as both movements were in flux. Revitalization movements change, especially when new organizational leadership takes over. After his ascension to the papacy in 1978, Pope John Paul II began to make a heavy conservative imprint on the Latin American church. He did this by appointing conservative or centrist bishops and by indicating lack of approval for some activist stances. Many bishops ceased to support CEBs and sought alternatives. The shift in policy shows up in Latin America in the statements from the Latin American bishops Conferences in Medellín (1968), Puebla (1979), and Santo Domingo (1992). Support for the CEBs begins with affirmation in 1968, ascends to ringing approval in 1979, and descends to faint praise in 1992. As noted, many CEBs were carriers of the theology of liberation that conservatives spurned. By contrast, movements that emphasized community and spirituality, such as Opus Dei, were praised and achieved growth and prominence.

Lay Movements

The greatest achievement of the Latin American Catholic church has been largely ignored: the church empowered laypersons to an extent unknown in most other regions of the world. Laypersons emerged in ways never dreamed possible; they were empowered for ministry in the church and for secular ministry. They performed functions previously reserved to priests and they created new ministries within the church.

Laypersons also exercised ministries to society through social service (providing help to individuals or families) or through social action (activities aimed at making the system more responsive to the needs of "outsiders" or at changing structures). In the case of social action, lay leaders typically began with a project that addressed an urgent need of the community, such as land distribution, school construction, or water supply. Before long they became aware of the larger realities of national, even transnational, economic and political life. Hence, an internal structural change in the church, empowerment of the laity, had larger social and political implications.

On the basis of reflection on their spiritual and temporal needs, laypersons and their clerical cooperators created new lay roles. While these new roles often match those described in the early Christian communities, contemporary invention bases itself on needs and structures of new groups, rather than imitation of ancient practice.

Lay leadership in the church is a larger and more complex issue than the creation of basic Christian communities, which is to be discussed. The empowerment of the laity for leadership in the Latin American church took place in many environments other than basic Christian communities. By way of example, the assembly of persons who worshipped at La Mansión in Santa Cruz, Bolivia, numbered about five thousand. This was more a mega-church than a base community. Laypersons at La Mansión assumed formally (by invitation) or informally (by initiative) a whole range of roles from liturgical music leadership to teaching groups of several hundred newer members ways to reflect on the Bible and to pray.

The way La Mansión and other communities operated represented a remarkable change from the past and a key to understanding the relative success of organizational changes in Latin America. Most basic to the new spirit, in organizational terms, was a sense of responsibility. To a considerable but yet unmeasured degree, the confidence that Latin Americans have in the Catholic Church came from this sense of shared responsibility.

Responsibility was expressed by sharing. One shared according to one's abilities and talents. There were drivers, mechanics, teachers, prayer leaders, cleaning squads, and a range of other helpers. At La Mansión, members of the community gave money or other resources in a manner that was uncommon in Santa Cruz, Bolivia, or in Latin America as a whole. They were able to build and maintain an impressive community worship structure. Each day they provided prepared food for the Dominican community that typically numbered four priests and brothers, plus a surplus for other hungry persons. In fifteen years, the community only missed one meal.

Small Communities

Small communities, weekly prayer groups, have a special place in the Charismatic movement. Without them the movement would not have flourished. They are, in effect, the driving force of the movement. They also represent the future of the Catholic Church. The Catholic Charismatic Renewal, after all, is the fastest growing and largest sector in the church. One of the innovations that the Charismatic movement emphasizes are what sociologists in the United States call small groups and sociologists in Latin America describe as small communities.[45] These communities are not new. Observers called attention to them in the 1970s when the progressive church in Latin America was fostering something new and special. These were typically referred to as Christian base communities or CEBs from their Spanish or Portuguese phraseologies. In fact there have been small groups in the Latin American church for decades. Catholic Action and the Legion of Mary functioned through small groups through much of the twentieth century. Those groups had specialized categories of members, such as students or farmers, while contemporary small communities were made up of ordinary parishioners, often from the same neighborhood or rural village. Be they CEBs or Charismatic prayer groups, these communities are living cells within a parish.

They offer a sense of community with support and encouragement but also much more. As Robert Wuthnow, a noted Princeton sociologist, wrote of small groups in the United States: "Their members care for each other, pray with one another, work together on community projects, and spark vitality in religious institutions."[46] Small communities in the Charismatic renewal act as a training ground in a new way to pray and to live. They act as safeguards for living in an environment that could distract their members from their new or renewed religious commitment. Religious leaders, noted Wuthnow, hope that small groups will foster spiritual growth in the United States where faith is often shallow and ineffective. Shallow faith is even more common in Latin America. Weak or uneducated faith is both the reason why many Catholics became Pentecostal by the millions in Latin America and the basic reason for evangelization—education in faith for Catholics—which forms the driving force of Catholic Charismatic evangelists.

Evangelization includes prayer, study, and testimony. As people pray communally they learn from the more experienced persons in their community how to pray. As people study scripture and theology together they begin to understand better the implications of these teachings in their own lives. As they recount to the community how they encountered Jesus and how that "changed their lives," they become more accountable about these alleged changes and more consistent in holding on to their values in their lives.

A specialized type of community, a covenant community, also has developed within Catholic Charismaticism. These are especially common in Brazil and are described at length in the chapters dealing with Brazil. These are especially significant because of the depth of their commitment to the church and the way they act as a strong foundation for the durability of the Charismatic movement.

Catholic Charismatics see themselves as living a *contra mundum* life (while often enjoying a middle-class and moderately consumerist lifestyle). They deemphasize drinking and life-in-the-streets machismo, and support the rule of law and obedience to authority. Their songs and dance are infectious and have entered mainstream entertainment. They offer alternatives to promiscuous sexual behavior and to easy contracting of HIV-AIDS. The CCR community offers support for youths who desire to remain celibate until marriage.

In a word, small groups act as a community in which conversions, often shaky at the start, are nurtured, protected, and deepened. (These groups are similar in many ways to the self-help groups that have grown in abundance in the United States and elsewhere and include Alcoholics Anonymous, Parents without Partners, and similar groups in which the group acts as a bulwark for maintaining convictions or finding one's way resolutely in difficult circumstances.)

Theoretical Overviews: Explaining Religious Change

The chief theories employed to explain the Catholic Charismatic movement have been concerned largely with its spread as a movement through Latin America. These are similar to the theories that furnish perspectives on the global Pentecostal movement. Catholic Charismaticism is viewed here as a religious movement engaged in by persons attempting to make sense of, and thus bring cognitive order to, a complex and sometimes hostile world.

It is defined as a social movement whose boundaries and membership, which consists of those who define themselves as Catholic and charismatic, are amorphous. It is a collectivity with an indefinite and shifting membership, with leadership whose position is determined more by informal response of the members than by formal procedures for legitimating authority.

In Latin America, the result of the coming together as a collectivity has been a hybrid religiosity. There is no "pure" Catholic Charismatic model. When one asks "What is Catholic and Charismatic," the response to a large degree depends on who furnishes the answer. Thus there is a need for a commonly accepted methodology for investigating and evaluating the words and actions of members of the movement and their interactions among themselves and with the larger institution.

Globally social and political scientists have furnished several theories to deal with Charismaticism as a transnational social movement: 1) modernization and secularization; 2) relative deprivation; 3) globalization; and 4) social movement theory. But only two have received much attention with regard to Latin America. Thus far the main theoretical attempt to explain the Charismatic renewal within the Latin American Catholic Church has been by rational choice practitioners. They offer a corrective to the modernization perspective, which brings with it secularization theory.[47] While rational choice theory has been central to political science, political and other social scientists were tardy in applying it to the field of religion in Latin America. They have followed rational choice practitioners who have focused on the U.S. "religious marketplace."

One of the leading advocates, Laurence Iannaccone, explained rational choice: "Religious consumers are said to shop for churches much as they shop for cars; weighing costs and benefits, and seeking the highest return on their investment." More important, though, for explaining the behavior of religious groups and movements are statements about the producers rather than the consumers: "religious 'producers,' erstwhile clergy, struggle to provide a commodity" at least as attractive as their competitors. "Religion is advertised and marketed, produced and consumed, demanded and supplied."[48] We are here concerned with the supply-side of the market.[49]

The first notable attempt to explain Latin American religion and the Catholic Church in Latin America through rational choice theory, also known as the rational actor theory, was made by Anthony Gill of the University of Washington. His *Rendering Unto Caesar: The Catholic Church and the State in Latin America* caused a notable stir among academics when it was published in 1998. Gill argued through selected evidence and rational choice theory that there was a causal connection between religious competition and the rise of progressive Catholicism. He also argued that in places where evangelical Protestantism and spirit sects made inroads among poor Catholics, local leaders of the Catholic Church championed the rights of the poor and turned against authoritarian regimes to retain parishioners. Where competition was minimal, bishops maintained good relations with military rulers. Applying economic reasoning to an entirely new setting, the book, the publishers said, offered an original theory of religious competition.[50]

The appearance of the book stimulated a great deal of discussion among North American academics devoted to the study of Latin American religion. At that time it was typical of many academics in the field to study only the Catholic or Protestant churches and seldom to include a full-scale analysis of the whole religious field. Thus, the first and incontestable achievement of Gill was to show the necessity of viewing the whole field of religious groups. Viewing the actors in that field as competitors also provided a dynamic and valuable perspective that was previously underutilized.

Gill built on the work of notable sociologists using rational actor theory to analyze religion in the United States: Roger Finke, Rodney Stark, Laurence Iannacone, and William Bainbridge.[51] Several years of discussion followed the publication of Gill's book. Eight rounds in the debate were posted at a Web site that became number one on Google's search engine for the category of religion in Latin America.[52] One of the first to respond to Gill in this debate was Professor Manuel Vásquez from the University of Florida, who wrote that he agreed with the general assumption that rational choice approaches are useful tools for the study of religious behavior. "He [Gill] is right to challenge the untenable notion that religion is irrational or, at very least, non-rational and that it is purely other-worldly." As Gill and Vásquez both noted, leaders of religious institutions are subject to the same concerns and constraints as their secular counterparts.

Primary among these concerns is the need for their church to survive and expand—that is, to preserve the institution and increase membership.[53]

Rational choice, or rational actor, theory as employed by Gill in *Rendering Unto Caesar* also received much criticism for Gill's historical interpretations of military governments and the Catholic Church's responses to them, as is clear from the scholarly opinions expressed after publication of the book.

A historian used rational actor theory in a more focused fashion than Gill. Andrew Chesnut, at the University of Houston, reported his investigations of religion at Belém, Brazil, in his *Born Again in Brazil* and his *Competitive Spirits*. Both works spelled out his views of religion as existing in a marketplace in which there are winners and losers. He was one the very few scholars writing in English to treat the Catholic Charismatic Renewal, which appeared as a chapter in his *Competitive Spirits*.

Chesnut saw that Protestant Pentecostals were running away with convert after convert from the Catholic Church in Latin America, especially in Brazil, Chesnut's area of special expertise. The millions of Catholics who had left the church to join the Pentecostals had done so in Chesnut's view because Pentecostals offered a better product (for example, a sense of community and the promise of healing and prosperity). Therefore, to meet the competition, the Catholic Church had to promote a similar product—that is, Catholic Charismatics who were seen as a direct imitation of Protestant Pentecostals.

Chesnut refined his views in his essay in a later, edited volume, *Conversion of a Continent*: "Religious market analysis must be combined with life-cycle information, network analysis, and other approaches to conversion outlined in this volume."[54] Such a more integrated approach is utilized in this work. The construction of culture in which religion is embedded is also taken into account.[55] Thus, while the rational choice became a common approach to explaining U.S. religious competition, religious actors were also seen, as Christian Smith has argued, as human beings who are "moral believing animals."[56]

A wider and, perhaps, more useful view, that of globalization, has been provided by various social scientists, such as Roland Robertson, and has been well exploited by the scholars Anna Peterson, Manuel Vásquez, and Philip Williams in their *Christianity, Social Change, and Globalization in the Americas* and later works. Similarly, in the following chapters, placing Charismaticism within the framework of globalization is central. The accounts of a transnational movement becoming embedded in local groups within their cultures will be the framework for explaining much of what has taken place in this eminently successful religious movement. The employment of social movement theory and of relative deprivation theory will not be fully exploited, leaving for future authors the opportunity to mine these fields. But, since social movements especially have to do with the construction of identity, the theme of identity from social movement theory is crucial to this work.[57]

Conversion among Catholic Charismatics

From the beginning of the Catholic Charismatic movement, conversion has occupied a central space as an entry point and lifelong process. In many places, people interested in the movement are invited to a Life in the Spirit retreat as the initial step. They are advised to go to confession or in some other way acknowledge their sins, resolve to improve their lives, and dispose themselves for the indwelling of the Holy Spirit. (In Catholic theology a person cannot force God to act but can only open himself or herself to divine action.) In the Life in the Spirit retreat many participants experience a coming of the Spirit as a joyful awareness of God's presence within themselves. This conversion is experienced as illumination, many say, which makes the bonding with God stronger and the moral path to the future clearer; that is, decisions are made that amount to a moral conversion.

In brief, conversion for Catholic Charismatics means a new way of life, a commitment with new elements, such as healing and what are called gifts of the Spirit. This depiction of a way of life accords with Henri Gooren's characterization of conversion careers and his five-level topology of religious activity.[58] For the most part, Charismatics are at the third and fourth levels of religious activity. They have gone through the ritual of affiliation/initiation, baptism, at an early age. But beyond mere affiliation, group membership now forms a central aspect of their lives and, indeed, of their identities. More, they report that they have experienced a radical change in the sense of a deepening of worldview and identity. They have advanced from indifferent or lukewarm affiliation. As Gooren has noted in his fourth level, that of confession, in the sense of proclamation,

Charismatics tend to practice a high level of proclamation within their religious group and have developed a missionary attitude toward non-members outside their group.

The Charismatic movement also appears to be an excellent exemplification of what David Smilde explains in his relational analysis of religious network and publics; that is, Charismatics were led to the movement by neighbors and relatives.[59] This is not a movement or activity that started from above. At its inception, the hierarchy of the Catholic Church neither mandated the movement nor initially sponsored the movement. Quite the contrary, the bishops typically delayed granting approval. Rather, the renewal began from the mid-level workforce and from the grass roots. Priests, sisters, and laypersons working in Latin America picked up the core ideas and practices in the United States or Canada and communicated what they knew to small groups in Latin America whose members in turn recruited others. Family members or neighbors recruited their acquaintances for membership in prayer groups. Or, charismatic personalities communicated through television or live performances the main ideas and practices to adherents who in turn recruited friends, relatives, and associates.

The movement in Latin America at first did not develop much reflective thought (theology) on conversion but relied on a very long tradition and on twentieth-century interpretations of thought about conversion. Through the centuries of Christian theology from medieval theology onward, Catholic writers commonly spoke of first and second conversions. First conversion was said to occur at baptism, in which one was dedicated to a life in God. This initial dedication to God was reinforced typically in adolescence by the sacrament of confirmation. Many persons lived good lives without evidence of a second conversion. But a second conversion occurred in many lives.

Some people, such as Saint Teresa of Ávila, lived mediocre lives until some further, life-altering event occurred. In Teresa's case an image of Jesus appeared to her and triggered a mystical experience. This event produced a deeper insight or sense of God and an enthusiastic response in the form of a commitment to live a deeper spiritual life. "What this [Charismatic] movement seeks to do," said the noted theologian Yves Congar, "is to ask the Lord to actualize what the Christian people have already received."[60]

In sum, there is an initial, intense experience of God, with the gifts of the Holy Spirit being received by many persons, as in healing and speaking in tongues. This is followed by dedication to personal renewal and ongoing growth in a life of holiness. After the Life in the Spirit retreat, participants typically join small prayer groups. The groups serve to instruct, encourage, and challenge members to greater spiritual growth. The groups act as communities and resemble extended families. Members help one another to grow in holiness and to build stronger relationships with God and with their neighbors. Social justice activism is not generally emphasized, although CCR groups in some Spanish-speaking countries, such as Colombia, have stressed issues such as working against the drug trade or joining in emergency aid after disasters.

Theologians have been drawn into theoretical debates about conversion within the CCR, with practical implications. These discussions about the understandings of conversion illuminate key differences between Catholics and Protestants, that is, between what are called in this volume Charismatics and Pentecostals. Among Catholics generally, conversion is a process that takes place over time; conversion can be "lost" or diminished. Among many Latin American Protestants, conversion is a once-and-for-all-time event, as it is for some American evangelicals. The idea that a person, such as the North American evangelist Billy Graham, could be converted and "saved" with many years yet to live is foreign to many Catholics.

Theological disputes show clearly the wide pluralism of the movement in which there has not been a unified view of conversion. Nor, say some theologians and practitioners, should there be a single understanding. In the light of the theology of the renowned Bernard Lonergan, the theologian Donald Gelpi, who has observed the Charismatic renewal for years, believes that there are at least four different types of conversion and that the interplay of these types helps to explain personal growth. Within the conversion process, one may, then, speak not only of religious conversion but of affective, intellectual, and moral conversion as well.[61]

Nonetheless, the main thread of understanding of conversion is clear: it is the conscious decision to turn to a life faithful to God and to turn from evil. Conversion is thus defined here as a change of mentality.

Conversion is also a lifelong process. In "Ecclesia in America," John Paul II's fullest statement about the church in the Western Hemisphere, he repeats the common understanding of conversion as a process that is never finished; it is a continual challenge and is always under threat of being lost.[62]

One should note, too, that there has been an evolution among Catholic Charismatics in many regions away from the initial Protestant emphases of the movement to perspectives that are more distinctly Catholic. While Pentecostal and Catholic groups hold much in common, forty years of history has shown a growing recognition by Catholic Charismatics of their distinctive identity.[63]

This evolution is marked first by Catholics becoming more fully aware of their mystical and spiritual theological traditions. This awareness was aided by research into their tradition of previous manifestations of the Spirit through the centuries.[64] A wide renaissance of interest in mysticism occurred in Spain, Germany, and Britain in the 1950s, centered in the study of spiritual masters, such as John of the Cross, Meister Eckhardt, and Julian of Norwich. Second, Spirit baptism has been seen as fitting in within traditional sacramental theology, especially the sacraments of baptism and confirmation; that is, Spirit baptism does not take the place of other sacraments, but it does represent a decisively new work of grace in a believer's life. Third, most Catholics tend not to see speaking in tongues as evidence of Spirit baptism, as do Pentecostals. Catholics also argue for a wider range of spiritual gifts beyond those typically cited by Protestants. Fourth, the Eucharist and the Mass are central practices in which the divine presence in the Eucharist is acknowledged, and charismata, including healing, are often received during the Mass. Lastly, devotion to Mary, the Mother of God, is an integral part of many Catholics' spiritual lives. This is especially evident among the numerous adherents to the movement in Mexico.

One of the gifts of the Spirit, healing, is central to many in the Charismatic movement, so the link between healing and conversion is crucial to the discussion here. Healing that is born of faith takes several forms. Conversion itself induces healing. The unconverted individual is diminished as a person by a disordered relationship with God and with other persons. Conversion is believed to bring about the reordering of social and religious attitudes in line with what God wishes. The theologian Donald Gelpi believes this reordering heals the human heart in its deepest center.[65]

Given the Catholic view of the precarious quality of conversion, the community assumes a responsibility to nurture the newly initiated. It does this through mentorship in prayer and in helping new members assume roles in the church and through strong emotional support and example. For their part, new members are expected to attend community meetings frequently, have docility toward spiritual masters, and eventually to bring in new members, once they have gained some experience in living as a Charismatic.

The main thrust of life after the initial intense religious experience, called here a second conversion, is *revisión de vida*, a change of life, avoiding what is considered evil and the occasions that will lead to slips and falls and attempting to be active and generous in relations with others. This program is morally demanding and time consuming. Many participate for some years but drop out of prayer-group participation. These people are called "postcharismatics" by the researchers David Barrett and Todd Johnson, who define them as "formerly active Charismatics who have become irregular, or less active, or inactive, or elsewhere active."[66] My interviews with Charismatic leaders through forty years lead to a tentative conclusion that most dropouts remain Catholic and continue to attend church with a bit more fervor and a greatly enhanced musical repertoire. Many dropouts from Pentecostalism fall into the category of "no religion," a growing pool of persons in Latin America. This does not seem to be the case with Catholic Charismatics.

Reading New Testament scriptures that were written within the context of the Roman culture of hedonism reinforces for members of small communities the sense of struggle in their own world against what they perceive as dangerous to their own moral integrity. They are certainly not opposed to pleasure or joy. They have incorporated music, dance, and celebration for enhancing their positive needs to appreciate, acknowledge, praise, and engage in thanksgiving. Often it looks like they are having a party. They are, but the means are not illegal (although they sometimes are too loud for the neighbors).

Conclusion

Of the 73 million Latin American Charismatic Catholics, 43 million live in Brazil and Mexico, the two largest countries, and 12 million live in Argentina and Colombia, the next two largest countries. Thus these four countries account for 55 million of the 73 million, or 75 percent of Catho-

Table I.1. Countries Ranked by Number of Charismatic Catholics (in Millions)

Brazil	33.7
Colombia	11.3
Mexico	9.2
Argentina	4.7
Venezuela	3.1
Peru	2.4
Chile	1.6
Ecuador	1.2
Bolivia	.881
Guatemala	.864
Haiti	.782
Dominican Republic	.752
Puerto Rico	.522
Honduras	.503
El Salvador	.400
Cuba	.349
Nicaragua	.216
Uruguay	.208
Panama	.198
Costa Rica	.183
Paraguay	.099

Source: Barrett and Johnson, "The Catholic Charismatic Renewal, 1959–2025," 119–22.

lic Charismatics. The remaining 18 million are spread throughout Latin America.

It is important to note that the boundaries of the movement are extremely flexible. Who is in and who is out is largely a question of affinity, of belonging, which is indicated by attendance at some Charismatic events. Thus, in addition to active, involved adult Catholics, their children are included in the count, as are what Barrett and Johnson call Catholic "postcharismatics."

Barrett and Johnson collected and published the statistics for the Catholic Charismatic movement for their World Christian Encyclopedia. Both scholars have been long engaged in viewing and evaluating religious statistics. They noted that Catholic statistics are the best documented membership data of the sets of data available within the larger Pentecostal/Charismatic renewal. Their reporting on the Catholic Charismatic Renewal was

Table I.2. Countries Ranked by Percentage of Catholics Who Are Charismatic

Colombia	28
Brazil	22
Puerto Rico	18
Argentina	14
Chile	14
Venezuela	14
Bolivia	12
Honduras	12
Haiti	12
Mexico	10
Ecuador	10
Dominican Republic	10
Peru	10
Guatemala	9
Panama	9
Cuba	8
Uruguay	8
El Salvador	7
Nicaragua	5
Paraguay	2

Source: Barrett and Johnson, "The Catholic Charismatic Renewal, 1959–2025," 119–22.

the result of a four-year survey carried out by the International Catholic Charismatic Renewal Services, which sent the survey instrument to the movement's coordinators or correspondents in every country of the world. The results were faxed back to Rome. Johnson and Barrett also reviewed public opinion polls in which adults identified themselves as Catholic Charismatics or as otherwise involved in the renewal. Todd Johnson continued his statistical appraisals of the movement as the director of the World Christian Database.

Table I.3. Countries Ranked by Percentage of Priests Who Are Charismatic

Dominican Republic	23
Brazil	11
Guatemala	11
Nicaragua	10
Argentina	9
El Salvador	9
Haiti	9
Puerto Rico	9
Cuba	5
Colombia	3
Bolivia	3
Mexico	2
Ecuador	2
Honduras	2
Chile	1
Peru	1
Venezuela	1
Costa Rica	1
Panama	1
Paraguay	0
Uruguay	0

Source: Barrett and Johnson, "The Catholic Charismatic Renewal, 1959–2025," 119–22.

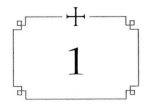

BOLIVIA

Learning While Doing

Father Francis MacNutt, a midwestern Dominican friar, provided the first spark for the Catholic Charismatic movement in several Latin American countries. Notably he preached the initial Life in the Spirit retreats with a team of Catholics and Protestants, men and women. His impetus for starting the movement was felt in the following countries: Bolivia and Peru, 1970; the Dominican Republic, 1971; Guatemala, Mexico, and Costa Rica, 1972; and Colombia and Chile, 1972.[1]

A radically different paradigm in any field, such as medicine or theology, can be challenging for people to accept. This was especially evident in Bolivia. MacNutt, who proposed the new paradigm of the Charismatic Renewal, recalled many years later the resistance he encountered while giving several dozen retreats in Latin America in the 1970s: "My main theme for retreats was usually the Holy Spirit—especially as shown in healing. Most of these Catholic missionaries were strongly identified with the poor and were working for greater social justice. Initially they were prejudiced against what I was saying because they associated my themes with those emphasized by some North American televangelists who stressed the 'health and wealth' gospel. It always took several days to convince the missionaries that I was not preaching a gospel that is too comfortable to be real. But many of them eventually put the double emphasis of the baptism of the Spirit and social justice together in one vision."[2]

He believed that "particularly in Bolivia, several missionaries understood the vision of combining the message of the Church's preferential option for the poor, together with the need of the power of the Spirit."[3]

He had in mind especially work that was going on in Santa Cruz, where a few Dominican missionaries were forming Christian base communities (CEBs) among the numerous poor.

MacNutt and his preaching companions gave the first Charismatic retreat in Bolivia in May 1970. They followed with two more retreats in English, attended almost exclusively by Catholic missionaries, with a few Bolivians and a handful of Protestants. After Francis MacNutt left Bolivia, the persons who experienced the baptism of the Spirit (not all did) at his retreats carried his emphasis on the power of the Spirit to Spanish-speaking persons in the ministries where they were working. This was especially true of the Dominican priests and sisters, who knew MacNutt from their earlier days in the central United States and were later working in the Santa Cruz area.

In the early 1970s, Santa Cruz was a dusty provincial capital that was becoming a sprawling city without the oppressive presence (at that time) of Bolivia's superheated political parties in the many barrios, the slum neighborhoods. In the rapid urban spread over the empty grasslands, the city found itself with four new rings, encirclements of tens of thousands of new migrants. The Catholic Church had no adequate way to give them pastoral care. As elsewhere in Latin America, grass-roots Christian communities, with their Bible study and communal prayer, arose to meet this need. Parishes in their traditional form were ineffectual organizational units for meeting the spiritual demands of Catholics.[4]

A great many Latin American Catholics, even in the late twentieth century, had little understanding of their faith. Many of the requests of ordinary Catholics for ritualistic services, such as baptism and the sacrament of marriage, were without much theological meaning. For some Catholics, rituals were clearly a matter of magic and superstition. They had almost no education in the faith. Even among those who had a more educated attitude, questions arose about a service station approach: one that had Catholics coming to a *patrón* who dispensed favors and services. Further questions were raised by Vatican Council II about conferring sacraments on those who had almost no instruction. Indeed, many came to believe that the emphasis on performing ecclesiastical rites without strong instruction was the curse of the Latin American church.

Major changes were called for: reduction in scale, instruction in depth, a sense of belonging with a community, new ministries, and the emergence of lay leaders. Some observers felt that the church had no choice in the 1960s but to create grass-roots communities. Father Ralph Rogawski and Sister Helen Raycraft, both Dominicans, were among those who shared this dissatisfaction. A few years before the Charismatic renewal was introduced to Bolivia, they approached their priest-friends from LaCrosse, Wisconsin, who headed the parish called Santa Cruz on the first ring of the outskirts of the city of Santa Cruz. They proposed a plan to these pastors for assisting them in pastoral care.

The parish was considered one of the most active in the city, with a packed church for Sunday liturgies. However, the parish only drew to Sunday Masses about 5 percent of the thirty thousand persons within the parish's boundaries. A small community of Dominican priests and brothers rented a house within the parish but at some distance from the church and a mile from the Dominican sisters, who also rented a house away from the parish center. From these points on the margins of the parish they promoted credit unions and cooperatives, organized clinics, and fostered neighborhood committees for health, electricity, burial, and garbage collection. A host of other projects grew up to include youth clubs, soccer teams, and employment agencies.

But while the Dominicans had a spiritual, interior life, the people they worked with often did not. The priests and sisters became acutely aware of this deficiency and conducted an evangelization retreat at one of the neighborhood districts, which contained some five thousand inhabitants. Several dozen people attended the retreat, which extended over ten evenings. The retreat sparked the desire among the participants to continue on as a community in their efforts to understand and practice their faith. This was a crucial moment, a life-changing event. From those attending the evening retreat meetings, a Christian base community (*comunidad eclesial de base*—CEB) was formed. This innovation of a small faith community spread to many other neighborhoods.

The CEBs were later used as vehicles for the spread of Charismatic renewal. Key aspects of this work included reliance on the Holy Spirit as a source of unity among fragmented lives and families and as a source of *healing*. Father Rogawski and Sister Raycraft attended Francis MacNutt's retreat and incorporated his ideas into their own retreats for the grass-roots communities. Through MacNutt's mentorship they felt they were recovering the primitive Christian understanding of healing that had been deemphasized through the centuries.

At Santa Cruz, by early 1974, the Dominican missionaries had established twenty-three prayer groups in the barrios and four at La Mansión, the latter to be described later. At Cochabamba Father Patrick Rearden, who was also one of MacNutt's disciples, and Rearden's associates turned the Dominican pastoral center in the heart of the city into a Charismatic center for prayer groups and for training teachers in evangelization. Padre Rearden concentrated on providing some ten Life in the Spirit seminars a year. He utilized these as the first step toward bringing Catholics into the Charismatic movement. The work in healing led him and new entrants into the movement to establish a rehabilitation house for drug addicts. This rehabilitation work continued to be supported in large part by Charismatic participants in Cochabamba. Rearden also helped initiate the movement in Peru. After Rearden returned permanently to the United States in the 2000s, the movement dwindled in Cochabamba.

Rogawski, Raycraft, and team members felt that lay leadership in their barrios had matured enough for them to leave Bolivia to foster the movement in Colombia and elsewhere. Both Rearden and Rogawski would join the revived tradition of itinerant preaching that characterizes the Charismatic renewal and would spend long years on the road.

The movement also spread in the early 1970s to two parishes in La Paz and one in Tarija. The Charismatic movement received a great boost in interest in 1973 when Julio César Ruibal, a nineteen-year-old Bolivian Protestant Pentecostal, took the country by storm with massive rallies and many reported healings. While studying in the United States, he had became a disciple of Kathyrn Kuhlman, the famed woman Pentecostal healer and preacher.[5] He incorporated her flamboyant preaching style, conducting rallies in stadiums and drawing maximum media coverage.[6] In such an isolated country as Bolivia this brought new attention to both Pentecostalism and the Catholic counterpart to Pentecostalism, the Charismatic movement. The main region that benefitted from this massive media attention was Santa Cruz, where a Charismatic center called La Mansión was created. The center is described here to focus on special issues that arose in Catholicism in adopting the Charismatic renewal.

La Mansión in Santa Cruz, Bolivia: Doing While Learning

In Bolivia, Cris Geraets, a Dominican missionary, wrote many articles and preached on the movement. He was conscious of making sense for himself as a Catholic of Pentecostal ideas and of having to adapt what was coming from North America to different cultures. He was intellectually well equipped.

Geraets was regarded as the best mind in his ordination class. He taught, wrote, and served as the president of the Bolivian Institute of Social Study and Action at La Paz for ten years and moved to Santa Cruz, where he started a Catholic parish and center for university students at Gabriel René Moreno University. He was shifting from social-justice education and activism to greater spiritual concerns. Geraets had been immersed in the philosophy and theology of Thomas Aquinas as taught at the pinnacle of its historical ascendency before Vatican Council II.

He followed the pattern of spreading the movement that he had learned from watching MacNutt. Or rather, he half watched the rituals of healing and praise that MacNutt followed and paid more attention to the spirit of what MacNutt was doing, conscious that he had to adapt MacNutt's practices of the movement to his own contexts. What was remarkable was Geraets's transition from the rigidity of a highly structured theological vision to Charismatic spontaneity in personal and public prayer.

Once Geraets's own initial adaptation to the new paradigm was made, he faced the cultural issues of spreading the renewal among the Bolivians among whom he ministered. This shift from an emphasis on Thomism (the philosophy and theology of Thomas Aquinas) and the orthodox Catholicism of the 1950s to a post–Vatican Council II manner cost him years of study. He calculated that he spent four hours a day for some six years in the effort. His new vision was acquired systematically, moving from theme to related theme. He put his ideas in print, largely in the style of reflections on a single theme.[7]

Some of the major topics—none of which had come up in his seminary training—included speaking in tongues, baptism in the Spirit, and healing as part of the ministry of priesthood. Later topics would include demonic possession, tithing, and other themes. His studies were backed by a small but prized community library acquired at the considerable effort of transporting books from distant lands and preserving books in hot and damp climates with paper-chewing insects. His studies were steeped in a seven-hundred-year Dominican tradition of study, mysticism, and spiritual discernment.

Geraets focused his study on the pastoral issues raised in his work as a pastor to the Santa Cruz parish and center. A central practical concern involved how one celebrated a Charismatic Mass. Father Geraets and his co-pastor, Father Dan Roach (another Dominican disciple of MacNutt), felt this was the most urgent question they addressed in the earlier years of their involvement in the movement. Lay parish community members glimpsed something of the intellectual struggle the priests faced. In the open environment of subtropical Santa Cruz, where doors and windows were typically open, they could see that their pastors scrupulously observed their study periods and were not available for idle conversation during these times. Further, Geraets had the look of an epiphany when he reached a new insight and communicated it to the parish community. This was a distinct period of learning while doing, including some trial and error, not unlike the early Christians trying to adjoin Christian worship to Jewish synagogue services. Fortunately for Geraets and Roach, Vatican Council II had allowed for a measure of experimentation with the centuries-old rituals of the Mass.[8]

Geraets and Roach had the twin tasks of retaining the Catholic essentials while not losing the spirit of Pentecostalism, especially a heightened sense of worship and ecstatic spirituality. The adaptation that these two priests made could be seen in what took place at the main worship service on Sundays at Santa Cruz.[9]

The service began with prayers by lay ministers for pardon, liberation from the power of the devil, and mental and physical healing. This was followed by "a prudent length of time" for spontaneous testimonials.[10] Each testimonial was typically limited to three minutes—but frequently ran longer with more intense recitations—and basically consisted of individuals relating their encounters with Jesus Christ and how those experiences changed their lives. The celebrant counted on being in tune with the Spirit to know when to shift from this first preparatory part to the traditional body of the ritual of the Mass.

The rest of the liturgy was fundamentally the Mass as celebrated after Vatican Council II but carried out more amply and joyfully than was typical. At the time of the Agnus Dei's Greeting of Peace, for example, most persons left their seats in church and exchanged handshakes and hugs with perhaps thirty other people within easy range on weekdays. This ceremony was more expansive on Sundays and could easily last twenty minutes since this bonding played an important role, including the exchange of more urgent news, such as sickness in the family. After Mass, most persons vacated the church building, but others remained for more specific prayers for their problems and for the imposition of hands for healing.[11]

Preaching was carried out on weekdays and more expansively on Sundays. Both Fathers Cris and Dan acquired the Latin American manner of preaching described as proclamation. Their homilies were focused and were not rambling in the Iberian tradition. Since both pastors were in the process of learning about the Charismatic renewal, their homilies became the fruits of their ongoing studies. The homilies were received by many as small nuggets of information, clues to how one might live one's new life as a Charismatic.

Francis MacNutt, Preaching, and the Spread of the Movement

Preaching as an art had fallen on hard times in the Latin America Catholic Church during the first two-thirds of the twentieth century before Vatican Council II. The professional training of priests as preachers was virtually nonexistent.[12] The Sunday homily thus was a poorly practiced craft, rambling and for the most part boring.[13] Several factors contributed to a renaissance of preaching: foreign missionaries, Vatican Council II, the example of televangelists, and the Charismatic movement. The Charismatic movement was a major factor in making preaching a better craft than it had been, in part because of its practitioners' careful attention to biblical texts and themes.

Francis MacNutt, who was a carrier of the movement from North to South America, was himself a well-tuned example of a preacher. Born in 1925, he was in his late forties and had been a priest for fourteen years when he first promoted the movement. He came to the renewal with a wealth of talents and experiences. He had hoped to study medicine at Washington University Medical School in St. Louis, but he was drafted into the U.S. army ten days before he was to begin classes there. After his discharge from the army, he spent his undergraduate years at Harvard, where he dedicated himself to intensive religious searching and from which he graduated with honors. He continued this search at the Catholic University of America, where he was much influenced by his reading of Thomas Merton's *Seven Storey Mountain*, which drew him into thinking of the priesthood.

At Catholic University his professional training was in the Master of Fine Arts program in dramatic arts. He joined the Dominican Order in

1950 and advanced to the priesthood in 1956. Along with his scholastic achievements, he was a gifted athlete (tennis and baseball) with a wide interest in humane pursuits (especially cinema and bird watching). At the Aquinas Institute of Theology he earned a Ph.D. in theology. He was appointed to teach preaching at Aquinas. During his seven years of teaching, he wrote three books on preaching and helped to found the Catholic Homiletic Society.

These experiences led him to interact with networks of Protestant teachers of preaching and through them he was invited to a weeklong Protestant Charismatic retreat in 1967. Among the leaders of that retreat were Tommy Tyson and Agnes Sanford, Protestants who remained life-long friends of his. It was at the retreat that he asked for prayers that he would be baptized in the Holy Spirit. Not long after he received what he described simply as a "dramatic turning point in his ministry" (baptism in the Spirit). Agnes Sanford told him that he would bring healing prayer back to the Catholic Church. This became the principal driving force in his life thereafter.

MacNutt began praying for the sick and he believed that they were often completely healed or noticeably improved. More and more he realized that an important part of Jesus' ministry of healing and deliverance through the power of the Holy Spirit had been commonplace in the early church but had been largely overlooked or ignored in the modern church.

He was one of the first Roman Catholic priests to be involved in the Charismatic renewal and in an active healing ministry. Thus MacNutt entered the Charismatic movement apart from the so-called foundational events at Duquesne University, but he quickly became integrated with other priests and lay leaders involved in the renewal. With them he helped found the Charismatic Concerns Committee (CCC) in the United States. This committee was renamed the Charismatic Leaders Fellowship and MacNutt served as the chairman of the group for several years in the twenty-first century.

As the Charismatic movement gained momentum in the early 1970s, MacNutt became widely known among Catholics and Protestants for his teachings about healing prayer and the power of the Holy Spirit to transform lives. He took on a full-time traveling ministry, preaching and teaching with teams that included Catholics and Protestants. The team membership shifted often—depending on the availability of team members—and frequently included Father Michael Scanlon, later the president of Steubenville Franciscan University, and Ruth Carter Stapleton, President Jimmy Carter's sister.

Using Merton House in St. Louis as his base, MacNutt traveled to thirty-one countries in a few short years in the 1970s. In 1977, he was a major participant at the Kansas City Charismatic Conference, which is often called the Arrowhead Conference (after the name of the stadium in which it was held). With forty thousand participants, this was then the largest Charismatic event in the United States and is generally regarded as the high point in the larger Protestant-Catholic Charismatic movement.[14] MacNutt took his place among what Vinson Synan called the Charismatic Hall of Fame preachers, which included Cardinal Suenens.[15]

MacNutt, however, largely lost influence within the Catholic wing of the larger Charismatic movement at the end of the 1970s. He met Judith Sewell at a Charismatic conference in Jerusalem in 1975 and married her outside of the Catholic Church in 1980. They settled in Clearwater, Florida, where they established the Christian Healing Ministries. No longer an active Catholic priest, Francis MacNutt and his wife, Judith, traveled widely, preaching and ministering, largely to Protestants. In 1987 the Episcopal diocese of Jacksonville invited them to move there and expand their healing center for prayer ministry and preaching. In 1993 MacNutt received a long-delayed dispensation of his priestly vows from the Catholic Church. The Catholic bishop of St. Augustine, John Snyder, celebrated a Catholic marriage ceremony for the MacNutts at a retreat house in Jacksonville.

MacNutt thereafter became increasingly reincorporated within the worldwide Catholic wing of the Charismatic renewal. Healing had again become a central interest of the global movement. In Jacksonville in 2007, the global leadership group called the International Catholic Charismatic Renewal Service Committee (ICCRS), located in Rome, co-sponsored with the MacNutts' Christian Healing Ministries an international conference, the School for Healing Prayers for Leaders. Four hundred and fifty Catholic leaders, lay and clerical, from forty-two countries attended the six-day event to bring the teachings of the couple to the larger Catholic Church.

Enthusiasm for the conference resulted in an invitation for Francis MacNutt to go to Rome the following year to be a major contributor to the Second International Institute for Catholic Charismatic Leadership Formation, which included the members of the Central Coordinating

Committee as learner-participants. The visit to Rome also brought an invitation from Cardinal Jozef Tomko, formerly the prefect of the Congregation for the Evangelization of Peoples and a person keenly interested in ecumenical affairs, for a private audience with him. Also in 2008, the ICCRS renewed its co-sponsorship of the Second School for Healing Prayers for Leaders at Jacksonville. This brought another large and diverse group of Catholic leaders from many countries to Jacksonville.

By 2008 Francis MacNutt, then eighty-three, had become the director emeritus of the School of Healing Prayer and Judith had assumed the full directorship. The two Jacksonville workshops for the global Catholic Charismatic Renewal and Francis's visit to the Vatican in 2008 were the crowning touches for his efforts to spread the movement and to fulfill in part the expectations that Agnes Sanford had of his bringing healing back as a ministry in the Catholic Church.

MacNutt had been a trailblazer in the professionalization of homiletic training of priests in the United States[16] and he incorporated his own training in dramatic arts and speech from Northwestern's speech department and the Catholic University of America's dramatic arts school with his familiarity with mainline Protestant biblical preaching. The Charismatic renewal helped change the art of preaching in a large segment of the Latin American Catholic Church through more expressive style and through more biblically based exegesis.

At La Mansión, daily liturgies took about forty minutes; Sundays, two hours. Masses on Pentecost and other important feasts went on for four hours. Singing was hearty and musicians provided more interludes and background than most Catholic liturgies provided. Music was especially prized by Charismatic participants. Parishioners grew to know many contemporary Christian hymns and songs by heart and did not need hymnals, although these were available. Many participants also sang or listened to religious music outside of church. Church was an important venue for religious music, but it wasn't the only venue. Local or international groups regularly performed within Mass and in separate shows in the afternoon or evening for Catholic Charismatic audiences.

For Fathers Cris and Dan music became a major innovation in their ministry. In their emphasis on celebration it was natural that music supported what was going on in the Eucharist. Specific music was fitted to the distinct parts of the Sunday celebrations. For more than twenty years what are called at La Mansión "professional" musical groups supported the Sunday music. The number of the groups had grown to fourteen by 2007 and the groups took turns performing during Sunday and feast-day Masses. The groups were made up on average of twelve performers per group. Frequently new ballads and interpretations were added to the common repertoire of the congregation. That there would be that number and quality of groups and new compositions went far beyond the expectations of the priests.

As the musical groups became more numerous, they not only vied for the slots available to them at La Mansión but also were encouraged to act as musical missionaries, going out to the many small *plazuelas* (small plazas) in Santa Cruz and the countryside, using the message of Christian music to revitalize Catholics. Other Catholic musical groups were organizing themselves in Santa Cruz's parishes, drawing in the pastors to the movement and linking up with Charismatic prayer groups.

An extensive network of Christian musicians grew, with layers of local and regional groups, and national and international performers. Word of mouth and Web logs passed on informal ratings of performers. These informal evaluations along with performer Web sites serve as the two parts needed to guide audiences and parish music advisors (ministers of music) toward finding one another to fill out programs for special occasions.

A theater group also grew up at La Mansión, as theater groups did elsewhere in the renewal. (There was a parallel development among adherents of liberation theology.)[17] Again, the emphasis was on using cultural mediums that carry messages. Theater does this effectively, directly, and emotionally. The impetus and performers for theatrical performances were provided by members of a prayer group and not by plans by the pastors and La Mansión's staff.

One of the first innovations inaugurated by Padre Cris was street preaching. While this was brought on by direct competition with Pentecostals and evangelicals, he had long harbored the notion of itinerant public preaching as a revival of the tradition of the first Dominicans in southern Europe who were attempting to evangelize the unchurched and religiously uneducated in the thirteenth century. As noted, Father Rogawski, Sister Helen, and their preaching team preceded Geraets in this outside-of-the-church ministry.

In the 1980s three younger Bolivian priests at La Mansión, along with Father Cris, began traveling to Bolivian villages where priests seldom visited and carried on weeklong preaching campaigns. The Bolivian priests were fluent in one or another of the Bolivian native languages and preached publicly while Father Geraets mentored them behind the scenes. Sometimes they found themselves in the same location with roving Pentecostal preachers and—to quote one of the Bolivian Dominicans—a battle of loudspeakers would take place. Itinerant preaching and traveling over Bolivia's rough terrain was grueling work and became curtailed in part due to Geraets's advancing health problems from Parkinson's disease. But street preaching campaigns in and around Santa Cruz became common on weekends. Here a confluence of music and preaching was used to attract and hold on to audiences. With some effort, the various *conjuntos* (musical groups) from La Mansión transported instruments and sound equipment to open-air venues.

Roughly the same sort of networking that took place among Catholic musicians occurred with Charismatic preachers. Word of mouth, e-mail, and Web sites sustained a circuit of guest preachers. Padre Rafael Lisandro Chávez from Venezuela was the featured preacher at La Mansión in November 2007. He was also billed as an expert in the systematic use of music for evangelization. But the favorite visiting preacher for many in Santa Cruz was Padre Jaime Burke, a Dominican itinerant preacher based in Houston, Texas. Padre Jaime stayed for a month and a half during the winter season in Santa Cruz, interrupting his travels to the Dominican Republic, Ireland, and other countries.

Padre Chávez, the Venezuelan priest, was the special guest for the eighteenth Gran Encuentro Internacional (2007), an event that acted each year as a revival meeting and drew participants from mostly neighboring countries. This Gran Encuentro and the feast of Pentecost were crowning events for parishioners, "alumni," relatives, and foreign Charismatics who were drawn to Santa Cruz. The Gran Encuentro served as a demonstration project, showing priests and lay leaders from other parts of Bolivia or the other Andean countries how to do Charismatic religious celebrations. Father Al Caprio, a Dominican from Chimbote, Peru, went to La Mansión several times to see how to celebrate Charismatic Masses and how to conduct street preaching. He adapted the Gran Encuentro to Chimbote by conducting monthly celebrations that brought together the disparate prayer groups in the city. He also conducted Gran Encuentros for northern Peru.

Amplification of the Movement

The Mass was a centerpiece leading to satellite activities. The prayer groups emerged as a central organizational feature of La Mansión in addition to the Mass. By 2008 some 140 groups were functioning. Each had contact persons, schedules, and distinct personalities. The prayer groups followed the pattern of the liturgical year with the seasons, such as Advent and Lent, and the biblical readings assigned for each day by the universal Catholic Church. These groups thus formed the living tissue of La Mansión. Through the universal calendar and readings, prayer group members also perceived themselves as part of the global church.

These prayer groups tended to develop spontaneously but the pastors kept a measure of accountability. They posted hints on bulletin boards on how to form prayer groups since this issue came up regularly. Groups grew too large and needed to divide. Loyal participants moved to other parishes. In each case the new groups were to make themselves known to pastors of the respective parishes, especially since many groups were presumed to want to take part in evangelization within parishes.

The quality of pastoral care in Latin America changed dramatically with the Charismatic movement. Until then, the criticism of the Catholic Church by thoughtful evangelicals—that the church did not offer adequate pastoral care—rang true.[18]

Adequate spiritual growth, many believed, implied personal contact with pastors and spiritual directors. This personal counseling would have to occur outside or alongside public liturgical services. Fathers Cris and Dan set aside every afternoon for long hours of listening and counseling. Personal struggles had to be dealt with on a one-to-one basis. The Catholic sacrament of confession also was administered at this time if clients so wished. Both priests acquired reputations in these counseling sessions for wisdom and holiness. When Father Cris died in 2001, his funeral procession reached a length of five miles.[19]

The array of lay ministers who participated in liturgies or paraliturgies at Santa Cruz grew impressively through the 1980s when making music, preaching of various sorts, praying, going in processions, controlling crowds, passing out books, picking up trash, taking collections, and a host of other activities needed to be carried out. Through time these lay offices or roles were refined and expanded.

Some lay ministries were distinctly Catholic, in contrast to the Pentecostal antecedents to Catholic Charismaticism. The Eucharist service (the Mass) was a defining difference between Catholics and historical Protestants and Pentecostals. Before the Catholic Charismatic Renewal, the customary parish Mass stood in strong contrast to the Pentecostal service in terms of having a ritualized commemoration of the Last Supper. Although the Charismatic Mass looked increasingly like a Pentecostal service, the Eucharist remained a strong element for Catholics. For a number of congregants at La Mansión, one of their most coveted positions was the office of extraordinary minister of the Eucharist and the taking of Communion to the sick.

Another aspect that makes Catholic Pentecostalism different from its Protestant progenitor is the emphasis on conversion as an ongoing process, as mentioned in the introduction. Conversion was clearly the emphasis each day at La Mansión, where the Mass was seen by Geraets and Roach as the reenactment of the Passion of Jesus and whose first effect, in the language of Thomas Aquinas, is the forgiveness of sins, demanding each day an attitude of conversion on the part of Christians. This is captured in the first part of the introduction to the Eucharist, in the prayers for pardon.

La Mansión increasingly identified itself as Catholic in a number of ways and its Web site makes clear its Catholic identity. In the more than thirty years since its founding the lay members of the community have deepened their own Catholic identity, especially through study and courses. Informal education—that is, education especially of adults outside of schools—has been part of the history of the center as will be noted.

The Long Emergence of a Lay Leadership Corps

Fathers Cris and Dan believed in delegating as many responsibilities as possible to the laity. Fifteen years before moving to Santa Cruz, the two priests along with the other Dominicans in Bolivia settled on the policy of acting as *asesores* (advisors) to lay movements rather than as directors of those movements. The Charismatic renewal, in their view, was primarily a lay movement. Various ministries, alongside those connected to liturgies, grew up quickly. Two of the most important were teaching prayer and teaching doctrine. On a typical Sunday in 1980, after the noon meal and siesta, some 150 persons would go to La Mansión for classes on prayer conducted by more experienced and trusted lay leaders. Other classes on prayer were held on weekdays.

In discovering Charismaticism laypeople also discovered that they did not know much about the faith, either through the Bible or through orthodox Catholic teaching. They saw that they were ignorant in ways they had never seen before. (If nothing else, the Charismatic movement holds up a mirror to ordinary Catholics to show them their deficiencies.) They felt deeply that they needed to fill this void and turned to educating themselves and to evangelization, the effort to educate others.

This awareness of their own ignorance of the faith led to two major changes. Adult lay parishioners took up reading on their own and they supported a continuing education institute at La Mansión. Their newly awakened desire for intense study reflected what parishioners viewed in the study habits of their pastors, Fathers Cris and Dan. Many of the working poor among the parishioners perceived for themselves that books were instruments that led to greater understanding and a better life. Reading books was not what most people did with spare time in subtropical Santa Cruz. It was commonly said that virtually the only books people in Santa Cruz read in the 1970s before the Charismatic renewal were pornographic. Further, a very high percentage of the adults were borderline illiterates. Many homes, even middle-class ones, had not a single book. One clear change among both older Pentecostal groups and Catholic Charismatics was the greatly increased buying and reading of religious literature. Catholic Charismatics read at a greater pace than their fellow Catholics. It is no surprise, then, that many Charismatic centers have bookstores.

The evolution of reading as a personal habit began typically with small doses—articles and reflection pieces—and moved to pamphlets, graphic (illustrated) stories, and then short and long books. With Charismatic festivals and music performances in the 1990s came booths for displaying and selling books. But the main venue for literature sales was Life in the Spirit seminars. Stirred to personal conversion and new ways of living, participants in the seminars and retreats felt they needed guidebooks. They also wanted their own copies of the Bible.

This new audience meant that virtually all notable Charismatic leaders have written at least one book. The best known have written dozens of books and pamphlets. Padre Diego Jaramillo of Colombia wrote more than one hundred books and pamphlets. Second-generation preachers have typically produced their first book by the time they are thirty-five. Books by preachers are roughly equivalent in the Charismatic movement to musical CDs for Christian musicians.

In the case of La Mansión, the crowning touch was the publication of a handsome, professionally packaged book called *La vida de los Padres Cris y Daniel*, a 420-page volume.[20] Two hundred of its pages were filled with theological and practical principles and a theological essay on the movement. This was not so much a commemorative volume as a well-perused manual for living as a committed Charismatic; it was the reinforcement of a conversion. The parishioners of La Mansión became "people of the book," that is, disposed to reading in ways they had never dreamed possible.

The result has been the formation of a corps of well-informed laity who are comfortable in their Catholic identity because it has been reflected upon, and who are able to meet the various challenges of other religions and of local and national culture that might draw them away from their chosen values.

This greatly increased personal study was enhanced by the center's major pillar of adult education, the Instituto Pastoral Santo Tomás de Aquino. The creation of the Institute filled an immediate need, gaining a wide base of students from all over the city. From the original enrollment of 150, enrollment shot up to 700 students. Clearly a hunger for deeper knowledge of the Catholic faith was being met.

The priests and lay leaders were not prepared, however, for some of the students who wanted to enroll. They were illiterate. Many came from indigenous backgrounds and were from the recent migrant population from the highlands to Santa Cruz's then dominant mestizo culture. If many of La Mansión's first adult parishioners were humble lower-class working poor, these new clients were even poorer. Thus began an unanticipated ministry that continues that of the teaching of reading and writing and then incorporating these newly literate students into the classes of the institute. As elsewhere in Latin America, a deep desire to read the Bible for one's self and not merely to listen to it being read was engendered by the movement.[21]

Evangelization and Reaching Out

Since 1980 the Instituto Pastoral has been aimed at the re-education of adult Catholics at three levels over a three-year period, with the highest level being aimed at sending lay catechists and lay missionaries into service of the church. In 2007 three hundred students were enrolled in the institute, a very large number for the parish considering the specialized courses and the time expended as students. Classes were held each weekday evening for two and a half hours. Graduates gained a robust education in theology, biblical studies, history, and a variety of other subjects.[22]

They formed a corps of lay catechists and other lay ministers. The education received is roughly the same as or better than the education received by many Pentecostal pastors.[23] The argument forcibly made by critics of the Catholic Church that Pentecostal pastors far outnumber Catholic priests ignores the enormous corps of lay catechists.[24] Further, if one follows the argument about laity in the church put forward by the great Catholic theologian Karl Rahner, a large part of these catechists are equivalently clerics.[25]

Many of the teachers at the institute were drawn from laypersons who were faculty members at the regional national university and from doctors and lawyers who, at early middle age, generously took on additional responsibilities. This generosity might have been tapped before but was not. Both in terms of giving time and money Latin American lay Catholics underperformed,[26] depending for centuries on the state or on the very wealthy to provide financial support and a tiny lay corps of sacristans and janitors. La Mansión notably turned that lack of generosity around.

Several aspects can be seen to this new-found generosity. The current large church building with spacious and clean bathrooms, unusual in the tropics, was built from local generosity, not from foreign mission funds. The evening school and most other classes were free. The meals for the Dominican community were provided each day by volunteers, in imitation of early Christian communities. As older groups of Pentecostals found out long ago in Central America, Latin Americans can be turned into generous givers in terms of human and financial resources and contribute even out of their own scarcity.[27]

The implications of personal study and adult education, including literacy training for national and international development, were noteworthy.

The Charismatic movement at Santa Cruz and elsewhere has contributed to human resource development through literacy and other skills that will aid in technical work. Whether it has contributed to a fuller ability to think critically remains an open question.

Healing

The emphasis placed by leaders and pastors within the Charismatic movement on healing extended their consciousness of the amount of suffering among parish members present at Charismatic services as well as those unable to be present because of physical illness, including addiction. The intercessory prayers by persons in the congregation at the beginning of daily and Sunday Mass made one acutely aware of what was going on in people's lives, both the present and the absent. At the very least a bonding in need and suffering was created. Persons attending daily Mass—and they tended to be repeaters—frequently seemed to be aware of persons with afflictions in the neighborhood who were not present. Knowing names and stories plus the sense of shared hope for them contributed to building community in ways that generalized petitions did not contribute.

Besides the emphasis on healing at every liturgy, a weekly healing Mass was also held on Friday afternoons. From the looks of the four thousand or so who attended on an afternoon in June 2004, the healing Mass was a family affair, with couples in their thirties and forties with young children, and elderly couples with extended families. Many participants were professional or government workers who took a half day from work. Healing drove them to church with as much force as it did to doctors' offices. While well-dressed professionals and their families attended, the majority of those present were the working poor.

The few researchers who have looked into the Catholic Charismatic Renewal have stressed problem solving as a central motivation for persons to join the movement. Illness, addiction, suffering in many forms—this is an almost universal condition among the poor and is common for other classes in Latin America—also drew many into the movement. Andrew Chesnut, in one of his early works, describes this universal condition as the "pathogens of poverty," the rotting food, dirty water, tattered clothing, frequent illnesses, and lack of schools, police, and clinics.[28]

Janneke Brouwer found that in Nicaragua almost all of her informants had become members of the Charismatic movement under the influence of certain needs, such as recognition of addiction or feelings of alienation, in their lives.[29] The Pentecostal scholar David Smilde argues that network location provides the most robust explanation of who addresses these needs through religious participation. He argues that other persons with similar needs find something other than religious means to address problems or continue suffering or explain them away. Smilde suggests that seeking solutions is situated in sites where networks are bridged, new understandings arise, and coalitions develop.[30]

For Pentecostals and Charismatics these sites include both services in churches and interactions in the streets. People in warmer climates of Latin America live a notable part of their lives on the streets, so Pentecostals and Charismatic Catholics frequent outdoor spaces. In other words, gathering together is done not only in churches but on the streets, or more accurately, in the numerous small plazas of Latin America.

While preaching on the streets is central for Pentecostals and Catholic Charismatics, it is probably less important than the informal ways that the message is spread in the plazas. At La Mansión, people come to the plazas around the campus to hear what is going on, exchange information, study in groups or alone, and practice music. The architects of the gradual gentrification of the aging La Mansión building and its surrounding space had a whole environment in mind. They built not only a church but also the peripheries of the church building as plazas where the above activities take place. Counseling and spiritual direction occur in the former mansion adjacent to the main church plaza and separate from the church. Here the Charismatic movement clearly overflowed traditional church structures into sites that are public and serve as the grounds for network activity.

Tried and Abandoned

Several other ministries were attempted. Radio and television programs from La Mansión reached city and regional audiences in the 1980s but the fragmentation and weakly capitalized nature of the Bolivian broadcast industry worked against sustained efforts in that field. As Pentecostals learned, church groups needed their own broadcast licenses and stations if they were to convey their message on a consistent basis. The communications branch and the technical equipment of La Mansión became recording studios for Christian musical groups rather than broadcast production facilities. As noted, itinerant preaching in native languages at remote indigenous villages dwindled.

Fathers Cris and Dan, for a long time, believed existing seminaries and schools of theology were incapable of training Charismatic priests. They sought to train students for the priesthood from La Mansión, under their own hands, at the Pastoral Institute, but this plan was nixed in the late 1980s by higher Dominican authorities. The few priests who emerged from this experiment were judged to be notably lacking in theological depth by their religious superiors.[31]

The Social-Justice Issue

As was noted at the beginning of this chapter, Francis MacNutt's Charismatic message was strongly resisted by missionaries who were committed to the active building of a society of justice and peace. Many of the participants in MacNutt's retreats in Latin America came from an activist social-justice background. Some, notably Colombians, found that the movement supplied them and their collaborators with a strong spiritual basis that they felt had been missing in their busy lives. In a word, for these activists, transforming society demanded a new attitude (conversion) and a new mindset for the new structures to be effective. Still, there was ambiguity in the issue of changing hearts since having a new spirituality did not eliminate the need for the activism required to advocate laws fostering justice (such as those against discrimination of various kinds) or creating new structures (such as those granted access to education).

Social justice as a major thrust of La Mansión did not occur, despite the activist background of the two founders. Gone were previous efforts at cooperatives, credit unions, union organizing, or strong organizing of neighborhood improvement projects. Gone, too, was prophecy, speaking out on a regular basis against governmental or corporate abuses.

What remained of the founders' expression of social-justice convictions was important but not the same. Fathers Cris and Dan did succeed in emphasizing the preferential option for the poor, a central focus for Latin American activists, and they made special provision for the poor in their literacy programs. Furthermore, the teaching of the social doctrine of the church became an integral part of the Pastoral Institute's curriculum, though this was more classroom lecturing than a prelude to action. The pastors did not advocate escape from the world, but, by default, justice, human rights, democracy, and citizenship were issues that they did not address. In general, a definite pulling back from the public sphere occurred.

Within the larger Bolivian church, older foreign and native priests saw an apparent lack of justice orientation in these priests, who had been prominent nationally in promoting unions, cooperatives, and credit unions and in denouncing Gulf Oil and its semi-secret signing of contracts with the Bolivian state, as unfortunate compromises.[32] It appeared that conversion to the Charismatic renewal meant otherworldliness and dependence on miraculous powers. This contrasted with these critics' views that Christians needed to work hard at making the structures of this world serve all persons better.

The criticism was met by the common argument of Catholic Charismatics and Pentecostals that the only secure way to improve society was by conversion of individuals. The question, simply stated, was changing hearts or changing structures and hearts? This was one of the great debates of Catholicism in the twentieth century. It would remain unresolved.

Perhaps, as shown here, the general effect of Catholic Charismatic Renewal is in line with what the noted Latin Americanist Daniel Levine sees as the future of the Catholic Church in Latin America: withdrawal from political confrontation.[33] However, one might also read the early twenty-first century as an interim period awaiting the consolidation of social justice and spirituality in the blending of liberation theology and Charismaticism.

Maturing

Over time, La Mansión has changed and notably matured in four ways. First and most significant is the emergence of strong and dedicated lay leaders. In part this was by design of the founders and was hastened by the death of Father Cris and the reduced health of Father Dan. Thus clerical leadership diminished. If nothing else had been accomplished, this would remain notable. The issue of clericalism in a lay movement was a strong concern for some time in the renewal movement. Clericalism could have perpetuated itself at La Mansión through its Pastoral Institute because Fathers Cris and Dan wished to educate their own candidates for the priesthood at the institute.

The resolution of the issue of training recruits for the priesthood from the Charismatic movement in Latin America has followed three paths: traditional seminaries that have made some accommodation to Charismatic ways (such as styles of celebrating Mass); special seminaries for Charismatic priests such as were created in Colombia; or national branches of religious orders, such as Eudists in Colombia or Missionaries of the Sacred Heart in the Dominican Republic, that became identified with promoting the Charismatic movement. The seminaries in Brazil seem to have made the most adjustments to Charismatic entrants while the national theological school in Bolivia appeared to abrade Charismatic propensities in theological students.[34]

The results of these differences in training were evident in the availability or lack thereof of young performers among young clergy. Year by year a newly ordained priest performer or preacher seemed to appear at one Charismatic festival or other in Brazil while Bolivia has had to import young Charismatic priest performers.

The absence of young priest-celebrants and priest-chaplains dedicated to the movement occurred at La Mansión as no young priest has joined the staff in twenty years. The three active priests at the center in 2008 were in their fifties, with no young priests as apprentices. However, the notable flourishing of lay leadership appeared to offset the previous clerical presence of five priests.

Second, evangelization as a major effort has paid off in terms of radical improvement in the intellectual grasp of the faith on the part of the laity. Third, Catholic identity steadily and explicitly increased. The intellectual and spiritual strengthening of a critical mass of laity in Santa Cruz gave the Catholic Church a core group to support the church in the face of growing challenges. While Bolivia saw a wide range of religious competitors enter the country in the twentieth century, it was not until the 1970s that evangelicals and especially Pentecostals began to make considerable inroads. Pentecostals gained about 10 percent of the Bolivian population by 2000. Fairly large numbers of switches in religious affiliation by Catholics and mainline Protestants occurred especially in the national capital, La Paz, through aggressive evangelistic and healing campaigns.

A major national event occurred in Santa Cruz, Bolivia's second most populous city, when Franklin Graham came to the city for the four-day Bolivia for Christ rally in 1999. This was the first time that a rally of the

Billy Graham Association was held in Bolivia. Probably one in every eight persons in greater Santa Cruz—some 138,000 persons—attended the high-energy event. Three hundred and fifty Protestant churches from around the country sponsored the event. Just the organizing of the event in itself showed the arrival of a matured Protestant presence in the country as nothing else would. (Here the mix of Pentecostals and evangelicals was conflated in the minds of most Bolivians. Both groups were called *evangélicos*.)

Religious challengers had been gaining acceptance in Santa Cruz for years. Now they publicly announced their desire to convert the whole region to their vision. La Mansión's Pastoral Institute had been preparing its students for thirty years for contact with Protestants by inculcating in them the ability to understand Protestant diversity and to live with religious pluralism without brushing their challengers off as "sects" and "ravenous wolves." More, the graduates of the institute were Catholics prepared to *convert Pentecostals*. Force was meeting force.

Fourth, financial support by the laity has remained strong. In general La Mansión has made itself into a thriving center.

Conclusion

Globalization played a large part in the process of the Catholic Charismatic Renewal taking root in Latin America. Those who have theorized about religious change and globalization—Roland Robertson, David Martin, Anna Peterson, and Manuel Vasquez, for example—have seen both the global and the local as taking part in bringing forth religion as expressed in a particular context.

This religious movement was not externally imposed upon adherents who joined the movement. Arguing that Charismaticism was imposed from above would ignore the popular and indigenous nature of the movement, deny the agency of individual members, and question the validity of individuals' religious experiences. Also to be noted against the argument of external imposition is the fact that the vast majority—well into the twenty-first century—of Latin America's local and national Charismatic movements are led by Latin Americans.

Competition brings vibrancy. Competition between religious competitors has contributed to a religious renaissance in the region that has been flooded by both Pentecostal and Catholic churches. In the case of

Bolivia, a moribund church has come alive. Priests, now mostly nationals, stood at 1,235 in 2007, a great increase over the 200 or so national priests of thirty years ago.[35] Seminarians, the hope of the future, increased from 49 in 1972 to 712 in 2007, more than a 1,300 percent increase.

Clearly the outstanding issue for the Catholic Charismatic movement in Latin America has been enculturation, the adaptation of a foreign innovation into the routinized practice of religion in another cultural context. Roland Robertson, one of the main framers of theories about globalization and religion, defines enculturation as the establishment of reciprocity between local beliefs and Western Christianity.[36] This process consisted in filtering what was acceptable from that which was not acceptable to the orthodox practice of Catholicism. The process is very similar to what has occurred in the acceptance of indigenous religious practices within the Catholic and Protestant churches in countries where a large segment of the population is indigenous, as in Bolivia and Guatemala.

Overall in Bolivia, the country ranked seventh in percentage of Charismatics, tied with Honduras and Haiti. The movement coordinators reported six hundred prayer groups and thirty-five priests active in the movement.[37]

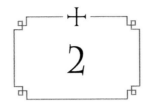

COLOMBIA

Social Justice and Pneuma

No other country in Latin America better exemplified the social-justice orientation possible within the movement than Colombia. The movement was built around two centers, one in Bogotá, the capital, and the other in Sonsón–Río Negro, an area of dispersed small towns near Medellín. In the first case, the urban poor were the target population of the movement's promoters; in the second case, peasant farmers were. In each case the poor of God were emphasized. In neither case was the theology of liberation involved—it never really took hold in Colombia—but rather a generalized effort ensued to take care of the poor when neither the state nor political parties had the vision or policies to do so.

That Charismatic movement's leaders and members embraced a social-justice orientation. The main criticism of the Charismatic movement by progressive Catholics had been that it turned its back on this-worldly orientations and the vision of the church at the service of the world. Latin American theologians and intellectuals pictured the Charismatic renewal as destroying the soul of Christianity, which they said must include concern for the poor and vulnerable. Without this concern for the poor and action on their behalf, Catholics as well as historical Protestants said that Pentecostal and Charismatic Christianity were not authentic. But both elements—an orientation to this world and service to this world, including the poor and the vulnerable within it—became the hallmarks of the Latin American Catholic Church after drastic changes in outlook and action took place at a historical meeting, the Latin American Bishops Conference (CELAM) at Medellín in 1968.

The First Colombian Pillar: Minuto de Dios

The Charismatic movement began in Colombia at Minuto de Dios, a thriving low-cost housing cooperative in Bogotá. Minuto de Dios was an effort by activist priests to call attention to the desperate needs of the lowest segment of Colombian society. Colombia's majority poor were being increasingly ignored as middle- and upper-class members made a rush toward prosperity in the 1970s. (This was before Colombia was engulfed in taking coca from Peru and Bolivia and processing the leaves into cocaine to form a profitable drug trade.)

In the early 1970s Colombians were doing well with a diversified economy; an advantageous geographic position that made them only short hours away by air from the U.S. market, thus able to airlift flowers and boutique agricultural products to the United States; and a large educated sector needed by a modern economy. But not all Colombians were educated or in an occupational stream that would lead to economic sufficiency. These were the many marginal persons in Colombian society.

The Charismatic movement started in Bogotá without a direct connection to the historic starting point for the Catholic segment of the Charismatic movement at Pittsburgh. In October 1967 a group of *Protestant* Charismatics, which included persons from the United States and Canada, was visiting Colombia.[1] Two of the visitors were housed in Barrio Minuto de Dios. One of them, Samuel Ballesteros, of Mexican descent, was a youth leader of a Baptist church in Chula Vista, California. He was impressed with the housing project and its community spirit and expressed interest in joining the project by adding his own contribution, evangelization, an element that was not well developed at that time in the project or in Colombia as a whole. Ballesteros became friends with Padre Rafael García-Herreros, the leader of Minuto de Dios, and carried on long conversations with him about the Charismatic understanding of the Holy Spirit and his gifts.[2]

Eventually in the early 1970s—the exact date is not clear—Padre Rafael received baptism in the Spirit.[3] This, along with further influences from Bolivia, helped ignite the movement, which spread through the Minuto de Dios community in Bogotá and then to other parts of the country. The two centers of diffusion, Bogotá and Sonsón, would be the power sources of the Colombian segment of the movement at its inception.

Minuto's Wide Social Enterprises

Minuto de Dios's name comes from a popular short radio and television message that ran for years in Colombia. The radio program was produced first at a provincial city and later moved its production to Bogotá. The program was devoted to a brief commentary and reflection on religious matters. The idea was to give God an uninterrupted moment of one's time to think not only about him but about what he would want for the poor in this world.

In the 1950s, housing for the lower classes was a neglected area. The Colombian Catholic Church of that time was predominantly other-worldly.[4] The vision of a church and of its professionals being engaged in socioeconomic development work was just beginning to gain traction. A few priests, on their own initiatives, began making the first small steps to develop programs for economic betterment and to motivate their parishioners to social activism. This education and development work was to be done as a group activity, as a community of believers.

Rafael García-Herreros was one of the first priests in Colombia in the 1950s to take up development work. He wanted to build with his parishioners low-cost housing. Together they planned a model housing project but with a utopian ideal of a Christian community, somewhat similar at that time to a kibbutz in its organization. García-Herreros emphasized simplicity and de-emphasized consumerism. His views were another reminder that strong emphasis on community was to become a hallmark of Latin American Christianity, especially Christian base communities and Charismatic prayer groups.[5]

Two wealthy benefactors contributed a parcel of land on the fringe of Bogotá near the River Juan Amarillo. The undeveloped land would become a housing development and a distinct neighborhood in Bogotá called Minuto de Dios. Between 80th and 90th Streets and 72nd and 75th Avenues they constructed a small city with many parks and gardens, a theater, a school for four thousand students, child-care centers, a health clinic, and a parish church of which García-Herreros became the pastor in 1965. Fifteen years later President Pastrana inaugurated the Minuto de Dios Museum of Contemporary Art, which had some valuable pieces and was itself of architectural interest. Minuto de Dios was built up over many years, with at least eleven distinct historical phases.

What was once an isolated site in exurbia became part of the expanding city. Fifty years after its founding Barrio Minuto de Dios was a stop on the metropolitan transportation system. The model cooperative community became nationally known to the extent that it was commemorated by a Colombian postage stamp with the designation "Barrio Minuto de Dios—50 años [years]." This then is no ordinary city neighborhood but a national icon. It is also a brand name that has been affixed to various enterprises, such as the museum and the university, as they grew up in the neighborhood.

One of the reasons the project became an icon came from imaginative fundraising. For example, in 1961 García-Herreros organized the first Banquete de Milliones at $5,000 a ticket, an astronomical sum in any country of the world at the time. For that sum attendees received a cup of consommé and bread (the food of the poor). Against dire predictions that the event would fail it continued as an annual event and grew in popularity. The *banquetes* concept brought the upper levels of Colombian society into the process—and the media along with them. All of the presidents of the country, starting with Alberto Lleras Camargo, supported the event. And from the very first year the reigning beauty queen, Miss Colombia, attended. Hence Minuto de Dios was much more than a project taking place on the margins of society. Its leaders intended it to become part of the conscience of the nation.[6] As an indication of the event's success in that regard, a spin-off from the event was the creation of a model neighborhood in Cartagena called el Barrio de las Reinas—the neighborhood of the beauty queens. In 1992, García-Herreros died on the day the banquet was held at the Salon Rojo of Bogotá's Hotel Tequendama Intercontinental.

By that time, the banquet had become an event that was spreading overseas, first to New York with its very large Colombian community and then to other cities in the United States with large Colombian populations. Tickets to the banquet were running at $100 in places like Atlanta. In Tampa in 2007 the event was already in its fourth year and was covered by a Mexican news agency and by local television channels. Banquets in seven U.S. cities that year were expected to pull in $300,000. Again, the main focus of the fundraising was the construction of low-cost, cooperative housing, but funding presumably went also to the Minuto de Dios Charismatic Center in Bogotá, Lumen 2000 television, and other projects that carried the Charismatic message.

Minuto de Dios enterprises increasingly acquired a Charismatic spirit.

The *banquete* concept spread to many Colombian cities and was going well through the 1960s and early 1970s. Then in 1972, years after the Duquesne events and apart from them, Padre Rafael, Minuto's founder, experienced baptism in the Spirit through Protestant colleagues, as noted. Thereafter Minuto de Dios became an important center for the spread of the Charismatic movement. It was not the only Catholic Charismatic center in Colombia, but it was the best known one. The center added Charismatic to its formal title, becoming known as the Corporación Centro Carismático Minuto de Dios.

Grounding in the Lay Apostolate

Much of García-Herreros's early professional life was devoted to seminary teaching, but he found time to work with laypersons in Catholic Action. Collaboration with the laity in joint projects was to mark his entire life. The role he played with them was essentially that of *asesor*, advisor-counselor. As was the case with virtually all other pioneers of the Catholic Charismatic Renewal (CCR), García-Herreros recognized from the beginning the importance of utilizing mass media.[7] He began with a "Catholic Hour" on Radio Fuentes in Cartagena, a provincial capital, in the 1950s.

He moved from Cartagena to Cali, where he began to put his social vision into practice early in his priestly life. In Cali he provided the leadership for construction of a new *barrio popular* (low-income neighborhood). This housing project for the poor was funded in large part by contributions from local influential families and sales of his own books. García-Herreros was the son of a Colombian army general and moved easily in upper social-class circles. His financing of lower-class projects through funding from the rich formed a partnership of rich and poor and a pattern that continued throughout his ministry.

When García-Herreros moved to Cali, he continued his radio messages of social justice. He became a popular but controversial figure. His radio messages were carried by outdoor loudspeakers in the market plaza. His views were commented on frequently by the local press. Before long, though, he was criticized and then increasingly condemned. Critics said his ideas "clearly had a communist flavor or were, at very least socialist."[8]

His superiors moved him for a short time to Medellín and then to Bogotá, where he spent most of the rest of his life. He arrived in Bogotá in 1955 just as television was making its appearance in the country. He experimented with several styles of programs and then settled on the Minuto de Dios format. Every evening at 7:30 on Channel 7 he delivered a short message along with his famous tagline, "Placing in God's hands this day that is passing and the night that is arriving."[9]

His goal was not only to deliver a spiritual message but one that would awaken the social conscience in the country. People referred to him as the Home Minister (*Ministro de Hacienda*) of the poor. Controversy about the content of Minuto de Dios's messages followed him for years, periodically flaming to crisis points. One of his first crises occurred in 1955 when he discussed the death penalty, raising ethical questions about its practice. In 1963 another controversy—the topic long forgotten—became so heated that the president of the country, Guillermo León Valencia, had to intervene to forestall suspension of the television program. Further flash points occurred in 1968 and in the early 1990s, but the program continued. With the death of Padre Rafael, the Minuto de Dios television spot seamlessly passed into the hands of Padre Diego Jaramillo.

Minuto de Dios proved to be a brilliant idea. Until Padre Rafael and his associates could afford ownership of a radio station, he had to bargain with commercial radio and television owners and managers for air time. While he obtained rather easily an hour of airtime on radio in provincial cities in the 1950s, the radio and television markets in Bogotá were fiercely competitive. Station managers consistently refused Padre Rafael's request for large blocks of time. Finally, in desperation, García-Herreros argued: "Just give me, just give God, a brief period of your air time. And let it be toward the end of the day."[10]

In 1955 he was given a brief interlude on the air each day—a brilliant idea that blossomed into a toehold in popular culture. The television program became familiar to Colombians, opening with a wooden cross and García-Herreros in a poncho over his clerical garb and ending with his famous tagline, mentioned above. This went on for fifty years and became the longest running program on Colombian television.

Minuto de Dios acquired its own radio station in 1985. The station reached a wide audience in north central Colombia through on-air coverage, but it quickly moved toward satellite and Web broadcasting to cover the whole country. Seven regional radio outlets had sprung up by 2008. The central station aimed to evangelize—educate its audience in Catholic doctrine—and found a place for an emphasis on healing and on its signature goal of "Christian solidarity with the poor" (*compromiso cristiano con los pobres*). This latter emphasis contrasted with many other Charismatic personalities and leaders whose work has been mostly with the middle classes. Signs appeared in the 2000s, however, that this distinct emphasis on social activism would be diluted in the next generation of Charismatic leaders.

With evangelization in mind, Minuto's personnel moved into television production work toward the beginning of the new century and formed a subsidiary corporation, Lumen 2000, now called Lumen TV, with help from a Dutch philanthropist. Similar to that of other Charismatics, the goal was to provide positive messages and to promote Christian and human values. In other words, Lumen TV attempted to be countercultural, supportive of Charismatic lives within a secular culture.

Padre Rafael's work grew to the extent that he brought in another priest, Diego Jaramillo, to share in the home construction, community building, and media work. Padre Diego did not come to this work as a convinced Charismatic but only became a Charismatic priest over time. His critical time of conversion to the movement seems to have occurred in 1973 at the first meeting of the Encuentros Carismáticos Católicos Latinoamericanos (ECCLA), to be discussed later in this chapter.[11]

Together García-Herreros and Jaramillo used press, radio, and television to spread information about and to generate enthusiasm for the movement. This effort was at the mass media level, but their most direct and effective work was conducting basic retreats in the Life in the Spirit, assemblies, congresses, Masses, and other activities. Life in the Spirit retreats were consistently emphasized, at least at the beginning of the movement, as a crucial step toward entrance into the movement. This is a far distant experience from communicating from the pulpit or a television stage. Persons who conduct these retreats are engulfed in listening to life histories, counseling, reconciling family members, and a host of other interactions that occur on the threshold of conversion.

García-Herreros died in 1992 at the age of eighty-three and Jaramillo took over as the president of Minuto de Dios. He expanded the effort toward more construction and media projects and obtained from the government permission to establish a university in the Minuto de Dios neighborhood for lower-class students who had few educational opportunities. The municipality of Minuto de Dios had created, at the time the model city was formed, an ordinance, somewhat unusual in Colombia in the 1960s, requiring elementary education of all children. Minuto had also created a high school with the same name and with more than ten branches around Colombia. A university was the logical outcome of these initiatives. Creation of the Universidad Minuto de Dios (Uniminuto) with regional branches was another huge task for the administrators of Minuto de Dios. The tapping into the generous support of the Colombian migrant community in the United States facilitated this wider growth.

It was not clear how deeply or widely the Charismatic spirit penetrated Uniminuto, the new university. Most Catholic universities in Latin America were not very Catholic in their mission or in the penetration of a strong theological spirit within the curriculum. Nonetheless, the president of Uniminuto in the early 2000s, Father Camilo Bernal Hadad, was a noted Charismatic priest and a leader in international renewal circles who sat on the board of the International Catholic Charismatic Renewal Services (ICCRS). If Uniminuto becomes a "Charismatic university," it would be one of the few in the world. Thus far, for most observers, the Franciscan University of Steubenville, Ohio, is one of the few to have qualified for that designation. In 2007, the new rector of the main branch of Uniminuto was an eminently qualified layperson with a special interest in conflict resolution and human rights. Thus the religious-secular character of the university was still being defined in practice.

In the evolution of Minuto de Dios in the twenty-first century, the shifts in its thinking about human development and specific ways to achieve that diffuse goal have been nimble and up-to-date with thinking in international development circles. While providing housing remained a priority, in 2008 Minuto de Dios was emphasizing microcredit, technical training, and a wide area of interest called "attention to the vulnerable." This latter area included humanitarian aid for persons displaced by Colombia's civil war (called *"la violencia"*), which intensified in the 1990s with billions of dollars of military aid from the United States coming for Plan Colombia. It also aimed at the eradication of child labor. Minuto de Dios took up a modest program of sponsoring individual children still living with their families but whose parents were unable to fund their primary or secondary education. Sponsors were asked to provide twenty dollars a month.

Padre Diego Jaramillo became the best-known international leader of Latin American Charismatics from 1977 to 1990 when he was a member of the International Catholic Charismatic Renewal Service Council, serving as its president from 1988 to 1990.[12] He preached in many countries. He wrote more than one hundred books and pamphlets to foster knowledge about the main aspects of the movement that, for most Catholics at the time, were unfamiliar.

The Second Colombian Pillar: Sonsón–Río Negro

The other great pioneer of Colombian Charismatic Renewal was Bishop Alfonso Uribe Jaramillo from the Medellín region. He was ordained in 1937 and taught for a while before going to the University of Montreal to obtain a doctorate in moral theology. As did many other priests who would have a strong influence on the future direction of the Latin American church, he worked in the 1940s in Catholic Action.[13]

This experience taught him how to work with laypersons and to value their contributions without clerical domination. The experience also showed him the benefit of lay leadership, especially in the engagement of the church with secular institutions. Participation in Catholic Action refined the sense of social justice that he had developed at the University of Montreal and engendered a propensity to see the day-by-day problems of the vulnerable sectors of the population.[14]

One practical aspect of that refined sensitivity to marginal groups was his founding a house for prostitutes who wished to find another occupation and the establishment of a shelter for street children. As García-Herreros did, he too started a fund to provide housing for the poor. To push this effort along he opened a brick factory.

He also wished to see more persons from peasant backgrounds as priests and in 1967 he founded a *campesino* (peasant farmer) seminary in Sonsón that later moved to Yarumal. The seminary was highly unusual in the lay and clerical mixture of its student body and its orientation, especially since it was aimed at providing leaders for farming communities, some as priests and others as laypersons. These future leaders were to promote both spiritual and economic development.

The campus included a huge classroom and a residence building as well as a large barn to store the fruit of the students' labors. It may have been the only dedicated Catholic farmer seminary in the world. Many graduates served the Colombian church and by 1990 more than two hundred graduates were serving as missionaries overseas.

The list of projects Uribe started—schools, hospitals, brick factories—would grow. What would remain impressive throughout his life was not only the wide social and spiritual vision Uribe showed but his ability to pull in others to put into practice his fertile ideas, often with no funded budget. The farmer seminary flourished because a series of rectors were willing to assume the leadership necessary to turn Uribe's ideas into buildings and curricula. This was the pattern of leadership by ideas and persuasion that Uribe followed throughout his life.

Although he was less well known in Europe and other continents than Padre Diego Jaramillo of Minuto de Dios, Uribe had a strong influence on the Charismatic movement, especially through the formation of priests. As a teacher and a seminary rector, he had a hand in the education of more than one thousand priests. He also took time to compose basic theological and spiritual works on the Charismatic movement at a time when his position as bishop gave legitimacy to the movement and brought an open-minded reception of new ideas associated with Charismatics that would have been overlooked or rejected without his sponsorship.

The Medellín region, before it became notorious for drug lords, was considered the most Catholic region of the country and—it was asserted—therefore, the most Catholic in Latin America.[15] That argument was put forward in terms of church participation and the number of priests, even if it was not fully convincing because the Catholicism in question was a traditional Catholicism unreformed by the church's social teaching, which began in the 1890s. What was noteworthy about Bishop Uribe was his ability to build upon the spiritual fervor that resided in the region. In the 1970s there was an abundance of priestly vocations in the region, especially in his diocese of Sonsón–Río Negro, an area mostly of small farms fifty to one hundred miles from the modern metropolis of Medellín.

The awareness of the need of a seminary with a special Charismatic character grew from several sources. First, many requests for sharing his clergy came to Uribe from other dioceses in the country and from abroad, places where there was a shortage of priests. Second, the Charismatic renewal was advancing through the Colombian church with Uribe as one of the best-known and forceful Charismatic leaders in the country. Third, a number of young men from the movement wished to join the priesthood but could not find a seminary that would welcome students from the Charismatic renewal because of the newness and strangeness of the movement and the generally conservative bent of the Colombian church, which was not ready to accept innovations. The country, Uribe felt, needed a Charismatic seminary. He took the bold step of approaching the archbishop of Medellín, the highly influential Alfonso López Trujillo, and the other bishops of the Antioquia ecclesiastical jurisdiction to approve this new seminary. Uribe had a strong reputation as a seminary teacher and rector in the region and they approved his initiative.

Uribe hoped that the new seminary would stress two special emphases needed in the Latin American church: evangelization and missions. With these goals in mind, in 1981 he founded the Missionary Seminary of the Holy Spirit. This was a vast undertaking in that he had to provide education for candidates starting in their high school years and proceeding several more years through philosophy before they entered theological studies and ordination to the priesthood. By 2002, some 220 students had become priests. Within that group a special association grew up of seminarians willing to serve in other dioceses and countries while remaining priests of the diocese of Sansón. Thirty-nine priests came from this group to become diocesan missionaries, that is, priests sent from the diocese to serve elsewhere.

Parallel to the effort of creating and running the Charismatic seminary, he created a corps of young priests dedicated to the spread of the Charismatic renewal, a group he called Servants of the Holy Spirit. He also created a congregation of sisters, Servants of the Divine Spirit, to work in evangelization in parishes where there was a shortage of priests. For lay leaders he started a university, la Universidad Católica del Oriente. He died in 1993 at the age of seventy-nine but his works flourished through the organizations he created and the dispersal of the men and women who were carriers of the Charismatic renewal.

Among writers within the renewal in Latin America, Bishop Uribe was one of the best known. His writings established him as a central figure of the movement. Seven of his books are still widely read, a tribute to the solidity and appeal of his theological presentations. But he will probably be best known for providing seminary educations to persons entering the priesthood from a Charismatic background when other seminaries would not accommodate them. With a more generalized support for the movement in the 2000s this issue of seminary training seemed to have dampened down.

Within the Latin American episcopate, Uribe played a key role in pulling bishops together to support the Charismatic movement at a crucial moment in its Latin American history when it needed support from higher ranks if it were to prosper. In 1987 he held in his diocese a meeting on the movement for Latin American bishops (Encuentro Episcopal Lati-noamericano). The meeting had no official status and lacked the sponsor-ship of the Latin American Bishops Conference (CELAM). The meeting depended on the suasion of Uribe and drew 109 archbishops, bishops, and prelates to La Ceja. The participants put together a strong statement called "The Catholic Charismatic Spiritual Renewal." The statement described the major elements of the movement in refined and succinct language. A wide range of bishops signed that statement. In many ways it provided the weighty document the movement then needed in Latin America. The statement was published on various Web sites and was read in places like Cuba where the movement was still in its infancy in 1987.

The Spread of the Movement in Colombia

Forty years after the movement came to Colombia, some organizational features persisted and others appeared as new. One of the strongest lasting emphases has been on work with youth. For example, by 1972 Minuto de Dios's urban community with that name had begun sending young vol-unteers as internal missionaries-evangelizers to other parts of the country, starting in Santander and Barbosa. Soon groups went evangelizing all over Colombia and to neighboring countries.

In Minuto itself numerous prayer groups sprung up throughout the barrio. Sunday Charismatic liturgy became the focal point for the week and on each Tuesday Father Rafael held a special Mass for the sick, one of the constant preoccupations of the movement. An evolution not well doc-umented but only hinted at has taken place in the prayer groups of Minuto barrio. Padre Diego described a number of groups becoming consolidated into Christian communities, presumably of the type closer to the Word of God community in Ann Arbor, Michigan, than Brazil's *comunidades de vida*, since there were close ties and numerous visitors from Ann Arbor in the early 1970s. In sum, some Minuto prayer groups grew into covenant communities with shared daily life and shared pastoral goals. Five of the youth prayer groups evolved into houses with special names and were the base of operation for those who wished to devote a full year to voluntary service in spreading the Charismatic movement and in evangelization.

To back up these and other efforts the Centro Carismático Minuto de Dios created a school, la Escuela de Servidores, to provide educa-tion in faith and to provide housing for its students. The Servidores sent out enough graduates that it became useful to hold a series of national meetings for alumni. The school had blossomed into a three-year program for teachers and lay catechists by 2008. As if these activities were not enough, Centro Carismático Minuto de Dios became the site for the Colombian national offices and the Latin American offices of the Charismatic movement in 1982. For a time García-Herreros appeared to be the solitary leader of the Charismatic movement in Bogotá, but the spread of the movement in the 1990s showed that the Colombian church and its bishops were catching up.[16]

That the movement had reached into the highest ranks of the bishops in Colombia and Latin America became clear when Bishop Jorge Jiménez Carvajal became the president of the Latin American Bishops Conference (CELAM). Bishop Jiménez attended the first ECCLA meeting in Bogotá and became bishop of a region partly under control of Colombian guerrillas. He was kidnapped (and eventually released) by guerrillas while president of CELAM.

A New Generation and Change

Colombia has always been a country marked by strong regionalism, with Medellín, Cali, and Baranquilla as rivals to Bogotá as centers of influence. Minuto's directors felt they needed to reach out from Bogotá. One of their first efforts was to establish a branch in Medellín. The Medellín branch of Minuto de Dios had prayer groups, not social-action projects, as the human basis of the movement there. Every activity and event appears to be centered in the dynamism of the prayer groups. Minuto de Dios hoped to have thousands of these groups in Medellín by 2010, with evangelization as the main goal. Minuto's central building in Medellín is called a prayer center—Casa de Oración Tierra Nueva, with a radio station and a bookstore. In early 2008 the house of prayer had eleven groups dedicated to evangelization, each with its own name and ethos, including prayer of intercession as the main focus of one of the groups. The central house offered a place for prayer groups to meet and for courses in evangelization with the hopes that members of prayer groups and other recruits would become missionary, that is active in reaching out to disengaged Catholics and to Protestant Pentecostals.

The curriculum of informal education provided at Medellín appears to offer evidence that the Minuto de Dios segment of the Charismatic movement—now in its second or third generation—was becoming more other-worldly and, in many ways, evangelical without social action. There were no model housing projects or anything similar. Charismatics at Minuto de Dios in Medellín looked like Charismatics in Brazil and other places: more mystical than mundane. The social-justice orientation that drove Padre Rafael to feverish activity and no little controversy was diminished in Medellín. The phrase that was repeated everywhere in García-Herreros's various statements of purpose, *"compromiso cristiano con los pobres"* (Christian commitment with the poor), is notably missing at Medellín.

Father John Montoya, a priest from the same religious congregation as Fathers García-Herreros and Jaramillo, was the director of the Minutos radio station in Medellín and the pastor of a parish. He preached at festivals and he was clearly part of the new generation of Charismatic priests in Colombia: he sang on public stages and he de-emphasized social issues. He sang and performed well enough to be posted as a singer at YouTube, where he and a singing group appeared as Padre John and Charisma Verde (Green Charisma).[17]

His views on social issues are typically vague and unfocused in contrast to García-Herreros's distinct views. No social or economic issues and certainly not housing for the poor, the signature issue of Minuto de Dios in the past, were mentioned as concerns on the group's Medellín Web site and its posted reflections on the Bible. In response to the question of what one does after a personal encounter with Jesus, Montoya said, "Be grateful and give your life in service."[18] In stating the mission of the radio station of which he is the director, he replied that Padre García-Herreros, the founder of Minuto de Dios, believed that "the ultimate word for the country is that we return to God . . . that we not have a superficial religion."[19] One could argue that this is a selective memory at work.

At another branch of Minuto de Dios, at Cartagena, the radio station was likewise the center of Charismatic activity. No house of prayer or ties to prayer groups were emphasized. What was similar to Medellín was the director of the station. He was Padre Alberto Linero, and like Father Montoya, he too was a Eudist priest. At the age of thirty-five, he was already a well-known preacher from the second generation of Charismatic priests before becoming the director. While he has not recorded music, he was known for his great support of the popular regional musical star Pillao Rodríguez. As other present-day Charismatics he saw (and wrote about) the value of the Christian message being conveyed in regional music, in this case, *vallenato*, music native to the Colombian Caribbean coast.[20] Linero was also a published author dealing with Charismatic themes. While Father Linero was a member of the same religious congregation as García-Herreros, he differed notably from him in not emphasizing the connection of Christianity and social justice.

One aspect that was relatively new to the Colombian movement was love of and support for religious rallies, called *festivales* in Colombia and other parts of Spanish America. These were mounted on stages in university auditoriums, parish halls, and the like. At Cartagena in February 2008 the festival sponsored by Minuto de Dios featured Padre Alberto as the preacher and Rafael Moreno as the singer. At Medellín the festival in February 2008 included as headliners Father John and Charisma Verde. The regional radio stations of Minuto de Dios served as excellent bases for messages of evangelization spoken or sung through the Christian music that is carried by local radio transmission and made available through streaming on the World Wide Web. The Festival Internacional de Alabanza at Medellín in February 2008, sponsored by the radio station, also included a Charismatic Cuban-American priest from New Orleans, Padre Pedro Nuñez.

The globalization of the movement showed up clearly in the various festivals that drew to its stages preachers, singers, and bands that crossed national boundaries. Nuñez concentrated on preaching engagements, but he has created one of the largest Charismatic festivals with music in the United States and one of the most popular overall in Louisiana. El Festival de Mensaje annually drew some forty-five thousand persons to two weekends of preaching, prayer, and music in New Orleans. Clearly what happens in Latin America will continue to influence the tastes and styles of being Catholic among the future Hispanic majority in the U.S. church.

Padre Pedro started his Hispanic ministry at the request of Archbishop Hannan in 1979 with a weekly page in Spanish in the diocesan newspaper. But his skills were more verbal than written and he quickly became a popular personality through radio and then television. His media work and other aspects of his ministry grew into an organization called Mensaje. By 2008, his radio and television programs were being carried widely in Latin America and the United States. He maintained an up-to-date Web site with a schedule of his preaching appearances and the times of his broadcasts as did so many other Charismatic leaders. His message did not consistently include concern for the poor or for social justice. The nearest his organization came to those issues was having a team that prayed for the needy (*necesitados*).

Regional Coordinating Agencies

Two streams of influence, one from Francis MacNutt, the other from Rafael García-Herreros, came together in the founding of the Latin American coordinating organization for the Charismatic movement in Latin America, the Encuentros Carismáticos Católicos Latinoamericanos (the Latin American Catholic Charismatic Encounter, or ECCLA). MacNutt had heard from sources in the Charismatic movements, mostly Protestant ones, that a dynamic start to the movement had been made at Bogotá but could probably use some assistance. In 1972, MacNutt made a stop there on his way back from solidifying the beginnings of the movement in Peru and Bolivia.

García-Herreros told MacNutt that, in MacNutt's words, "He was hesitant in communicating his conversion to the Charismatic movement until he could see how this would work out in the context of the Catholic community of 10,000 persons in Minuto de Dios neighborhood that he had helped to build up over the past fifteen years."[21] García-Herreros was stymied in not having the Charismatic movement catch on in the *barrios populares* (poor neighborhoods). MacNutt said he knew of priests working in *barrios populares* and could bring them to Bogotá. Thus for García-Herreros the main interest of the first meeting of the group was to have a small number of priests getting together to figure out how best to foster the movement among the poor. Or, in MacNutt's words, "to build Christian community, especially in poor barrios."[22]

From MacNutt's point of view, this meeting would be the beginning of the inter-American coordination of the movement. MacNutt, by then, was by the standards of the time a seasoned preacher in the movement while García-Herreros was just beginning. However, García-Herreros was Latin American and clearly had structures and people who would aid in organizing. García-Herreros was concentrating on "how the power of the Spirit might be expressed in a Catholic culture in order to bring the people of Colombia to Christ."[23] He was uncanny in understanding the culture and using it to the church's advantage.

The two agreed that MacNutt would convene the meeting, do most of the inviting of the original participants, and would turn the conduct of the meeting in Spanish over to a fellow Dominican, Father Ralph Rogawski. García-Herreros would host the meeting and thereafter would serve as the coordinator of the next Latin American meeting.

The founding of the ECCLA served many purposes. Most of all, it allowed participants to teach one another how to move about in the unknown terrain of Catholic Pentecostalism at the time. They faced two major intellectual issues. They were dealing with something that came to them from Protestant hands. The brand of Protestant Charismatic Christianity that was being offered them did not have a strong theological basis, at least one that they could deal with easily. They knew instinctively that they needed to set these Pentecostal ideas on Catholic footing if they intended to remain Catholic. They all did.

Then, too, Pentecostalism seemed to contradict what many of the Latin American Catholic founders of the movement were then doing at the time in social ministry or in teaching Catholic social doctrine. In fact, Pentecostalism seemed the direct theological opposite of the reform of the Latin American Catholic Church that had taken place three years earlier in Colombia at the historic meeting of the Latin American bishops in Medellín. There the church proclaimed its role as part of the socioeconomic and spiritual transformation of Latin America.[24]

That the adaptation of Pentecostalism to Catholicism in Latin America fell to their hands was clear evidence of the organizational looseness of the Charismatic movement and of the Catholic Church itself. Mid-level talent was putting forward a new way to be Catholic, somewhat apart from directives from upper-level managers, only informing them when necessary of their own entrepreneurial activities. Neither dioceses nor parishes typically took part in the origins of this life-altering movement for the church. This tolerance for entrepreneurial activity may explain why the Catholic Church allowed the Charismatic renewal to flourish while mainline Protestants did not typically have the same tolerance.[25]

MacNutt used his many contacts in Latin America and invited Catholic Charismatic leaders to Minuto de Dios in Bogotá in March 1973.[26] Twenty-three participants came from the Dominican Republic, Mexico, Puerto Rico, Costa Rica, and Venezuela in addition to Peru and Bolivia, which had been the main centers of attention for MacNutt. Notably, the only Protestant—and lay—person at the meeting, Sam Ballesteros, was elected chair for the second ECCLA meeting, which was to be held in Bogotá as well.

Recognition of the central role of laity—after all, this was to be a lay movement—brought many more laypersons to the second and subsequent meetings.[27] The second meeting of the ECCLA was held in Bogotá in 1974 and drew 220 participants from seventeen of the nineteen Latin American countries. Here was clear evidence of the velocity with which the movement spread in the seven years since the historic founding event at Pittsburgh in 1967. This was a movement of adults, mostly in their thirties, in which a conversion or at least a drastic change in their way of thinking and acting was involved.

Further, the transnational crossing from the culture of the modernized giant of the United States to cultures of third world environments was mostly seamless, if not, indeed, enhanced from passing from the north to the south. The movement would be enlarged surely by numbers and, perhaps, by what Latin America added to the movement. What was gained and what was lost in this transfer is a question that will act as a guiding theme through the analysis in this volume. In a word, did the movement become better by becoming Latin American?

Indeed, becoming Latin American was the main thread of what the movement accomplished for at least the first twenty years. Being open to the movement (in contrast to historical Protestantism) came from two special wellsprings: openness to magical realism deeply rooted in Catholic culture and openness surrounding the Vatican Council II. Colombia can be taken as an especially good place for magical realism. Few authors have been more adept at portraying magical realism than Colombia's Gabriel García Márquez, the Nobel Prize winner (and one of the authors anointed by Oprah Winfrey). Catholic Charismaticism appeared to be an appropriate embodiment of magical realism, with its willingness to suspend belief of what the eyes see in a world of unseen spirits and fantasy. In brief, this propensity can viewed as "Be ready for anything." In addition, no regional church, not even those in Africa or Asia, took Vatican Council II more seriously than the church in Latin America because no other church systematically applied Vatican Council II to its own region the way the Latin American church did. A tectonic change clearly took place beginning in 1962 (the start of Vatican Council II) and continuing intensely to 1968, when the Latin American Bishops Conference was held in Medellín. The Latin American church would not be the same. Others, especially Protestant observers, noted the changes and, for the most part, welcomed them.[28]

This Latin American openness to the Charismatic movement caused problems. Some problems were wrestled with and were resolved. Other issues remained insoluble. The first set of problems was contained in the task of putting Pentecostalism on a Catholic footing. A good start, already alluded to, was made in the United States and Europe by theologians such as Kilian McDonnell and Donald Gelpi, and most notably by the giant of Vatican Council II, Yves Congar.[29] MacNutt himself took the lead in providing a Catholic theological view on healing as a ministry practiced by early Christians but gradually lost in the church.[30] Specific Latin American concerns arising from the region's traditional or popular religion had to be dealt with more fully than had been done. Devotions to Mary, the Mother of God, and the saints certainly were not part of Pentecostalism, but they had to be included if Latin American Catholics were to join the movement in any significant numbers. Catholic sacraments and other issues were central but easier to deal with.

No historian has come forward to trace modern Latin American devotional life, as Eamon Duffy did for the centuries of English Catholic devotional life.[31] Such a history would show that Colombians and Mexicans included Mary in the Charismatic movement early on while further south in the lower Andes and the Southern Cone Catholic Charismatics included Mary after a period of neglect. The ECCLA group was not going to resolve these issues on the spot, but the discussants within the original group included better than average theologians. For example, MacNutt had a doctorate in theology from Aquinas Institute of Theology and García-Herreros did advanced graduate work in Rome and Switzerland. Furthermore, most participants had been actively keeping up for ten years with the new theology that flooded through the church during and after Vatican Council II (1962–65).

Thus Catholic Pentecostalism in Latin America fell into the hands of a special set of talented agents (and their immediate successors as leaders) whose array of talents, from theological insights to entrepreneurial skills to polished preaching, may not be duplicated for a long time. Within three decades, under their hands and those of others, Latin American Charismaticism would increasingly take on its own character.[32] One of the main mechanisms for stimulating and communicating these changes were the regular meetings of the ECCLA.[33]

As the movement grew, more countries, newly alive with the renewal, sent leaders to the meetings of the ECCLA. The site of the meeting then changed from Bogotá to Puerto Rico and thereafter to other countries. The move from Bogotá was made despite Bogotá having become the central location for the Latin American Bishops Conference.

Because of the mobile quality of the meetings and diffuse leadership a weak but central coordinating body, the Consejo Católico Carismático Latinoamericano (CONCCLAT), was created. This coordinating "center" moved every two years and was headed by a new person at each location. Its main functions were organizing the regular meetings and new activities, such as a transnational priest retreat and a music festival. A separate wing for a youth secretariat was created as well, with its first biennial meeting in 2003. The Consejo Católico Carismático Latinoamericano has no dedicated building for its headquarters, no board, no bishop advisor, and a minimally active Web site. Clearly no single organization or authority acts as the spokesperson for the movement in Latin America. This lack of bureaucracy gives the renewal a nimbleness for innovation, but it also deprives the movement of a voice and weight for lobbying its interests with the Latin American bishops at CELAM.

The Encuentros Carismáticos Católicos Latinoamericanos and its umbrella Consejo Católico Carismático Latinoamericano exist more in cyberspace and in the minds of their participants than in what social scientists describe as formal organizational expressions typical of a social or religious movement, with officers, a division of labor, and flow-of-responsibility charts. The Latin American Charismatic renewal in several aspects is thoroughly postmodern.

In many ways the direction followed and the emphases placed for future efforts in the Spanish-speaking countries were consolidated at the meeting in Bogotá in 1974. Reading through interviews and documents of the last forty years shows a remarkable consistency in vision carried forward to the present.

An almost immediate consequence of the first meeting in Bogotá was the organizing of the First Youth Council in April 1973. Some three hundred participants were expected, but some five thousand showed up, taxing the hospitality of host families at the Minuto de Dios community in Bogotá but serving as a spark for the creation of many spontaneous prayer groups and assemblies within the meeting.

Two of the core pastoral ideas discussed at the first meeting in Bogotá were the goals of forming small communities and the pursuit of social justice from the grass roots. The preferred form of small community at the time within the Latin American church was the Christian base communities, often called CEBs. During the meeting Father Ralph Rogawski and Sister Helen Marie Raycraft, both Dominicans working in the barrios of Santa Cruz, extolled the reception of the poor to this type of religious community working toward its own political goals.

At the meeting Rogawski and Raycraft received invitations to help initiate similar communities in the barrios of Colombia, Venezuela, and Mexico. Their Dominican Missionary Preaching Team responded to invitations by starting in Colombia. One of the first parishes they went to was located in Cali, one of the four major cities of Colombia. At Cali, a priest missionary from Idaho served as the pastor. Father William Kenneth Weigand, later the bishop of Sacramento, California, gave extraordinary support to the Dominican Missionary Preaching Team. The parish of St. John the Baptist in Barrio Guabal had sixty thousand residents, a relatively impossible number of persons to give pastoral care to. Clearly the parish needed intermediate structures—small communities—in which persons would have interaction with one another on the basis of their faith, would hear the word of God, and would attempt to improve their living conditions together. Over the years, with follow-up visits by the missionary team, some thirty-five CEBs had pulled together into functioning groups.

The pastor backed the initiative up by assigning Sunday Masses to his assistants so he could spend most of Sundays with leaders of the CEBs for their intellectual and spiritual formation, including basic education in the Charismatic way to be Christian. On a regular basis Father Weigand and small-community leaders went off on weekend encampments so they could avoid distractions and mutually work out how best to educate poorly trained Catholics in the basic truths of the Catholic faith. This process of re-education fostered a sense of urgency of communicating a message and pulling together as a parish team. Weigand used the small-community leaders as his parish council. In this way the mega-parish of St. John the Baptist grew from the ground up, its small communities acting as cells within a living body.

While the pastor was pleased with the reorganization of the parish and the moderate social activism that was growing among his parishioners, others were not. The local politicians, who were vigilant in maintaining their paternalistic control of Guabal, became hostile to the neighbors' organizing. They distributed leaflets denouncing the Dominicans and the local parish personnel. Weigand not only did not back down but supported the creation of lay preaching teams in his own parish. He further sent out teams of six to eight laypersons to conduct mission renewal weeks in other neighborhoods and parishes of the Cali area. These teams preached and helped to create small ecclesial communities that anchored the renewal in other places. A movement rather than a passing fad was taking shape.

By 2000, Colombia had one of the highest percentages, 28 percent, of Charismatics in the national Catholic population. The number of Charismatics, 11.3 million, was second to Brazil and exceeded Mexico's 9 million, although Mexico's Catholic population is more than twice that of Colombia. True to the intention of the Colombian founders of the movement that the movement be primarily lay in character, only 3 percent of Colombia's priests are counted by the national coordinating headquarters as Charismatic.[34]

One of the strategies that came out of the first ECCLA meeting was itinerant preaching to spark the movement. Those who already had acquired experience in the movement felt impelled to share it. Itinerant preachers would go on for many years to promote conversion and healing in other countries in much of Latin America and in the larger Catholic world. The best-known Charismatic missionary traveled from his base in the Dominican Republic. Emiliano Tardif, a Canadian priest, went as a missionary for the movement to seventy-one countries.

A number of other persons also operated as itinerant preachers and prime movers in the movement. Father Joe Kane, a Canadian oblate, developed a preaching mission with a team of laypersons in the barrios of Lima. They emphasized renewal and healing and formed small ecclesial communities. In a meeting Kane and Rogawski agreed that Kane and colleagues would accept invitations from Peru, Chile, and Ecuador, while Rogawski and companions would go to Colombia, Venezuela, and Mexico.

Ralph Rogawski and Helen Raycraft refined their approach as the Dominican Missionary Preaching Team, working first in Latin America and then through most of the United States. After they helped to establish communities in Colombia, they moved on to Venezuela and Mexico. They gave priests' retreats in Puerto Rico where the renewal experienced a fast start.

Conclusion

In contrast to many other Latin American countries, the Catholic Charismatic Renewal thrived in a country with perhaps the least religious competition. A twenty-year review of studies on religion in Colombia yields a 4 percent estimate of Protestants in the country, of whom Pentecostals are presumed to be about half.[35] Nonetheless, competition appeared to be at a high pitch with numerous Pentecostal and evangelical groups in the country vying for attention and for new members in a turbulent environment of a civil war and the state's incapacity to protect its citizens. During the late 1990s, Protestants, previously politically quiescent in the country, chose to enter widely publicized "religious wars" in the national elections of 1994,[36] so that whatever was their percentage in the population, their influence seemed strong and threatening. Thus a case could be made that competition contributed to a great increase in Catholic Charismatics as a way to confront Pentecostal growth. But alternative explanations that include the influence of globalization of culture, as from the United States (especially given Colombia's proximity to the United States), seem more appropriate.

The issue of social class also comes up in the Colombian case. David Martin, one of the world's leading authorities on the Pentecostal/Charismatic movement and on secularization theory, characterized Catholic Charismatic Renewal as middle class dipping down to lower class (while in his view Pentecostalism trended up from the lower class to the middle class).[37] This was not borne out in Colombia. Minuto de Dios, where the movement commenced in the country, was a lower-class area and the Colombian movement has maintained a strong allegiance of lower-class members into the 1990s and beyond, shown by Minuto's efforts to extend educational opportunities to the poor, including Uniminuto, its university.

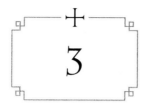

THE DOMINICAN
REPUBLIC

The Preacher and His Island

The Catholic Church in the Dominican Republic was a little-known part of the Latin American church for most of its history. But in the late twentieth century a confluence of influences brought new life to the Dominican church. Lay vitalization movements were particularly important. One of these movements, the Catholic Charismatic Renewal, took hold early in the movement's history and the Dominican Republic formed one of the main pillars of the movement in the region.

Charismatic preachers who have visited most of Latin America regard the Dominican Republic as one of the most intensively Catholic Charismatic countries. In fact, it was a major base from which the movement radiated to Latin America and other parts of the globe. The fame as the greatest national apostle of the movement would have to go to Padre Emiliano Tardif. The Dominican Republic was his adopted country. He was believed by many to be a saint and some thought he worked miracles.

That the Dominican Republic would contain one of the most widely diffused Charismatic movements is easily understood since the country is rather narrowly confined and a preacher's influence could easily reach to most corners of the country. Moreover, the Catholic Church there quietly built up strong formal and informal networks of bishops, small communities, and lay leaders through twentieth-century missionaries.

The advance of the Charismatic renewal, however, has come at a price: the movement seems to have diverted away generalized support of Dominican Catholics for a social-justice orientation. This orientation was finally taking hold in the 1990s after decades of what looked like social quietism under the Trujillo dictatorship.[1]

Whereas the Catholic Church in many other Latin American countries came alive socially and politically during the military era (1969–85),[2] the church in the Dominican Republic was just coming out of the dark ages under the Trujillo family dictatorship in 1961. The forces for change in the church mandated by the Latin American Bishops Conference (CELAM) held in Medellín in 1968 were at work in the country, enhanced by a special group of talented and visionary missionaries and most of all by an unusual closeness of parish priest and people in many areas of the island.[3] The Trujillo dictatorship paradoxically drew people and church more closely together. This closeness would be the foundation for the future church. When asked in the 1980s about the difference between the Catholic Church in the Dominican Republic and in Puerto Rico, the papal nuncio to both countries at the time said that the church in the Dominican Republic was accessible; that is, the bishops were available and disposed to listen to their people while the Puerto Rican church leadership (since changed) was authoritarian and distant from the people.[4] To a considerable extent the Dominican bishops reflected the solid foundation of parish priest and people.

The foundation for a strong church was decades in the making. In the early twentieth century the Catholic Church was a shell of an institution. The church had almost no native clergy. Foreign Catholics, especially Canadians, came to its rescue. They also put a foreign stamp on the culture and organization of the church. From the 1940s through the 1960s Canadian priests staffed fully one-third of the rural parishes of the country.

The Influx of Missionaries

The Dominican Republic anticipated by thirty years the great missionary influx from the North Atlantic countries to Latin America that came to be called a missionary crusade of the 1960–70s.[5] In the mid-1930s when the Trujillo family was consolidating its control of the island, the Dominican archbishop Ricardo Pittini sought and obtained permission from the senior Rafael Trujillo to invite fourteen foreign orders and missionary groups to the country. From the native church's point of view, this was to make up for a dearth of priests and sisters in the country. From

Trujillo's point of view, this import was expected to give the country an international luster and a stronger Catholic Church that it badly needed.

From the beginning of this initiative the Trujillo family had a proprietary interest in the church and in its new foreign mission partners. This alliance would eventually create grave problems of independence for action by the foreign missionary groups, but despite central governmental control the missionary groups adeptly put their own stamp on the parishes, schools, and hospitals where they worked.

The Trujillos desired and made clear to missionaries that they were to vivify Catholicism, strengthen church institutions, and administer rural parishes in outlying areas. The rural areas of most of Latin America at this time, notoriously the Dominican Republic, Bolivia, Guatemala, and Cuba, were in disastrous shape.[6] The commonly repeated histories of what the missionaries found in rural areas at this time were that of no priests resident in the countryside and of peasants seeing a visiting priest in a run-down church every four or five years. For complex reasons, Rafael Trujillo proclaimed himself Protector of the Church, with special interest in the rural poor.

Two Canadian foreign mission societies, one English-speaking, the Scarboro Society, and one French-speaking, the Missionaries of the Sacred Heart, accepted the invitation.[7] Both were important, especially in later stages of resistance to the Trujillo family dictatorship. In the turbulent period after Trujillo's death, Father Arthur MacKinnon of Scarboro was killed during the U.S. invasion in 1965 under mysterious circumstances.[8]

The emphasis here is on the Sacred Heart Fathers because it is from them that the Charismatic movement achieved unusual fruition. In 1935, these missionaries based in Quebec City accepted twelve parishes in the Cibao and Samaná regions of the northern part of the country. Most of these parishes were enormous, being two hundred to four hundred square miles, each with between twelve thousand and twenty-five thousand inhabitants. Parishioners were, for the most part, nominal Catholics, having very little understanding of the faith. They practiced an unlettered popular religion learned at home. This religion was a mixture of a sense of awe for God and creation, devotion to the saints, and a relationship to God that was close to magical bargaining. Both parties, missionaries and parishioners, had a lot to learn from one another. After eighty years of interaction, laypersons from the Dominican Republic would become missionaries to other countries. They would also represent a new kind of Latin American Catholic, aggressively evangelizing.

In part because the Trujillos limited a public voice for the church, Canadian missionaries emphasized building the church up from the base, away from the gaze of the Trujillos' sycophant followers in the capital. This would eventually have a strong payoff in terms of church vitality fifty years later. They worked at creating parish structures and religious practices with churches, chapels, and services and with teaching about God, prayer, and the sacraments. But the Canadians also were used to dealing with the poor in Canada and were leaders in self-empowerment programs such as cooperatives and credit unions. From the 1960s onward they had a vision of the missionary as an agent of socioeconomic development, or as it came to be called in the Dominican Republic *social pastoral*.

The heart of the Canadian vision came from the Coady Institute for cooperatives at Antigonish and the Maritime Provinces. During the terrible days of the Great Depression there and repeated for the poor of the Dominican Republic at a later date, parish priests formed study groups in communities that led to cooperatives. These groups met to reflect on economic problems, to strengthen common people's confidence in their abilities to solve their own problems, to foster the emergence of local leaders, and to improve their lives, materially and spiritually. The formation of small groups and the imparted conviction by the missionaries that they needed to do things together were crucial for the future of the church. Out of these cooperatives and other groups grew the small base communities and a leadership class, the *presidentes de la asamblea*, that came to be the backbone of the Dominican church. In some ways, too, the prayer groups and covenant communities of the Charismatic movement built on this foundation.

The cooperatives were viewed as Christian communities. They spread literacy and small-business skills. But, in retrospect, Father Tardif and other missionaries believed that something was missing. While people bonded together on the basis of religious identity, the spiritual dimension of that identity was not stressed. In fact, in many cooperative members, religious faith was not deeply rooted in understanding or devotion. This became clear as cooperative members faltered in the performance of their shared duties or drifted away from the church.

In Tardif's case, sickness brought him to a crisis point at which he was forced to consider the course of his life and pastoral activity. He was, he said in later remembrances, killing himself with one activity after another, facing up to one practical problem after the other. He fell sick in 1973 with a virulent form of tuberculosis in both lungs, returned to Canada, and expected to die. In Quebec he was visited by five laypersons from the Catholic Charismatic movement, which was still in its early days.[9] That they should pray for him and expect his healing through these prayers jolted him. He felt ridiculous and asked them to close the door so that he would not be seen in what he then considered awkward circumstances. Despite his lack of confidence in healing prayer, he experienced a sudden cure, as certified by his doctors.

From then on, he gave himself to learning about and spreading the movement. He visited major Charismatic centers in the province of Quebec and at Pittsburgh and Notre Dame. He was a changed person when he returned to the Dominican Republic. In the parish work he took up in 1974 he placed greatest emphasis on forming prayer groups so that the members of the groups would become evangelizers and would have regard for the poor. Praying for healing of others was one of his main new roles, one that often seemed to bring results. As manifested earlier in his life, he had a strong ability to attract others to his projects.

He was assigned to the parish of Nagua. This was a town of some fifteen thousand, with thirty barrios surrounding the town. He was one of three parish priests there. One of them, Father Raymond-Marie Audet, had also become Charismatic in Canada. On the day of Tardif's arrival, Audet invited him to attend a meeting of a prayer group that Audet had founded. Tardif described his own healing at the meeting and invited suffering persons to come forward for their healing.

Two persons were reported as immediately cured. Word of the healings spread quickly in the town. The prayer group expanded and so too did interest in healing. Father Audet typically conducted Mass in barrios. In one of these neighborhoods, there were reputed to be more prostitutes than church-going Catholics. After the Mass there, Father Audet invited the sick to come forward so that he could pray with them for healing. Some fifteen persons were reported as healed but one cure was prominent for being instantaneous and dramatic. A woman with twisted fingers from rheumatoid arthritis was well known because she could not feed herself. During the prayers for healing she felt a burning sensation and experienced an opening of her fingers.

The religious climate of the barrio was reported to have changed as had that of the larger parish. The parish church building was too small to accommodate persons with renewed interest in religion. Furthermore, the three priests could not give adequate spiritual attention to individual persons so they formed small groups and appointed lay leaders. Some fifty-two prayer groups were formed in the town and barrios. The groups typically numbered between fifty and eighty persons; some grew to be more than one hundred persons. Groups had to split and to multiply because no available buildings would hold them and because everyone, it seemed, wanted to talk about their own lives, personal and spiritual, and to be helped into adjusting to the Charismatic movement.

This modification of behavior and change in thinking needed by the movement required instruction. Tardif believed that leaders and teachers would emerge among the laity. Catechists were already at hand. These were trained lay religious educators. He and the other priests entrusted the catechists with pastoral care of the prayer groups. They were to conduct a half-hour Bible study during each meeting. Tardif was building on solid foundations—trained catechists and Bible study as the basis of understanding. Thus, the priests maintained contact with large numbers of persons through dividing the parish into regions. They met with each region one evening a month for teaching and spiritual direction.

From the start Tardif envisioned healing as covering a wide range of ills. Beyond physical problems, he saw persons struggling with spiritual ills and being apparently healed from excessive guilt, anxiety, addictions, memories of rejection and abandonment, and damaged interpersonal relationships. This emphasis on better interpersonal relationships led thirty-two unmarried couples on one occasion to request the sacrament of matrimony. Nagua, with the reputation as a city of prostitution, saw some prostitutes abandon the profession and the city gained a new reputation as a city of prayer. This new fame brought thousands, including many outsiders, to weekly public prayer meetings. On several occasions attendance reached as high as forty thousand.

While he was assigned to Nagua, Tardif was asked by his superior to fill in for the parish priest at Pimentel while that priest was on home leave. This was the place that brought Tardif to the sudden and dramatic attention of the nation. On the first Sunday at Pimentel, a small village of wooden residences of farmers who worked the surrounding fields, Padre Tardif announced that he would give a conference each Wednesday for a few weeks about the Charismatic renewal. Among the two hundred who showed up the following Wednesday, one person was carried in on a stretcher, unable to walk, due to a back problem. After Tardif prayed over him, the man began to be *agitado* (physically agitated) and then stood up and walked for the first time in five years. In the midst of thanksgiving and more prayers, another ten persons were reported as healed of various sicknesses.

Word of these apparent healings spread quickly through the countryside and three thousand people showed up the following Wednesday. Seeing the crowd and sensing the presence of many curiosity seekers,[10] Tardif shifted his plan from a talk on the movement to holding a Mass for the sick. The church was too small to accommodate the crowd so he celebrated Mass outdoors with a microphone and loudspeakers. A blind woman began to see that day during the service and had a remarkable return of vision the next day. By the third week some seven thousand people were on hand for the outdoor Mass for the sick. Many who came were sick, blind, or paralyzed. The cars and trucks that brought them from outlying regions jammed the narrow highways and caused annoying problems for rural police, who were unaccustomed to chaos or to long hours on duty. They complained to the police chief, but he replied that his own wife was healed the previous week and the chief reportedly obtained eighteen extra policemen on loan from other stations for directing traffic.

The following Wednesday, June 9, was the anniversary of Tardif's return to the Dominican Republic and that was considered to be of significance for the multitude of persons who were coming from all over the country to see for themselves what was occurring. Twenty thousand people flooded the village. Tardif moved the altar and the microphone to the roof of the one-story rectory as a stage for the Mass and prayers for the sick. Some one hundred people were thought to have been healed that evening. By the time of the fifth week and the anticipated Wednesday Mass for the sick, people had come from Puerto Rico and Haiti as well as the Dominican Republic. The crowd was estimated at more than forty thousand and photos seem to confirm the number.

The sudden fame brought waves of criticism in the press and on television. Tardif was called a witch, a charlatan, a faker, and worse, but he remained serene. Throughout his priestly ministry, he never claimed to work miracles but said that God accomplished healing. Tardif attempted to deal with the notoriety and the gossip mechanisms embedded in Caribbean culture with as much public-relations savvy as he could manage.

After he returned to the parish at Nagua, rumors about him and the Charismatic movement ranged from political meddling in municipal politics to spiritism. Since some of his doubters were other priests and influential laypeople, Tardif was especially careful to meet regularly with the two bishops in the area, Juan Antonio Flores Santana of La Vega and Roque Adames Rodríguez of Santiago. Both continued to support him in his work. Their support was crucial for everything else that was to follow.

The Covenant Community

Padre Tardif promoted prayer groups as part of the pastoral plan for the spiritual renovation of the parish and began extending this effort to the nearby villages and rural areas. His efforts over a few years paid off with evidence of a spirit of prayer in parishioners and in a small group of laypersons who wanted to work full time in fostering the movement. In 1982 he founded his own covenant community called Siervos de Cristo Vivo (Servants of the Living Christ).

The idea for the community grew from the spiritual experiences of three laypersons who began working with Padre Tardif in Nagua and Pimentel. In 1976, they went with him as members of the Dominican delegation to the fourth Encuentros Carismáticos Católicos Latinoamericanos (ECCLA) at Caracas. The apparent healing powers of Father Tardif became known to delegates from other countries. From then on he and his small team received invitations to travel to other countries. In 1977, they were invited to what was billed as the first ecumenical Charismatic congress in the world at Kansas City. The congress drew fifty-five thousand people, including a large Spanish-speaking contingent.

The team went the following year to Miami. These joint ventures, demanding increased personal involvement for laypersons unaccustomed to travel and unaccustomed to ignoring their personal lives in provincial towns, made clear the need for forming a community. By 1982 seven laypersons, including two married couples, and Father Tardif agreed to form the Siervos de Cristo Vivo. This was a covenant community with shared common life and resources. The relatively long gestation for the community paid off in terms of compatibility for doing things together.[11] The Siervos became fully dedicated to evangelization.

With their previous experience of travel to North America and Europe, the Siervos had a much wider vision of what they wanted to do in the church. They also had been building up a reputation that would make it easier for foreigners to want to help them spread the Charismatic message. While they created ten houses for the community in the Dominican Republic,[12] by 2007 they had also established seven houses in Europe, four in the United States, two each in Cuba and Colombia, and single houses in Panama, Puerto Rico, and Argentina.

In the mid-1990s Padre Tardif and a Mexican layperson, Jose Prado Flores, agreed to create sister schools of evangelization. The ones in the Dominican Republic were called by various names. Their projected national Escuela de Evangelización Juan Pablo II functioned largely on paper until 2007 when the Santo Domingo campus for the school began to be constructed. The schools in the Dominican Republic were in contrast to the worldwide enterprise Prado had started from Mexico, the Escuelas de Evangelización San Andrés with branches in all regions of the world. Tardif and his Siervos de Cristo Vivo had a different emphasis for evangelization than Prado, one rooted in the houses and the communities of laypersons housed therein as schools of evangelization. Communities went to the trouble of formally organizing evangelization schools in seven of ten cities and towns where they had houses.

The covenant communities and their houses in the Dominican Republic also supported a medical clinic and a bookstore, but notably absent were the investments in radio and television production and the involvement in music that characterized Colombian and Brazilian Charismatics. On balance, comparing pastoral efforts before and after the Charismatic renewal came to the Dominican Republic, it appears that the renewal increased an interest in more intense spirituality, made Dominican laypersons aware of the need of religious education, created a large force of lay evangelizers to address that need, reduced Pentecostal competition by increasing religious knowledge and loyalty to the Catholic Church, increased candidates to the priesthood, and sent well-formed lay missionaries to other countries. It also reinforced the Dominican identity of the Catholic Church after almost a century of extensive foreign missionary presence.

The spirituality that intensified was other-worldly and personal, not this-worldly and oriented primarily to the common good. Thus what appeared to be diminished was the strong emphasis on *social pastoral* that had been built up over decades of efforts to spread the social teaching of the church. Charismatic leaders who had been in *social pastoral* believed that something better had taken its place. But older missionaries were not convinced. One could argue it was too early to tell, that emphasis on activism or prayers tends to swing through phases, and that there would eventually be a synthesis of both tendencies.

Dominican laypersons—not the traditional missionaries who were priests and sisters—were going to other countries as missionaries. As noted, this missionary activity reversed the historical missionary flow from other parts of the world to Latin America. After five hundred years of looking inward and being dependent on other countries for supplying intellectual, human, and financial resources, Latin Americans were reaching out, confidently. And laypersons were supplying the missionary push in ways that were not predicted.

Since many persons were drawn to Padre Tardif because of his growing reputation as being able to heal people, both he and his covenant community were deeply involved in explaining how a Christian should view healing. That healing was a common practice in the early Christian church was a theme that Francis MacNutt was delving into through book-long treatises, a corps of works that grew by further historical research, theological reflection, and extension to a new range of implications, including what seemed truly esoteric, as healing the family tree and deliverance from evil spirits.[13] Tardif could keep nuanced views about healing in his head. His disciples needed something in writing; this being the twenty-first century, they needed something specifically for the World Wide Web. So it was that the Siervos created on their Web site a compendium of information about healing.[14] There one finds authoritative statements from the Vatican's Congregation of the Doctrine of the Faith with a straightforward reflection on prayer to obtain healing from God. The long history of prayer and sickness over the centuries is summarized. The compendium has surprising theological depth. There are no instant answers or detailed steps but rather a description of how one disposes oneself before God for healing. And the Web site also shows how one should view illness with persistent pain, despite prayer, and, in many cases, impending death.

Many other aspects of healing were taken up. Some themes were quite striking and extended to include every possible aspect of wholeness: inner healing, pardoning enemies, healing of hate or fear, intergenerational healing, and the healing of negative self-image. Throughout, a sense of mystery and dependence on God is maintained. Without that sense, these Web pages could easily be the target of cynical humor or ridicule, along the lines of dialing up a cure. Professional theologians might wonder, though, about the excessive use of religion in an instrumental way. In their view, purity of religion tends toward regarding God in himself through praise, not primarily through seeking favors. Nonetheless, these views of suffering and the divine expressed by the Siervos stand in stark contrast to the health-and-wealth Pentecostals, the neo-Pentecostals who have grown by leaps and bounds by their extreme emphasis on the promise of healing as a reward.

When the Latin American bishops met in 1992 for their fourth general conference (general conferences are held every ten years or so), they went to the Dominican Republic not because the church there was a paragon of strength at that time but largely because the world was celebrating the fifth centenary of Columbus's arrival at the island. The *New York Times*, among others, found little to praise in the Dominican Catholic Church and plenty to worry about, especially the presence of lively Pentecostals. If reporters did note that the seminaries were full, they did not know what that abundance implied. Even though Charismatics had notable accomplishments in the country, they were largely overlooked, probably because the reporters believed the United States to be the measure of all things and were aware that the movement had declined in the United States.[15]

Divergent Paths: This-Worldly versus Other-Worldly

The emphases of the two Canadian missionary groups were decidedly different. The Scarboro priests stressed socioeconomic development and political action. They tended toward shorter commitments to the country. The Missionaries of the Sacred Heart Fathers—Father Tardif's group— put much deeper roots down, staying on in the same parish for decades. While they promoted cooperatives, they had as a long-term goal that of fostering native vocations to the priesthood. The lack of native clergy was so dire in the Dominican Republic that 80 percent of the clergy in the Trujillo period were foreign missionaries, even after four hundred years of the presence of the Catholic Church in the country. In 1960, 240 foreign priests and 70 native priests served 3 million Catholics.

The Quebecers took time to foster priestly vocations, both diocesan and religious. At considerable sacrifice in terms of human resources they set up a regional seminary at San José de las Matas in 1956. Eventually they had enough native recruits to their order that the Missionaries of the Sacred Heart formed a province in the Dominican Republic separate from the mother province in Quebec. By 2006, 55 Dominicans and 12 very old Canadians made up the province. A counterpart group of Canadian nuns did even better and had 120 sisters from the Dominican Republic.

The total number of native priests grew from 70 in 1960 to 890 in 2004, more than 1,000 percent. The trend-line was a steady upward climb, suggesting that no one policy was responsible for the growth. Dominican scholars agreed that promotion of spiritual renewal, moderate economic development, and lay leadership by the church all contributed to the increases.[16] The Charismatic renewal added further fuel to the increase in the priesthood just when new energy was needed due to the partial decline of other lay movements. Between 2001 and 2004 seminarians in the Dominican Republic increased by 20 percent while declining in North Atlantic countries.

The French Canadians' sensitivity to national culture seems pivotal to their various successes and what was to follow in the Charismatic renewal. For example, they demonstrated such sensitivity with their active collaboration with Bishop Roque Adames Rodríguez of Santiago, the second most important city of the country, and the creation of a center for training lay leaders for the rich rural areas surrounding Santiago. These leaders were called presidentes de la asamblea, leaders of small groups in whom a strong measure of spiritual leadership, as in prayer and works, was entrusted. José Luis Sáez, the Jesuit dean of Catholic historians, called them probably the most important innovation of the second half of the twentieth century.[17] The communities were empowered to elect leaders among the trusted and competent persons of the community to lead cell-like groups in liturgical services, prayer, and communion. They were more than catechists and were similar to the Delegates of the Word lay leaders in Honduras. Several Dominican commentators, including Sáez, believed that this innovation was a major cultural breakthrough in that it reduced the cultural distance between pastor and faithful.

The Sacred Heart Fathers of Quebec, increasingly native Dominicans themselves, strongly supported this sharing of authority with the presidentes de la asamblea. The latter innovation was seen as increasing the church's rootededness in the people and enhancing the church's Dominican identity. The Sacred Heart Fathers reinforced their actions in their widely read Amigo del Hogar, a monthly magazine with more than fifty years of publishing history.

Within this wide network of parishes, priests, lay leaders, magazine, cultural outlook that was increasingly Dominican, Father Tardif was able to build on years of collective achievements. Similarly, his own history before becoming Charismatic was useful. He had been known as a serious and hard-working person who was a provincial superior for a time of his own group and the president of the National Conference of Religious (persons who belonged to religious orders and congregations).

Despite his reputation, on his return to the Dominican Republic after his illness he found that a number of priests lacked trust in him because of what they were hearing about his strange behavior, like speaking in tongues. Every week, especially on Sundays, a parade of buses and cars went to the parish church where Tardif preached and prayed for healing. One Sunday, a priest from a neighboring parish took the unusual step to see for himself. He unobtrusively took a seat in the middle of one of the Sunday multitudes to take part and to observe what was going on. At the end of the Mass, Tardif prayed for the sick and then prayed and sang *in tongues*. This ancient practice, known as glossolalia, had been largely lost in Christian churches.

For an outsider to Catholic or Protestant Pentecostalism, praying in tongues sounded like babbling—in fact, the kind of babbling that psychotic or drunk persons might do. The neighboring priest left the church building. He was reported to have said that Padre Tardif may have had his lungs cured but that he was sick in the head. Padre Tardif believed that he was not going to convince other priests to accept the movement through discussions with them. They would have to hear the testimonials of those who lives were changed and to witness the fruits of the renewal.

With a mixture of doubt and some openness, an increasing number of priests in the Dominican Republic undertook the Life in the Spirit retreat that was the entry point into the movement in the country. This retreat became a central activity for Tardif. The retreats were typically conducted at a retreat house near Santo Domingo.

Tardif was continually playing out his role as preacher and healer on a much wider scale than just his adopted country. Early in his life as a Charismatic Tardif was invited to give a retreat just for bishops in Colombia, then considered an ultra-conservative national church. This was followed by participation in an ad hoc conference of just bishops from all over Latin America, meeting without official weight to discuss the pros and cons of the movement. Tardif spoke so confidently about the merits of the movement that the bishops requested that he conduct in the following year a Life in the Spirit retreat for them. While many Charismatic preachers were caught up with local audiences, Tardif moved easily and frequently across the world. In part, he did this because he felt confident in addressing bishops, priests, sisters, and laypersons in ways that other preachers did not. He received active encouragement from them as well.

Trying to persuade persons in those distinct audiences of a major paradigm change in the church was not easy. The line of argument Tardif followed was that the Charismatic renewal was very much in line with Vatican Council II. This seemed to be key. Tardif was faced with church professionals and many laypersons who had undergone major changes in perspectives caused by the changes brought about by Vatican Council II. They were not about to give up a change in orientation that cost them dearly to have made. Indeed, Tardif argued, you don't have to give up that dear treasure, you only add on, and do that generously. The serious business of reform was replaced by a joyous enterprise of reform. He supplied new energy when that was needed in the church.

Tardif went to Rome to meet with other leaders of the renewal's Consejo Internacional (International Council) on the twenty-fifth anniversary of the renewal and to a meeting with Pope John Paul II with the same confidence about the movement that he had in addressing everybody else. In many ways Tardif was the ideal salesperson for radically new ideas, making their acceptance appear to be a seamless evolution from the core of Christian orthodoxy. While other Charismatic leaders and groups emphasized the new (New Pentecost, New Song, New Creation), Tardif traced the ancient quality of healing within the early church.

He also rode on the backs of the theologians who were the acknowledged fathers of Vatican Council II. Tardif was intelligent enough to get inside what major theologians, such as Yves Congar and others, wrote in their treatises about the Holy Spirit. Tardif was at least a good journeyman theologian; more, he was a popularizer who planted the movement squarely on theological and biblical foundations. These foundations not only got him a hearing but helped to keep new adherents within the movement and within the church.

While many dropouts from the Charismatic movement remain Catholic, the equivalent is not true of Protestant Pentecostals.[18] Large numbers of them make up the new and growing pool of persons "with no religion," a polling category that in the 2000s included 10–15 percent of the general population in Latin America, depending on the region, as noted earlier.

Dropping out of the movement is a real danger. The older versions of Protestant Pentecostalism, with larger numbers than later versions, had very high dropout rates.[19] In some places, more than half of new recruits were gone by the third year. Pentecostalism, in the classical form, as in the Assemblies of God, is a perfectionist religion with high requirements. Furthermore, Pentecostal pastors in denominations like the Assemblies of God were demanding, kept track of attendance, and dropped backsliders from church rolls.

Catholic Charismaticism is also demanding in terms of minimal moral standards and high ideals, including financial generosity (previously a weak point in Latin American Catholics). Ideally, one should be out evangelizing and perhaps going some other place than one's home parish to be a missionary. To get one's mind and heart ready for those roles takes months and years. Many Charismatics decide against trying. But dropouts stay in the church, pray better, and give more than the typical minimum offering for church support.

The profound confidence Tardif had in what he was doing was well communicated in a variety of other cultures. He took the Life in the Spirit retreats to some seventy countries, a third of the entire world. In this he was backed up by the covenant community of laypersons he created, the Siervos de Cristo Vivo. They went with him as a team, sharing in the preaching, counseling, and praying, and playing other roles needed for retreats to have an impact.

Vocation as Personal and Collective

That some covenant team members were married couples and most team members were dedicated laypersons added to the image of the spiritual ideals of the movement as accessible to ordinary folk, not a spirituality only for those called to be priests or nuns. The concept of a special vocation for each person has been very strong in the Catholic Church. Furthermore, the notion of each person having a special vocation was central to the appeal of the Charismatic movement. Tardif used this theme as well as or more effectively than most Charismatic preachers. As shown, what Tardif did as a Charismatic was in many ways an extension of what he had been doing before his "conversion." During all those years as a parish priest, a seminary teacher, and a vocation recruiter he emphasized the special quality of being called by God to do something special as a particular person with whatever resources were given by God. He also stressed the process of discerning what that vocation was and how to nurture it. This process had been aimed at priestly vocations, but in contemporary times the discernment process was considered appropriate for lay vocations. This was a major change for Tardif and the laity. While it was assumed but not well emphasized that laypersons did in fact have individual callings, it certainly was not emphasized that they were called to preach, witness, evangelize, and go to foreign lands. Both the themes of individual vocation and the possibility of fulfilling new roles in the church were turned in Tardif's hands into an exciting message.

Perhaps he did not perceive immediately a notable perspective of this Catholic idea of vocation: acting collectively. He certainly believed that vocations were related to the benefiting of the people of God, as the church was increasingly called after Vatican Council II, but having a covenant community of laypersons of which he would be a member was an idea that only grew over some years. His primary community was then the Missionaries of the Sacred Heart. Would he now have two primary communities?

Tardif as Healer and "Saint"

The trips to foreign lands by Tardif and his associates also served the purpose of establishing Siervos de Cristo Vivo communities in other countries. Charismatics in other countries wanted to keep Tardif or at least his spirit among them, so they obtained properties, money, and other resources to establish communities in Miami, Madrid, Rome, and other locations. And some foreigners rather quickly joined them. The generosity on all sides was impressive.

One of the major attractions of Tardif was the popular belief that he was a miracle worker, although this term was almost never used by Canadians or *dominicanos* in their biographical descriptions of him. Nor, as noted, are most Charismatic preachers so described by serious journalists; rather they are described as "healers," persons whose prayers for healing seemed to be heard with some regularity.

Describing someone as a miracle worker in religion raises the bar of esteem to a very high level and implies holiness of an exceptional degree.

When asked if he was a miracle worker, Tardif replied that God works miracles, not he.[20] Furthermore, he consistently emphasized that good health, both spiritual and bodily, was the ordinary will of God; sickness was an evil; and healing was something one should commonly expect.

Still, there were those occasions in which instantaneous healing seemed to have occurred at a time when Father Tardif had prayed publicly or privately for some seriously ill person. These talked about, presumptive cures set him apart from many other Charismatic preachers. The rumors and gossip about them brought flocks of people, some of them loosely hinged psychologically. He seemed resigned to this notoriety, thankful for the large audiences it drew in.

"Miracle worker" was an appellation that surrounded him for perhaps ten years until his sudden death in 1999. That reputation continued after his death. Because the process of his canonization began in 2007 his life and writings will be scrutinized over some years. Some of the piecing together of his life history has been taking place in Quebec, and Canadians have been finding in him a star among remarkable missionaries and a holy person who also seemed to have worked some miracles in his home territory while conducting Life in the Spirit retreats. These retreats and his personality helped to re-energize the Charismatic movement in Quebec. Nonetheless, Professor Catherine LeGrand of McGill University reported that Tardif was "not well received by Church officials in Montreal."[21] Furthermore, Tardif, who was known as Pére Emilien at home, is part of the revisionist history that is being constructed and published about Catholicism in Quebec. The prevailing picture is one of the dark ages of Quebec during the first two-thirds of the twentieth century in which French Canada was depicted as traditional, inward-looking, and backward. This, it was asserted, was "la Grande Noirceur."[22] Revisionist historians, such as Catherine LeGrand of McGill University, have documented a contrary view of an enlightened clergy and a very wide range of Canadian grass-roots active support that supplied new intellectual visions, economic resources, innovative organizational structures, and financial and spiritual empowerment of native clergy and laity. These were no small accomplishments to note in the history of globalized religion.

The hold over the imaginations of the Dominican people that Father Tardif achieved was demonstrated with his unexpected death. While preaching a Life in the Spirit retreat for 250 priests in Argentina, he was seized by a heart attack and died. Seventy-one at the time, he appeared to be in full vigor of life. The death brought sudden shock and deep mourning when it was announced in the Dominican Republic. President Lionel Fernández called him the apostle of the Dominican Republic and declared a national day of mourning, reserved for national heroes. The length of his funeral procession was said to be many kilometers. Although resident outside of Canada for more than forty years, he was widely remembered in Canada as well.

Devotion to Padre Tardif continued after his death to such an extent that it seemed fitting to move his remains from the Missionaries of the Sacred Heart cemetery at Santiago de los Caballeros to Santo Domingo. He was reburied with ceremony beneath the altar of the lower chapel of the Escuela de Evangelización Juan Pablo II in the capital city, becoming thereby the site of a frequently visited shrine. A monument and more elaborate crypt were being planned. The project for establishing the school was unfinished work at the time of his death. The new campus and church, still under construction at the time of reburial, were also a reminder that his life was rooted in an ongoing process of re-educating Catholics.

The process for his beatification after his death was initiated officially by the Dominican Church and was approved by the Vatican. Not all healers are holy in the sense that they have achieved heroic sanctity. Whether Tardif's healings will be seen in the beatification process as supernatural is not important to many of Tardif's followers; what matters to them was his special goodness.

Conclusion

A major Catholic revival has been occurring in the Dominican Republic. Vitality is evident by many indicators. In 2002, among the laity there were 47,145 lay catechists, a high number in a small Catholic population of 5 million. The national church is second in Latin America in the percentage increase in priests, 2,529 percent, from 1957 to 2008 and third in the percentage increase of graduate-level seminarians, 1,339 percent, in the same period. The time period indicates mostly growth in native-born additions to the priesthood or ranks of seminarians and, by most accounts, reflects the vitality of the lay movements of the country, especially the Charismatic renewal.

What was most notable about the renewal in the Dominican Republic was, first, the ease with which the movement took hold, again showing its translatability from one culture to another. After initial resistance, especially on the part of clergy, the movement grew quickly. Tardif acted as a cultural broker for the transnational movement in its incorporation within the Dominican church.

Second, Tardif and the Dominican laity who traveled with him showed the ease with which this became a global movement. Tardif, often with associates, took what he practiced in the Dominican Republic, a small and not well-known country, to many countries in a relatively short time. A number of these countries had societies and cultures far different from the Dominican Republic but took in Tardif's message with an unusual ease. Furthermore, this was a message received from the fringes, not the metropole. Missionaries or movements' advocates used to spend decades of effort establishing movements. Tardif, spreading the movement to other countries, was more of a parachutist who dropped in and lighted a fire.

Third, a great change within the Dominican Church was extroversion, the movement toward evangelization, the proclamation of the Gospel in public, especially by laypersons. This, too, was stimulated by religious competitors, especially Pentecostals who had been working aggressively for some time on the island. Apparently, the Catholic Charismatic Renewal and evangelization efforts have held evangelicals and Pentecostals to less than 10 percent of the Dominican population. (The percentage of Protestants and other non-Catholics varied from 3 to 25 percent.)

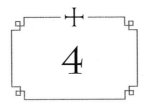

BRAZIL

The Charismatic Giant

The Charismatic renewal took hold in Brazil more widely than most countries in Latin America. That the renewal was extensive was largely ignored in the first three decades by progressives who did not agree with the reputed conservative qualities of Charismaticism. They also overlooked the word-of-mouth information about the movement. They could be excused for not having a comprehensive view of the movement because Brazil is so large geographically that very few observers had a full view of the religious situation in the country.

Now, however, foreign and domestic research resources have been put to use to poll Brazilians about important aspects of their religions. The Pew Forum on Religion and Public Life conducted a survey in 2006 that showed that about half of Brazilians identified themselves as Charismatic.[1] Some observers quibbled in interviews over the use of the word Charismatic, and one expert, who was based in Rio de Janeiro where the renewal is not nearly as extensive as elsewhere, said she thought many Brazilians who viewed one or two of Padre Marcelo Rossi's shows called themselves Charismatic.[2] That view does not match the grass-roots reporting from the national coordinating center for the movement. The center's figures show that of the eighty-six hundred Catholic parishes in the country, the renewal is present in six thousand through prayer groups. This is a very high number and a clear indicator of the widespread dispersal of the movement. The Charismatic renewal in Brazil cannot be ignored. It represents a radical shift in religion in the country.

In an earlier study of Brazil in 2000 David Barrett and Todd Johnson estimated that 33.7 million Catholics are Charismatics, representing 22 percent of the national Catholic population.[3] This estimate was made largely before the impact on the Catholic Church by Father Marcelo Rossi and other Charismatic performers occurred and one can safely presume that the number of Catholics identifying themselves as Charismatic increased considerably in the decade beginning in 2000.

In a continental perspective, Brazil represented 45 percent of the 73 million Catholic Charismatics in the region. The country is outsized and very different from other Latin American countries in many ways, including historical background (it was founded in 1500, not 1492) and language (Portuguese, not Spanish), that it merits separate treatment and two chapters in this volume.

Edward Dougherty and Harold Rahm

That the Catholic Charismatic Renewal was extraordinarily diverse in the character of its founders and the direction of their priestly careers has become clear in the forty years since the movement started in Brazil. Two priests from the United States may have looked alike in their black Jesuit cassocks when they arrived in Brazil in the 1960s. Both were members of the New Orleans Jesuit province and worked in Campinas, the second largest city of São Paulo state. But Harold J. Rahm from Tyler, Texas, and Edward John Dougherty from New Orleans could hardly have been more different. They were joined in founding the renewal in Brazil by a third priest, Jonas Abib, a Brazilian-Lebanese, who was also considerably different from the other two founders.

Rahm, who was already forty-five when he left as a missionary for Brazil, had a full and fruitful life working in the Segundo Barrio section of El Paso, Texas, with tough and troubled teenagers. He founded Our Lady's Youth Center, which attracted local teenagers for competitive sports, construction-apprenticeship projects, and life-skill experiences. Rahm drew in hundreds of older citizens to help carry on his projects. He and his effective youth work entered in south Texas history as recounted by the grass-roots historian C. L. Sonnichsen.[4]

Rahm was assigned to Brazil in 1964 by the New Orleans Jesuit province and worked with the popular Catholic revitalization movement called Cursillos da Cristâo (Short Courses in Christianity). Typical of his baroque approach to life, he combined techniques from the Jesuit Spiritual Exercises, Legion of Mary, Catholic Action, and other pastoral approaches to his work. The other New Orleans Jesuit province member, Edward Dougherty, went to Brazil two years later than Rahm, in 1966. He was twenty-two years younger than Rahm and still a nonordained student. From Brazil he went to Canada for theological studies, encountering the Charismatic renewal in nearby Michigan, where he had a Pentecostal experience in March 1969. He returned to Campinas, Brazil, three months later and shared his newfound Charismatic spirituality with Rahm. Conversing with Dougherty plus reading a classical Pentecostal work, *Aglow with the Spirit: How to Receive the Baptism in the Holy Spirit*, by Robert C. Scott, led Rahm to join Dougherty in embracing the Charismatic renewal in 1969. Dougherty was ordained to the priesthood the following year.

Both priests, along with Abib, were credited with founding the renewal in Brazil. Both became major figures in Brazil and in the Catholic Church, along different but complementary long-term career paths. Rahm devoted himself to healing people with addictions and thereby became a national and world figure in drug prevention and treatment. He became president of the Brazilian Therapeutic Communities. For his work, he received the coveted Harry Stoll Award from the World Federation of Therapeutic Communities.

When he arrived in Brazil he found few agencies for dealing with addiction and no formalized programs. He was instrumental in establishing a number of addiction centers in Brazil, including Our Lord's Ranch outside of Campinas and Our Lady of Guadalupe Prevention and Assistance Center for female addicts. He helped to create a successful ministry to street children in Campinas.

He increasingly became rooted in Brazil, became a naturalized citizen in 1985, and stimulated national efforts for drug treatment. He authored twenty-four books and assisted in founding over two thousand therapeutic communities in Brazil. Again embracing other people's ideas, he borrowed from the English-speaking Tough Love Program, creating a Brazilian version, Amor Exigente, that came to include more than fifteen hundred therapeutic communities. His spiritual views helped to inform his vision for prevention and rehabilitation from addiction, but he had from the beginning of his youth work insisted on physical labor for young persons, especially for recovering addicts. Even when he was in his seventies he was putting in time working in garden plots. One of his many endeavors was appropriately called the Promotional Association of Prayer and Work (APOT), better known as the Father Harold Institution.

Especially in his latter years he managed to draw into his drug-treatment work associates from sixty religious traditions and from groups as diverse as the Masons and the Rotarians.

Father Harold made it clear in professional addresses and writings that he saw that medical science and correct religion go hand in hand.[5] His emphasis on spirituality also is a revered tradition in alcoholic addiction treatment, with which Rahm was familiar personally and professionally.[6] Rahm thus repeated one of the earliest themes of the Catholic Charismatic Renewal as it began as a worldwide phenomenon spreading from the United States: the healing of seemingly intractable personal issues embedded in societal problems through prayer and inner renewal (combined, in his view, with professional help).

Rahm's work paralleled the book that the founders of the movement at Duquesne University cited as influential at the time in terms of their openness to the Holy Spirit. This was not a theological work but rather Ralph Wilkerson's *The Cross and the Switchblade*.[7] This book describes how a minister in the inner city fails in his work with gang members and addicts until his clients accept the Holy Spirit into their lives. The volume was one of the most circulated and eagerly read books by Charismatics, Catholics and Protestants, in the early days of the movement. Wilkerson's book, translated into Spanish, made its way quickly to Latin America and became one of the first volumes prospective adherents read in the 1970s. While interest in Wilkerson's book waned within the movement, the legacy of Charismatic Christianity as a healing force remained for all manner of illnesses in general and for addiction in particular.

Father Harold began spreading the Charismatic movement through retreats that have been a common feature of Catholic life especially since the Reformation. Retreats have been especially associated with Father Harold's religious congregation, the Jesuits, since they have used the spiritual discipline of their founder, Ignatius Loyola, distilled in what are called the Spiritual Exercises as the basis of weeklong (or longer) examinations of one's life and commitment to personal reform. These retreats are typically conducted in special retreat or renewal houses. Rahm used the form of retreats but substituted Pentecostal themes—such as baptism in the Spirit—for traditional ones. At Campinas he organized retreats for Catholics that he called Prayer Meetings in the Holy Spirit.

Rahm, knowing the need of new adherents of having something substantial to read in Portuguese, wrote *Sereis Batizados no Epírito* (You Will

Be Baptized in the Spirit) with María Lamego; it was published in 1972. The book had a strong impact and was passed from hand to hand by the new converts. It was regarded as the mechanism for advancing the movement in Brazil in the same way that *The Cross and the Switchblade* sparked the renewal in the United States. Furthermore, since the book was published with the stamp of church approval, called an imprimatur, from the bishop of Campinas that approval was taken as official legitimation for the nascent but then unusual movement.[8]

Dougherty's Whirlwind Tour and the Growth of Brazilian Charismaticism

Newly ordained Father Dougherty went to Toronto in 1971 to finish his theological degree. He returned in 1972 to Brazil and gave priests' retreats with a Charismatic emphasis. By the time he returned to Brazil, he had formed grand plans on how to spread the movement to all corners of the country. In 1972–73 he undertook flying to the state capitals in that vast country, which is larger than the contiguous United States.[9]

Father Dougherty would continue to concentrate his energies more directly within the movement than Rahm and he became, for a time, the main figure of the renewal in Brazil. In the retreats called Experience of the Holy Spirit and later known as Experience of Prayer he was joined by a fellow Jesuit, Father João Batista Malagâes Sales.[10]

At his various stops during his trips to state capitals, Dougherty invited a select group of priests and women religious to his retreats, which covered the fundamentals of the movement in an atmosphere of intense prayer and fellowship. Some participants received at that time baptism in the Spirit; others received that gift later. As Dougherty moved on to other cities, these first members furthered the spread of the movement by inviting select laypersons for retreats that they conducted, similar to the ones Dougherty gave. Thus the movement radiated out from hub cities and spread from priests to lay leaders, from a North American to Brazilians, in a remarkable way.[11]

The spread of the movement in Brazil was considerably more diffused throughout the national territory than most other countries due, in part, to Dougherty's early determination to recruit new members and give Charismatic retreats in all the states of Brazil. Dougherty's effort was not singular; rather, parallel efforts to start the movement came from George

Kosicki, Clemente Krug, Daniel Kiakarski, and other priests from the United States. By the middle of 1973 Dougherty felt the need of greater coordination for the movement. With Rahm and Juliette Schuckenbrock, the spiritual director of the Holy Cross Sisters, he organized the First National Congress of the Charismatic Renewal, which took place in Campinas. Fifty leaders came to the meeting. This was followed six months later in January 1974 by the Second National Congress of the Charismatic Renewal. Leaders from mostly the southern and central sections of Brazil came in increased numbers. Through 1974, Brazilian priests, sisters, and lay leaders increasingly joined the movement and began to fill in the empty spaces on the Charismatic expansion map.

After this initial flurry of igniting the movement in various parts of the country in the 1970s, Dougherty turned his efforts more directly toward mass media. He needed financing and a very large assemblage of lay collaborators for his work. In 1979[12] he founded the Associação do Senhor Jesus (Association of the Lord Jesus, ASJ), which included core members of covenant communities—almost all Charismatic Catholics—to produce mass media in Valinhos, outside of Campinas. In addition, he needed a much larger outer circle of members to support the work financially and by prayer. At first, major funding came from the United States, but later most financial support came from Brazilians, including seventy thousand member-contributors of the ASJ.

It is noteworthy how quickly both Pentecostalism and Charismatic Catholicism became indigenous movements with Brazilians taking over or at least sharing leadership in the movements. For centuries both Protestant and Catholic missionaries in their global missions lacked indigenous pastors, leaders, and cultural adaptations to local cultures. Lamin Sanneh, along with other scholars, has called attention to this special quality of Pentecostalism and its variants to foster indigenous leadership quickly.[13]

However, because communication in this vast developing country was limited, especially concerning national religious trends that are typically of marginal interest to national media, the movement did not become visible, discussed, dissected, and reacted to until very large numbers had joined the movement. Only in 1997 did *Veja*, a major national newsweekly, discover the Charismatic explosion.[14] Internationally this explosive growth would continue to remain largely unheralded for some time. Thus, when the Pew Forum on Religion and Public Life, based in Washington, D.C., found in its survey of Brazil in 2006 that about half of

Table 4.1. Growth of Brazilian Charismatic Catholics by Years

1970	10,000
1979	300,000
1984	1 million
1989	2 million
1994	4 million
1998	8 million
2004	12 million
2008	15–33 million

Sources: 1970, estimate of author based on interviews; 1979–2004, Veja (Aug. 4, 1998 and Dec. 8, 2004); and estimates based on Pew Forum survey and Christian Database, 2008.

Catholics identified themselves as Charismatic, a number of Brazilianists asked how that was possible since widespread affiliation had escaped their attention.[15]

Those closer to what was taking place chart the progress of the movement in table 4.1.

The above estimates include both ardent practitioners and sympathetic hangers-on. Cecília Mariz, one of Brazil's recognized authorities on Charismatics, believes that the numbers are probably inflated by persons who occasionally attend Charismatic services or have viewed Father Rossi on television and now call themselves Charismatic without having a deep commitment to the movement's ideals.[16]

These numbers also raise myriad questions, including why lay Charismatic leaders were not invited in 2007 to the Latin American Bishops Conference (CELAM) in Aparecida, the most important Latin American church meeting since 1992 (CELAM in Santo Domingo) and one held on Brazilian soil.[17] Other, more direct questions arose: How did the movement grow? How did the movement maintain its members? Charismatic ideals are hard to sustain. Pentecostals, the Charismatics' cousins, have a notoriously high dropout rate, as noted.[18] Would there not be similarly high numbers of Catholic dropouts? The typical follow-up for priests and laity to sustain them in their new spirituality included membership in prayer groups that met regularly. The prayer groups, as seen elsewhere, have been fundamental to the movement.

Organizing the first retreats and resultant prayer groups was fairly easy for Dougherty, who utilized the large membership lists of existing lay movements, especially the Cursillos da Cristão (Short Courses in Christianity), already mentioned. Many of the first members thus tended to be middle-class Catholics with at least a modest education in the Catholic faith. This recruiting base for Charismatics was typical throughout Latin America at the time

The first step of selecting active Catholics as candidates for Charismaticism was a momentous decision. By default at this time, the movement avoided direct recruitment from the majority of Latin Americans who were non-practicing Catholics, thus further opening the door to Protestant Pentecostals to attract these inactive Catholics by the millions to active faith within their fold.[19] It was precisely in these decades of the 1970s and 1980s that Catholic Charismaticism began taking shape as a movement and that Pentecostal groups on a parallel path began to accelerate toward their thundering growth of the 1990s and 2000s when they were believed to be making a million converts a year.

Social-class membership of religious groups has been a persistent theme for religious scholars. The gigantic growth of Catholic Charismatic Renewal in Brazil swept into the movement members of the social and economic elites. The family clan members—Simonsen, Vidigal, Cabrera, and Papa—of high society in São Paulo and in Brazil in general could be found in attendance at Charismatic services at Igreja Nossa Senhora do Brasil, a church in São Paulo frequented by what local gossip columnists writing in Portuguese called, borrowing the English term, *socialites*. Similarly, members of the social elite such as Carmen Mayrink Veiga and Gisella Amaral in Rio and Zilda Couto and Angela Gutierrez in Belo Horizonte were also associated with the renewal. At the national capital, Brasília, both high-level national government officials and local members of Brasília's elite were Charismatic Catholics. In 1998 government officials met weekly for Charismatic prayer meetings in the chapel of the Palácio da Alvorada, the residence of then president Fernando Enrique Cardoso.

The high visibility of these social elites in sumptuous churches contrasted with many of the humbler buildings of the neo-Pentecostal structures of Edir Madedo's Universal Church of the Kingdom of God, or simply the Universal Church, often found in the outlying exurban areas. The attraction for the socialites as well as humbler members in part had been healing. Carmen Mayrink Veiga suffered from persistent pain in one leg and sought expensive medical treatment. When this did not bring positive results, she had recourse to Charismatic prayer. This brought healing.

At that point, she realized that it was not a question of having money, but rather faith.[20]

Earlier studies of Brazilian Catholic Charismatics emphasized healing as the great attraction of Catholics both to the Charismatic movement and to Protestant Pentecostalism. Andrew Chesnut developed this theme in his *Born Again in Brazil* and again in *Competitive Spirit* where he described speaking in tongues and faith healing. He pointed out that for the poorer social classes healing was from the pathogens of poverty, such as illness, alcoholism, and chronic marital strife. That emphasis has certainly been pursued by Harold Rahm in his hundreds of therapeutic communities. But the Charismatic movement increasingly emphasized inner healing and afflictions that affect middle-class members, such as childhood traumas and crippling memories (such as of abuse). The centrality of healing to the movement diminished in the 2000s but still remained strong.

Praise, thanksgiving, and joy in living increasingly became centerpieces of the movement. Large events like Halleluya, a five-day Charismatic meeting sponsored by Shalom with some four hundred thousand people in attendance at the coastal city of Fortaleza, and Hosana Brasil, a three-day celebration sponsored by Canção Nova at Cochoeira Paulista, emphasized praise and joy. The program for Hosana began with a short dance, an *espetáculo*, then a two-hour Mass and an optional show with musical performers until midnight. Then followed a full routine of prayers, testimonies, and Masses for the next two days, with add-on shows for children and adults until 12:30 a.m. on the final night. Healing was not emphasized in the program or commented upon in the ninety posted e-mail comments after the event; rather e-mail commentaries ran along the lines of experiencing joy and pleasure in the events, especially in the motivational preaching. They sounded like the middle-class comments of the audiences of Joel Osteen that were recorded for an episode of CBS's *Sixty Minutes*, which aired in 2007.[21] In fact, the Canção Nova event resembled CBS's characterization of Osteen's service as an uninhibited celebration that is part rock concert and part spectacular,[22] except that it was Catholic.

Charismatics also grew in numbers among Brazil's intellectual elite and students. In the 1990s the movement became more visible within Brazil's universities. The desire to have an influence in the universities or at least among its students follows a long tradition in the Latin American Catholic Church of lay student movements. For one of these movements, Catholic

Action, the goal was influencing secular universities to provide a Christian perspective and was carried on by Juventud Universitaria Católica (JUC), the branch of Catholic Action that operated in university settings and produced great figures in liberation theology, such as Gustavo Gutiérrez and Paulo Freire. This goal of infiltrating a hostile or alien culture was reinforced by the contemporary campus Charismatic ministry's description of its basic prayer unit as a *cell*. This repeats usage by Catholic Action, which created interlocking cells with a secrecy (about who were members and what action strategies they employed) and solidarity among members that resembled the Communist movement.[23]

A university Charismatic initiative called Ministério Universidades Renovadas took shape in 1994 in several Brazilian states. Two years later the group held its first National Meeting of Catholic Charismatic University Students (ENUCC). The conference drew 250 university students, professors, and staff persons from 40 universities and 10 states. The alumni from the Charismatic ministry in the universities wished to keep alive the religious enthusiasm generated during their student years. In 1999, they organized the first national meeting for recent graduates.

By 1998 a marked international expansion had taken place with student representatives from Brazil attending the continent-wide meetings of Encuentros Carismáticos Católicos Latinoamericanos (ECCLA), described previously. Later, Brazilian students went in mission to other countries, such as Mexico and Peru, to expand the movement in universities there. This dynamism drew students from other countries to attend yearly conferences of ENUCC in Brazil, starting in 2000.

That same year saw the first National Festival of Music of the University Renewal Ministry. Students from various regions of Brazil sent in original musical compositions on the themes of university-level evangelization for the national competition. As if an essential part of their soul, Brazilians turned to producing popular songs to express their new or deepened faith.

The heart of the Charismatic university ministry was the formation of prayer groups, formally called Grupos de Oração Universitarios (GOUs) and bearing a certain gravitas. The members of the GOUs are not just acquaintances getting together to pray but students, professors, and recent graduates praying in the context of preparing for honored professions, ones to be carried out with dignity, a sense of justice, ethics, respect for others, and "a certainty that all social transformation will occur only after conversion of the heart."[24] At the end of 2007, there were 662 GOUs throughout the country and they might be better conceived as established chapters (as of fraternities and sororities) than as simple prayer groups.

In terms of form and organization these GOUs are classical socialization groups intent on reinforcing values and ideology (here meant in the sense of ideas plus action). Their counterparts can be found not only among young Muslims in Algeria and Egypt but among young evangelicals in the United States and Canada.

A Charismatic Giant: Jonas Abib and the Lure of Music

The third keystone in the building of the movement came into place when Father (later Monsignor)[25] Jonas Abib, a Brazilian-Lebanese priest, entered the picture.[26] Abib was working with young persons and teaching in Lorena, São Paulo state, as a priest in the 1960s. He reportedly was struggling in the work until he was introduced to the Catholic Charismatic Renewal in 1971, an event that marked the rest of his life. By 1978 he had established and organized with laypersons the Charismatic base for his activities, a covenant community called Comunidade Canção Nova (New Song Community).

One of the main missions of the community became the composing, recording, and marketing of Christian popular music (similar to Christian music on sale under the same heading at Target, Walmart, and other stores in the United States). By 1980 the group had established its own radio station, emphasizing contemporary religious music and other Charismatic programming. Before long, the popular station, bearing the name Radio Canção Nova (New Song Radio), gained a high-power transmission license and the ability to reach most of Brazil. With twenty years experience in radio, the community then moved into television production.

The New Song Community typified one of the organizational types regularly found in the Catholic Charismatic movement: covenant communities. These are groups of persons strongly drawn to the movement who find in the groups the spiritual direction, encouragement, and structures for living new lives. In the United States covenant communities became important features of the movement. Probably the best known was the Word of God Community in Ann Arbor, Michigan, which was associated with the leadership of Steve Clark. But largely similar groups also arose in other places like Providence, Rhode Island. Many groups formed, flourished for a few years, and dispersed with hardly a scrap of paper in an archive. "It was an important period in our life and we were better persons because of the community," two former participants of the Providence community told me.[27]

Whereas twenty years ago the number of these covenant communities in Brazil was about fifty, by 1998 they numbered about three hundred; by 2008 they were in the thousands. Six of them were considered especially influential in 1998 when special attention was drawn to them by national media. None had a greater reach than Abib's New Song Community, which in that year had twenty-three subsidiary communities in Brazil and four overseas (one each in the United States, Portugal, France, and Israel). Regina Novaes, an expert on Charismatics, believes that New Song is one of the most important Charismatic communities in the world.[28] (This group is not to be confused with New Song churches of the United States, a New Age initiative from California.)

Two types of affiliation to New Song are offered members. The first might be called radical in that members move to Cachoeira Paulista, give up their jobs, material possessions, and, in some cases, their families, to dedicate themselves to New Song's mission. Those who choose this path reside with the community, pool their income, and take up their share of the work of evangelization. They are divided up in subcommunities of priests, celibate single laypersons, and families with children. "I am a modern friar in jeans and t-shirt," said Heloísa de Paiva Calvalho, a forty-one-year-old trained nurse from Rio state who lived in Cachoeira Paulista for five years. "I couldn't stand any longer living in an environment of competition and individualism." She lives in a residence with fifty-seven other persons and is committed to chastity. This type of commitment is backed up by years of study and spiritual formation. A former mechanic, forty-year-old Francisco Jose dos Santos, moved to the community with his wife, Ednéia, and a son, spending fourteen years in the community. Some of the years were spent in formation, during which he abandoned alcohol and drugs and found a vocation as a singer (along with his wife, who is also a singer). He adopted the stage name Dungas and sold one million copies of his five CDs, marketed under the New Song label. Two of his three sons were born and all were raised at Cachoeira Paulista, away from the violence and chaos of inner-city life.

The vision for community held by Abib and other founders of covenant communities comes from the biblical book the Acts of the Apostles, wherein an early form of Christian community is described as all things being held in common. Brazilian leaders seemed to have picked up this important form of evangelical living, which was so different from traditional practices among laypersons in Brazil and did not entail conscious copying of the covenant community innovation from the United States and its checkered history of dominant leaders stifling the spread of the movement.[29] Brazilians read Acts, adapted what they read, and moved forward into a future with mega-churches, music, and television.

The second type of participation in the community is far more common and is called a *comunidade da aliança* (community of alliance). Members are linked to the core group but lead conventional lives. In 2007, the forty-six-year-old actress Myrian Rios, the former wife of the popular singer Roberto Carlos, had been associated with New Song for two years. She continued living in Rio with her two sons. She belonged to a branch community there but went at least once a month to Cachoeira Paulista to participate in weekend prayer encampments "because New Song changed [her] life," she said. "I was rudderless but I found peace when I sorted out my life." She contributed to New Song in part by conducting a talk show for its television network.

The crowning touch for the New Song Community was the construction of a mega-church at Cachoeira Paulista, the waterfall region in the Paraíba Valley, halfway between Brazil's major cities, Rio and São Paulo. This building is the largest Catholic Church in Latin America. With 22,000 square meters, it is large enough to hold 100,000 people (70,000 seated). It is reported to hold more people, sitting or standing, than the national shrine of Aparecida (75,000) or St. Peter's in Rome (60,000).[30] The building, called the Bishop João Hipólito de Moraes Evangelization Center, was designed for evangelization, the education of adults in Christian beliefs. The impressive structure sits on a large campus where the 600 members of the Charismatic community live and are served by banks, post offices, restaurants, and other urban facilities.

On weekends some 60,000 persons come to attend the Masses celebrated by Father Jonas, the president and founder, or another Charismatic priest. Each month more than 515,000 supporters regularly contribute—some persons give 10 percent of their income—to the community's needs, especially its expensive television productions and broadcasts.

Unfortunately, this effort may have been thirty years too late for reaching Catholics who were presumably in need of such evangelization but became Pentecostals. It may be a bulwark, though, against further erosion.

In sum, New Song's efforts demonstrated the vitality of the movement and of its independence with regard to foreign assistance.

Abib and fellow musicians pioneered popular Catholic music in Brazil, a type of music that would rival other Brazilian popular music in the 1990s. (This type of Christian music would skyrocket in sales when Padre Marcelo Rossi entered the field in the late 1990s.) When one speaks of the Pentecostalization of Brazilian Catholicism, the term often refers to the styles of public worship and (more or less) private prayer. Stellar examples of the Pentecostalized way some Brazilian Catholics "do their thing" in religion can be heard in the more than twenty music CDs produced by Abib and the members of his community. This music was intended for private devotion as well as public performance. Thus private prayer was no longer thought of as, for example, kneeling as a solitary person in a church but rather prayer sung or listened to with iPods at home, at a quiet time in a church, or virtually any place. Their musical ministry also melded with evangelization.

Women and the Renewal

The demand for this type of music has spawned a new singing nun with a far more profound repertoire than the Soeur Sourire (the Singing Nun), the short-lived phenomenon of the Belgian missionary sister promoted in the United States by the television empresario Ed Sullivan in 1964 and whose one-note music went to the top of the charts.[31] The Brazilian sister Miria Therezinha Kolling spent a number of years in musical training, including two years in Europe with master teachers, before devoting herself to composing, recording, and performing. She recorded some fifty LPs and CDs and has a large following. In 2004 she completed a singing tour of the eastern United States as a Brazilian singing for expatriate Brazilians. Indicative of this vibrant world of religious performance, Sister Miria maintains an active Web site with a monthly agenda of her appearances.

The important issue of women and religion was well researched in the country because Brazil's social scientists who are interested in religion are exceptionally well trained and have conducted empirical studies on the issue. In Brazil, as in most of Latin America (and the world), women predominate in the practice of religion. This is true in Afro-Brazilian religions, evangelical Protestantism, Pentecostalism and neo-Pentecostalism, Catholic Christian base communities (CEBs), and the Catholic Charismatic

Renewal, although the percentages of women may be less than expected. In terms of general attendance at Mass in 1990, the last year for which figures were available, 61.7 percent of those attending were women. Probably the percentage of women active in both CEBs and the Charismatic renewal was higher. As noted by Cecília Mariz, that proportion was a matter of considerable concern among religious leaders.[32] The issue of overrepresentation by women in religion has been debated for many years in Latin America. Cultural explanations were advanced in Brazil that women had more responsibility for *"coisas serias"* (serious concerns) and therefore were more likely to be found in church.

Better explanations than that stereotype came from Mariz and her fellow researcher María das Dores Machado, who concluded that the Pentecostal movement and the Charismatic renewal allowed women greater individual choice and freedom to participate in the group in the manner they preferred than traditional religions did. Mariz and Machado found that Pentecostal and Charismatic groups offered alternative spaces to the home and neighborhood for discussing family and women's problems, creating social networks, and helping women build self-esteem.

The Significance of Covenant Communities

Charismatic communities, like the ones described, are noteworthy for the relative autonomy from church authorities they have shown in organizing themselves. They also have experienced spontaneous growth, like the arid Brazilian northeast blooming after the first downpour of spring. While prayer groups are basic to the Charismatic movement and virtually everyone belonged in their first years in the movement to a prayer group, the covenant communities achieved prominent attention and enhanced status for their members in Brazil. Jonas Abib's New Song Community, already noted, was taking shape in the 1970s. Then Shalom and other covenant communities multiplied greatly in the 1980s and 1990s in Brazil and began drawing social researchers to look at their motivations and mechanisms of decision, commitment, and role in society.

The first thing researchers made clear was there were two types of these covenant groups (similar to what was noted in other countries but with different terminology): communities of life and communities of alliance. The members of the first live together and share income, resources, work, and prayer, largely in the manner of the radical, core community described above for the New Song Community. Members of the second type support the life of the first group with donations, voluntary work, and prayer but maintain their own lives and occupations.

Neither type of covenant community is an essential element of the organizational structure of the Charismatic renewal, but both types are evidence of the dynamism and flexibility of the Charismatic movement. They also show the common belief that "the Spirit breathes where he wishes"; that is, God is greater than what the human mind can know or predict what he will cause to happen next. The covenant communities came about from initiatives of entrepreneurial leadership as leaders arose in the movement. Typically these founders of communities were individual laypersons, but a few communities were founded by a married couple, some were founded by priests, and others were founded by a group of young laypersons. The spontaneity of their origins implies autonomy in relation to the organizational hierarchy of the church. Despite the real or imagined tight grip of Catholic bishops, Charismatics, as previously noted, have found a much greater home in the Catholic Church than historical Protestant ones.[33]

Each of the communities followed the charisma, the special vocation or talent of the founder, and had their own proper norms. They also tended to have a specific mission, such as work in mass media. In a landmark study, Mariz focused on five core groups ("communities of life") found in the metropolitan Rio de Janeiro region.[34] A key motivation for forming the groups was highly revealing. During interviews with Mariz's researchers or in postings on their Web sites, members of these core groups emphasized the fragility of the contemporary nuclear family in modern society that seemed to have lost its capacity to fulfill the functions one expects of a family in terms of offering support for individual personality development and affective care. In many ways the covenant communities were a search for an alternative to the model of the contemporary conjugal family. Mariz and her research associates found that this search was especially strong among young unmarried persons who were on the threshold of forming their own nuclear families and felt incapable of doing this well.

Of the five covenant communities Mariz studied in the Rio de Janeiro area, three had been founded in states other than Rio de Janeiro: two in São Paulo and one in Ceará. The first group studied was started in São Paulo by Father Abib as part of the New Song Community, the group noted above. In Rio this group at the time of the study concentrated mostly on radio and television rather than emphasizing community prayer and domestic life. They occupied several apartments, close by one another, but having little time for shared domestic life. Their lives were focused on the New Song Radio and TV network, an encompassing work. Thirty-four persons were in the core group (the community of life) and twenty were in the community of alliance in 2003.

The second community, Shalom, was founded in 1982 at Fortaleza, Ceará, in northern Brazil by a young person who had been influenced by Jonas Abib of New Song. He adopted (as Brazilians easily do) another name and became known as Moysés. He was joined in founding Shalom by a married woman who had been variously identified by informants for the Mariz study as Estela or María Emmer. The young man, a student of physiotherapy, participated in a prayer group in Fortaleza and was determined to start a snack bar where he could preach the Word of God to its customers. He believed that he, his co-founder, and their companions would transform this *lanchonete* (a snack bar of the type seen all over Latin America) into a means of attracting drifting young people to the love of God.[35] Others joined him and they decided to form a covenant community to support their work. The community is evolving into a religious congregation with religious vows taken by its core members.

Shalom as a movement caught fire and spread to other parts of Brazil. Members became foreign missionaries first in Italy and Israel and then elsewhere. Shalom began and continued as a movement of young Catholics organizing themselves for service in the church. The interests that they had in popular culture and music continued after entry into the covenant community. They staged large concert events, such as Halleluya, an annual show that drew four hundred thousand people to Fortaleza for five days. Their featured singer, Suely Façanha, was one of the attractions. Shalom was already remarkable in 1999 when the author Julia Miranda devoted considerable analysis of Shalom in her book on the Charismatic movement, even though Shalom captured few of the headlines that the works of other charismatic leaders did.[36]

By 2008 Shalom had established fifty-five community houses in Brazil and twelve houses overseas in Canada, Israel, Switzerland, France, and Italy. Their work was focused on evangelization, that is, informal religious education that took many forms, from weekend parish renewal events in numerous dioceses of Brazil to summer camps, magazine and book publishing, large musical shows, and a host of other activities.

A number of Brazilians have come across them as itinerant evangelizers, showing up in slums and remote villages, sometimes in direct competition with their street preaching Pentecostal counterparts. Shalom's members also go door-to-door, thinking of themselves not only as evangelizers but also as messengers of peace since their communal charism is expressed as *shalom*, the biblical word for peace. They continue to run snack bars and have added pizzerias. They provide hospital work, houses for unwed mothers, hospices, and their own kindergarten through middle school. At Fortaleza, their headquarters, their priest-members offered well-attended Charismatic Masses and conducted a healing Mass once a week. Much of their work was concentrated on fostering prayer groups. By 2007 they had established some 350 prayer groups. They owned four radio stations in large market areas and produced radio programs for a number of other stations. They, too, were producing and distributing musical CDs from their own talented performers.

The group was invited by the archbishop to establish a community in Rio. At first they settled in the Leme neighborhood and created a prayer group while being supported by a parish there. They moved before long to three houses in the Botafogo district, where one of the houses served as a center of evangelization. The leader in Rio, who had adopted the name Timbó, had a charismatic personality and his writings were posted on the group's local Web site.

The third group studied in Rio, Toca de Assis, was started in Campinas by a priest (then a seminarian), Roberto Jose Lettieri, in 1983. He was working alone in the streets with homeless persons until he caught the Charismatic spirit and formed a small community with the intention of establishing a new religious congregation and of living in the spirit of St. Francis of Assisi. This group has seen amazing growth, with one thousand male and female vowed members. This was not a clerical order but a lay congregation whose members were not highly educated in theology. They established 108 houses all over Brazil and had 46 houses alone in São Paulo state, with 10 houses in Campinas. This is no small accomplishment given the logistics of creating and supporting a household, especially in contemporary urban areas, but the group has the advantage of emphasizing simplicity in lifestyle, little expense for minimal theological education, and the free-spirited mobility of members. Their simplicity keeps the members close to life on the streets and to the homeless, the special target but not the only target of their evangelizing. Their outgoing missionary spirit led them to foreign mission activity at Balasar, Portugal and Quito, Ecuador. Music also marks their ministry. Their CD *Certeza de Céu* was fourth on the Catholic Music chart for 2006.

In contrast to the groups already described, the fourth group studied, Novo Maná e Mae do Redentor, was created in Rio de Janeiro. The founding couple organized in 1993 the covenant community group from a prayer group in a parish setting in the Nova Iguaçu district of Rio. They established four houses for its twenty-nine core members, supported by fifty to seventy persons in their community of alliance. Their special mission (charism) was distributing food, both material and spiritual.

Another group formed in Rio, the Comunidade Missionária Mãe do Redentor (Missionary Community of the Mother of the Redeemer), was started in 1996 by three young adults. The five core members were working in radio, television, and the Internet "to rescue lives from spiritual misery." They did this with the support of some six hundred associates.

Given the generalized ignorance of most Catholic and secular intellectuals of the largest and fastest growing religious movement in Brazil and much of Latin America, it is surprising and welcome that a small but important sector of Brazilian social scientists—one group was led by Cecília Mariz of Rio's state university and by her former students—has carefully studied and analyzed the Catholic Charismatic movement in Brazil. The analysis is not fully tested by comparative studies, but it is useful as a starting point.

Seeing the details of lived religion as supplied by studies, interviews, and numerous commentaries available on the Internet allows for a more careful look at what is taking place. In other words, if half of Brazil's Catholics are Charismatic, so what? Is this all just a matter of style (such as singing and shaking energetically)?

Although the movement is still evolving in Brazil, here are, in summary, the distinctive features of its historical development. First, Brazilians in very large numbers are devoting themselves to religion and religious practices in ways that they did not previously do. In other words, a religious revival is going on in Brazil and in much of Latin America and Catholics are part of the revival. Second, Brazilians—ordinary Brazilians—are spending a lot of money on Catholic enterprises in ways that they previously did not do. Third, the embrace by dedicated covenant community members of modern media—especially radio, television, and the Internet and to a lesser extent magazines and books—is fully in touch with the times. Fourth, popular music in the form of large concerts and home listening is being composed, produced, and consumed at an impressive rate. Popular religious music as a business flourishes in the church and society. Fifth, persons with strong Catholic identities have embraced popular culture—music, as noted, and other media as well. In addition, they moved into movies in the first decade of the twenty-first century. Sixth, they have been loyal to the wishes of John Paul II to flood into the areas of life young people prefer. Seventh, this is very much a youth phenomenon, but not only. Eighth, all socioeconomic classes are being reached. Ninth, the soul of Catholic beliefs—sacraments, Mass, Mary—makes Catholic Charismaticism distinct from Protestant Pentecostalism. Tenth, Catholics are becoming evangelical. Eleventh, Catholics have become missionary in their orientation at home and abroad.

Radio, Television, and the Response to Pentecostals

The First Wave of Media Efforts

To a considerable degree, the Catholic Church has lagged behind Protestants in Brazil and in most of Latin America in broadcast media. This was especially borne home when the neo-Pentecostal Universal Church of the Kingdom of God (IURD) bought the major TV Record network, one big enough to challenge the dominant network, O Globo, which, though a secular network, leaned toward giving space to Catholic Charismatics.[37] Symbolically it appeared as though the Catholic Church had been pushed aside from presence in the public eye. This pushing aside appeared to be confirmed when an IURD pastor kicked a statue of Mary, the patroness of Brazil, on TV Record. Catholics felt more strongly then ever their desire to own or control their own media so they could reply adequately to such an attack.

Prior to the massive entry of Charismatic Catholics into mass media in the 1980s the Catholic Church had some 126 radio stations (of a national total of 1,300). These stations served a modest audience and the enterprise was fragile financially and shaky in terms of structure. This situation of station ownership was common across Latin America, where among the 4,482 AM stations, 300 were Catholic, 7 percent of the total.

At the same time, Protestant stations had large audiences despite small Protestant presences in some countries in the middle of the twentieth century. Then toward the end of the twentieth century the Pentecostals made a major radio broadcasting initiative. They wanted to be in easy communication with their own members and to draw in non-practicing Catholics. These stations reached, so it seemed, all the remote corners of rural and urban Brazil.

Catholics worked hard to change the situation in radio with considerable success in terms of audience numbers, in part because the pool of Charismatic listeners grew dramatically. In the 1990s, of the 181 Catholic radio stations then operating, the majority of programming came from Charismatics. Whether they did this out of a sense of battling Pentecostals or from an inner drive to share their vision with others is a moot question but one that keeps surfacing.

Charismatics were at work in television before *chute da Santa* (the kicking of the Blessed Mother statue) occurred. Padre Eduardo Dougherty was the best-known pioneer in Catholic television work. He and his numerous lay collaborators of the Associação do Senhor Jesus (Association of the Lord Jesus) started television production work in a garage at Valinhos that was then used as a distribution center for Charismatic books. They began recording a television program at the Pontifical Catholic University in Campinas. Thus they created in 1980 a weekly Charismatic television show called *We Announce Jesus*, a program that continued for years. The production quality of the program was inferior but gradually improved. Several networks carried the program, which reached 60 percent of the national territory. The intended audience was narrowly Charismatic and the show had a strong emotional emphasis that made it seem similar to Pentecostal programming.

What Dougherty was doing—small as it was at the time—came under heavy criticism. The programming was called disembodied (from social reality), Pentecostal, other-worldly, authoritarian, and contrary to the pastoral orientations laid down by the Brazilian Bishops Conference. In part this assessment was repeated by an advisory group to the bishops when Dougherty sought sponsorship from the Brazilian Bishops Conference for the *We Announce Jesus* program. A small war over what would be emphasized in Catholic television programming was set off between Catholic Charismatics and advocates of the liberation theology. The advisory group harshly evaluated Dougherty's program. It was dominated by liberationists who saw media work as part of the popular education for liberation and as needing to be part of the democratization of media. (Brazil at the time was coming out of military dictatorship.)

Leaders from the progressive wing of the church were throwing their weight against the Charismatic renewal. Theologians and lay leaders committed to the Christian base communities (CEBs), the main carriers of liberation theology, lobbied mightily with the Brazilian Bishops Conference and with key bishops to keep the Charismatic movement at the margins of the church.

One of the first to attack was Leonardo Boff, the best-known Brazilian theologian and a major creator of liberation theology. The Catholic Charismatic renewal, as noted, began in Brazil in the early 1970s. By 1978 Boff was writing that the Brazilian Bishops Conference should never officially approve the Catholic Charismatic Renewal in its present state.

Probably no national church in Latin America, except for Nicaragua, was more politically partisan than the Brazilian church. Christian base communities had supplied solid support for the labor movement, for the Movimento Sem Terra (MST) movement, and the Partido dos Trabalhodores in Brazil. Some progressive leaders saw the Charismatic movement as a European Latin alliance against the CEBs and liberation theology. They began to sound alarm bells about projects of the Charismatic renewal. They viewed one project in particular, Evangelization 2000, a pet project of Padre Eduardo Dougherty, as a very expensive restorationist project designed to neutralize the activist social-justice movements of the church. Journalists wrote about Evangelization 2000 and a similar project, Lumen 2000, as having lots of money from unspecified foreign donors and as being planned behind closed doors. Thus progressives and their allies painted the Charismatic renewal as suspicious, as a foreign import.

Progressive bishops and theologians succeeded in calling attention to serious flaws in the Charismatic renewal.[38] When the Brazilian bishops approved a policy statement about the Charismatic movement, they did so belatedly in 1994. This was long after officials in Rome, European countries, and the United States had issued their statements. Some Brazilian Catholic leaders continued to express their grave reservations about the movement. The bishop who was then head of the Nova Iguaçu diocese,

Monsignor Hipólito Adriano, forbade praying in tongues and faith-healing ceremonies. He allowed worshipers to raise their arms in praise but they could not jump.

Dougherty and the Association of the Lord Jesus aimed at stimulating the formation of prayer groups and leaders for the renewal. They provided a wide range of written materials for the burgeoning movement. At the beginning Dougherty focused on television production work rather than establishing a network. A television production campus of some twenty-four thousand square meters emerged at Valinhos. His production studios changed names, came to be called Century 21, and began exporting television programs to other countries. He and his collaborators turned out a variety of television productions, including Christian soap operas, to counteract the sensual Brazilian *telenovelas*. Media reporters believed that his facilities were professionally sophisticated and ranked third in the country as a production company.

Charismatics were active in creating a second-tier television network, Redevida (Life Network). Redevida, with 503 stations, was the largest Catholic network. Industry sources reported that progessive Charismatics (not an oxymoron in their minds) dominated in programming. This was a commercial network, but since it emphasized "family values" it did not accept advertising for tobacco or alcoholic products.

Dougherty was the strength behind the Century 21 network, the first mentioned of the dedicated Charismatic television efforts. In 2003, it had fifty-eight stations in a satellite and UHF network, extending through much of Brazil. In 2008, it was on the air for a half day seven days a week. Dougherty was a central figure on camera especially during weekend programming. He appeared (in U.S.-style clerical garb) on many programs in the many ways that Pat Robertson appeared on the Christian Broadcasting Network and its centerpiece show, *The 700 Club*. He published *Brasil Cristão* (Christian Brazil), a magazine with a circulation of 184,000 to reinforce the television messages and to aid in fundraising. Graphics in the magazine ran toward pictures of statues of Mary and the Sacred Heart of Jesus, the direct opposite of Pentecostal and neo-Pentecostal publications.

The centerpiece of the week's activity was the five-hour Sunday show. An American Jesuit who knew Dougherty as an average Jesuit student describes the show as "amazing," both in its production values and in the blossoming of Dougherty into a television personality. The show is taped in a stadium-style studio that holds two thousand people—white and black, middle class and poor—in its enthusiastic audience. A layman acts as master of ceremonies. Padre Eduardo runs in and out of view of the camera during the five-hour program. Back stage he walks quickly to the counseling center with its banks of telephones to deal with individual cases or he speaks to clients on a cell phone. A sister in habit acts as a personal secretary and arrangements manager.

During the show he appears in Sunday celebrant vestments or a clerical suit. He speaks Portuguese almost perfectly. The show includes a Catholic Mass. The rest of the show includes Padre Eduardo speaking in tongues; ten Carmelite nuns in habit praying for the healing of those in the audience who come forward; and a break in the seriousness with an interlude given to a stand-up comic. The show has a dramatic conclusion the audience has been awaiting for four hours and fifteen minutes. This is the benediction ceremony. Dougherty in full ceremonial cope appears before the host from Mass, which is placed in a monstrance at the altar. Incense is used in abundance and discreetly placed smoke machines increase the cloudlike atmosphere. Petitions sent in by listeners or from the studio audience are read out.

As in many Pentecostal ceremonies of petition, many of the petitions are heart rendering: seemingly hopeless cases of unemployment, injury, addiction, marital infidelity. "It is wrong *not* to believe that God has the power to do something. I can't add any conditions like: 'If you will, God,'" one Charismatic viewer said. He added, "But secretly I would be pleased if he changed my heart to accept what seems inevitable."

A time for a possible successor to Dougherty had arrived; Padre Eduardo was advancing into his seventies and was not a singing attraction. Taking Dougherty's place at Sunday Mass on Century 21 in early 2008 was a rising Charismatic star, Padre Reginaldo Manzotti. Padre Reginaldo, from Brazil's Northeast, is a Carmelite friar who studied theology in Rome and returned to Brazil to be ordained a priest in 1995. He dedicated himself especially to evangelization, appealing to the young and enlisting them in evangelism. In the process he won the trust of various bishops. He also created Missa e Shows (Mass and Musical Shows), recorded several CDs, and had an attractive Web site labeled "Padre Reginaldo Remix," where he was pictured in a lime green t-shirt with polychromatic identifying graphics for the Web site.

Century 21 was under Dougherty's control, whereas Redevida was a joint commercial network between the media impresario João Filho and the Brazilian Bishops Conference, with a fairly wide variety of programming. Estimates of the amount of Charismatic programming on Redevida ran from 60 to 80 percent while its audience clearly was the "Charismatic, middle class." The commercial network carries no advertising that is not in line with Christian family life. For a time Redevida carried Padre Eduardo's Mass segment of his five-hour Sunday show. In 2008 the network carried Sunday and weekday Masses from the national shrine at Aparecida.

The Second Wave

Jonas Abib and his Canção Nova community expanded their broadcast media efforts from their years of successful radio efforts to television. In 2003, TV Canção Nova had 254 stations in its network and plans for 160 more stations by the end of that year. As with much of television broadcasting in developing countries, this is not twenty-four-hour programming. The network had a commercial license but was kept afloat by donations from the faithful.

After some forty years of planning, a fourth Catholic enterprise, TV Aparecida, went on the air in 2005. This UHF station is located in São Paulo state in the headquarters of the main shrine of Brazil, where the statue of Brazil's patron Our Lady of Aparecida is located and where the Latin American Bishops Conference took place in 2007. Through open-air transmission, cable, and satellite the station claimed to cover Brazil's highly populated southeast.

TV Globo, Brazil's largest secular network, opened itself to Charismatics, especially Padre Marcelo Rossi (to be treated later), who regularly appeared on the *Faustão Show*. At the time of TV Record's sale to Edir Macedo and his IURD, newspapers reported the strong opposition of O Globo to the acquisition. O Globo and Padre Marcelo were portrayed as allies in battle with Pentecostals (TV Record network and Edir Macedo), or else it was just considered Marcelo versus Macedo. A constant question for a while involved who had the highest ratings. The ratings fight—if there was one—was more often between persons in the same time slots. In head-to-head competition TV Record was frequently represented by Bishop Crevelli, a pastor with the IURD, not Macedo, and in that competition Rossi seemed to have the edge. And overall, Rossi was sailing along in top record sales and two successful movies. Furthermore, the battle of the numbers was fundamentally taking place at the filling of the pews and not only or especially on the large or small screens. The results of the Charismatic challenge to Pentecostals at the grass-roots level were not clear and will probably take a decade to measure.

What were clear were changes within the Catholic Church. The Charismatic renewal is a major sector for implementing two new emphases: evangelization and mission. If there is a single guiding impulse of the Charismatic renewal in its current phase it is to go out to others. Charismatics channel this impulse into becoming evangelizers and missionaries (the former word being familiar to Protestants but not to Catholics).

Evangelization became a catch phrase for the re-education of Catholics, young and old, who were deemed to be largely ignorant of the content of their faith and were holding on to the practice of Catholicism largely through popular devotions. As one Latin American scholar wrote of his childhood and dead faith: "We had no clue about [religious faith or themes] ... despite years of Catholic school and prayer books and the first communion training and the daily Masses, all mandatory, perfunctory exercises, empty of meaning, interest, and above all devotion."[39] Andre de Souza reported that numerous sociological studies showed that Pentecostalism grew principally by attracting cultural Catholics who never internalized their Catholicism as did many participants in the various movements of Catholic revitalization that have existed in Brazil over the last few decades.[40] Cultural, non-practicing Catholics became easy targets for challengers from other religions when in-migration became a common fact for millions of Latin Americans.

Especially from the 1960s onward, migrants to cities typically became untied from family and religion (which came to them from their families) at their previous locations and were free to choose religions other than Catholicism. Pentecostalism, which had been present in key Latin American countries—Brazil, Chile, and Guatemala—since the 1910s now found itself in a position to attract many Catholics (and historical Protestants). Few well-educated Catholics left the church, but millions of non-church-going Catholics who had only a superficial understanding of their faith flocked by the hundreds of thousands to Pentecostalism, the modern variant of Protestantism that emphasized healing, and later to neo-Pentecostalism, the newest version of Pentecostalism, which emphasized a gospel of wealth and prosperity, similar to some core messages of Joel Osteen, who was called by CBS News "America's Preacher,"[41] a title previously reserved for Billy Graham.

Evangelization thus became a priority for the Latin American Catholic Church. The loss of millions of marginal Catholics in the 1990s and 2000s only confirmed earlier indications that a storm was brewing. Lay Catholics responded to the call for volunteers in re-educating the region's Catholics. They also took the lead, along with clergy, in the effort. The centerpiece of this massive campaign was lay catechists.[42] How extensively active the laity have been in twentieth- and twenty-first-century evangelization can be seen in the numbers: 1.2 million laypersons had qualified to become catechists by 2006.[43] This extraordinary number was probably five times what it was in the 1980s when statistics on the office of catechist did not exist in part because it was thought to be an office dealing with Indians. Thus, for decades "catechists" in Latin America referred largely to indigenous laypersons working as interpreters and teachers among Latin American's indigenous millions.

In fact, catechist is an ancient and honored office in the church. That the office of catechist is recognized by the church matters to the officeholder, the institution, and the people served because it offers status, affirmation, and the "right" to play an important role in the church. The ranks of catechists have been filled especially by Charismatics, who, as noted earlier, are eager to share what they consider the precious message of faith. This eagerness gives many bishops and most progressive Catholics pause because they feel that many Charismatics are partial in selecting which parts of the Christian message they communicate to others. Some Charismatics have expressed little conviction about the social-justice message of the Latin American church that was one of its hallmarks.

From the sidelines—and judging only on the basis of effectiveness— Charismatics, as deeply convinced participants in the Pentecostal movement, are probably an even match with many but not all Pentecostal challengers and proselytizers in the battle to retain, lose, or regain the Brazilian faithful. Pentecostal challengers are highly fragmented, offering no united front or underlying vision of God or the way to approach a supreme being. But Pentecostal scholars (and Vatican observers) tend to point to two general types of Pentecostals: the older churches, such as the Assemblies of God in Brazil, and the newer prosperity or health and wealth churches, such as the IURD.

The match up of Catholic Charismatics and older Pentecostals is played on fairly similar theological terrain. The contest of Catholic Charismatics and health and wealth churches is not. These churches make claims about

God that Catholics and historical Protestants believe to be erroneous interpretations of Christian revelation. This contrarian view was made clear in CBS's news coverage of Joel Osteen in 2007 through interviews with Protestant intellectuals and it does not require special intellectual abilities or esoteric theological knowledge to understand.[44] Prosperity gospelers preach that God is a loving, forgiving God *who will reward believers with health, wealth, and happiness.* Or, simply put, "prosperity gospel" is the teaching that God will reward faithful followers with material wealth.[45] This is an airy, fairy tale, according to most Protestant theologians.[46] They strongly opposed this stance, although they preferred that the congressional committee to investigate six prosperity churches in 2008 not cross into what they see as church territory.

In Europe where the IURD has spread and in its native Brazil, such preaching and the church itself have received scathing criticism from secular observers and the press, as Virginia Garrard-Burnett, a historian at the University of Texas, has observed: "In England it has been described as a bizarre cult. In Belgium the Parliament put the church under investigation. Most notably in Brazil the church is almost under constant attack."[47] Despite criticisms and investigations, the IURD is one of the fastest growing churches in the world. Only long-term evangelization efforts by Catholic Charismatics are likely to counter effectively the IURD and similar prosperity churches (especially in periods of economic downturn). So far, the Charismatic effort to counter Pentecostals seems to be based more on positive attraction than direct confrontation. If there is a war, it is more like that of opposing bandstands than boxers in a ring, except for the surprising event in the 1990s of the kicking of the statue of the Blessed Mother, as noted above.

Politics and Charismatics

Similar to the first academic characterizations of Pentecostals, Catholic Charismatics were described unvaryingly as apolitical and spiritual in their approach to society. This was true in France, the United States, and Canada where, for a time at least, Charismatics had a strong influence. On closer look one could find social works, such as hospitals and drug rehab centers, but not support of labor unions and not typically partisan politics.

While the older, classical Pentecostal congregations in Brazil, such as the Assemblies of God and their eight million members, tended to avoid politics, more recent health-and-wealth ones, such as Macedo's Universal Church, plunged right in, creating their own political parties or supporting distinct candidates from established parties in the hopes of using politics to protect the interests their own churches, which were frequently beleaguered by investigations into their finances and practices. These political endeavors have been widely covered by the press and by trusted academics, such as Pau! Freston.[48] The most talked about achievement from this effort of Macedo's was *la bancada evangélica,* the Protestant back bench.

The election of Osmar Pereira, the Brazilian Charismatic renewal's presiding coordinator, as federal deputy from Minas Gerais in the late 1970s was the first big step of Catholic Charismatics into politics. A decade later, Padre Eduardo Dougherty pushed the election of the Charismatic Salvador Filho as city alderman for two terms. Then, starting in 1992 with municipal elections in Fortaleza in northeastern Brazil, Charismatics accelerated their partisan political activities and won federal posts in Belo Horizonte, Curitiba, and other places.[49] With this push and efforts to put forward federal presidential candidates, commentators arrived at a point of speaking of a *bancada carismática.* The energetic this-worldly effort gave pause to reflective Charismatics who wondered if this was out of line: the idea that there were *spokespersons* for the renewal was not well accepted, even less that the specific elected politicians would be those spokespersons for the values of Charismatics.

Those questions caused the participants of the National Congress of the Renewal of 1995 to take up political activity in the movement as a major issue. The renewal congress created a new department for communication about religion and politics. Considerable debate took place within an advisory group that had been formed to give direction to the department, including the comments of a theologian who attempted to point out that the theology of liberation had been especially aimed at Christian reflection on political policy and practice. For a time, the department continued grandiloquently to present itself as promoting the social teaching of the church.

But by 2008 the coordinator of the department, Marizete Nunes do Nascimento, and associates seemed to have but a single focus: abortion. The department and the movement sponsored a national demonstration against abortion similar to the March for Life in the United States. Other social and political issues, for which the Brazilian church leaders were famed, such as the plights of the landless and the indigenous, received no attention. The abortion agenda and the rationale of the department looked like ideas borrowed from an evangelical think tank (if one existed) in Washington, D.C.

While the movement's coordinators were emphasizing no partisan politics and no Charismatic party, second-generation Charismatics wholeheartedly embraced political careers. Three of the more flamboyant showed themselves on their Web sites in full possession of Charismatic credentials. The state deputy Eros Biondini made much of his sixteen years of participating in the mission of TV Canção Novo, "transmitting for the whole state of Minas Gerais the message of the Gospel."[50]

Brazil has had a tradition of separation of church and state since 1889 and this naked use of the religion card in politics by Biondini and others seemed to mark a new stage of partisan politics on the part of Catholic laity. However, the change probably can be dated to the time of the neo-Pentecostal Universal Church's purchase and use of the TV Record network and its aggressive religious programming on commercial television. More, the TV Record network also broadcast defiantly anti-Catholic comments and actions. In other words, there were taunts and responses.

As most commentators said, war was declared by the Universal Church and Catholic Charismatics, not by the aging liberationists, and this war was responded to in a forceful way in television and politics, the two arenas chosen by the Universal Church for battle. One could make the case that Charismatics were acting not only in imitation of neo-Pentecostals, as Chesnut has argued throughout his *Competitive Spirits*, but also out of their own pneumatic experience and exuberant spirituality.

Deputy Biondini put himself forward *politically* as "an evangelizer." This would have been a questionable credential for a Catholic in the 1970s but no longer. Biondini had an array of talents appropriate to a postmodern context. He is a horse doctor—with a degree in veterinary medicine—and a musician. He wants to improve the world by Christians exercising their professions well—he created Missão Nova Mundo (New World Mission) to promote that argument—and he is most proud of being part of *Christ Is the Show*. This annual show was created by the musical group Nova Aliança in 1991. It has drawn fifteen thousand fans a year, is listed on the archdiocesan calendar of Belo Horizonte, and is said by Biondini to be one of the largest shows in the country.

In 2007 Deputy Biondini addressed the Minas Gerais State Assembly to honor the fortieth anniversary of the birth of the movement (in Pittsburgh, which was not mentioned), with the archbishop of Belo Horizonte present. If one had doubts about the conquering sweep of the Charismatic movement in Brazil, Biondini proclaimed the brazen truth to the contrary. If neo-Pentecostals wanted to fight, they would find worthy contenders not in somber clerics but in high-energy lay Catholics. Biondini, as noted, is not alone in his efforts to counter neo-Pentecostal political moves.

Missionary and Evangelizing Charismatics

The Latin American Catholic Church also became actively missionary in the late twentieth century. The rise of the Catholic Charismatic movement began in Latin America just as a missionary spirit was being generally expressed in the region.[51] Charismatics were adding to this effort but neither careful statistics nor sociological studies as yet exist to delineate the full extent of Charismatic Catholic mission efforts.

That Latin America needed evangelization became clearest in 2007 when the Latin American bishops held their major conference, as they did every decade or so to assess their condition. The meeting was held in Aparecida, Brazil, and it was there on the home soil of the world's largest Catholic country that the losses to the church were clearest. Seven years previously the national census—which included questions about religion that the U.S. census does not include—showed undisputedly that millions of Brazilian Catholics had shifted to Protestant groups. These non-Catholic groups were variously defined, but experts agreed that the vast majority were Pentecostal.

However, this information only confirmed what was well known by church leaders in Latin America and by the Vatican. In the previous general conference of bishops and with the pope in attendance at Santo Domingo in 1992, John Paul II called for new evangelization as the top priority of the church. Leaders agreed that the first evangelization by Spanish and Portuguese missionaries had never fully succeeded and that deeper knowledge, enlightenment, and conversion to an adult faith were needed by many Latin American Catholics. John Paul II made himself heard in the sense that strong personalities—charismatic figures often not in church leadership positions—picked up the challenge of evangelizing the continent. Many of them came from new movements in the church, including the Legionnaires of Christ, but none came forward as forcefully or effectively as members of the Catholic Charismatic Renewal.

The covenant groups previously described all emphasized evangelization. New Song built the largest Catholic structure in Latin America, the Bishop João Hipólito de Moraes Evangelization Center. At the heart of its statement of purpose New Song placed statements from *Evangelii Nuntiandi*, the declaration of Paul VI in 1975 that is taken as the Magna Carta of contemporary evangelization efforts. Virtually all the Charismatic covenant communities express their purpose as evangelization, though the forms for attempting to accomplish that differ widely and are typically imaginative.

While Latin American theologians were taking up themes of evangelization and debating ways to accomplish it, Charismatics, along with others, felt they knew exactly what to do—use mass media—although they were not always clear about how best to do that. They embraced radio and television, co-natural elements for an expressive religion, a religion tending toward performance, testimony, and witness. They learned almost as quickly as some American presidential candidates the value of the Internet, including a strong presence on YouTube.[52] They—Pentecostal and Charismatic—turned successfully to the composition and performance of music. And one, Marcelo Rossi, became a superstar. Furthermore, he kept millions of young Catholics in the church. He also reinforced their enthusiasm for their future as Christians and the future of the church.

As the covenant communities evangelize in various kinds of environments and with their own "charisma," virtually all have had music as a special emphasis for their work. This emphasis was all up-front and remarkable for Catholics who were not accustomed to their members being on bestseller lists for popular music, either in the category of overall bestsellers or in the category of Christian music, a territory then foreign to most Catholics who listened to and bought music. In 2006, Father Marcelo Rossi was number one overall in music for his bestselling musical CD in Brazil, *Nova Bendicâo*. Toca de Assis, Shalom, and Canção Nova all have singers or groups that have sold well in the category of Christian music.

From its inception Canção Nova emphasized the writing and performing of songs as a special charisma of the group. Hence the logo Canção Nova (New Song) being carried on virtually all of its enterprises, including radio and television. Shalom has a different history, but music is one of its main ministries. While Canção Nova does not explain to outsiders why the emphasis on song and singing is central to its members' lives, Shalom has an elaborate rationale for its emphasis on music available on its Web site. Music is seen as part of God's plan. It is, in Shalom's vision, a highly efficacious method of dialoging with God. Furthermore, music is a fundamental element in building human society. In a word, good music elevates and unites men and women with God and with each other; bad music alienates humans from God. Shalom has attempted to be inside popular culture and channel it and not stand on the sidelines with an ineffectual wringing of hands about music putatively leading men and women away from God.

Music is seen by Shalom's members as part of the divine plan and is to be used in the service of the church. However, it has its own integrity as an art. It is to be practiced with reverence, putting forth a word or sound made when others are ready to listen. Shalom sees musicians as steeped in silence, listening for the opportune moment to employ song, doing this for the sake of others. Clothing was to be modest: not too colorful, and without short skirts or too much cleavage. Music, argues Shalom, does not emphasize exuberance but simplicity. The whole body is to be employed but not in exaggerated movements and certainly not in a sexually suggestive manner. (Bono, who is often cited as a Christian music practitioner, warned about the use of music for winning converts through music. Shalom has stated no position on that.)

Evangelization clearly was growing as a major priority of the Catholic Church in Latin America, but missionary activity from Latin America was not until recently seen as a needed effort from the whole Latin American church. Latin American Catholics were concerned with themselves since they were not even able to take care of their own pastoral and spiritual needs. But something changed in the late twentieth century in the Latin American Catholic psyche. Some of the impetus for missionary outlook came from long-term efforts, such as that of the Mexican church as will be noted, to look outward to Asia, Africa, and the global church.[53] But more recent efforts mark the start of a new stage in the extroversion of the Latin American Catholic Church. Charismatic covenant communities spontaneously opened missions in foreign countries, as did Shalom with twelve houses overseas in the first twenty-five years of its history. Canção Nova established mission houses in the United States, France, Portugal, and Israel. Toca de Assis established missions in Ecuador and Portugal.

The infusion of Charismatics from the global south to Europe has brought new energy to northern regions described as being in spiritual winter. It also breathed new life into the church in the United States.

The most profound sign of vitality of the Latin American church, one beyond growth in priests and seminarians and commitment of hundreds of thousands of lay ministers, is the recent sending of missionaries. When the church in the United States switched from being a missionary-receiving church to a missionary-sending church, this signaled the final stage of its coming of age. In this same way, then, the Latin American church was reaching a key point in its maturity.

This new outreach of the Latin American church stands in contrast to its historical tendency, which was to focus largely on itself. After five hundred years of Catholicism, Latin America was extremely slow in developing a missionary outreach. A major reason for this deficiency came about in the nineteenth century when the church was decimated of its clergy by the independent republics that were formed out of the Spanish empire. These governments forced Spanish priests to leave the continent. Furthermore, the anticlerical governments in many countries severely restricted the church in terms of income, participation in public life, and education.

One accepted test of authentic Christianity is mission. This is the willingness to share the gift of faith with others at some cost to oneself. Through centuries mission was defined as going to non-Christian people, *missio ad gentes*, generally in a distant region. By the twentieth century, this meaning of mission had expanded to mean leaving one's home to go to another region of the world even if the mission-receiving area was generally Christian. More recently mission has also meant leaving one's home for another part of the same country or for some other country in Latin America.

This change from receiving missionaries to sending them occurred directly from the education of Latin American Catholics in their responsibility to the whole church and not just to their region. But it also occurred by an overflow of generosity. Members of Shalom, Canção Nova, and Toca Assis, who were either responding to invitations from abroad or sensing great needs elsewhere—and having a globe rather than a country as their internal map—crossed borders or oceans to evangelize: this is one of the classical definitions of a missionary. Some four thousand to five thousand Latin Americans have carried on this foreign missionary work.[54]

It surprises some observers that many of the new Latin American missionaries are laypersons because the majority of foreign missionaries in the past have been priests or religious sisters. But by looking at the ranks of Brazilian Charismatics and seeing mostly enthusiastic laypersons eager to spread their faith, one would understand better this new complexion of the missionary force.

Foreign missionaries are only a small segment of missionary activity. Thousands of internal missionaries became active in Brazil.

Internal missionaries began going door to door to invite persons to the local prayer group or the local parish. They did so more from internal compulsion than slavish imitation of what the Pentecostals did. Members of Toca de Assis routinely work and virtually live in the streets. Shalom's community members' desire to start a snack bar in Toulouse and talk about the Catholic faith with un-churched French men and women seem like a case of being driven to new frontiers rather than copying Pentecostal tactics, as Andrew Chesnut and some advocates of rational choice theory have argued.[55]

Conclusion

If the popular press is to be believed, then the Brazilian Catholic Church was under siege as perhaps few other churches have been. Competition with non-Catholic religious groups, particularly the Pentecostals, seemed more like war than brotherly rivalries. But this competition has generated a vibrancy that is exceptional. Major gains have been made in the numbers of priests and seminarians. The number of priests has been rising steadily. From 1957 to 2007, priests increased by 1,019 percent and seminarians by 898 percent.[56] But most impressive has been the mobilization of people in the pews who have come forward to evangelize and leave home to become missionaries.

In explaining why Latin America is so different from Europe in terms of religious fervor, David Martin believes that "Latin America became a hybrid, incorporating an Anglo-Saxon type of trajectory, with Pentecostalism emerging as the vehicle of a major mobilization of the poor."[57] Brazilian (and Latin American) Catholic Charismaticism similarly became a hybrid of U.S. and Brazilian religious cultures incorporating an Anglo-Saxon type of religious trajectory. Charismaticism travels well, especially where there is freedom to innovate.

In terms of globalization, outside influences have brought a global Charismatic culture but with creative local adaptations. Anthony Smith, writing about global culture, notes that new traditions must hew closely to vernacular motifs. "It is one thing," Smith says, "to package imagery and diffuse it. . . . It is quite another to ensure the power to move and to inspire."[58] The Brazilian Catholic cultural adeptness has brought a new stage in the enculturation of Catholicism in the country. The Charismatic renewal has penetrated youth culture, assimilated musical styles, and adopted secular communications media for its message. It has also renewed religious language and reinforced religion as an everyday part of life rather than a marginal or Sunday event for Brazilians.

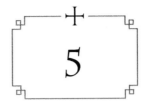

BRAZIL

Superstar and Competition with Pentecostals

When Father Marcelo Rossi became a recognized superstar in Brazilian public life, his various publics were invested in him with many different interests and issues. That a Catholic priest could sing well enough to gain popular attention is little more than a trivial celebrity fact, that he would want to sing and dance before hundreds of thousands of participants in Catholic Mass is a mystery to be delved into here.

Without question, Father Marcelo possessed superstar status both among people in the pews and in the wide and vibrant world of Brazilian popular culture. His status tended to obscure the true character of Catholic Charismatics in Latin America because the media have focused on him and not what is behind him. However, as I have shown previously, he was not a founder of the movement and he does not represent more than one aspect—a prominent tip of the iceberg—of the movement.

The movement is built on the strong foundation of prayer groups and covenant communities. Most have a slim connection to Father Rossi. The movement has spread all over Brazil and the conversions many members make in joining the movement were little influenced by his or any other Charismatic singer on stage. He is not the only leader but one among many. It makes good press to stress the glitz and glitter of celebrity life and to pitch the religious picture as most journalists do as a struggle between Catholics and Pentecostals. As noted, this is presumably embodied in a war over television ratings and imagined to be centered in whether Rossi (Catholic) draws more listeners than Crivelli (a Pentecostal preacher from the Universal Church of the Kingdom of God). Furthermore, the numerical indicators of popular culture are by news media, in part because they have few other ways to picture for readers religious phenomena happening in public. By contrast, much of the movement has taken place out of sight.

Nonetheless Father Rossi is pivotal to evaluating what is going on. More, he and his career, his personality, and his message are inherently intriguing in part because religion and culture may mix differently in the Global south and may hold the key to understanding the future of the largest church in Catholicism within the context of global Pentecostalism. In other words, Rossi brings to focus many of the main issues in religion and society in the contemporary world and especially in the Global south.

How Rossi arrived at a pinnacle of popular culture and why he should be there are among the questions ordinary people, cultural commentators, and theologians ask. When his first CDs became runaway bestsellers in the late 1990s, national and international attention was drawn to Rossi. Rossi's sales figures are even more impressive because Brazilian CDs are more expensive than most others in Latin America or in the United States. In 2004 when popular music CDs in the United States were running at about U.S.$12, popular music CDs in Brazil cost U.S.$18 (in a country with a much lower median income).

Rossi's appeal has held up from the late 1990s. In 2006 his *Minha Benção* topped the popular music charts for the year. His appeal has spread to Brazilians overseas, with his CDs (in Portuguese) easily available through Amazon.com and other sources. Even though his CDs sell better than those of most singers in Brazil, he does not have an extraordinary voice. He is attractive but not exceptional. What is special for most of his followers—and they are in the millions—is his message, a Charismatic Catholic message.

The Message and the Medium

Father Rossi comes from a recent history of priests and other religious performers in public, that is, performances of religious music outside of churches. For Catholics, at least, this is a relatively new phenomenon. One could date the start-up year as 1967 when Padre Zezinho began his singing career. Padre Zezinho (whose legal name is Jose Fernandes de Oliveira) broke the ground for Christian music in Brazil. "During this period not one singer sang the music I composed or religious music. [Forty years later], the great names seek to sing and record it," he recalled in an interview.[1] Born in the state of Minas Gerais, an up-and-at-'em area, he gained his love and skill in music from his violinist father. And then in the 1960s the superiors of his small religious Congregation of the Sacred Heart sent him to the United States for several years to further his skills in theater, music, and other media.[2]

He composed his first songs for the congregation of his first parish assignment in São Paulo's San Judas's parish. "Nobody had ever heard or imagined there could be a priest-musical artist," he said.[3] This was the beginning of an extensive career as a singer and songwriter. Eventually he wrote some fifteen hundred religious songs (songs of the interior life, as he described them)[4] and recorded almost one hundred records and CDs, some translated into five languages, and all told distributed in forty countries. Through the years he combined what he knew of U.S. country music, nonmilitary parade marches, Germanic waltzes, and music from southern Minas Gerais. His music caught on early and he was soon selling one hundred thousand records a year, plus having his music recorded by famous artists, such as Roberto Carlos's hit record "Prayer for the Family," which sold one million copies.

Padre Zezinho and virtually all the priest-singers came to be known by their first names. Brazilians prefer simple, endearing names for performers, athletes, and friends, as in Pelé or Reinaldo, two world-class Brazilian soccer players. One can also invent one's *nome creativo* (stage or creative artist name). Names are often in the diminutive, implying being familiarly known and loveable. So instead of Padre Zé (Father Joe), the priest-performer became known as Padre Zezinho (Father Joey). Or people just use Zezinho if no one will be left guessing about his clerical identity. Occasionally the diminutive does not fit the body type so the augmentative is used. Thus Rio's Father George became Padre Jorjão (Big Father George).

Priests in Brazil have more latitude in choosing their garb for performing than they might elsewhere. In most of Brazil priests tended in the twentieth century to wear secular clothes on the street, often with a small cross or another religious symbol on the shirt collar or chest pocket. In 2009, Padre Zezinho, who was born in 1941, looked like Dick Clark, the seemingly ageless U.S. music show host. On his CD covers, he had a full head of black hair with a few gray streaks, wore a patterned sweater over an open-collar, long-sleeve white shirt, and dark blue slacks.

Padre Zezinho and some of the other recording priests further adorn themselves with chains and crosses but typically no rings. One priest-singer in a black clerical suit (a black suit was somewhat usual for clerics, except for bishops) appeared on a CD cover with a pectoral cross larger than any worn by a bishop thus far observed. By contrast, Zezinho wears a small silver cross of four equal arms and a heart cut out of the center of the cross. This logo is repeated on CD covers, which allows for quick recognition of Zezinho's disks in the CD bins.

The puzzle of priest-performers has several hints of answers. First, Padre Zezinho was in the United States learning evangelism through mass media when Christian contemporary music was about to burst into full-scale competition with other categories of recorded music, selling by 2005 some 750 million recordings a year.[5] In 1974, a landmark year for Christian contemporary music, a group called the Second Chapter of Acts, using contemporary pop idioms, sold 250,000 records in contrast to older evangelical singers who were lucky to sell 100,000 copies.[6] Zezinho was witnessing the modern birth of Christian contemporary music and carried back to Brazil many of its characteristics.

Second was the presence in Latin America, ten years after Zezinho's modest beginnings in Brazil, of Jimmy Swaggert, a cousin and virtual duplicate of the rocker and country music star Jerry Lee Lewis. Swaggert, of the Assemblies of God Pentecostal wing of the U.S. church, showed Brazilians how to present religion to large groups *outside of churches*. In contrast to most Christian music performers in the United States, Swaggert was an ordained minister. He opened his show/religious service with his own singing and piano playing, then paused and launched into spoken prayer and dramatic preaching. When in Brazil, he drew one hundred thousand people to the Maracaná in Rio, Brazil's largest stadium. This show/religious service was carried on television and satellite. Swaggert also sang and recorded music, showing yet another way to reach a popular audience beyond the style of rally utilized by Billy Graham and others.

At the parish where he started his ministry, Padre Zezinho attracted other musicians and began small but popular musical shows with local bands and singers in a parish hall. This setting was too small and localized for all the persons who wanted to hear him and he was soon on the road. This was the beginning of a steady career of performing on the road, doing about forty shows a year in Brazil and other countries. By some estimates 120 million Brazilians have heard his music. Some of the shows were mega-productions. Perhaps typical of these larger shows that were produced just as Rossi came on the scene was Zezinho's *Tenderness and*

Peace Show in 1996 at Recife. At this event the heralded retired archbishop of the Northeast, Dom Helder Câmara, made a special appearance on stage.[7] Câmara was but one of five guests to appear, flanked by lead and backup singers, members of a chorus, and a band.

The presence of Câmara, who was nominated for the Nobel Peace Prize, might have shocked observers who remembered his unflinching demands for social justice for Brazil's poor and believed that present-day priest-performers had their appeal primarily because of a message of otherworldliness. Zezinho did not fit well within that mold. His songs tugged at the heart over abandoned children, his paraplegic parents, a murdered land-reform proponent, and an end to social violence in Brazil. He did, at times, appear to be in the Charismatic mold: one of his bestselling CDs dealt with divine healing. But he is a priest of Vatican Council II, open to various tendencies, ecumenical in relation to other Christians, and actively fostering this-worldly concerns of justice and peace.

He composed two complete Masses. He also wrote several works of catechesis. He broadcast for thirty years on radio. In television, he limited himself to the Catholic networks with lesser audiences than the main O Globo or TV Record television networks. He and his brother singer-priest, Padre Joâozinho, described below, both conscientiously avoided commercial television outlets. By the time of his fortieth anniversary as a performer, Zezinho had sold more than five million records.

Zezinho was a pioneer who opened up the world of religious music in Brazil. By the late 2000s some twenty-five hundred Catholic bands had been formed; thirty thousand singers had been selected to lead congregations at Mass in popular religious music; and more than five hundred religious music CDs were being cut and distributed annually. Zezinho calculated that more than five hundred artists were making a living singing religious music in Brazil. He also believed that music acts as an instrument for dialogue between churches and has stimulated many persons to pursue the priesthood or Christian marriage. Later Charismatic priest-performers would not share his ecumenical convictions.

A lesser light but nonetheless important in pioneering music as ministry was another priest who used as his stage name Padre Antonio Maria. He began his professional life in the Jaraguá district of São Paulo, working with orphans. During his first four years of priesthood, which were spent in Portugal, he was already known as a young priest who could sing exceptionally well. In Brazil, in contrast to those who mostly sang in churches or on stages, Padre Antonio Maria sang at large open spaces, such as gas stations and city plazas. He also gained national attention through friendship with some of Brazil's top pop singers.

This innovation of using an impromptu setting such as a gas station probably began with the Jesus People in the United States in the 1960s. They liked to make music with Christian lyrics "wherever" for the enjoyment of others. This was in the spirit of a serendipitous happening of joy and peace. "Wherever" frequently meant a coffeehouse. There was an informal network of these Christian coffeehouses across the United States in the 1960s and 1970s. Bands traveled around, typically in VW buses, and dropped in at the coffeehouses, expecting little more than a burger and gas money in return for the pleasure of performing and enlightening.

In addition, their innovation, one carried out also in Brazil, was the incorporation of rock sounds into Christian music. It was as if George Beverly Shea, Billy Graham's favorite singer, had picked up an electronic guitar. The entrance of rock music came with the conversion of young people from the Haight-Ashbury generation to evangelical Christian churches. When they came into the church, their music came with them. They saw no reason to leave behind their beloved sound and associated instrumentation. Their job was to adjust the drug and sex messages frequently conveyed by rockers at that time. This they did with a manic zeal shared by their listeners. The same was true of country and folk music: there is a Christian guitar "community" of some one hundred thousand persons gathered at a common Web site.[8]

Padre Antonio Maria moved into the high realms of the celebrity entertainment and sports world and found himself burned by bad publicity in 2005 when he attempted to bless the illicit marriage in France of the Brazilian soccer star Ronaldo and a television actress. Media attention on priest-singers intensified as their popularity grew.

Simultaneously, a third generation of priest-singers was coming on stage, virtually all from the Catholic Charismatic wing of the church. One of them already mentioned, Padre Joãozinho, was inspired by Padre Zezinho and was from the same Congregation of the Sacred Heart. He was much more focused inwardly on Charismatic audiences, was openly critical of some popular musical styles (as others were about the saccharine *pogode* music), and avoided commercial television appearances.

Among other newcomers was Padre Zeca in hip Rio.[9] He also made missteps, going too far to be "with it." A surfer from childhood, he became known as the suntanned Marcelo Rossi. His dream was to carry the church to where the people lived, having been inspired by Pope John Paul's visit to Brazil and the pope's informal conference at that time with young priests and seminarians. In 1997, Padre Zeca organized the first Young Catholic Gospel Meeting called "God Is a Ten" at Post 10, the pole marker for a section of the famed Ipanema beach.[10] He helped to organize Charismatic prayer groups at the Catholic University of Rio, recorded various CDs that sold well, especially *God Is a Ten*. His recording label EMI was so impressed with these successes that the company created a separate internal department for popular religious music.[11]

Rio, a key archdiocese within Brazil, gave support to the Charismatic movement through its leader, Cardinal Eugenio Sales, but Padre Zeca eventually went beyond the comfort zone of the archdiocese of Rio because of his unorthodox beach liturgies. Rio is regarded as the least Catholic city in the country and Zeca felt driven to meeting the un-churched where they were likely to congregate. Assigned as a young priest to a parish in the heart of the beach community at Copacabana, he brought together "Catholic bands" for the immensely popular Rock in Rio Café musical festival (held in an area that could accommodate five Woodstocks) and at open spaces at the Rio beach areas that drew very large crowds. He held the fourth of these events at Ipanema beach in 2000, an event that *Epoca* magazine reported as drawing seventy thousand people.[12] He told a newspaper, "This is a spectacle and within the spectacle is the Mass. In the show that precedes the Mass, spectators jump around and dance . . . and then the silence that young people create during the Mass time is impressive. I know well how to separate the liturgical celebration from the show."[13] After much criticism, Father Zeca's beach Masses came to an abrupt halt. The press said he was disciplined in some unspecified way and he disappeared from public view. In fact, he went to Rome for four years to complete a doctorate in theology and returned to Rio to work in a parish. He wrote his dissertation on a basic Pentecostal theme, religious experience, focusing on the thought of St. Augustine.

Other priests in this new generation also sang and performed. From time to time aggregate pictures of priest-singers appeared in Sunday supplements. They numbered between nine and twenty. These would be the front ranks, with national CD sales. Others were singing for only local audiences. Young men wishing to emulate them were apparently entering the seminaries, guaranteeing perhaps a future for the church of priest-singers. But the epicenter was held by Padre Rossi and sometimes it seemed like the future of priest-singers and that of the church rested on his wide shoulders.

Some large social forces are at work here. Brazilian parishes are changing. A Brazilian researcher has noted an internal change in parishes and a change in the way priesthood is expressed. Alberto Antoniazzi, a priest-researcher and advisor to the Brazilian Bishops Conference, has traced the evolution of parishes from the traditional dispensing of rituals until the 1960s, to the emphasis on community in the 1970s and 1980s, to the prevalence of religious expression and personalized religion in the 1990s. In the 1990s the pastor changed from being the animator of a community to a "personality" whose *performance* was judged by the value of the emotional expression he generated.[14]

The parish, Antoniazzi believed, was affected by what Brazilians saw in the mass media, bringing the parishes toward emotional expression and experience to match in a general way what Brazilians viewed on television. However, only some parishes and priests have changed toward a performance style. Priest-performers come from various Catholic tendencies, but the two major tendencies seem to be at war with one another. Even more sharply than in other countries, a number of Brazilian priests reflected either Charismatic Catholicism or liberation theology ideologies.

While several other priests and at least one religious sister were performing in public for years, somehow Rossi pulled it altogether to become number one. But the questions piled up, and one in particular stood out. In a country such as Brazil, which contained a libertarian cultural form known for its hedonism—Carnival and scanty clothes, beach living and easy sexual mores—how did a religious message fit?

Father Rossi's Own Mega-Church

No one in Brazil thirty years ago predicted that Catholics would be building mega-churches devoted to the ministries of superstar priests. But the two largest churches in Latin America will be the homes for the ministries of Father Jonas Abib and Father Marcelo Rossi. No sooner in the mid-2000s had Abib built his church with a capacity of one hundred thousand people than Rossi was announcing plans for a structure with a similar capacity.[15] The only differences seem to be aesthetic: Rossi's architect is one of those internationally known imaginative ones while a compromising committee seems to have designed Abib's structure. Rossi's architect is Ruy Ohtake, a former Buddhist, now Catholic, who designed a striking hotel and other commercial properties in São Paulo. Through the late 2000s Rossi has remained rector of Santuario Mãe de Deus, where thousands flock to his weekday and Sunday Masses. Thirty thousand participants are not uncommon, especially on special feasts. Sunday liturgies are carried by the commercial network, O Globo Internacional, to more than forty countries, including many in Africa and Europe.

Father Rossi has drawn 2.5 million people to a Charismatic celebration, needing a racetrack because a soccer stadium was not large enough. "He drew as many people as John Paul II did when he came to Brazil," a middle-of-the-road Catholic priest said. He was not thinking of John Paul II as a performer, but many observers have seen Pope John Paul's appeal as similar to that of a rock star. Whatever else he did, John Paul II showed another way to be a priest in his large gatherings of faithful on visits all over the world even when suffering from Parkinson's disease. When Pope John Paul II spoke to young priests in Brazil about reaching out to young people in contemporary forms, Rossi and other priests listened and responded.

In Rossi's case, he incorporated singing and movement into both stadium-like events and daily Mass. He became a singing star. One of his first CDs, *Music to Praise the Lord*, sold extremely well, some 3.2 million copies. Other hits followed as his CDs rose to the top of the charts. He also dances, in the sense of moving to the music. These are the surface qualities that have attracted attention, but one cannot explain Rossi without his message. He is trying to lead his listeners, especially the younger ones, to commit themselves to Jesus, allow the divine spirit to enter their lives, and live according to a Christian code of ethics. The message is one of personal conversion in an atmosphere of joy and hope.

Rossi was born in 1967 under military rule that was turning nasty, with social-justice activists and moderate politicians suffering from military repression in the 1970s and 1980s. He grew up in Santana in the northern section of São Paulo city, which was becoming one of the largest cities in the world. He was not a pious child and like many Brazilians drifted into religious indifference. Given his physical talents, he specialized in physical education and spent a short time in the air force as a physical education instructor. At the age of twenty-one and basically rootless in terms of belief, he suffered two shocks that affected him deeply. A cousin suffered sudden death in an accident and an aunt developed a deadly form of cancer. In his grief he sought comfort in the church he had abandoned for five years. He recounted in his personal history that he found peace through a personal encounter with God. His viewing of a television mini-series about the life of Pope John Paul II led him to consider imitating him by joining the priesthood. This was just the first step in following in John Paul's footsteps. After studies in philosophy he moved on to the Salesian School of Theology at Lorena in São Paulo state, which was a hotbed of the Catholic Charismatic Renewal where Jonas Abib and his disciples were working with young persons.

By the time he was ordained in 1994 at an older age than most seminarians at that time, Brazil had passed from military to civilian governments and was entering a long period of opening out to the world in global trade, especially in commodities. China and other countries would begin to vie with one another for Brazil's soybeans, orange juice, and similar products. For many Brazilians—but not all—the future looked wide open.

Padre Marcelo, as Rossi is commonly called, was first assigned as an assistant pastor to a church in a slum area in the Santo Amaro diocese on the fringe of the city of São Paulo. By then the legendary archdiocese of São Paulo under the ecumenical and social-justice leadership of Cardinal Evaristo Arns had been broken up into several dioceses and Rossi's diocese ended up with a relatively conservative bishop. As young adult, Rossi had stopped attending church out of boredom. He resolved as a young priest never to bore his listeners. This universal hope of new ministers was backed up by his strong assets: a six-feet-four-inch athletic build, fair hair, good looks, and an abundance of energy.

In the parish where he was an assistant pastor, Rossi's preaching and services soon attracted larger audiences. Catholics were formerly expected to join the territorial parishes where they lived. Records of birth, marriage, and death—all important in modern societies—were kept in the local parish churches. Contemporary Catholics tend to choose parishes by what they see as most congenial to themselves, a notable trend in religion. People began overflowing the church where Rossi was assigned as an assistant pastor. Before long, he was made the pastor of his own parish, one at a distance from his first assignment. People followed. As his parish church proved quickly to be inadequate for the crowds at his Masses, the diocese moved his Sunday services to a rented dance hall. Then the diocese provided him with money for refitting an old glass factory. This hangarlike structure accommodated thirty thousand people. Five days a week he celebrated Mass at what he called Santuario Terço Vizentino (Sanctuary of the Byzantine Rosary). The sanctuary held more people than Madison Square Garden. The thirty thousand people for a weekday parish Mass could find a place in a mythical Guinness Book of Religious Records.

Larger numbers came on Sundays and special occasions. Doors were left open because of the subtropical heat. The loudspeakers were turned up for the crowd of listeners. Traffic jammed the residential area surrounding the church building. Soon neighbors complained effectively to the municipal government about the disruption of the crowds and especially the noise. The diocese had to pay a fine to the municipality of some $U.S.5,000 every day that the sound exceeded the 50–55 decibel range. Rossi stopped using the building in December 2000. Four months later he moved to another rehabbed structure, a gigantic former metalworking plant with sixty thousand square meters of floor space. This location provided less congested traffic patterns, greater parking facilities, and better ventilation.

All of these changes of location occurred relatively rapidly. Large numbers of people were drawn to Rossi's Masses not only by word of mouth in Rio but also by an event that brought Rossi to the national stage. In 1997, three years into his priestly career, he was the central attraction at a religious rally called "I Am Happy to Be Catholic" at Morumbí stadium in São Paulo. Seventy thousand people attended.

To carry his message to a larger number of people, Rossi decided to cut a record that would in some fashion convey the unique experience of being present at his Masses. He put together *Music to Praise God* in 1998. This first CD became a hit and Rossi's face appeared on the covers of national news magazines. He found a niche in preaching through music. The next year, 1999, he put out his second CD, *A Present for Jesus*. It was followed in 2000 by his third CD, *Songs for the New Millennium*. Then in 2001, his fourth CD, *Peace*, was released with music from the noted artists Roberto Carlos and Erasmo Carlos. With this kind of collaboration he was now an insider within the world of popular culture. That same year the major commercial network O Globo began carrying his Sunday Mass live to Brazil and twelve other countries. In 2002 his fifth CD, *Angels*, appeared. He became rector of the Santuario, which then was named Terço Bizantino, and Rossi was looking toward the movies, gathering around him an informal group of film people.

In addition to music, the Charismatic movement contributed to changing—for better or worse—the art of preaching in Brazil and Latin America. As noted previously, preaching as an art had fallen into a steep decline in Latin America. It began improving with the biblical studies revival in the Latin American Catholic Church in the 1970s and with the new style of the oral "presentation of the Word" (reading Scripture and preaching) that came to be summarized as *proclamation*. The Charismatic movement added fire and animation to preaching homilies, but key carriers of the movement, such as Francis MacNutt, also brought two additional characteristics: professional expertise from speech and drama schools and Catholic revivalism.[16] The professionalism added rhetorical structure, awareness of the audiences' needs, and emphasis on being heard through up-to-date sound equipment, which was not typically found in many Latin American Catholic church buildings. In the United States Catholic revivalism moved beyond annual retreats in parishes to places like baseball stadiums. MacNutt was one among many Catholic Charismatics to grace the infields of Shea Stadium and other baseball parks for revivals.

The language used by Charismatic preachers, especially young ones, has been noted for its appeal to young audiences. Members of these audiences have often been quoted by newspaper interviewers and have written in their own blogs of the simple, direct language preachers use to explain God, the Holy Spirit, and prayer. It is almost as if they have mastered "youth talk." The Colombian and Brazilian preachers especially have gained enthusiastic followings as indicated in numerous posted e-mails soliciting evaluations after weekends sponsored by Minuto de Dios or Canção Nova. Word of mouth and e-mails have created an informal rating system of preachers.

Rossi became the major cultural carrier of the Catholic Charismatic Renewal in Brazil. On the west coast of South America and the Caribbean many Spanish-speaking Catholics have never heard of him. In 2008 he was securely established at Santuario Mãe de Deus on United Nations Boulevard in São Paulo with access by subway and bus. A steady flow of participants reached him from all over the city and often from other parts of the country.

The mobilization of the human infrastructure to support the Charismatic movement was remarkable. In Rossi's case, most persons attending his Masses came by public transportation. But a system of shared rides to the Masses was facilitated by a large network to bring the faithful to the Santuario Mãe de Deus.[17] Charismatic phone directories in Rio de Janeiro, four hundred miles from São Paulo, offered the numbers of ninety contacts (persons or couples) who arranged rides to the Santuario from most sections of Rio. Similar networks of contacts and rides were available within São Paulo and other parts of the country.

Rossi was carefully watched for improprieties for several reasons. First, Brazilians have a strong strain of anticlericalism. They had the Catholic Church as a state or a sponsored church for four hundred years[18] and this long symbiosis typically generates a distinct strain of anticlericalism. Among Brazilians this strain often means deep skepticism about the institutional church while maintaining confidence in God. Second, Brazilians had evidence of religion being used for apparent gain in the case of the Universal Church of the Kingdom of God (IURD), the third largest Pentecostal church in Brazil, whose finances and practices have been investigated in Brazil and other countries. Third, they have seen the rise and fall of Jimmy Swaggert, who cut a notable path through Brazil. Last, Brazilians live in a country with a long history of charismatic and mystical characters that were thoroughly enshrouded in religion in one form or another.

Money was presumed to be coming to Rossi at a high rate. His CDs brought in millions of cruzeiros. Then, as journalists of various stripes have pointed out, Rossi was an empresario in the sense that family members managed what seemed to be a lucrative business at his Santuario of selling religious goods. That his Web site also includes a category of "shopping" did little to counter the impression of money piling up. As a secular priest with no vow of poverty, Rossi is entitled to retain money he makes in side ventures as an artist or a writer. Secular priests, such as the bestselling author Father Andrew Greeley, have on occasion gained considerable private wealth from earnings or inheritance. From the beginning of his musical career Rossi made it clear that profits from his recordings went to benefit the needy of his diocese. More, a large portion was presumed to be going toward the planned mega-church that would cost multimillions of dollars and would hold thousands of persons.

The situation was somewhat similar to that of Joel Osteen in which money piled up from his book deals and from weekly contributions;

family members were trusted instruments in administration; and his large church was rebuilt from the shell of an athletic stadium in Houston at considerable expense. With 47,000 people in weekly attendance, Osteen's Lakewood Church was the largest mega-church community in the United States. ("Mega-church" is defined as a church with 2,000 people in weekly attendance.) Rossi's attendance exceeded Osteen's by a wide margin: Rossi's weekly attendance ran about 190,000. Weekly attendance will probably top that when the new structure is built. His plans for the monumental Ohtake-designed mega-church were put on hold while money was being collected. In the meantime Rossi announced in 2007 that he was producing another major motion picture, one based on the life of Christ. He planned to use profits from the movie to finance the mega-church.

In the early 2000s Rossi moved into movie making. In 2003, money raised from his various enterprises helped fund his first film, *Maria, Mae do Filho de Deus*. Financing also came from a partnership of Columbia Pictures, Sony, O Globo, and Diller Productions. The film, despite being a religious movie about Mary, the Mother of Jesus, was a box office success. Measuring success at movie box offices is relative to the country in question. The producer said that 2.5 million people saw the film and that about 280,000 DVDs of the film were sold. This placed the film sixth among pictures produced nationally in 1995–2004. Rossi followed that in 2004 with another film, *Irmãos de Fe*, also co-produced with Columbia. The film was a portrayal of the conversion of St. Paul to Christianity. Rossi played a leading role on-screen in this further commercial success.

Until the 2000s, religious films had the same mixed commercial history in Brazil as in the United States. Then Mel Gibson's mix of blood and Bible in *The Passion of the Christ* (2004) proved a blockbuster hit that set records around the world. In Brazil his film drew seven million viewers. Rossi's films began appearing in Brazil slightly before Gibson's and avoided overly graphic violence but not a muted controversy over the portrayal of Jews in a Rossi film. The controversy was softened by a politically correct ending promoting peace between Christians and Jews. This was in contrast to Gibson's alleged anti-Semitism and the strong controversy that followed Gibson's film. Both Rossi's and Gibson's successes occurred at roughly the same time, which seemed to prove that religious films were marketable, and for Rossi, at least, their successes offered proof that prime cultural media could be used for evangelization, or perhaps proselytism. Film critics saw *Irmãos de Fe* as showing that all persons are welcomed into the Catholic Church no matter what their previous faith was.[19] (The latter was perhaps an indirect message that Pentecostals would be welcomed back to Catholicism.)

Rossi moved agilely among many activities. With daily programs on Radio América he had three hundred thousand listeners in the São Paulo area and seven million in Brazil. (His radio broadcasts set audience records.) He had weekly television programs on Redevida and TV Globo and participated daily in Radio Jovem Pan Am. On radio he was interviewed or participated in chat shows. Furthermore, he was in constant demand for other television talk shows and as a guest for variety programs. His appearances doubled the typical listenership. In 2001 he added his own Web site (http://www.padremarcelorossiline.com.br) where he receives high-density traffic.

Rossi's Message

Rossi's appeal does not mean universal admiration. One of Brazil's most read writers expressed his grave doubts about Rossi's message. Frei Betto, a non-ordained Dominican brother, wrote both bestselling fiction (*Hotel Brasil*) and nonfiction (*Bautismo de sangue*). Both Betto and Rossi are based in the São Paulo area. In 1998 in *A Folha de São Paulo*, a high-circulation daily with national distribution, Betto took Padre Rossi to task for missing opportunities to promote social justice.[20] Betto's criticism was that Rossi had immense audiences but did not say a word to remind audiences of the situation of millions of suffering poor in the country. To Betto it was a waste of opportunities.

As if to answer Betto, Rossi framed the second film, *Irmãos de Fe*, of which he was the principal producer, around the story of young poor persons caught up in a highly corrupt justice system. The difference between Betto's and Rossi's perspectives was not thereby resolved because Betto's long career as a Brazilian intellectual has been aimed at changing structural inequities along with the human heart, while Rossi sees societal improvement as dependent on personal conversion, without discussion of changing social structures.[21] In many ways, this was at the heart of the differences between liberation theology, Christian base communities, and political activism on the one hand, and Charismatic renewal, covenant communities, and political neutrality on the other that underlay the tensions of major groups attempting to revitalize the church.

Liberation theology held sway among the leaders in the Brazilian Bishops Conference and among the most vocal of Brazilian Catholic intellectuals. For some time liberation theologians and prominent church journals largely ignored the Catholic Charismatic Renewal, apparently regarding it as beneath the dignity of serious theological investigation. A change occurred in 2000 when Clovodis Boff, a major and highly respected Brazilian theologian, wrote with appreciation of the Charismatic movement.[22] By then the movement had not only gained numerical importance but acceptance or tolerance from the majority of bishops. This represents an erosion of the caution the Brazilian Bishops Conference expressed in 1994 when it viewed the Charismatic movement with "serious reservations."[23]

However, one can understand that when Father Rossi began performing at large public gatherings, his bishop was often visible on or near the stage as a sign of approbation. The Charismatic renewal later appeared as the chosen instrument of a large number of conservative bishops to turn the Brazilian church away from what they viewed as excessive and damaging activism. These bishops looked upon liberation theology and its popular expression, Christian base communities (CEBs), as failed strategies that drove millions of Catholics to Pentecostalism and other religions. Nor did liberation theology or the CEBs please the last two popes, another reason for strong opposition by conservatives.

Even Clovodis Boff's more radical brother theologian, Leonardo Boff, changed his mind and pictured the Charismatic renewal becoming "a singular expression of Christianity in the Twenty-First Century."[24] However, many Catholic leaders remained adamantly opposed to the Charismatic movement, including what they regarded as the movement's fostering of immature psychological dependencies. Some, such as the ecumenist Jorge Atilio Silva Iulianetta, saw good on both sides. But another religious intellectual, Pedro Ribeiro da Oliveira, viewed the conflict as a war of titans. As a Brazilian with a propensity for dialectical analysis in oppositional terms, Ribeiro saw CEBs and the Charismatic renewal as dialectical *contradictions*. (For a Brazilian, a contradiction involves two beings that cannot occupy the same space at the same time.) They will compete until one becomes dominant. He wrote in the heavyweight *Revista Eclesiástica Brasileira*: "Probably they will coexist for some time until one of them shows greater plausibility, incorporates the other, and creates a new Catholic synthesis for the Twenty-First Century."[25]

The most noteworthy characteristic of Padre Marcelo Rossi's services is his attraction of young Brazilians. For a while it looked like Catholic youth, primarily the religiously indifferent ones, would be swept up into Pentecostal churches. "Somehow Father Marcelo has cut through to the young," a Brazilian pastor remarked. He continued: "Young people need to be led and Marcelo does that, as nobody else."[26] David Barrett estimated that more than half of regular Catholic Charismatics are less than twenty-five years old.

Padre Marcelo is an athletic event. He spins, twists, and speaks directly through a hand mike that looks like part of his large hand. His weightlessness—lack of intellectual gravitas—made it easy to believe that he and at least some of the other priest-performers would blow away before long. Brazilian Charismaticism has plenty of academic skeptics, such as J. Reginaldo Prandi, who viewed Rossi as trivializing religion.[27] They believe not only that Rossi will pass away as a fad but also that he will damage religion's role as a carrier of needed values, such as justice. They feel the same about the "beach priests."

Music as a Key to Judging Religion

The historian Edith Blumhofer, who was educated at Hunter College and Harvard University and who directs the Center for the Study of Evangelicals at Wheaton College at Naperville, Illinois, believes music is a key for judging religion. She believes that if one wants to understand the deep character of a religious movement, one should study its hymns. As previous chapters have shown, music entered the core of religion as practiced by Charismatics. Music has always been an integral part of Christianity, but it seems now to have acquired or reacquired a place as fundamental as spoken language. It is a language, perhaps better than words alone, for some aspects of praise and celebration.

From the beginnings of Christianity, Christians have expressed their faith in song. In modern history this tendency is evident among Protestants and Catholics. They made hymns part of family and private devotions as well as church services. Blumhofer explains their importance as indicators of what is taking place: "Hymn texts provide metaphors for understanding theology, articulating deep emotions, and elaborating the practical consequences of belief. Hymnody offers an underutilized lens on the religious life of ordinary people and the language that sustains popular faith."[28]

With music as an indicator, one could say that with popular Catholic music Brazilians achieved a more enculturated worship than during many other periods in their five hundred years of Christianity. It may not be classically beautiful music or always pleasing to foreign tastes but it is Brazilian. It is Christian in joy, peace, sorrow. It is diverse. It is theirs, as Catholics and Brazilians.

The great global innovation of Charismatic Catholicism was that religious music and praise cannot be contained within churches. This was increasingly true across Latin America. In Brazil Padre Zezinho moved (or restored) religious music to street corners, kitchen-sink areas, and concert stages. In Bolivia, when Father Dan Roach said that the people of La Mansión did not need hymn books at the Pentecost vigil because they knew the lyrics and melody better than the top forty, he meant that they were singing them "all the time" without regard to place.

The strangeness for many North Americans of religious music becoming the everyday song in the head was less so for Latinos. Here in summary is what *Latin Beat*, a mainline music magazine, said of sacred music wrapped in secular Caribbean rhythms (within the context of Puerto Rico, where Catholic Charismatics were numerous): "There has been an abiding tie between music of the people and popular religion. Where does the religious element stop and the secular begin? Maybe in this case differences don't exist, because music is, among other things, a manifestation of the heart, the culture, and the conscience, places where the roots of religion are."[29]

Throughout Latin America, religion permeates its culture. Its magical realism in literature and everyday speech in which God is recognized (*"si Dios quiere," "vaya con Dios,"* and hundreds of other phrases) give testimony to widespread acceptance of a world of spirits. Even in Brazil with its world-class economy and a highly modernized sector, a very high percentage of the population believes in God. Cocktail conversations there include religion routinely and without embarrassment.

Popular religion is the soil in which much Latin American religious sensibilities grow. It may be more appropriate to describe this as religiosity, the habit of carrying out religious practices, rather than as spirituality, whose focus is on a supreme being more than on the routine of practices. This description also implies a continuum of this religiosity, ranging from persons who view religion primarily as a source of favors to those more held in awe of God, who also happens to be the source of favors.

The history of this religiosity also helps explain a paradox: most Latin Americans do not regularly attend church. In a word, popular religion needs to be understood in order to understand the soul of Latin America. Popular religion is not the whole soul, but it is an essential component for probably the majority of Latin Americans. What is meant here by popular religion is religion as practiced by ordinary Catholics in contrast to official religion delineated by religious elites (bishops and theologians). At the heart of popular religion is concern with the material world: "with bodily nourishment and healing, with birth and death, with mundane concerns, as getting a job or having good fortune on examinations, with warding off misfortune," as Cristián Parker has described it.[30]

In many ways Vatican Council II marked a major shift in moving the institution away from traditional and popular religion. It forced decisions among church policymakers and pastoral leaders about what to safeguard and modify and what to discard from the past. Here is one of the characteristics marking the soul of the Latin American church and making it different from the churches of the North Atlantic: the Latin American church held on to popular religion, albeit after considerable controversy. Novenas, processions, devotion to Jesus the miracle worker, Mary, and the saints continue.

The now comfortable position of popular religion in most national churches was attained only after fierce debates. After Vatican Council II ended in 1965 and through the 1970s, progressive leaders and theologians argued that popular religion encouraged fatalism, conservatism, and excessive emphasis on a life after death while largely ignoring the building of a just society in this world. The debate also became confused because one aspect of popular religion, fiestas, was sometimes surrounded by binge drinking and resultant violence, including sexual violence and violent macho competition between men. Concern about the drinking and violence continued, as exemplified among Catholic Mayas who have become teetotalers in Chiapas and some Catholic Aymaras in Bolivia's altiplano. However, the debate about the negative qualities of popular religion moderated as theologians began noting positive aspects of popular religion, including its potentially liberating aspects. By the time of the Latin American Bishops Conference (CELAM) at Puebla in 1979 bishops had noted both negative and positive aspects.

The appeal of nuns, priests, and laypersons singing and selling CDs by the hundreds of thousands "is the message they bring," said Richard

Strasser, a professor of music as a business at Northeastern University.[31] "The types of music—samba, rock, country—do not make much difference. People are listening to the message," he continued.[32] Others agree but add that the typical environment of the young is noise. Father Nicanor Austriaco, a biologist-theologian at Providence College, explained that whatever takes place in religion for the young has to begin from noise-music-sound; they do not understand or like silence. "They are surrounded by noise-crowds-chatter. They can pray in silence but it's much easier beginning with sound and then maturing to silence. Their prayer has to begin with noise. Christian music fills this space. In a word, they have to pray with music. This is natural to them. Music allows them to pray easily. Further music amplifies praise. Praise of God [through music] thus comes easily to them."[33]

Religious music sung outside of churches is ingrained in popular culture, especially for the young but not only for them, and has a renewed place in society. And, to hear Brazilians tell it, music helps to save souls.

Conclusion

Now entering his third decade in celebrity life, Father Marcelo Rossi has evident signs of aging. His light hair has darkened with pronounced gray appearing at his temples. But his appeal has continued to grow, not decline, and his high-energy projects have continued. At the end of 2007 he gathered thirty-five singing performers for an all-day event billed as a Missa/show to be staged at a motor racetrack. Four million concertgoers/Mass attenders were expected. In the end, Frei Betto said that Padre Marcelo accomplished what liberation theology could not do: capture the attention of society for Christianity.

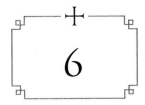

MEXICO

Number One Exporter to the United States

Latin America's other large country, a growing power in world trade, especially as a producer of oil, also enjoyed a great expansion of the Catholic Charismatic Renewal within its borders. Its 9.2 million Catholic Charismatics as of 2000 represent a substantial presence within its population of some 100 million persons, all but 12 percent of them Catholic.[1]

Despite the relatively small percentage of evangelicals in Mexico, Mexican Catholics have felt themselves under siege from them, as well as from Pentecostals, Mormons, and traditional indigenous religions, during most of the twentieth and twenty-first centuries. But despite the numbers and resources of many Protestant missionaries, Mexican Catholics have mostly managed to hold their own; that is, in spite of numerous newspaper reports in the United States of Catholic losses, especially in rural areas, the census data on religion in Mexico has shown little change of membership.[2] This overall steady trend may be due in part to the high apostasy rate among Mexican evangelicals, as shown by Kurt Bowen in his landmark *Evangelism and Apostasy*.[3] Clearly in this prolonged struggle with religious competitors, competition seems to have been good for the Catholic Church. Furthermore, the question of Catholic identity has been actively tested for decades. Thus Catholics found the resources necessary to retain their Catholic identity and loyalty to the church. Lay organizations, including in recent times the Catholic Charismatic Renewal, have been a major factor in this loyalty.

"No one can study or visit Mexico without being besieged by the religiosity of the culture," wrote Martin Austin Nesvig in his edited volume, *Religious Culture in Modern Mexico*.[4] He also notes that "despite this clear religiosity, North American scholars are sometimes reluctant to discuss the category of religion in modern Mexico." Furthermore, "In examining the available scholarly discussions one often finds [that] this process of *secularization* [emphasis mine] is assumed to be an inextricable part of the linear and forward-moving process of social and political history."[5]

Mexico matters a great deal to the United States in terms of religion. Mexico is the major exporter of migrants and, while they may assimilate into North American life by the third or fourth generation, their preferences for a more extroverted worship, communal activity, and missionary outlook will be played out in the religious marketplace of the United States. Charismatics from Mexico and other countries will strongly affect the churches of the United States, Catholic and otherwise.

The Spread of the Renewal in Mexico

Similar to Brazil, the Catholic Charismatic Renewal spread in Mexico more universally than in most other countries. The movement was not centered in a single person, as in smaller countries. It enjoyed the support of the bishops from the beginning in part because bishops were active initiators of the movement. But the movement has been largely in the hands of laypersons for at least the last three decades, with a strong clerical base but with diminishing clerical intervention in key innovations. The movement has been anchored in its maturity by adult covenant communities. Furthermore, the Mexican Charismatic leaders have picked up the fervor for evangelization and missionary expansion as few other national churches have.

The soil in which the movement grew was fertile, with both an extremely strong popular religion and a dedicated, educated middle class. Mexican Catholics practiced their religion by going to church at a high rate.[6] Catholic Action and other lay movements helped create a militant and loyal base of lay Catholics that were under attack from anticlerical governments. Mexico was waiting for the Charismatic movement as the next step in its long march from deeply embedded popular religion to militant Catholicism to more comfortable stasis with the state.

The renewal came to Mexico from a variety of persons, almost by osmosis from the United States. However, a homegrown religious order is credited with being the first group—with Father Alfonso Navarro Catellanos as principal among them—to introduce the renewal to Mexico. The

Missionaries of the Holy Spirit used their church and center for spirituality at Iglesia Altillo in Mexico City to diffuse the movement.

Alfonso Navarro from the Missionaries of the Holy Spirit was a key promoter of the movement. He had special talents and training that lent further weight to the organizing of the movement in Mexico and Latin America. With a doctorate in philosophy and an advanced degree in theology obtained at European universities during the time of great intellectual ferment there in the 1960s, Navarro (not to be confused with the martyr-priest in El Salvador with a similar name) aided greatly in modifying "Protestant" aspects of Pentecostalism and making the movement acceptable to Catholics who wished to remain orthodox in the practice of their faith. (This did not preclude an ecumenical perspective. On the basis of lengthy research on Father Navarro, Bryan Reising, a disciple of Father Navarro and a diocesan director of evangelization in Minnesota, wrote that Navarro was "involved ecumenically with other Christian churches and well respected in their circles.")[7]

While centered in Altillo, Navarro was also put in charge of the Charismatic renewal groups of all the houses of the Missionaries of the Holy Spirit in Mexico. In 1974, he was invited to the intercontinental meeting of the movement, the Latin American Charismatic Conference (ECCLA), and in preparation for the meeting, according to Reising, Navarro had a major intellectual insight into the central message of Christianity, *kerygma*, in the tradition of the early church. He promoted his insight at the meeting without evident acceptance on the part of the other leaders of the movement.

Thereafter a divergence in the Latin American wing (the largest of the global sectors of the renewal) appeared. Navarro substituted education in the *kerygma* for Life in the Spirit seminars as an initiation into the renewal.[8] However, he had an early effect on the mainstream when he identified renewal with catechesis and mission in the 1970s, long before these themes were common for many Latin Americans. (Many were then taken up with dealing with repressive Latin American governments.) It was at the Altillo center and church that José (Pepe) Prado Flores, the most successful of Mexicans in spreading the movement, experienced a conversion in the Holy Spirit. Thus both great Mexican evangelizers were associated with that important center.

That the Mexican church should have picked up the Charismatic movement early and with more universal spread than other countries can be easily understood by its proximity to the United States. Within a short time—it seemed like hours and minutes rather than years—of the start of the movement, Mexican Catholics resident in the United States were carrying the movement to Mexico. In their travels to the United States, Mexican priests and bishops also saw for themselves the vitality of the movement and wanted the same for themselves and their parishioners.

The other unique characteristic of the movement in Mexico was the rapid enfolding of the movement within a wide range of the hierarchy. It was described by early historians of the movement as being adopted and directed from the Mexican Social Secretariat.[9] Bishop Carlos Talavera Ramírez from the secretariat was one of the first notables to join the movement. He represented the Mexican segment of the movement at the first Latin American Charismatic Conference (ECCLA) called by Father Francis MacNutt and held at Bogotá in 1973.

The Mexican Catholic Church was a deeply conservative church and its bishops kept control of the innovations that entered the country. When the renewal was getting under way in the 1960s and 1970s, organizational oversight through the secretariat allowed the hierarchy to watch over its initial growth and *suavizar* (to modify) some of its Protestant characteristics in order to avoid the creation of a parallel church that could have grown independently of the larger institution. From Mexico City the renewal, as noted, spread to other parts of the country, aided by the constant flow of persons and ideas to and from central Mexico to the central part of the United States. (The Midwest was then the strongest region for the renewal, anchored by Notre Dame, Indiana, and Ann Arbor, Michigan.)

Early involvement and support by the bishops was key to everything that happened subsequently in Mexico. Through the lengthy persecution of the church in the twentieth century by the government and control of religion by the ruling party, Mexican Catholics were forced to take stands against the state and its secularizing pressures and they learned to accept loyally the lead of their bishops in the accommodations of church and state that took place especially after 1940, when Manuel Avila Camacho, the president at the time, reached an understanding with church leaders that effectively allowed the church to operate publicly as long as it did not engage in sectarian political stands. The last handicaps placed on the church—such as prohibitions against clerical garb and voting by clerics— were done away with by the state only in 1996.

Not long after the major founding event of Catholic Charismaticism at Pittsburgh in 1967, Mexican Charismatics had formed the Renovation Movement of Catholic Charismatics in the Holy Spirit (MRCCES), perhaps the longest title for a national Charismatic movement in the world. Mexico was becoming at this time a movement society[10] and the Charismatic movement clearly showed what movement analysts call nodes and networks that sprang up quickly and coalesced into an effective movement. From the 1970s forward, the movement held annual national conferences. It did so effectively and quickly. Given Mexico's status as the second most populated country of Latin America, with a population of about 100 million, the National Pastoral Team, the national coordinating body of the movement, proved to be most important. The group met annually. At the forty-first meeting of the national conference in 2008 representatives from sixty dioceses, almost all of the dioceses of the country, were present.

Top leadership of the National Pastoral Team has typically passed from one married couple to another. Members of the team brought with them years of experience of organizing as business people or professionals and as Catholics in one organization, such as Catholic Action, or another. Mexican lay Catholics had decades of participating in organizations of Catholic lawyers, entrepreneurs and managers, teachers, and armed forces officers. The Charismatic renewal reaped the harvest of these decades of organizational experiences and lay involvement in the Mexican church.

Various bishops circulated in and out of membership in the National Pastoral Team as episcopal advisors to the movement. The rotating membership guaranteed a wide base of support among Mexican bishops. The papal nuncio, a key person in the Mexican church, also attended national meetings.

Despite the best intentions of the Mexican bishops and the oversight of the Social Secretariat, confrontations between laypersons involved in the movement and bishops arose. From the beginning of the movement, one could see three trouble spots: First, this was a movement that some members perceived as initiated and directed primarily if not exclusively by laypersons. Second, Charismatics introduced new practices and forms of conduct traditionally not seen among Catholics and let alone viewed within church buildings. Third, Charismatics employed a new discourse that emphasized the priesthood of the faithful and openness that even the least significant person could receive and exercise extraordinary gifts bestowed by the Holy Spirit. (Small schisms related to Charismatics would occur in Guatemala, Peru, and Costa Rica as will be noted.)[11]

The jarring encounters between innovators and gatekeepers were frequent occurrences but were seldom systematically recorded either in the United States, Mexico, or elsewhere. One of the few carefully observed confrontations in Mexico took place at Zamora in Michoacán. The confrontations were centered in the acceptance of a new paradigm of charisma within the church—in other words, greater space being opened in the church for lay preachers, teachers, and leaders to be heard. The movement offered a space in which priests were gradually moderating their views that theirs were the only authorized voices for speaking with and about God. The Charismatic movement was far from the only influence that modified this view. But clearly lay Charismatics began preaching, teaching, giving testimonials to faith, and acting as spiritual counselors with a sense of entitlement for actions and offices typically considered the province of ordained ministers.

In Zamora this pressure for enhanced space for laity in the church came about through a clash of the discourses—ways of talking about the right to speak—between Charismatic lay leaders and priests. Lay leaders in the movement, after some years of experience, felt they had a right to talk about policy and practice in the church on the basis of possession of a gift or charisma. They had been baptized in the Spirit. They possessed lived experience. They thought this experience was something better than book learning. Priests, in contrast, had been trained to believe that they were the authorized voices to speak for the church. They felt they were also appointed by the bishops to avoid "excesses."[12] This conviction was reinforced by many questionable aspects of Charismaticism: it came from the United States, a country perceived by Mexicans to be Protestant, and was clothed in what looked like Protestant wrappings.

Most of all, Charismaticism was reputed to have various emotional excesses. Mexico has a very long history of excesses in religion, typically practiced out of direct view of parish priests, such as actually whipping persons representing Christ during Holy Week in 2008.[13] This practice was outlawed by the church, which also outlawed other customary ceremonies, such as the burning of the effigy of Judas, a practice that was still taking place in the heart of Mexico City well into the twenty-first century. Penitential practices of this sort and other strange beliefs have long existed within Mexico side by side with orthodox practices conducted inside most Catholic church buildings.[14]

The key bishop in the early acceptance of the movement in Mexico was Carlos Talavera Ramírez, a leader within the Mexican bishops. He was a strong voice for social justice and was often the president of the Episcopal Commission on Social Pastoral of the Mexican Bishops Conference. As a key symbol of the modest attempts at social and political action by the Mexican church, his conversion to the renewal gave progressive and other Catholics the open-mindedness they needed toward a movement that could have been viewed as a gringo invention or as something too Protestant for them to embrace.

The Social Secretariat, with branches operating within individual dioceses, kept track of lay movements. Typically a priest named by the bishop exercised this oversight. The lay leader Pepe Prado, with his wide-ranging enterprises of evangelization schools, which will be discussed later in this chapter, was careful to have a trustworthy Mexican priest as a long-term ecclesiastical advisor for his initiatives in the movement.

Of all the key early risers to the movement who had been deeply involved in social questions, Talavera appeared never to have lost the desire to fight actively for social justice. Even after his retirement as bishop of Coatzacoalcos in the state of Veracruz because of mandatory age restrictions, he continued as bishop emeritus to take up the political fight. Well into his eighties he was still fighting for more just treatment of immigrants and was meeting with the bishops of Florida to find common ground in this struggle. He supported international retreats for priests, passing along his dual convictions of Charismatic spirituality and social-justice activism.

As the movements have matured within countries, covenant communities have arisen in several but not all Latin American countries. In Mexico they began appearing in 1980. Father Pablo Cárdenas Cantú, a Mexican Franciscan, took the lead in forming the first covenant community (called in the Mexican church, comunidades de alianza) in San Luis Potosí. This pivotal covenant community was the Comunidad Nueva Alianza de San Luis Potosí. The community had the guidance of the Word of God Community, one of the first and best-known covenant communities, located at Ann Arbor, Michigan, for this creation.

Cárdenas and his community wanted to stimulate other prayer groups in the country to form covenant communities. In 1985 they held the Week for Communities at San Luis Potosí. Seven groups from diverse parts of Mexico and from Brownsville, Texas, listened to Cárdenas and members of Nueva Alianza describe their experiences in forming and living by the rules for shared lives that were adopted by the groups. Several of the visiting groups took formal steps toward founding covenant communities. They and new groups came together the next year for a repetition of the Week for Communities. By then seven covenant communities had formed and served as the base for the national Federation of Communities of Alliance, with Father Cárdenas as president. The national meetings continued on an annual basis as the number of communities grew. A husband and wife team was elected president of the federation in 1995 and lay leadership became the norm.

This group became the Mexican Federation of Alliance Communities and aligned itself with the International Fraternity of Alliance Communities. Both groups had become increasingly lay in membership, leadership, and orientation. In lifestyle this meant that most members were carrying out work-a-day jobs, often as professionals, while sharing housing and financial resources with other members of the covenant community. They maintained communication with the national church through sympathetic bishop-moderators of the federation. Bishop Talavera served in this post until his death at the age of eighty-five in 2006, followed by the archbishop of Tijuana. By 2007 there were twenty-seven covenant communities in nineteen dioceses of the country and in Texas.

The Mexican Church: A Leader in Missions and Evangelization

Missions became a major theme in the Latin American church in the twenty-first century. Recent studies make clear that 1) most countries in Latin America sent some missionaries overseas; 2) the numbers of missionaries from a country tended to reflect the size of the country's population so that one could say that this is a generalized phenomenon; and 3) Mexico led the way with the largest number of foreign missionaries. Its numbers were disproportionately larger than Brazil, the region's most populous nation.

One should note that the Mexican church has had a larger corps of native priests and seminarians than most Latin American churches relative to its population for at least the last fifty years. This corps furnished a larger foundation upon which to build mission-sending activities. That the Mexican church had this clerical foundation surprises older Americans who had heard tales of the twentieth-century Mexican persecution of priests and presumed that Mexican seminaries had collapsed. After President Avila Comacho granted a measure of peaceful coexistence to the church in the 1940s, Mexican seminaries, unnoticed by hardly anyone, began to flourish. Mexico's seminarians reached a relatively high baseline of some twenty-two hundred in 1972.

One accepted test of authentic Christianity is mission, as previously mentioned. A central question for any diocese or parish, regardless of its geographical or economic situation, is this: Does it have a missionary consciousness? The church, local or national, is by its nature missionary. Every bishop and his subjects have responsibility for the whole church. The Latin American church recognized this responsibility in 1979 when it said that it "would have to produce missionaries out of [its] poverty."[15]

By the ancient criterion of going to another part of the world, how is Latin America doing? For at least ten years, Latin America has sent some 4,000 missionaries to foreign parts, in addition to the very large sector of missionaries working within Latin America itself. The substantial foreign missionary activity is a notable milestone in the Latin American church's journey to maturity. In addition, large numbers have left their homes to become internal missionaries, sometimes short-term but nonetheless at some sacrifice. Thus, 118,784 Catholics acted as lay missionaries, mostly within Latin America, in 2000.[16] Lay missionaries are understood to be laymen and women (excluding clergy and men and women religious) who are serving as missionaries at home or abroad.[17]

These foreign and domestic missionaries represent a solid achievement for the Latin American church that is almost never mentioned by the host of commentators on the Latin American church who are fixated only on competing evangelical growth and who are blind to the general religious revival of Latin America that also affects Catholicism.

Two strong impulses for mission affected Latin America. The stimulus within the region for mission came from an effort noted previously: foreign missionaries who took charge of most of the indigenous areas of Latin America in the mid-twentieth century found that religious practice had fallen into the control of a native non-Christian religious hierarchy. In other words, the missionaries had to undertake a second evangelization. The new catechesis with its strongly biblical basis and with a new appreciation of the religious values of native cultures gave dynamism to the religious (and political) resurgence of the indigenous sector of the church.[18] Latin American missionary impulses have their roots in this revival.

The other powerful influence was external and only slowly affected the Latin American church. Vatican Council II created the Decree on the Church's Missionary Activity, known as *Ad Gentes* (1965). The decree made it clear that the entire church is missionary, that mission was not just the concern of missionary orders, and, by implication, that the Latin American church was highly deficient in this regard.

Of all the regional churches, the Latin American church responded the most wholeheartedly to Vatican Council II. As already noted, no other church systematically applied the council's teaching to its region as happened at the Latin American Bishops Conference (CELAM) in Medellín in 1968. But the church lagged in implementing missionary activity because it had neither internalized the vision of mission nor had at hand the organizational resources it needed. (The journey from the dependency thinking that has plagued the church has been long and painful.) Nonetheless, in 1966, a year after Vatican Council II, the Latin American Bishops Conference dutifully put in place the Departamento de Misiones (Department of Missions, DEMIS). This department organized meetings in the two following years to identify the situations in Latin America that called for missionary activity. In doing so, it made a contribution to mission theory. Participants at the meetings rejected the traditional definitions of what was "mission territory," understood as a region where the majority of inhabitants were non-Christian, to emphasize instead "missionary situations." Some groups need missionary activity rather than just typical pastoral care because their cultures had not yet encountered what the mission expert John Gorski calls the life-giving force of the Gospel.[19]

The Departamento de Misiones, of course, found targets for missionary activity among Latin America's indigenous population. Unfortunately, the organization thereby became known informally as the Department of Indian Affairs. Since most Latin American countries had small minorities of indigenous peoples and since the president of DEMIS from 1969 to 1974 was Mexico's Bishop Samuel Ruiz García in Chiapas (who was considered untrustworthy at the time because of his implementation of reforms but who was eventually vindicated), most church leaders focused on what they considered more urgent questions. Typical of the times, these leaders considered the indigenous to be socially marginalized groups; the leaders did not yet perceive them as peoples with ancient cultures worthy of detailed attention.

That outmoded view was to change dramatically at the Latin American Bishops Conference (CELAM) at Puebla in 1979. Following their methodology of see-judge-act, which required a wide and accurate description and analysis of the continent, the bishops acknowledged several missionary situations in the region: not only the indigenous (who, by then, had made great progress) but also the African Latin Americans and the numerous out-of-place and often unwanted migrants within Latin America. Furthermore, the church recognized groups—politicians, titans of business and industry, the military, and others—who were presumed to be in difficult missionary situations not merely because they might be indifferent to evangelization but also because they might be resistant to or impeding of missionary efforts.

The CELAM meeting in Puebla thus not only contributed something original in conveying a sense of mission to the regional church, it also opened the door to other initiatives for mission to persons and agencies outside of the Department of Missions. Momentum toward growth in missions shifted to groups outside the department. This was especially true in the indigenous mission sphere where organic intellectuals now were themselves indigenous.

The church had changed its policy from *pastoral indigenista* to *pastoral indígena*, from paternalism to empowerment.[20] The notable growth of indigenous intellectuals and church leaders was the fruit of this policy change. The indigenous theologians' creative efforts have brought forth *teología india*, a major theological development that is distinct from liberation theology in its emphasis on culture but is dependent on liberation theology's emphasis on context.[21] Here, then, are Indians creating theology from the margins of Latin American society but adding to the general richness of universal theology through contributing insights into God as male and female and into the care of the earth as an ethical responsibility. Indigenous peoples took the lead in their creation of an organization for ecumenical dialogue, the Latin American Articulation of the Indigenous Apostolate (AELAPI). The group has sponsored six continental encounter-workshops and several subregional meetings. This small but important movement brings together leaders from both Christian (Catholic and historical Protestant) and non-Christian indigenous sectors, especially from the more numerous highland groups of Mayan or Incan backgrounds. The dialogue has highly unequal partners, given the academic sophistication of the Catholic and Protestant partners in contrast to many native non-Christian leaders, but it has survived more than twenty-five years of ups and downs.[22]

Responsibility for World Missions

One of the more notable changes in the pastoral vision of the Latin American church in recent times has been its inclusion of foreign missions as one of its goals. The change also includes a surprise: laypeople form the majority of persons within this movement.

If one can mark progress in the missionary outlook of the church by national and regional missionary congresses, then Mexico took the lead. National missionary congresses have been held in Mexico since the 1940s to awaken and focus a world mission spirit within Mexican Catholics. This activity took place in a church aware of its own scarcity of resources. In 1997 the seventh congress took place at Torreón. This meeting marked the beginning of inclusion of persons from other Latin American countries and became simultaneously the First Latin American Mission Congress, marking the historical takeoff point for Latin America's turning toward the larger world and its needs.

Organizational structures had an impact on furthering the change in outlook and channeling zeal. By church law every diocese, even the weakest, is expected to create and support a mission office. Then, too, national churches that mostly pulled themselves together in the 1950s into more or less effective national bishops conferences had to appoint national directors of the Pontifical Mission Societies. Local and national structures were thus in place for what was to take place, even though resources and widespread motivation were lacking. Only a small number of non-Mexican bishops and national directors of the Pontifical Mission Societies attended the first continental meeting at Torreón. From then on, sizable national delegations from all countries not only attended but did so with prepared participation and follow-up programs in their own countries, using the newly installed organizational structures.

These continental meetings, held every four years, reinforced the vision of every diocese as being the basis of missionary activity in the church. By the Third Congress in Bogotá in 1987 a major step had been taken in recognizing the missionary commitment of *laypeople* and in establishing various missionary institutes. Alongside these initiatives, Pope John Paul

II issued a comprehensive encyclical on world mission, *Redemptoris Missio*. This was taken to heart at the next congress in Lima in 1991 and also fueled renewed discussion of new evangelization, the main theme of the Latin American Bishops Conference (CELAM) at Santo Domingo in 1992. While it appeared to be going over ground already traveled in previous meetings, the next mission congress in Brazil paid special attention to indigenous and African cultures at home and the question of enculturation. Getting straight the church's approach to these cultures and to enculturation strengthened its hand in sending missionaries overseas.

Mexico's taking the lead among Latin American countries in sending foreign missionaries was owed not only to the pioneering Guadalupe Missionaries and the national missionary congresses but also was due to the strong push to evangelize the 14 percent of Mexicans who identified themselves as indigenous—over twelve million people.[23] As John Gorski, a major authority in Latin American missiology, pointed out, the great effort to evangelize Latin America's indigenous populations from the 1960s onward served as a stepping stone to missionary activity farther afield.[24] Pastoral work with the indigenous—the programs at Chiapas and Oaxaca were the best known—was vigorously carried out after a slow start while the innovators of this movement underwent their own conversion to seeing valuable aspects to religious cosmovisions other than orthodox Catholicism.

The great achievement of the Mexican church—one almost never alluded to by scholars—is that the church in Mexico had produced 171,719 lay catechists by 2000.[25] Two major themes of the contemporary Latin American church are captured by lay catechists and by the melding of Charismatics with catechesis work: first and foremost, the employment of laity; and second, the marriage of evangelization and internal and external mission. A historical point of transition from focusing on indigenous evangelization to amplifying evangelization for the majority population took place in Mexico.

The need in Mexico for evangelization was not always recognized because of the real or presumptive loyalty of most Mexicans to the church. But some pastors were acutely aware of dangers. Luis Butera, an older Italian missionary working in Mexico but with dreams of providing missionary help for Africa, became caught up in trying to improve the level of religious knowledge and commitment among non-indigenous Mexicans. He saw the danger of many Mexicans leaving the church. In other words, many Mexican Catholics had a strong attachment to the church, which had been reinforced by their family's choosing the side of the church in the church-state conflicts during the long Mexican revolutionary period. But most of the middle and lower classes were educated in strongly secular public schools. Thus they had a weak intellectual appreciation of the church's teachings; were challenged by conflicting viewpoints; and were being attracted by evangelical and Pentecostal churches.

The religious environment in many areas of Mexico became over-heated. After decades of fighting the state over the place of religion in a lay state, loyal Mexican Catholics felt they had reached a peaceful phase in this relationship in the 1990s. Just then, it seemed that evangelicals and Pentecostals assaulted them. Ordinary Catholics found that they had to give reasons to these challengers for their faith in God and their loyalty to the church. Charismatics and other active Catholic laity were revving up in the 1990s and in the new century to help them.

Furthermore, the structural size of the Mexican parish was a major problem. Priests could not fully attend the vast territorial expanse especially of rural parishes in Mexico, many with twenty to thirty chapels (way stations that priests could only occasionally visit) and territories being filled in with evangelical churches. As one missionary priest said, "One can only respond by utilizing laity to aid in responding to the great demand for religious formation, liturgical services, pre-sacramental courses, and preparation of catechists."[26]

Thus Mexico became a giant mobilizer of laity in ministry. The Catholic Church had commissioned, as noted, 171,719 lay catechists by 2003.[27] The number is second to the remarkable 491,000 catechists in Brazil and considerably ahead of other countries. Froehle and Gautier calculated that Mexico had an average of 30 catechists per parish, a number far higher than any other country in the Americas.[28] These catechists now work with all sectors of the Mexican church, not just the indigenous.

This large trained lay catechetical workforce has been engaged in evangelization. The confluence of the catechistical mobilization with the wide expansion of the Charismatic movement in Mexico also followed the priority of evangelization of Pope John Paul II, which was expressed in 1992 at the Latin American Bishops' Conference at Santo Domingo. The 9 million Charismatics and the 171,000 catechists (the numbers overlap to a degree no one knows) add weight and vibrancy to the Mexican church, a vitality most observers of Latin America overlook.

Growth also has taken place among priests, whose numbers doubled between 1975 and 2003.[29] Religious sisters continued a steady increase over the years to 23,232 in 2001. Together the Brazilian and Mexican church have put together a solid and growing workforce. Mexico stands as another strong pillar of the Charismatic movement alongside Brazil.

Because Mexico has furnished a large proportion of newly arriving Catholics to the church in the United States—28 percent of all immigrants in 2000 to the United States were born in Mexico and persons of Mexican descent probably make up half of Latinos who are Catholics in the United States—what happens in the Mexican church will affect the U.S. church in a major fashion. In interviews with Catholic pastoral leaders in the United States, few had more than shadowy knowledge of the Mexican church.[30] Some thought Mexican Catholics come from a situation of state persecution similar to that in Russia. Mexican Catholics were viewed as having been beaten down but nonetheless passively remaining as minimal Catholics. In contrast to that view, millions of Mexican Catholics exuberantly practice their faith, preach the Word, and go out to others as missionaries.

Mexico's Contribution to Global Evangelization

The Latin American Bishops Conference at Puebla in 1979 clearly stated the goal of the whole church as evangelization.[31] In the 1980s, persons in lay renewal movements in the Latin American church—movements already described—reached a level of maturity at which they wished to share their intensified faith and spirituality with other Catholics. Members of the Catholic Charismatic Renewal, especially their clerical advisors, were in the forefront of this impetus. Father Emiliano Tardif and others from the Dominican Republic were early leaders in linking Charismatics and evangelization.

However, they were minor leaguers compared to the efforts of a Mexican lay Catholic evangelist and preacher, Pepe Prado, who established the Escuelas de Evangelización San Andrés (San Andres Schools of Evangelization). Hundreds of these schools were founded in sixty countries on five continents. They exist all over Mexico and were advancing in the United States in places as far-flung as Santa Rosa, California, San Antonio, and New Orleans. The number of his schools is believed to have doubled in ten years.

Thus Mexican laity from the renewal served as catalysts for the largest network of schools of evangelization in Catholicism, if not Christianity. These Escuelas de Evangelización San Andrés were the strongest evidence of the two special marks of the renewal, especially as it has unfolded in Latin America: evangelization and mission.

The charismatic person behind the schools was Pepe Prado. Born in 1947 at Morelia in Central Mexico, he pursued philosophical, biblical, theological, and catechetical studies in Mexico and Belgium, taught biblical studies in Mexico City as a layperson, and experienced the presence of the Holy Spirit in 1971, apparently apart from the Duquesne lineage of Catholic Charismatics. He shifted the emphasis from dwelling on the Pentecostal experience to putting more energy into evangelization. He has proven himself to be a great entrepreneur for evangelization, carrying not only the message that *lay* Catholics need to be evangelizers and missionaries but putting in place evangelization schools around the world.

Pepe Prado credited Bill Finke, a Protestant Pentecostal pastor, and Father Emiliano Tardif, the great Canadian apostle working primarily in the Dominican Republic, with being co-creators of the Escuelas de Evangelización San Andres. Presumably he meant that they served as his advisors. In 1980 Prado started the first school in Mexico. The schools spread quickly in Mexico and Colombia and two headquarters for the great expansion that was to follow were established in those countries. Prado, who had been working mainly in Mexico City, set up world headquarters at Guadalajara, where he benefitted from the sponsorship of the archbishop. Guadalajara also had very strong Protestant Pentecostal competition. The archbishop, for a time, was greeted daily as he entered the cathedral with shouts from a heckler that he was the anti-Christ and that the church was the whore of Babylon. Pentecostals were distinctly a minority in the country, with less than 5 percent of the population, but they were growing and they were vocal, preaching in the streets as well as in their numerous chapels.

By 2007 Prado's schools had been established in countries of the Americas, Europe, Africa, Asia, and Oceania. The organization claimed to have established two thousand schools worldwide by 2006.[32] The schools followed the same vision, curriculum, and methodology for teaching evangelization. Inasmuch as was possible, the aim of the schools was to multiply themselves by creating teachers of teachers.

In several countries the schools were in multiple locations, as in the United States. The principal work in the United States started at San Antonio in 1996 with the cooperation of Archbishop Patricio Flores and Bishop Thomas Flanagan. By 2002, more than twenty-three hundred persons at San Antonio had taken courses on evangelization.

Prado followed the lead of another great Mexican promoter of evangelization, Alfonso Navarro, already mentioned as a missionary of the Holy Spirit who was associated with their center at Altillo. Navarro promoted the *kerygma* initiation-experience as entry into the renewal but carried his vision much further through the Sistema Integral de Evangelización (SINE), a system of catechesis of varying levels to follow up the initial experience.

Furthermore, he reimagined the parish from the typical service-station approach of Latin American parishes of that time, dispensing services to clients who bothered to come to the parish church, to that of an evangelizing parish, with laity and priests radiating out to others their religious message. Navarro was tireless in this promotion, going to various parts of the world, including Mexico's northern neighbor. His ideas caught on to a greater or lesser extent from El Paso, Texas to Argentina. The implementation of his ideas was highlighted in the United States by Paul Wilkes in his *Excellent Catholic Parishes* and Ernesto Elizondo, a priest in the diocese of Austin, Texas, in "Transforming the Sacramental Parish into an Evangelizing Community."[33] Navarro's disciples were also notably effective in Estelí, Nicaragua; Pereira, Colombia; and São Jose dos Campos, Brazil. In all, it was estimated that SINE spread to one thousand parishes, schools, hospitals, and prisons in twenty-four countries. Navarro died at the age of sixty-seven in 2003 but SINE's offices and disciples carried on his work.

Navarro's vision remained as a disputed question among Catholic pastoral planners and activists on several scores. Critics were not pleased with what they perceived as a notable absence of a social-justice perspective in the content in the proposed courses and with what they deemed a totalizing approach to a parish that allowed little diversity. Nonetheless, both Prado and Navarro put Mexico in the forefront of evangelizers and missionaries.

Lay Preaching

Prado was remarkable for being a lay preacher, an office virtually unknown (or unacknowledged) in the Catholic Church. Preaching from the pulpit was strictly limited to priests and deacons. After Vatican Council II, a period of some confusion ensued about who might occupy the pulpit, but in 2008 Juan Diego Brunetta, a Dominican priest and information officer for the Knights of Columbus, wrote with confidence that preaching homilies from the pulpit was limited to priests and deacons.[34] Less formal preaching than Sunday homilies spread as a practice to include a number of gifted laypersons, among them Eamon Duffy, the famed Cambridge University scholar.[35] But everyday preaching by Catholic women, aside from preaching homilies from the pulpit, has been a common practice especially in Charismatic prayer meetings for decades. The Charismatic movement was notable from the beginning of the movement in Latin America for routinely including women, lay and religious, on preaching teams. Sister Helen Raycraft, a Dominican sister from Chicago, has preached for years in Latin America and the United States and has written about her experiences in that regard.[36]

Prado's organization supports the efforts of a young Brazilian lay preacher, Vilma Stanislavski. She discovered her talents as a preacher and an evangelist as a young adult in the Charismatic movement in Brazil, moved for five years to the headquarters of Escuelas de Evangelización San Andrés in Guadalajara, Mexico, and then returned to Brazil. In her twenties and thirties she preached in Brazil, Mexico, the United States, and other countries.

Laypersons increasingly preached during spiritual retreats in the latter third of the twentieth century and none more frequently and fervently than lay Catholic Charismatics. Two from Latin America became internationally prominent. Pepe Prado was one of them. By 2008 he had preached in fifty-two countries on five continents, including the Vatican. More, he preached retreats over several days to exclusive audiences of priests in seventeen countries.

Another lay preacher from Central America, Salvador Gómez, not only preached widely across Latin America and the United States, but also wrote a guide for lay preachers.[37] Lay preaching has become such a regular aspect of Charismaticism that an Argentine school of evangelization also advertises itself as a school for (lay) preaching.[38] Escuelas de Evangelización San Andrés has come to include the preparation of lay preachers as one of its main objectives.

That Charismaticism promotes lay preaching could be seen in the Web directory of prominent Charismatic preachers worldwide.[39] Of the forty-nine individuals or married couples listed, thirty-one were lay while eighteen were priests or deacons. Eleven were individual women or partners of a married couple; most of these women were lay, while one was a religious sister. This listing was only one of the more prominent international preachers. Missing from this view were thousands of religious sisters and laymen and women who routinely preach at Charismatic and evangelization meetings.

A Major Exporter of Migrants and Charismatics

The Charismatic resurgence from Mexico expanded to the United States. There the numerous members of the renewal have been leading a major shift in the U.S. church away from a traditional style of prayer and worship toward a more Charismatic style and practice. Three directions of influence from Latin America have entered into this shift. First, migrants from Latin America brought with them a preference for Charismatic practices. Second, U.S. missionaries who were active in the movement in Latin America stimulated new growth among Charismatics when they returned for duty in the United States. Third, missionary groups from Latin America—often with a Charismatic bent—are working as missionaries to revitalize the church in the United States.

The Charismatic renewal of the Catholic Church started in the United States but began fading after its notable beginning at Pittsburgh and its rapid spread through most of the country. In 1987 one million Catholics attended 10,500 prayer groups. Furthermore, there was great cultural diversity with prayer groups that were being conducted in twelve major languages. By the early 1990s signs of decline appeared as membership in prayer groups decreased, covenant communities collapsed, and, in general, the movement in the country diminished.[40] By 2000 some 200,000 Catholics were participating in 4,800 prayer groups.[41] A somewhat similar decline occurred in Australia, Germany, and the Netherlands. Those countries did not benefit, as did the church in the United States, from the very large influx of Charismatic Catholics from Latin America.

Reports and commentaries began appearing after the American Religious Identification Survey of 2001 showed that the percentage of U.S. Hispanic adult Catholics had dropped from 66 percent in 1990 to 57 percent in 2001.[42] Strong danger signs seemed to be posted, but Charismatic leaders interviewed at the time felt that the survey may have measured the immediate past without picking up the great surge in Hispanic, Haitian, and Brazilian Catholic immigrants who were bringing with them enthusiasm for the Charismatic renewal, a trend that was highlighted later in stories in the *Washington Post* and other media sources about the new liveliness in Catholic parishes in Washington, New York, and elsewhere due to the renewal.

Latino Catholics (including here also Haitian and Brazilian expatriates) took the lead in bringing a new stage to the movement in the new century. Hispanics are the fastest growing population group in the U.S. Catholic Church. They form one-third of all Catholics and they are projected to be half the Catholic population within a generation. In terms of exposure to U.S. culture, they are of two basic types: natives and migrants. Native are persons born in the United States of Hispanic heritage. In the case of families from New Mexico, some trace twenty generations of residence in what is now the United States but once was Spanish territory. Puerto Ricans have almost a century of incorporation as citizens. Migrants are foreign-born Hispanics who may or may not have acquired U.S. citizenship.[43] The Hispanic population grew significantly from the census of 1990, increasing by 22 million to 35.2 million at the time of the census of 2000. While both native and foreign-born groups grew in size, the foreign-born Hispanic population experienced extraordinary growth. Many of the new immigrants came from countries where the Catholic Charismatic Renewal was strongest, such as Mexico, the Dominican Republic, Colombia, and El Salvador.

Mexicans, native and foreign born, form the largest sector, being roughly two-thirds of the Hispanic population. They form a strong conduit through which the renewal runs. Mexicans came from a land where San Andrés Schools of Evangelization, SINE, and other organizations evangelized Mexicans widely. Of course, many Mexican migrants came from regions not touched by evangelization efforts, but the majority came from regions, such as central Mexico, where the renewal was strong.[44]

What is most striking about Hispanics is that more than half of all Hispanic Catholics in the United States identify themselves as Charismatics.[45] Investigators, with the help of large foundation grants, have been looking into migrant religion, especially in the southeastern United States, for some years and were reporting their extensive findings in 2009.[46] They found not only notable growth among migrants who are Charismatic but also tensions between the social-justice and Charismatic modalities of Catholicism, a now familiar theme.[47]

The presence of Charismatics cannot be ignored, not only because of their numbers but also for their strong preference for a distinctive form of Christianity. As a highly revealing Pew Hispanic Study made clear, religious expressions associated with the Pentecostal and Charismatic movements are a key attribute of Hispanics.[48]

Presumably the numerous parishes, schools, and other institutions of the church will have to take this attribute into account. If bishops and parish priests ignore this preference, these Catholics may join Pentecostal churches, as they have in large numbers in Latin America and in smaller numbers already in the United States. If, in contrast, bishops and priests warmly welcome Hispanic Charismatics, the church itself may change. Authors of the Pew Hispanic Project argued in their report that "Hispanics are transforming the nation's religious landscape, especially the Catholic Church."[49]

Conclusion

The Mexican Catholic Charismatic Renewal became a socioreligious laboratory that is remarkable for several findings. First, to the surprise of many, Mexican Catholicism in the twenty-first century began showing a more open door to ecumenical activities within the Pentecostal world. Pepe Prado became well known in international circles. He became a professor of an institute for Charismatic leaders in Rome in 2005. But he, more than most other Charismatic leaders in Latin America, maintained active contacts with Protestants. He has been a longtime member of the ecumenical International Charismatic Consultation on World Evangelization (ICCOWE). Similarly, Father Navarro, noted for his wide and effective evangelization program, was highly ecumenical. As will be seen in the case of Argentina, if Christian unity is to be achieved, Catholic Charismatics are likely to be agents in this venture.

Second, the new theoretical approaches to cultural history described by Adrian Bantjes for Mexico showed that focusing on local forms of religiosity was useful for demonstrating how Mexican popular religion served a strong personal and social purpose.[50] Borrowing the same frame of analysis for Catholic Charismaticism that had been used by historians for popular religion shows here how Charismatic religiosity informed and empowered subaltern groups in their struggles to shape their own destinies in a contentious environment.

Third, this account also shows that local religion is by no means static. Eamon Duffy showed that in the case of English traditional religion, religious culture was "capable of enormous flexibility and variety."[51] A similar flexibility is shown in the embrace in Mexico of Mary, the Virgin of Guadalupe. While Protestant Pentecostals seemingly had no place for the veneration of the saints, Mexican Charismatic Catholics have shown the capacity for the hybridization of apparently contrary religious traditions (Pentecostalism and popular religion) as did their ancestors in combining Aztec, Toltec, and other indigenous religiocultural elements together with Christianity in a way that made sense to them.

Syncretism has outlived its usefulness in its utility to define the indigenous Catholicism of an earlier age, as well as now. Persons operate comfortably "in more than one tradition at a time, enlarging their cosmovision and repertoire of world renewing," as William Taylor wrote of Catholics in eighteenth-century Mexico.[52] He could say the same in the twenty-first century.

Last, one should note that one of the remarkable aspects in the new Mexican Charismatic missionary outreach and in most of the enterprises of the contemporary Latin American church is the reliance on having to reflect theologically on virtually everything that is undertaken. It is a "vision thing" and, if the recounting of history herein has been correct, Latin Americans excel in providing a vision for the church and its activities. At very least, after five hundred years, Latin Americans have internalized responsibility for the global church in ways that are new and promising.

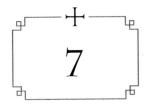

7

THE STRONG MIDDLE COUNTRIES

Beyond Brazil and Mexico, five other South American countries have shown a remarkable growth of Catholic Charismatics:[1]

Argentina	4.7 million
Venezuela	3.1 million
Peru	2.4 million
Chile	1.6 million
Ecuador	1.2 million

These countries form an exceptionally strong middle sector of the Charismatic renewal. They ranked fourth to eighth in the number of Charismatics reported among Latin American countries. They are also relatively high in percentages of Catholics who are Charismatic. Argentina, Venezuela, and Chile have 14 percent Charismatics in the Catholic population, while Peru and Ecuador have 10 percent.[2]

Argentina

No Latin American country had a more ragged, diffuse beginning for its Catholic Charismatic Renewal than Argentina. However, few match its contemporary growth. And none in 2008 matched its ecumenical connections. Argentina has grown into a country worth watching for its religious situation and ecumenical leadership in ways that the nation previously did not warrant.

The movement came in part through Protestant pastors, not typically a trustworthy source for traditional Argentine Catholics, a sector that seemed to have been the dominant element of the laity and clergy in the Argentine Catholic Church for much of the twentieth century.[3] Juan Carlos Ortiz, who would later come to the attention of North Americans for his work with the televangelist Robert Schuller's Crystal Cathedral at Garden Grove, California, was serving as an Assemblies of God pastor in Argentina. He was strongly influential in spurring interest in the renewal among Catholics.

Ortiz was part of an interdenominational group called Movimiento de Renovación Espiritual (Movement for Spiritual Renewal, MRE), which started as a small group of some two dozen persons meeting in the upper-middle-class Belgrano section of Buenos Aires in 1967. The number of members expanded and in 1972 the group held an ecumenical Charismatic retreat in which Catholics participated.

An Argentine Jesuit, Father Alberto Ibañez Padilla, had become a Charismatic Catholic through contact with the movement in Medellín, Colombia and in the United States. He was one of the Catholic participants in that ecumenical retreat. At the same time Father Ibañez was the advisor to a somewhat esoteric spiritual movement called Refugios del Sagrado Corazón (Refuges of the Sacred Heart). This movement practiced the spirituality of St. Francis de Sales (a moderate form of Christian asceticism) and came to number 120 groups for lay Catholics in Argentina, Uruguay, and Paraguay. The movement split in two and Father Ibañez headed up one of the resulting groups, incorporating it in 1973 with the same name as that of a Protestant movement of 1967, the Movement for Spiritual Renewal (MRE). The MRE coexisted with the other splinter group from Ibañez's previous spiritual movement. This second group was growing in membership in the Buenos Aires region and was called Convivencia con Cristo (Living with Christ). Other Catholic Charismatic groups started up in the remote provinces of Salta and Corrientes with no strong connection to the capital, Buenos Aires. In general, the 1970s were marked by isolated groups that were created by a layperson or priest who had come in contact with the movement in another country, such as Puerto Rico, the United States, or Colombia. Also, the groups tended to be in close contact with Protestant groups that were operating as the Charismatic wing of Protestant churches.

The MRE (the Catholic version headed by Father Ibañez) was investigated by the Jesuits and questioned by the archdiocesan offices in Buenos Aires about Charismatic practices, especially the practice of speaking in tongues. A little later Archbishop Adolfo Tortolo of Paraná raised questions about the movement because of participation by a controversial Pentecostal pastor, Omar Cabrera.

Questioning on the part of Argentine church authorities diminished as the growing acknowledgment and approval of the movement by Pope Paul VI occurred, especially in his addresses to leaders of the movement in 1973 and 1975.[4] In the minds of Argentine Charismatic leaders the crowning approval of the statutes of the movement by the universal church was granted by the Pontifical Council for the Laity in 1993 after the landmark International Charismatic Leaders Retreat in Assisi.

The 1980s unfolded in Argentina as the nation was rebuilding after the state-sponsored terrorism of the Dirty War (1976–83) and the humiliating loss of the Malvinas/Falklands War to Great Britain (1982). The decade witnessed a generalized spiritual awakening in which the Catholic Charismatic Renewal was an expression. In 1985 Father Felicísimo Vicente promoted the movement in a strategic location in Buenos Aires, the Shrine of the Sacred Heart of Jesus in the San Justo district, making the church building a central gathering place for the movement.

By contrast with the cosmopolitan environment of Buenos Aires, a strong beginning of the renewal also took place among working-class Catholics at Santiago del Estero, northwest of Buenos Aires. There the renewal enlivened popular religion and filled soccer stadiums and churches with provincial conferences, healing campaigns, and other mass events. Similar events began to take place at the end of the 1980s in other outlying provinces of Formosa, Corrientes, Entre Ríos, La Rioja, and the Patagonian region.

Despite the growth of the movement around the country in the 1980s, the majority of bishops maintained serious reservations about the movement. The sole prominent exception was the archbishop of Salta, who supported the movement enthusiastically, in part because Salta was a northwestern province perhaps closer to Bolivia in its religiosity and its tolerance for innovations in religion. In 1989 the Argentine Bishops Conference issued two complementary documents dealing with the Charismatic renewal. The first of these, "Los Lineamentos Básicos" (Basic Guidelines), delineated what should be the objectives of the movement and the general principles for its functioning, along with formal recognition of a national team of coordinators. The second document, "Criterios Fundamentales" (Fundamental Criteria), was a doctrinal evaluation of the movement and described its fruits and risks.

In 1998 the renewal was authorized to function by individual bishops in every diocese of the country, with the single exception of the diocese of San Rafael. Being allowed to function within a diocese meant a measure of tolerance on the part of the bishop rather than that the bishop was personally supportive of the movement. This tolerance was a factor in the growth of the movement into the largest and most active Catholic movement in the country.

Through the end of the 1980s and until 1992 the movement lacked structures and national and provincial leadership. According to Father Salvador Guerrieri, a national advisor to the movement, in the national meetings of Charismatic leaders before 1992 attendance was haphazard: those who were free of pressing obligations came to the meetings while many others did not attend in a particular year. The meetings themselves were conducted without any programmatic planning. Participants—typically one hundred in most years—simply came to discuss mutual interests and offer support for one another in a movement lacking strong hierarchical support.[5]

Notable changes in the structuring of the movement occurred in 1992 when separate national meetings were projected that year for five specialized groups within the movement: priest-advisors, diocesan coordinators, adult leaders, youth leaders, and married couples. In a national church historically dominated by bishops and priests and without the extensive lay participation evident in other national churches, as in Brazil and Chile, the participation of priests in the movement seemed crucial to the continuation of the renewal. Abelardo Jorge Soneira, a sociologist from the Jesuit Universidad del Salvador, noted that about 10 percent of all Argentine priests took part in the national meetings of priest-advisors. Barrett and Johnson estimated 9 percent. In fact, in comparison with other countries, the percentage of priests in the movement is high. Argentina shares the fifth place in Latin America with three other countries in the percentage of priests, according to estimates of Barrett and Johnson.[6]

Colombia, with a national population roughly equivalent to that of Argentina, had more than twice as many Catholic Charismatics and only 3 percent participation of priests. Mexico, with some 9.2 million

Charismatic Catholics, had only 2 percent participation of priests. Again, the movement is principally a lay movement, not a clerical one. The understanding of this aspect of the movement had been difficult in Argentina, where lay movements, such as Catholic Action, had a strong clerical hand.

In a closer look at clergy in one of his later studies of the movement, Soneria came to the realization that attendance by priests at the national conferences for priests does not mean that the priest-attenders are themselves Charismatic. He quotes the national chaplain for the movement as observing that few priests "truly understand what the movement involves. Most of the priests-attenders have a Charismatic prayer group in their parishes. They have these prayer groups because the members do not bother anybody and the groups are a way for the old ladies to pray a little and to be together. Throughout the world the movement started despite the priests or more recently with the priests. But priests who truly understand the movement are few."[7]

Argentine social researchers of religion attempted no systematic study of the movement until Soneira's studies of the movement began appearing in the late 1990s. Fortunato Mallimaci, the national doyen of Catholic lay movements and the longtime dean of social sciences at the Catholic University of Buenos Aires, confirmed in 1995 that systematic studies of the renewal had not taken place. His own reservations about the movement were clear (and may have acted as an admonition to younger researchers not to take up the topic). The movement, he wrote, citing the French author Jean Seguy, "Weakens the gifts of the Holy Spirit, leads to excessive emotionalism, excessive emphasis on experience, and Biblical fundamentalism. These are the constant risks to which members of the movement are exposed."[8]

Abelardo Soneira's published studies of the Argentine movement include no participant observation or reflection on direct observation, although one of his major studies on the topic was published in an ethnographic journal.[9] This stands in marked contrast to Alejandro Frigerio, María Julia Carozzi, and Daniel Míguez, major Argentine researchers of religion who employed ethnographic methods to further the understanding of new religious phenomena.

As the movement expanded, lay members began organizing national meetings according to their special interests. Health professionals, members of religious congregations, music ministers, and other groups began holding national conferences in the 1990s. Furthermore, regional structures came into place with their own annual conferences, often packed with eager participants.

Preachers—most of them priests—from other countries acted as keynote speakers for the national and regional congresses and for leading the crucial Seminars in the Life in the Spirit. Many of them were Colombians, indicating the leading role of Colombia in the Latin American movement. But the visiting preachers also included Father James Burke, a priest from the United States who had been a missionary in Bolivia. These itinerant preachers did not run in and out of Argentina but tended to stay for periods long enough to allow for effective preaching.[10] They also tended to return to Argentina to reinforce their teachings of the fundamentals of the movement.

The foreign preacher most prominent in Argentina was Father Darío Betancourt, a Colombian-born priest with his main residence in the United States. In the evangelistic style popularized by Billy Graham, Betancourt organized Charismatic campaigns. These were held in soccer stadiums or open spaces in parks or auto racetracks where he emphasized Charismatic views of healing. He carried the same message to separate national conferences of health professionals and to priests. Betancourt was especially strong in his emphasis on evangelization as part of the Charismatic movement. He preached that the charisms of the Holy Spirit, especially healing, were what Jesus meant should be included in the "new" evangelization. In other words the Vatican's push for evangelization fit perfectly into the Charismatic movement. But Betancourt had more in mind than the Vatican proposed: "words accompanied by signs and wonders."

Betancourt was remembered in Argentina especially for his prolonged stay in that country in 1994–95. The high point of that stay was the Charismatic rally at Vélez soccer stadium where fifty thousand people gathered to hear his message and observe "signs and wonders" (presumably events of healing).[11] Leaders in the Argentine renewal considered the rally at Vélez one of the historical high points of the movement, in which, in their view, the country took notice.

In the late 1990s, the freelance activity of foreign preachers, especially Father Betancourt, was being viewed by the national clerical and lay coordinators of the movement in Argentina as a negative enterprise outside of their control. The national directors did not want the organization of events, especially Charismatic preaching campaigns by foreigners such as Betancourt, to take place independently of Argentine control. Soneira, the social scientist, concluded that the national team, headed by Father Ibañez, had become *"sumamente centralista"* (supremely centralist, or controlling).[12] Soneira saw the Argentine organizational Charismatic leaders as running a tight ecclesial ship in contrast to other national leadership groups and to the international coordinating leadership in Rome, which viewed themselves as service providers rather than as authoritative commanders.

The preacher who emerged within the movement in Argentina and became an international celebrity was a layperson. Osvaldo Cuadro Moreno had a long career as a Catholic active in Catholic Action and the Cursillos de Cristiandad movements before becoming Charismatic. His more than twenty books sold more than three hundred thousand copies, a large number for religious books in Latin America.[13] He used radio and television as a spokesperson for the Argentine Bishops Commission on Media. His long experience in Catholic lay movements convinced him of the value of small communities similar to the first Christian communities. He also became an itinerant preacher with an emphasis on marriage and family relations, traveling to Mexico, Peru, and the United States.

The most significant feature of the Argentine movement has been its active ecumenism in the first decade of the twenty-first century. In 2003, the spark for notable public and ecumenical sharing with Protestants was the visit of Professor Mateo Callisi, the leader of Italian Charismatic Catholics, to Argentina. The Federación Argentina de Iglesias Evangélicas (Argentine Federation of Protestant Evangelical Churches, FAIE) sponsored a meeting between leaders of Pentecostal churches associated with the FAIE and national Catholic Charismatic leaders at the FAIE's headquarters. It was especially significant that a Catholic bishop, Monseñor Abel Bulotta, the bishop of San Justo, was active in the meeting. Callisi had two messages that were reported by the FAIE. The first was his argument that ecumenism for Catholics had to be based on the Decree on Ecumenism, *Unitatis Redintegratio*, of Vatican Council II. Callisi saw in that decree acknowledgment of the influence of evangelicals and the Protestant Reformation in four aspects: communities of prayer, experience of the baptism in the Spirit, and the notions of universal priesthood of the faithful and the "invisible church" in the sense of a "pact." The latter (not further explained) was considered by the Protestant participants to be well understood by them.[14] Callisi believed that there were great possibilities for dialogue for the Protestant Pentecostals and Catholic Charismatics in Argentina, something Callisi thought would be less likely to succeed in Italy.

Callisi's second message was that the Catholic Charismatic movement should not be "institutionalized," a message that had been long overlooked and continued to be overlooked by the national Catholic Charismatic leaders. In fact, institutionalization gave organizational backbone and credence to key events in the journey to ecumenical cooperation in Argentina. In fact, three joint Pentecostal-Catholic worship services were held in the mid-1970s.

Then in 2007 at Luna Park, a domed Buenos Aires sport and concert venue, a joyous Pentecostal-Charismatic event took place that received prominent coverage in major newspapers. *El Clarín* noted that Argentina's leading Catholic figure, Cardinal Jorge Bergoglio, a person thought to be a candidate for pope a few years ago, attended and threw himself into the arm-raising, spontaneous spirit of Pentecostal praise.[15]

The event went on for hours and demonstrated, according to the reporter for *El Clarín*, confirmation that "Catholics and Protestants—after decades of distance and recriminations—were each year growing closer together spiritually." The reporter went on to say that religious analysts viewed these meetings as "evidence of the excellent interreligious climate in the country." He also noted that it was not so long ago that Protestants preaching in the streets or in parks found themselves targets of stones thrown by Catholics. He pointed out as well that Protestants, on their part, had managed to put aside doubts about Catholic devotions to Mary and the saints.

The Comunión Renovada de Evangélicos y Católicos en el Espíritu Santo (Ecumenical Communion of Catholics and Protestants in the Holy Spirit, CRECES) was the organizing force behind the four events. The group grew directly out of the warm relations between Catholics and Protestants created by Callisi during his visit to Argentina. The CRECES was modeled after an Italian ecumenical initiative, Consultazione Carismatica Italiana, created by Callisi and Pastor Giovanni Traettino, Callisi's Protestant counterpart in Italy. After Callisi's visit, four Catholic lay leaders met with four Protestant pastors at the Buenos Aires Catholic Social Pastoral Center for lunch. From this grew monthly luncheons, then joint prayer services at a downtown Protestant church, and then the formation of CRECES. The group sponsored the increasingly large annual get-togethers called Encuentros Fraternales (Brotherhood Celebrations).

Both sides, Protestant and Catholic, brought unusual strengths to the partnership. One of the key Protestant partners was Pastor J. Norberto Saracco, an Argentine who had obtained a doctorate in theology from the University of Birmingham, where the Center for Pentecostal and Charismatic Studies had set a high intellectual standard for the religious movements often disdained for their lack of theological scholarship. Faculty members of the center at Birmingham were also well informed of the twenty-five-year Vatican-Pentecostal Dialogue. Upon his return to Argentina, Saracco founded the Facultad Internacional de Educación Teológico (International School for Theological Education) with branches in several countries, including the United States, to help spread his ecumenical views.[16] Saracco was the main preacher at the II Encuentro Fraternal in 2005.

On the Catholic side, Callisi, who had long been involved in the Catholic-Pentecostal theological dialogues, returned to Argentina as a featured speaker for a special retreat for priests and Protestant pastors. He was followed from Italy to Argentina in 2006 by the Charismatic theologian Father Raniero Catalamessa, the preacher of the papal household. With this strong Roman backing, it became easier for the typically cautious cardinal of Buenos Aires to express his enthusiasm for the Charismatic-Pentecostal joint celebrations in 2007. At one point in the celebration at Lima Park stadium the cardinal spoke loudly of "not privatizing the Gospel." No one could have predicted thirty years ago that Argentina would be the venue for a great ecumenical breakthrough. Latin America was one of the weakest places in the world for ecumenism and Argentina one of the worst bets.[17]

Venezuela

In direct contrast to Argentina and Brazil, the Charismatic renewal in Venezuela has been a lower-key movement. The wide issues associated with the start-up of an Argentine movement, with the mixture of Protestant and Catholic Pentecostals, were largely missing in Venezuela. High-profile priest-performers who appear regularly on television, similar to Padre Marcelo Rossi and Padre Eduardo Doughtery (among many others) in

Brazil, have not been a prominent feature of the movement in Venezuela. Despite these differences, the movement in Venezuela has prospered.

Venezuela stood in fifth place among Latin American nations with an estimated 3.1 million Catholic participants. This places the country immediately after Argentina and before Peru in the number of Catholic Charismatics. To a far greater extent than Argentina, Venezuela's movement has been led by laity. Less than 1 percent of Venezuela's priests are Charismatic in contrast to Argentina's 9 percent. This lay leadership may be the key to describing virtually everything about the movement in Venezuela.[18]

To start, the national office was a bare bones operation with a staff of three to five persons, who defined themselves as largely reactive to the requests of members throughout the country and selectively proactive in terms of coordinating some large events.[19] They appeared not to be interested in controlling large Charismatic campaigns by foreign or domestic preachers in the manner of Argentina's national coordinators.

Rather than authoritarian control what marked Venezuela was spontaneity: large and small national meetings were organized by groups throughout the country. These ranged from the National Workshop for Journalists and Public Speakers to national get-togethers for seminarians.

The national headquarters was glad to know about the events but felt no need to assume control or exercise sponsorship. As a result the official written history of the movement is a narrative jumble of apparently unrelated events.[20]

Covenant communities have been the backbone of the movement. In Venezuela these are called *comunidades eclesiales de renovación* (ecclesial communities of renewal, CERs). It is highly significant that the designation sounds like but differs from the controversial *comunidades eclesiales de base* (Christian base communities, CEBs), the carriers of liberation theology that were very important in Latin America, including Venezuela, beginning in the 1970s. Christian base communities were fostered especially among the lower classes in the slums of Caracas and were advocates of social justice. They may also have been causes for friction, if not fissures, in the Venezuelan national church, which had come to depend for its economic and numerical support on the middle classes through the extensive provision of Catholic grade and high schools in the first two-thirds of the twentieth century.[21]

These CERs gave the church in the capital city a different ideological coloring from that of the Catholic Church in some other parts of the country that were not especially attuned to justice issues. Caracas was also the seat of the influential and theologically progressive Universidad Andrés Bello, where one of its top administrators, Father Luis Ugalde, S.J., was known for his courageous social-justice positions, as was the Jesuit monthly, *SIC*, and its editor, Arturo Sosa, S.J. The magazine acted as a center for Catholic intellectuals and activists. Other progressive Catholic movements, such as the human rights movement, also flourished in Caracas and seemed not to have much resonance in other dioceses of the Venezuelan church.[22]

In general a variety of lay movements were quietly active but largely went unnoticed by observers of the Latin American Catholic Church who were focused on church-state conflicts in other countries in the latter third of the twentieth century. Nonetheless, considerable vitality was occurring in what was once a moribund national church. One indicator of progress and vitality has been the growth in the number of seminarians. They increased 764 percent between 1972 and 2001 and continued to grow by 13 percent from 2001 through 2004.[23] This growth helped consolidate a national church, as young Venezuelan priests replaced departing missionaries who were returning to their home countries in their declining years.

After the election of Hugo Chavez in 1999, Caracas seemed to be a beehive of overheated politics while other large cities seemed relatively tranquil. Fostering one of Venezuela's famed youth orchestras and other cultural endeavors, Barquisimeto was such a place, where the national office of the movement came to reside.[24] The archbishop of Barquisimeto was an early and ardent supporter of the Charismatic renewal. His enthusiasm was shared by laypersons who were important for the spread of the movement in the area around Barquisimeto and in fostering the movement from Barquisimeto as though it were the center of energy radiating out to other parts of the country. Some of the earliest large gatherings of Charismatics, drawing thousands of eager participants, were held in the city at its soccer stadium.

It should be noted as an important aside that in the early days of the Charismatic movement in Venezuela a gifted U.S. missionary, Father Tom Maney, made one of the more successful personal integrations of the two major Catholic tendencies of the twentieth century—liberation theology and the Catholic Charismatic Renewal. He was already convinced of the social-justice orientation of liberation theology and was active in educating lay Catholics in Venezuela in this perspective. He, along with some other progressive Catholic missionaries, was searching in the early 1970s for something more.

Maney, a Maryknoll missionary, felt called to carry back to the United States the value of small communities for enlivening the U.S. church. He teamed up with Sister Joan Geraeds and they became an itinerant preaching team dedicated to the renewal of North American parishes. He published a book on the theme of small renewal communities within parishes that was received by appreciative English-language readers, many of whom attempted to put his ideas into practice in their communities.[25] Maney's move to the United States helped a number of Catholics in that country but left Venezuela, for a time, without a high-profile and articulate spokesperson for the integration of justice and Charismatic perspectives.

An emphasis other than justice, evangelization, was being promoted among Venezuelan Catholics. One aspect was schooling for the poor; another was the generalized trend in Latin America for the re-education of adult Catholics. Venezuela was home to the great innovation in education called the Escuelas de Fé y Alegría (Schools of Faith and Happiness).

Fé y Alegría marked a prominent new direction of work for the benefit of the poor. This large educational movement began in 1955 through a visionary Spanish Jesuit who wished to expand the long-standing focus of Jesuit education toward the formation of elite members of society in Latin America. Whereas half of the twenty-eight Jesuit universities of the United States in the 1950s had labor institutes with close ties to working-class movements, Jesuit universities in Latin America typically lacked such connections. In Venezuela, Jose Maria Velaz, in his first pastoral steps as a Jesuit priest, focused on the poor of the country and viewed education as a major transformative instrument. Basic education for the poor, he believed, would take them from being a dominated, vulnerable group to a people that would be proactive in their own destinies.

Using the energies of university students and recent college graduates as teachers and aides, Velaz created primary schools within recycled buildings. These schools, he promised, would be directed to the most impoverished and excluded sectors of the population in order to empower them in their personal development and their participation in society. From the start of his activity, Velaz foresaw a movement that would include wide goals, such as nutrition, housing, and cultural learning for improving the condition of the poor.

These goals would never be achieved on a large scale without financial aid from the state. Furthermore, the fundamental obligation to educate its citizens fell on the state. In country after country in Latin America, a deal was struck whereby the state would provide buildings, maintenance, and salaries while the church would train, recruit, and supervise teachers and helpers. Typically Jesuits have acted as administrators, recruiters, and animators for these schools. For the Jesuits as a group this meant a monumental commitment in terms of personnel and energy. For national societies this meant a contribution from a group with almost five centuries of notable educational experience. As the Latin American church began using the expression "option for the poor" in the late 1960s, the Fé y Alegría movement easily assumed this perspective into its discourse.

This cooperation of church and state was highly unusual in Latin America, where separation of church and state has been the norm for decades. The cooperation was especially unusual in more secular nations such as Venezuela, where many immigrants had come to the country in the nineteenth and twentieth centuries as un-churched persons from Europe. The Fé y Alegría program expressed what became known in the United States under Presidents Clinton and Bush as faith-based initiatives but without many of the evangelical issues.[26] Opposition to Fé y Alegría by secularists, competing religionists, Freemasons, and Marxists has been remarkably muted in most Latin American countries. However, opposition from long entrenched anticlerical groups probably means the movement will not take hold in countries with deeply embedded anticlerical traditions, such as Mexico or Uruguay.

By 2003, 1.2 million students were participating in Fé y Alegría programs in fourteen countries. This represented a fivefold gain in little more than twenty years from 1981. Leaders of the movement extended educational activities to the secondary level in selected areas and used radio schools to extend instruction to sparsely populated areas.

The recruitment of lay Catholics to teach in these schools implied a greater grasp of Catholicism than was typical of teachers in the past. So the need to upgrade adult teachers in basic understandings of the faith occurred at about the same time as the impetus toward new evangelization, already discussed, was occurring. The Charismatic movement coming to Venezuela then fit in well with both catechesis (especially of children) and evangelization (mostly of adults). Members of *comunidades de renovación*, the local designation of Charismatic communities, underwent an evolution from being centered on their own spiritual growth to turning out toward the larger church and engaging in evangelization/catechesis. This change moved adept Charismatics to classroom teaching and retreat preaching.

The spread of covenant communities to many dioceses in Venezuela assured a degree of stability to the movement that was missing in a number of countries. These intentional communities added depth to the movement and anchored it securely. Prayer groups are more transitory groupings. Barrett and Johnson, who have been compiling for many years estimates of participation in prayer groups, confirmed what was being observed by leaders early in the movement—that there was "revolving door" syndrome. Large numbers of active Charismatics, Barrett and Johnson said, "Ceased to be attenders of prayer groups or specifically Charismatic parish activities after three or four years." They were also called "alumni or post-charismatics. Most still regarded themselves as Charismatics and were also often found to be active in other less visible areas of the church's mission."[27]

In sum, many former attenders of Charismatic group meetings—be these meetings of prayer groups or large parishwide or citywide meetings—moved into teaching catechism, conducting youth groups, and other parish or extra-parish activities. In the view of some veteran promoters of the Charismatic movement, such as Francis MacNutt, James Burke, and Ralph Rogawski, this is a typical evolution. Burke and Rogawski witnessed some ten thousand men and women pass through Cursillos de Cristiandad at a center in La Paz, Bolivia, where the missionaries taught. These Cursillistas then became teachers in the Catholic labor school or weekend evangelizers (preachers) on *misiones volantes* (visits of doctors and teachers on Saturdays or Sundays to remote priestless areas outside of urban areas), or made themselves available for service within a parish.

Thus, a wide range of being Charismatic exists: from regular attendance at a Charismatic prayer group to forgoing Charismatic group meetings while still attending Charismatic Masses. After years of looking over the data from the Charismatic movement, Barrett and Johnson concluded that there were several categories of Charismatics. Among active involved adults are the weekly attenders. They are adults typically enrolled and attending the renewal's officially recognized prayer meetings. "These," Barrett and Johnson said, "have been called the 'shock troops' of the movement."[28] Other adult Charismatics attend prayer meetings monthly or yearly and often attend the yearly national conferences. Barrett and Johnson also included "self-identifying adult Charismatics" who identify themselves in public opinion polls either as Catholic Charismatics or as involved in some fashion in the renewal. To these Barrett and Johnson add a fifth category of children and infants, members of families of Charismatics. Last, there exists a large fringe of Catholic post-Charismatics (formerly active Charismatics who have become less active, or active elsewhere as Christians). In the case of Venezuela, the renewal counted 60,000 core adult prayer group attenders in 2000. Adding less frequent attenders, children, and post-Charismatics in the country increases the total to 3,136,000. This amounted to 14 percent of the national Catholic population, tied for fourth place in Latin America. Again, the number and the percentage of priests (20 of 2,406, or less than 1 percent) were low, extraordinarily low.

Nonetheless, priest-preachers, especially ones with the reputation for having an apparent gift of healing, have been central to the movement in terms of being the centerpiece of large gatherings, as at the national or diocesan congresses. Emiliano Tardif from the Dominican Republic was an important presence in Venezuela during the early days of the movement. Father Hugo Estrada from Guatemala came in 2008 for the Charismatic Priests Retreat. But as the movement found its footing in Venezuela, a star priest emerged among the missionaries present in the country. Father Jaime Kelly, an Irish member of the Missionaries of the Sacred Heart, became a much-sought preacher within the country. As the priest-advisor to the Venezuelan movement, he also was consulted by laity on a variety of questions, especially about the religious ideas and pseudo-religions that flow through the Caribbean (of which much of Venezuela is a part).

With so few priests participating in the Venezuelan movement, it is little surprise that preaching has been taken up by some lay members of the movement. Lay preaching had an outlet on Radio Lumen and other stations open to religious broadcasting. As of 2008 Venezuela had not reached the higher density of Charismatic use of radio and television, as, say, Brazil or Guatemala.

Peru

Similar to Argentina, the influence of Protestant Charismatics in igniting the Catholic Charismatic Renewal was especially clear in the case of Peru.

Hobart Vann, a Baptist pastor from California, made his way to Lima, moved by a vision he had of spreading the Charismatic movement to foreign lands and for reasons that were unclear, specifically to Peru. Vann had been working since his "conversion" within the movement in 1966 to spread the Charismatic movement among Protestants of various denominations in California. In 1968 he experienced a strong desire to go to Latin America, but he needed Spanish-language training first. When there was no room for him and his family at a Protestant language school in Mexico, he found space at the Catholic language school in Lima conducted by the priests of the Saint James Society and sponsored by the Catholic archdiocese of Boston.[29]

In the welcoming atmosphere there he proposed giving the first Life in the Spirit seminar in Peru. He was advised that he would need to have a Catholic partner for the seminar if it were to draw Catholic priests and sisters. At that time Patrick Rearden, a Dominican priest-disciple of Frank MacNutt, was assigned to Bolivia but was staying temporarily in Lima, and he agreed to co-direct with Vann the Life in the Spirit seminar.[30]

In 1970, Vann arranged for the Union Church, a nondenominational Protestant church in the Miraflores section of Lima, to be the site of the first Charismatic retreat in the country. Virtually all of the Protestant and Catholic parishes or congregations of greater Lima received invitations to participate. Some one hundred priests and sisters attended but only four or five Protestants.

From the start of the movement in Peru the sisters from the Immaculate Heart of Mary in Philadelphia offered their centrally located school as the site of the first and most important Charismatic prayer group in Lima. The group served as the incubation center of the movement among Catholic priests and sisters. In effect, the prayer meetings there served as a warm-up for the second (English-language) Charismatic retreat in the country, May 19–24, 1970, at the Union Church. Again Hobart Vann recruited many of the retreatants. The retreat was directed by Father Frank MacNutt and a team of three Methodist ministers: Joseph Petree from Greensboro, North Carolina; Tommy Tyson, a Methodist evangelist; and Raúl Zevala, a Peruvian pastor. Again, mostly Catholic priests and sisters—some two hundred missionaries largely from the United States and Canada—attended. The majority received baptism in the Spirit at that time.

Since they came from all over Peru, this helped to insure a more uniform geographical beginning to the movement than was true in many other countries. (Not all of the enthusiastic beginnings were sustained in Peru, however.) From these groups some notable Charismatic clerical preachers emerged. Equally important, priests and sisters went back to their parishes and schools to recruit lay leaders for the movement.

The third Charismatic retreat a year later was partly in Spanish and some two hundred lay Catholic Peruvians attended. Preaching the entry-level Life in the Spirit retreats in Spanish opened the doors of the movement to the majority of Peruvians who spoke Spanish. The diffusion of the movement thereafter took place at the grass roots through these new lay disciples and at the regional level through priests, brothers, and sisters using networks already established among missionaries who had become incorporated within informal networks of pastoral agents during their stay in the country.

The movement thus started with a variety of agents. Furthermore, many priests and sisters had encountered the movement and made their first steps in the movement in the United States from multiple sources other than Vann, Rearden, or MacNutt. Peru at that time probably had the highest percentage of Catholic missionaries from the United States of any country in Latin America.[31] Some missionaries, such as the Marianists and Maryknoll priests and sisters, had been established in Peru for decades; most came in the great missionary influx of the 1960s and 1970s. These missionaries had initiated and consolidated their parishes, schools, and hospitals by the time the Charismatic renewal started. These missionaries recruited Peruvian laypersons for the movement. Thus priests and religious sisters from the United States carried the movement from the United States to Peru in greater numbers than was true in most other Latin American countries.

Among the Charismatic leaders that emerged from that group was Father George DiPrizio, a Holy Cross priest. He became caught up in the movement and thereafter dedicated his priestly ministry to its spread. He joined with a Dominican priest from Bolivia, Father Jim Burke, to help start the movement in Puerto Rico. The Charismatic preaching ministry took DiPrizio to other countries as well since he was a gifted keynote speaker and retreat director. His book, *Dios Mío, Necesito Algo!* (My God, I'm Lacking Something!), published in 1987, was aimed at Spanish-speakers and at explaining major themes of the movement. It served as a handbook for individuals and prayer groups looking for enlightenment on spiritual growth.

DiPrizio had an especially strong theological training and was typical of many religious order priests formed in the religious seminaries of the United States and Europe in the 1940s and 1950s. DiPrizio received a first-class theological education at the University of Notre Dame. He made good use of this theological formation in formulating his vision in Spanish of the Charismatic movement for his large audiences in Peru and for readers of his Spanish-language book on the movement. It was not a coincidence that a fellow Holy Cross priest, Edward D. O'Connor, became a much-read author of English-language books on the Charismatic movement[32] or that Notre Dame became a major home to the movement as it spread from its major point of origin at Pittsburgh.[33]

English-speaking Canadian priests were active in spreading the movement in Peru. One of the most successful was Father Joe Kane, an Oblate missionary. In ways parallel to Father Rogawski in Santa Cruz, Bolivia, Kane had been working to create small ecclesial communities in Lima's rough neighborhoods, *los barrios limeños*, with a team of laypersons. He also learned a great deal about the Charismatic movement as an apprentice Charismatic, preaching alongside Pastor Vann. Vann worked especially hard in 1973–75 to spread the movement among Protestants and Catholics throughout Peru, with Father Kane often at his side. After carrying on Charismatic activities for some time in and around Lima and working on the road with Vann, Kane formed an itinerant preaching team to carry the movement to other parts of Peru and to neighboring Ecuador and Chile. The Catholic Charismatic movement was receiving enthusiastic word-of-mouth notices in church circles and invitations for speaking engagements, leading retreats, and advising on best pastoral practices were being received by notable preachers like Kane and Rogawski. The two priests reached a friendly agreement: Rogawski would respond to invitations north of Ecuador and Kane would take the ones to the south. In the latter part of his life Kane returned to Canada, where he served as a chaplain and a Charismatic leader among laypersons working with the poor in the Ottawa region.

However, the missionary priests and sisters from North America were coming to the end of the typical missionary career through age and declining health and were beginning to be reassigned back to the United

States and Canada. As a result, leadership passed rather quickly from person to person with very little stability. Young Peruvian priests did not come forward at this time with forceful leadership. On the surface, at least, it appeared that Peru, the country that spawned liberation theology through one of its principal creators, Gustavo Gutiérrez of Lima, was not especially receptive to an other-worldly message from the United States. Gutiérrez, unlike some other major liberation theologians, such as Leonardo Boff, did not speak out publicly against the Charismatic movement, but it was well known in Peru and elsewhere that he shared no enthusiasm and offered no public support for the movement.[34] Gutiérrez was a defining figure in Peruvian society and taught thousands of Peruvians in his popular summer courses at the Pontifical Catholic University in Lima. That lack of support probably held back many laypersons and priests and sisters from joining or persisting in the Charismatic movement.

The two—liberation theology and the Charismatic movement—were both major movements of Christianity and Catholicism in the twentieth century. On the surface, at least, they appeared to be contradictory, although a number of persons seemed to have been able to reconcile for themselves the apparent contradictions.

The Peruvian priests who took over leadership of the Charismatic movement in the country as the North Americans departed did not have the same interest in the theological aspects of the movement as their predecessors nor were they able to avoid serious fissures in the movement. Father Rómulo Falcón, who had been working in Trujillo, became the national coordinating leader of the movement in Peru in 1984. While he was in this position, the Charismatic movement began dividing along two tendencies, the "renewed Charismatics," who spurned traditional Catholic practices, such as devotion to the Mother of Jesus and the saints, and "traditional Charismatics" (so labeled by their rivals). When Falcón was called to Europe by his missionary congregation, the movement was left adrift. It split, with self-described "renewed Charismatics" mostly leaving the Catholic Church either to join existing Pentecostal churches or to form small independent churches. The numbers of participants in the breakaway groups seemed to have dwindled in the ensuing years.

Peter Hocken, the priest-historian of the wider Charismatic movement, noted that in some regions in the 1980s lay-clerical tensions brought fissures. He wrote that in the process of Catholic structuring, pioneer lay leaders were often unhappy with the clerical authority provided for them.

As a result, a number of Charismatic groups that were formed in the first wave of the renewal did not continue within the Catholic Church but became independent Charismatic assemblies under their former lay leaders.[35] These schisms occurred in Peru, Costa Rica, and Guatemala in the relatively early days of the movement but have not occurred noticeably in Latin America since then. (Wide variation in the countries in question with regard to clerical leadership could be noted much later: in 2000 only 1 percent or less of priests in Peru and Costa Rica were Charismatics while 11 percent of the priests in Guatemala were Charismatics.)

After large initial growth, by 2005, the Charismatic movement in Peru appeared to have diminished to a relatively low level. Some 338 prayer groups with about 10,000 members were reported by the central coordinating headquarters of the movement.[36] The movement appeared to have reached most departments (states) of the country, but only two, Chiclayo and Chimbote, reported anything close to 2,000 members. Leadership at Chimbote had a late start and largely passed to lay initiative after the Charismatic preacher, Father Al Caprio, an Eastern Province Dominican, returned to the United States. The personal course of Caprio's involvement in the movement shows how many priests and laypersons entered the movement indirectly and not through what some have portrayed as the sine qua non entry point for Catholic Charismatics: the Life in the Spirit seminar.

Father Caprio was a latecomer to Catholic mission life. He had worked as a youth minister in the United States and then in Peru. For this work he borrowed methods that were successfully employed by the Salesian priests and brothers in the Los Angeles area, replicating in his own way intensive retreats called Youth Encounters Spirit (YES). This innovative work made it easier for him to be open to the Charismatic renewal when he went to Peru and eventually became pastor of the large traditional Dominican parish of San Pedro in Chimbote, then a somewhat ramshackle steel-mill and fishing boomtown in northern coastal Peru. Given the Dominican ties to Chimbote,[37] Father Francis MacNutt was willing to fit into his tight schedule a Life in the Spirit retreat there. It was through contact with participants in that seminar or similar retreats being held in the country that Caprio heard of the movement. Most of them were then members of small prayer groups in the city.

During a celebration of Sunday Mass in 1975 Caprio experienced what he recalled as a spiritual awakening to the role of the Holy Spirit in the life of the church and in his own life. As he recalls it, during Mass he was suddenly struck by "how good Thou Art," words he had read hundreds of times without special attention. This time, however, he felt a strong and warm light enveloping him to the point of embarrassment since the congregation had no awareness of why he was pausing overly long during the familiar words of the Mass. From then on he became deeply immersed in the Charismatic movement, helping to give retreats and lending his gifts as an organizer, and becoming the regional coordinator and religious director for the movement's adherents, drawing on members of the existing prayer groups to expand the movement among the 150,000 or so inhabitants of Chimbote and its environs.

He was learning on the job but felt the need for greater depth in theology and a surer knowledge of the best pastoral practices for Charismatics. He went to La Mansión, the Charismatic center in Santa Cruz, Bolivia, described earlier, to see for himself a successful center and to have Fathers Cris Geraets and Dan Roach act as his mentors. He stayed there for extended periods. Father Geraets, as already noted, had spent years in study, formulating a theological and pastoral vision for the then new and somewhat raw Charismatic movement. Since Caprio shared basically the same theological training as a Dominican, he was a quick and willing learner.[38] He also increasingly felt that he was on solid ground. (By this time, too, some of the great Dominican theologians of the twentieth century, such as Yves Congar, were formulating and publishing their theological perspectives on the Holy Spirit.)

The apprenticeship served him well. He recalled in 2008 that the main thing he gained from the visits to Santa Cruz was being able to give a reason for what he was attempting to do in the Charismatic movement. He was questioned frequently by Catholics who were ignorant of the movement. He was accused by Catholics in a neighboring parish of being Protestant, a not unusual thought harbored by insular Latin American Catholics of priests from the "Protestant" United States. Caprio created a Sunday evening Charismatic Mass that became the centerpiece of the movement for Chimbote, drawing persons from other parishes beyond San Pedro. The work week that followed was filled with activities designed to create lay leaders and to draw in indifferent Catholics. On Mondays, Caprio met with leaders of the parish and the movement. On Thursdays he devoted himself to youth work and on Saturdays he and team members went to other parts of the city to start prayer groups and to preach in the streets. Singing and musical groups grew up mostly spontaneously.

Street preaching was one of the innovations copied through Caprio's observations of the Charismatic center in Santa Cruz and utilized deliberately by him as a response to what he perceived to be the very large number of baptized Catholics who were unreached by the church. In Santa Cruz, as Father Caprio remembered it, one night a week was mission night. Priests and seasoned lay members of La Mansión went out to areas of Santa Cruz that they believed to be underserved by the Catholic Church or threatened by aggressive Pentecostal street preachers. Caprio followed the same pattern in Chimbote. Caprio was, in a word, a street priest instead of a sacristy priest. He and individuals from youth groups he had formed often discussed how to reach the hundreds of young people hanging out on the streets of Chimbote at most times but especially evident on Sunday when they appeared to be unreached by the church.

In process of the Dominicans' turning the diocese over to the national church, Luis Bambarén, a Peruvian Jesuit, was named bishop of the diocese. Bambarén was one of the best known "justice priests" in the country. He did not oppose the Charismatic movement in the diocese. Neither did he make any gesture toward supporting it. He did maintain friendly relations with Caprio so that it was clear that the movement was tolerated in the diocese.

When Dominicans from the United States turned the Chimbote diocese back to the care of the Peruvian church, Caprio returned to the United States in late 1989. He turned over directorship of the Chimbote section of the renewal to another Charismatic priest who enthusiastically carried on the Charismatic Masses and retreats until dying of hepatitis five years later. A married couple, Luis Gutiérrez and María Gozzer de Gutiérrez, expanded on ideas that Caprio had passed on, especially emphasizing the extroverted character of the movement through courses on evangelization and on defense of the faith in the face of the Pentecostal challenge. No strong clerical leadership for the movement was available so Caprio returned as often as he could—every few years—from his duties at Rutgers University Catholic Center or later assignments in the United States to preside at Charismatic Masses and to conduct retreats. He was received by ardent followers he had inspired to commit themselves to the church and to the movement. These occasions reinforced what the priest had begun. The movement at Chimbote remained something of a hot spot in the country, but overall in Peru the movement was adding only small numbers of new members while older members dropped out.[39]

As priest-leaders who were missionaries left the country to return home and Peruvian priests did not join the movement in substantial numbers, the informal initiative for spreading the movement in Peru largely passed into lay hands, apart from officially designated positions. Laypeople effectively and largely unnoticed spread the movement. Barrett and Johnson estimated in 2000 that Charismatic Catholics numbered 2.4 million people and 10 percent of the Peruvian Catholic population. They also calculated that only 1 percent of the 2,514 priests in the country that year were Charismatic, one of the lowest percentages of priests associated with the movement in Latin America.[40]

Chile

Word of mouth among U.S. missionaries carried enthusiastic notices from Peru and Bolivia to Chile. Francis MacNutt accepted an invitation from missionaries in Santiago as soon as he was able to offer the first Life in the Spirit seminar in Chile. In the early 1970s his ministry was expanding to Africa and other parts of the world, as well as Latin America. After Peru and Bolivia he felt a special obligation to accept invitations from his midwestern Dominican brothers working in various parts of Nigeria. The earliest opportunity to go to Chile came in 1972 when he was able to direct a seminar in the Life of the Spirit at the retreat house at Las Rosas in Santiago. By then MacNutt had mentored two Dominican priests, Fathers Jim Burke and Pat Rearden, who had been working for some time in Bolivia and were adept in Spanish. The three Dominican men, along with the Dominican sister Ana Felix and an unnamed Methodist pastor, conducted the retreat conferences and spiritual direction in Spanish and English at Las Rosas.

The Chilean church, then as now, was extraordinarily well organized relative to most other Latin American countries. Chilean priests, sisters, and laity typically belonged to multiple organizations and networks in the church and society. Furthermore, they were accustomed to innovations and typically kept open minds about new pastoral ideas from other countries. The Charismatic movement, however, was "made in the U.S.A.," making it probably less attractive than Action Catholique and other French pastoral innovations to Chile's bishops and priests, who then tended to be Francophiles.

The movement had to pass scrutiny by its bishops and clergy. In general they were considered by many observers to have the best theologically educated clergy in Latin America, led both by Jesuit and diocesan seminary professors. This theological culture may have dampened somewhat the reception of a "hot" (highly emotional) pastoral innovation. The same Chilean culture that prized equanimity also spared Chile some of the deviations, hard divisions, and small schisms that some countries experienced with the Charismatic movement.

Among Chilean priests who helped to anchor the movement theologically was Carlos Aldunate Lyon. An older Jesuit priest ordained in 1944, he had been the rector of various Jesuit schools in the country. His main contribution to the movement was his philosophical and theological depth, including a doctorate from Louvain and decades spent in spiritual direction and retreats. When the renewal came to Chile, Aldunate turned to his learning to interpret for Chileans such major Charismatic notions as healing and charisms.

By 2008 the national secretariat of the movement noted that "more than 700 prayer communities existed in the country from Arica to Punta Arenas." In other words, it was definitely part of the religious fabric of the country from one end to the other. Moreover, the early and enthusiastic start to the movement seems to have paid off in a very large body of post-Charismatics. Barrett and Johnson estimated the number in 2000 as 1.965 million Chilean Catholic Charismatics. This placed Chile seventh on the number of Charismatics, just behind Peru and ahead of Ecuador. Here, too, the movement definitely was led by laity, with less than 1 percent of its clergy being listed as members. Only 20 clergy were listed by the coordinators of the national renewal in Chile as active members in 2000.[41]

Chileans had many options for spiritual growth, ranging from the conservative Opus Dei to ardent followers of liberation theology within Christian base communities. What is likely is that the Charismatic style of prayer within public worship will become more common. What is not likely is that there will be a Chilean Marcelo Rossi.

Ecuador

The movement had an early start in Ecuador, beginning in 1970. Growth took place among high school and university youth groups, so that a number of young Ecuadorian laypersons were familiar with the movement in the larger cities of Quito, Guayaquil, and Cuenca. Many later became part of the large pool of post-Charismatics in Ecuador. The movement in the country has been relatively impressive, both in terms of numbers and percentages of the Catholic population. The movement also has been strongly lay in character with only 2 percent of priests in 2000.[42] Some priest-participants of a more recent generation became star preachers.

In Quito the two strongest Charismatic proto-covenant communities discussed consolidation. But, as was typical of the movement in Ecuador in the early 1980s, there was, according to informants in Quito, "a lack of leadership with a clear vision [of the movement] that could be communicated to followers."[43]

In Ecuador's principal cities the lack of clear leadership led lay activists to seek help from places where the movement was thriving. In Guayaquil a strong lay group within the Charismatic movement decided to live as a covenant community with support of several priests. Several of the group went to Colombia's Minuto de Dios to see how the covenant community associated with that group was organized and modeled their own efforts on the Colombian experience.

About the same time in Quito, a married couple, Jorge and Hortensia Espinoza, decided to go to what they perceived as the main wellspring at that time of the Catholic Charismatic Renewal: the Word of God community in Ann Arbor, Michigan. This covenant community warmly received the Espinozas and their children and acted as mentors in Charismatic spirituality while Jorge also pursued professional studies at the University of Michigan. The Espinozas returned to Quito to help establish the covenant community called Jesús es el Señor (Jesus Is Lord). In preparing for this, Osvaldo Cuadro Moreno, a lay preacher-teacher from the movement in Argentina, counseled the Quito group about the dynamics of forming a covenant community among themselves. Twenty-two people formed the initial community in August 1983. Their average age was twenty-five. A second covenant community also called Jesus Is Lord was founded in Guayaquil a year later. In 1985 the leaders from the Quito community went to San José, Costa Rica, to visit a nascent community there that became incorporated under the name Arbol de Vida (Tree of Life).

Also in that year, the Quito community began to emphasize communal rather than individual ministries. Evangelization was one of the principal ministries. The community formalized this effort in the Corporación Comunión y Vida (Communion and Life Corporation) as a legal entity for its ministries. Again it is notable that the ministries the community chose to emphasize, evangelization and missionary work, were activities barely spoken about for lay Catholics in Latin America at that time.

The covenant community sought from the archbishop of Quito a priest-advisor and was fortunate to enlist an older Spanish Jesuit, Father Francisco Ramos, who was a biblical and theological professor, for this position. His mentorship helped to moderate some of the questionable mystical language and tendencies derived from the Word of God community in Ann Arbor. Another covenant community grew up in Cuenca in southern Ecuador. Fuente de Vida (Fountain of Life) Community sponsored large public concerts and workshops in basic Charismatic themes for married couples and young unmarried Catholics, as well as in inner healing.

The Eudist religious congregation of men in Colombia that furnished the human and institutional support behind Minuto de Dios and was the mainspring of the Charismatic renewal in Colombia also influenced the movement in neighboring Ecuador. The Eudists conducted the San León Magno seminary at Cuenca where one of the younger priest-performers, Father Wilson Sossa, was a teacher. The Santa Teresa de Monay parish of the Eudists in Cuenca was also a Charismatic center for the city.

Another Eudist is probably *número uno* in name recognition among priest-evangelists from Ecuador. Padre Charly García was pastor of the San Juan Eudes parish in Quito, but he maintained a highly active life on the road. In October 2008 he spent three days preaching at the Archdiocesan Hispanic Congress in Houston, Texas, and a week at the International Congress on Healing at Jacksonville, Florida, followed by a week in November at the International New Pentecost Congress at Santa Cruz, Bolivia. García began an itinerant life during his younger days as a layperson in a Charismatic prayer group in his native Lima, Peru. After graduating in economics from the Catholic University in Lima, he migrated to Bogotá, where he became familiar with Minuto de Dios, entered the Eudistas, was ordained in 1992, and was sent to Rome for graduate studies in marriage and family.[44]

Conclusion

The five countries thus form a strong middle sector of the Charismatic renewal. Argentina had a large clerical presence in the movement: 9 percent. The lack of clerical presence is notable in all the other countries under consideration here. That liberation theology had a strong acceptance among the clergy in these countries, especially the foreign missionary clergy, may account for lack of recruitment of clergy. But, focusing more on lay leadership, a central theme running through this volume, these countries tended to have an abundance of lay revitalization movements, especially Cursillos de Cristiandad, small community movements, and indigenous resurgence movements. While Chile did not have a national indigenous movement, it did have significant indigenous activism sponsored by the church, but, above all, it had a wide array of late twentieth-century lay movements.[45] Argentina lagged in the abundance of lay movements but was one of the earliest strongholds of Catholic Action and a core lay leadership sector centered in Fortunato Mallimaci, a noted Argentine social scientist.

The Catholic lay population had already shown a propensity to accept global movements, such as the Catholic Charismatic Renewal, through previous and contemporaneous participation in various transnational lay movements. Charismaticism, too, showed again its ability to take hold locally, its translatability, as Lamin Sanneh and others have called its adaptability.

Charismaticism is like a musical genre, say jazz. Chilean Catholic Charismatics are clearly the vibrant practitioners of Charismaticism that one expects to find in Latin America, but Chilean Catholic Charismatic rhythm differs from its Brazilian counterpart, as much as Brazilian jazz differs from jazz performed by Chilean musicians like Claudia Acuña.

While the percentage increase in the priest workforce in these countries has been positive, the greatest increases have been among seminary students in the last years of education for priestly ministry. They offer hope for a vibrant future for the church. Some of them probably have been influenced by the Charismatic movement—no one knows for certain. The percentage increase of seminarians from 1957 to 2008[46] ranges from Argentina's 481 percent increase to Venezuela's 1,064 percent increase. These increases are in great contrast to the precipitous drops in recruits for the priesthood in the United States during this long period.

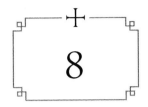

THE LESSER GROWTH
COUNTRIES

All of the countries of Latin America were enlivened by the Charismatic renewal but not all had the same level of growth. Five countries of Central America and two in the Southern Cone of South America experienced lesser growth in numbers. All were relatively small in area and population.

Central America gained world attention in the latter third of the twentieth century. Internal wars that were waged in Guatemala, Nicaragua, and El Salvador affected neighboring countries and pulled in the United States, Cuba, the Soviet Union, and other countries. Central America became an unfortunate battleground of the cold war. However, once Central American peace accords were signed in 1996, most of the world, including the United States, turned its attention to other regions. Nonetheless, a religious revival took place in Central America during the last four decades amid many martyrdoms, such as that of Archbishop Oscar Romero.

What is the situation now? All six countries of Central America and Panama[1] show an unusual strengthening of their core workforce, the priest-pastors of the Catholic Church. Most of these are native-born additions.[2] Here is the growth in priests, in terms of percentage increase, from north to south, from 1957 to 2008.

Guatemala	2,649 percent
El Salvador	1,810
Honduras	1,978
Nicaragua	1,565
Costa Rica	2,293
Panama	2,698

That kind of growth among priests in contemporary times is worth reflecting upon, since it is the opposite of what has happened in the United States and Europe. But other forms of spiritual growth and vibrancy have appeared in Central America that also need investigating. A variety of religious influences affected the region. Notable among them were an influx of historical and Pentecostal Protestants offering strong competition to the Catholic Church and the response by Catholic missionaries and laypeople in the form of lay revitalization movements, such as Catholic Action and the Cursillos de Cristiandad. Thus, in the twentieth century, laity and innovative movements in these countries brought new life to the church.[3]

The percentages of the Catholics in Central America who were Charismatic were among the lowest, ranging from 5 to 12 percent. "Charismatics may draw considerable attention—they certainly want attention—but their percentages are nothing like South American and Caribbean countries," one long-term observer said in an interview.[4] No satisfactory explanation has been given for this relative lack of success.

Guatemala is a notable exception and merits its own treatment in the concluding chapter. But the other Central American countries merit passing attention for important aspects, positive and negative, within the Charismatic renewal and because the countries supplied a steady river of immigration to the United States. There Charismatics were having an impact in places as diverse as Washington, D.C. and Houston.

Costa Rica

Costa Rica was one of the first countries visited by Francis MacNutt in 1972. The movement fluctuated with ups and downs in membership in various locations, especially in the capital city of San José near where MacNutt and his companions conducted the first seminar in Life in the Spirit, the customary entry point for new members and the occasion of second conversions for many.

In the early 1970s Costa Rica had a strong strain of ecumenical sharing in prayer services and common projects. MacNutt came to the country with an ecumenical team. About the same time two Protestant pastors from Charismatic churches in Argentina, Carlos Ortiz from the Assemblies of God and Alberto Mottesi, a Baptist, visited Costa Rica to promote the Charismatic movement among Protestants. When these Charismatic leaders from north and south arrived in San José they concentrated on meeting with English- and Spanish-speaking Costa Ricans in their homes, in addition to some public conferences. From these home groups grew more public meetings between Catholics and Protestants at the Templo Bíblico of San José, a church affiliated with the Asociación de Iglesias Bíblicas Costaricenses (Association of Costa Rican Biblical Churches, AIBC), a denomination that was not Charismatic at that time.

While these ecumenical meetings were occurring, Father Reginald Pol began offering pastoral leadership and coordination to the nascent Catholic renewal in the country.[5] Pol recounted his experience as one of the first priests to interest himself in the movement in a long essay on the Charismatic movement in Costa Rica written by Alberto Pozo Córdova.[6] Pol recalled nothing like persecution of the movement at its beginning; rather, he believed there was incomprehension and a sense that the movement harbored "crazies." The bishops of the country, in his view, were but one sector of persons at all levels who did not understand the movement. Pol himself became known as "the Charismatic priest who embodied the movement in himself," an identification he resisted.

Incomprehension on the part of the bishops gave way to their desire to control the movement, which they perceived as a freewheeling movement with very slim theological underpinnings. After an initial burst in membership, the Costa Rican bishops, in the words of the journalist-anthropologist David Stoll, "became repressive toward the end of the 1970s." Stoll reported that whole groups of Charismatics saw contradictions between their free interpretations and subjective mystical experiences and what the Catholic Church wanted to impose on them. A large number of them were reported to have become Protestant. (How many remained Protestant was not addressed.) Stoll also indicated that the bishops placed an unnamed popular priest as the coordinator of the movement. The priest, Stoll said, emphasized distinctly Catholic elements for the movement's members.[7]

An observer of the national movement better situated than the itinerant Stoll was Professor Pablo Richard, an expatriate Chilean resident in Costa Rica over decades. He was a highly respected Catholic theologian of the Department of Ecumenical Investigations at the National University of Costa Rica. Richard reported that the Charismatic movement had begun with fundamentalist leanings and an exaggerated spirituality but had matured into an organized ecclesial movement. The movement, he believed, also had shown the capacity to be reborn especially among the poor and marginalized sectors of society, with structures more adapted to their needs than had been the case in the beginning of the movement.[8]

As an indicator of its limited acceptance by the church and people, the Costa Rican movement in 2000 reported 183,000 members in a Catholic population of some 3 million persons. In terms of the percentage of membership, the renewal in Costa Rica, with 5 percent of the Catholic population, was one of the lowest in Latin America.

The Charismatic movement thus began in the country as an indiscriminate intermingling of Catholic and widely divergent Protestant intellectual tendencies.[9] The Catholic sector of the Charismatic movement in Costa Rica invited noted preachers who were deeply rooted in the foundations of Catholic theology to stay in Costa Rica for prolonged periods and to impart to Costa Ricans what the preachers had worked out through extensive study on the theology of the Holy Spirit and his gifts to the church. One of these was Father James Burke, a Dominican priest who had pursued doctoral studies at the University of Saint Thomas (the Angelicum) in Rome, taught theology, and was the rector at the Bolivian national seminary for a number of years. He began in the 1950s to share his theological insights with thousands of lay leaders in Bolivia through the Cursillos de Cristiandad (Short Courses in Christianity) movement. Although somewhat older than MacNutt, Burke accepted MacNutt's mentorship, listened carefully to MacNutt's early teaching about the Holy Spirit, and added depth to those teachings through years of further study, delving into recent biblical and patristic scholarship on the Holy Spirit, along with the Dominican tradition of contemplative prayer that included reliance on the Holy Spirit.

Following these years of midlife redirection, Burke felt impelled to carry what he had learned around the world. After years of a life being rooted in a single place, he put aside the security of having a home to start in his early fifties to move each year to various Charismatic centers. In 2008 he went for four- to six-week stays in Santa Cruz, Bolivia; Dublin, Ireland; San Isidro, Costa Rica; and Santo Domingo, the Dominican Republic, with stops for preaching in other countries.

The weakness of the idea of the itinerant preacher is a lack of continuity and reinforcement of a message that needs time to be absorbed by the hearers.[10] Burke sought to overcome that weakness by lengthy stays, return visits, and personal attention given to individuals through tutoring and spiritual counseling. The best assessments of his continued contribution to the theological deepening of the renewal are the repeated invitations by host countries for his return, as well as invitations from new destinations each year. Burke was eighty-five years old in 2008.

By the end of the 2000s the national epicenter of the movement was San Isidro, a relatively new diocesan territory cut out from other dioceses and located southwest of San José. Father Burke told me that one thousand people had attended his renewal seminars in 2008 at San Isidro, where a retreat center served as the base for these adult renewal programs.

Many strands of a new and different—that is, extroverted—church came together in these adult programs of renewal. The two most obvious characteristics of its outward-looking spirit were evangelization and mission, as noted elsewhere. Catholics needed to reach out to one another and to non-believers in evangelization and they needed to become missionaries. The new evangelization put in motion by Pope Paul in the 1970s was catching fire first in South America in the late 1990s and then in the backwaters of the church in Central America in the 2000s. Catholics, the pope argued, did not possess a deep and solid understanding of the faith. There were millions of nominal Catholics with superficial Christianity. When asked in a national religious survey in 2007, 45 percent of the Costa Rican population replied that they were practicing Catholics and 25 percent said they were non-practicing Catholics.[11] Costa Rican Catholics are probably better in their practice of the faith than many Catholics in other countries but nonetheless lack comprehensive religious knowledge. The one million Catholics who count themselves as non-practicing are targets for conversion to other denominations or, as is increasingly the case in Latin America, become "persons of no religion." Neither practicing nor non-practicing Catholics will remain Catholic without better intellectual grounding in the faith and personal conviction.

Burke's goal was greater personal conversion to God and commitment to the church. But there were personal obstacles within some individuals to this (second) conversion, so Burke emphasized the repair of the frayed relations of an individual with God and with all the persons the individual had to live with, seeing other persons as part of the divine web; that is, other humans had divine qualities and were in effect God at hand. These relations needed to be set right, that is, healed. Physical problems also acted as barriers to full human lives and needed healing.

Both types of healing and conversion went hand in hand for Burke. He, as well as his mentor, Frank MacNutt, found themselves incorporating healing as an integral part of the ministry. Some extraordinary events took place. Burke recounts how a young laywoman at the San Isidro retreat center had asked him for healing prayer for her eyes, which were becoming blind. He complied and seven years later when she met Burke, she recounted how her doctors could not explain how she regained normal eyesight and was able to shed her thick eyeglasses.

Again it should be noted that conversion for Burke and for Catholics generally differs from Pentecostal conversion, especially as described by many ardent Pentecostal preachers. For Pentecostals conversion was once and total whereas Burke recognized that a conversion, a turning from evil and choosing God, occurs at baptism and needs to be nurtured over time. For many Catholics this includes a renewal of the baptismal commitment to God and church through a second conversion and is followed by regular study of the Bible and Christian doctrine, prayer, and an extroverted turning out to others in (spiritual as well as physical) need.

Honduras

Many participants in the Charismatic seminars led by Father Burke were Delegados de la Palabra (Delegates of the Word), that is, leaders of small Christian communities in Central America. These leaders were more than village elders; they also led by teaching and preaching a biblical message. Hence the Charismatic movement was having an important impact in several regards: it was reaching and influencing young community leaders at the beginning of their careers as part of the volunteer church workforce and as leaders within the church. The movement would radiate through the communities from the Delegados to followers. Furthermore, many Delegados engaged in preaching. This engagement in lay preaching acted as a complement to preaching done at Sunday liturgies by priests. It also had several effects on the lay preachers. Preparation for preaching and the act of preaching itself tended to reinforce the message being preached and commitment to the organization.[12] Having to appear before one's peers increased the likelihood of thoughtful preparation, avoiding the danger of being judged unprepared or foolish by listeners. Assuming the office of preacher increased the likelihood of living an ethical life because of the preacher being measured by Christian standards and observed by others.

Apart from the Delegados, other laity became preachers. John Allen recounts in *The Future Church* the conversion of perhaps the best-known Catholic layperson in Honduras, Oscar Osorio, a star preacher on the Catholic cable channel in the country. His high-energy, expressive preaching opened each morning's programming. Osorio became a full-time preacher after years of studying the teachings, practices, and traditions of the church. Originally a Seventh-Day Adventist, he became a Catholic at mid-life through his Catholic wife, participation in a Catholic Bible study group, and time spent in Mexico with Catholic Charismatics. He felt called to full-time ministry as a preacher, sought counsel from the bishop, and found financial support for this from a Charismatic parish priest and his parishioners.

He roamed from parish to parish, "preaching," Allen said, "to any audience that would have him" (including seminarians). Similar to what he observed in Mexico, he helped create schools of evangelization in Tegucigalpa, the capital city, to bring along others into his ministry, a ministry that faces tough competition from very large numbers of Pentecostals in the country.

The theology of the Holy Spirit in Catholic thought also includes the view that the Spirit is present in the listeners to help them discern whether the message they hear is authentic. This aspect of Spiritan theology has been barely acknowledged in most Catholic Pentecostal writings viewed over the last forty years.[13]

Delegados de la Palabra began as an ecclesial innovation in Honduras and spread to Costa Rica and elsewhere. This innovation forms a variant in the Latin American movement that began in the 1960s and was generally described as the Christian base community (CEB) movement. These CEBs became especially prominent during the 1970s and 1980s under military dictatorships in the region and were often associated with liberation theology. In their Honduran origins, though, this was not the intent of their original promoters. Rather, lacking priests in many places, Honduran laity petitioned the bishop of Choluteca to deputize lay leaders to read and teach the word of God to them so that they would not be deprived of that gift of hearing the word of God, even though no ordained minister was available. What began as a Lenten practice was expanded to the full year.[14] In turn, this brought the need for educational programs for leaders, including literacy programs and Bible and theology classes. The results were outstanding in terms of increasing religious knowledge and commitment to the church, of creating a leadership class, and of making available to people at the grass roots vernacular intellectuals.

The lay leadership and lay spirituality programs that had been growing in Honduras made it easier to recruit candidates there for the Charismatic renewal than in countries without this basis. By 2000 Barrett and Johnson estimated that there were slightly more than half a million Catholic Charismatics in the country, or about 12 percent of the Catholic population, with only 2 percent of Catholic priests as members, confirming the largely lay character of the renewal in Honduras.

El Salvador

The movement spread from Costa Rica to the north into El Salvador when a priest from Costa Rica who was working in a parish in the western part of the main city, San Salvador, started the movement in 1983, rather late in the trajectory of the movement. Father Miguel Angel Zamora formed Charismatic prayer groups in the middle-class parish of Iglesia La Carmen. The following year he, then assistant pastor, and a group of laypersons from El Carmen took the unusual step of traveling to Los Angeles to meet with a former pastor of the Assemblies of God (a classical or traditional form of Protestant Pentecostalism) who had converted to Catholicism and who had become active in the Catholic Charismatic Renewal. From him they became increasingly dedicated to making the movement grow. Peterson and Vásquez noted in their treatment of the Salvadoran Charismatic renewal that the pastor of El Carmen had not encouraged the movement and that it was only when Zamora was appointed pastor that the movement flourished in the parish and radiated outward.[15]

Before long, El Carmen drew many persons from other parishes to participate in retreats and large gatherings. Leaders of the movement, given their mentor's past history as a former pastor in the Assemblies of God, developed the strategy of *campos de misión* (mission fields). El Carmen became a center where recruits received training and returned to their home parishes to form numerous Charismatic groups. If their pastors were lukewarm toward the movement, El Carmen supplied their necessary encouragement for continuing in the renewal. Thus Zamora and associates drew some twelve thousand Salvadorans into the renewal. Evangelization, the re-education of adult Catholics, also reached from El Carmen into a poor neighborhood, Colonia Fortaleza. The renewal helped to stem the loss of Catholics to Pentecostal churches, no small achievement in a country where Pentecostal growth was as great as that of neighboring Guatemala.

A somewhat similar Charismatic center was started in San Salvador at María Auxiliadora parish by persons who had experienced the movement first at El Carmen. Catholic Charismatics moved freely between the two centers with little competition between them (in contrast to Protestant Pentecostals among whom the shunning of backsliders was common). Both centers helped to spawn several smaller centers in other parishes in the San Salvador area. These Charismatics were clearly tied to church growth and evangelization. In this they were joined by the lay Charismatic Missionaries of the Sacred Heart of Jesus from Mexico. Their founder, Josué David Cruz Urrutia, started one of his first Catholic Missionary Centers outside of Mexico in San Salvador in 2000. The group's three lay missionaries were carrying on a whirlwind of activities dealing with spiritual growth and missionary outreach.[16]

That this was occurring in the place where Archbishop Oscar Romero was killed and is still venerated actively as a holy man by local citizens and visitors should be noted. The archdiocese of San Salvador, under Romero and his successor, Archbishop Arturo Rivera y Damas, was the hotbed of the Christian base community movement with strong ties to liberation theology. While vestiges of those tendencies still exist, the context and church leadership have both changed.

The long and arduous turn toward negotiated peace seemed to have diminished the participation of Christians in efforts toward liberation expressed through social and political activism. Within top church leadership, a change toward a deeply conservative tendency took place in 1995 with the new appointed archbishop, Fernando Sáenz la Calle, who was a member of the traditionalist Opus Dei movement. Sáenz became archbishop following the age-based resignation of the moderately progressive Arturo Rivera y Damas. Sáenz made several signature moves, including the removal of Rodolfo Cardenal, the Jesuit pastor of Cristo Resusitado parish, which indicated no support by the archbishop for liberation tendencies but rather enthusiastic support for the Charismatic movement.[17] Nonetheless, things are not so simple as to summarize levels of analysis of the church through depiction of the persona and actions of bishops (or popes, for that matter). Rather, it is better to say that whatever the disposition of the archbishop, large numbers of Salvadorans sought what the renewal had to offer: personal transformation and greater contact with God.

This tendency of desiring greater spiritual growth was not new historically for the Catholic laity of El Salvador or generally throughout Central America where the Cursillos de Cristiandad (Short Courses in Christianity) flourished before and during Vatican Council II (1962–65). The Cursillos as practiced in Costa Rica offered a series of courses and rituals leading to greater spiritual growth. (In many other countries, the Cursillos were largely utilized as shock-and-bonding experiences for new recruits into more permanent activism in Catholic Action or other groups.)

As viewed in El Salvador Catholic Charismatics emphasize spiritual growth (*crecimiento*) and have an elaborate program of moving through stages similar to the Cursillo participant advancing through stages of study and ritual participation. For growth within the Charismatic movement Salvadorans attend eight to twelve weekly classes and finish with a weekend retreat.

Peterson and Vásquez note, "Many of the CCR participants we interviewed spent years passing through stages of growth, which evolve elaborate programs of Bible study, prayer, and small group participation, all supervised by lay and clerical pastoral agents. The successful completion of each step is cause for celebration and for increased responsibility in the movement."[18] The Salvadoran movement leaders reported four hundred thousand adherents by 2000, amounting to 7 percent of the Catholic population and 9 percent participation by priests.

Nicaragua

The Charismatic movement became involved in politics in Nicaragua as no other country in Latin America. The movement began in the country in 1972 and was soon intermingled in the hard stances taken by Catholics. Some were deeply involved in the Sandinist revolutionary movement, a movement said to be Christian, Marxist, and Nicaraguan,[19] and some were conservative anti-revolutionaries led by Cardinal Miguel Obando y Bravo, the archbishop of Managua. As noted in the introduction, the conflict of left and right became centered in the presidency of Violeta Barrios de Chamorro.

The Sandinists held power from 1979 to 1990. The presidential election of 1990 brought Barrios de Chamorro to power and with her a large contingent of conservative Catholics to government. One of the main conflicts at that time was over the curriculum of the national education system. Anti-Sandinists wanted to restore moral values in the curriculum. They were led by Nicaraguan Catholic Charismatics who had the strong support of Tom Monaghan, the billionaire founder of Domino's Pizza. The Sword in the Spirit, an international community formed partly by a Catholic Charismatic covenant community based in Ann Arbor, Michigan,[20] where Monaghan grew up, was strongly influential in the Chamorro government. The educational issue was highly contentious in the country.[21]

In 2009, three alliance communities of the Sword in the Spirit still existed in the country. In the late 2000s, Monaghan established a branch campus of his Ave Maria University in Nicaragua, with Humberto Belli as its president. Belli was a former atheist and contentious spokesperson for the turn toward Catholic conservatism.

Perhaps the imbroglio led to Nicaragua's having one of the lowest percentages of Charismatics within the Catholic population. In 2000 only 5 percent of the Catholic population was estimated by Barrett and Johnson as being Charismatic: some 216,000 in a population of 4.3 million Catholics. This occurred despite a high 10 percent of priests being counted by the movement as Charismatic.

Panama

The movement began two years later in Panama than in its neighbors, Colombia and Costa Rica, and it began through Mexican, not U.S. intermediaries, perhaps because of the strong presence of U.S. priests who favored a social-justice orientation and rejected the other-worldly quality of the Charismatic renewal as preached by its leading exponents at the time. Some English-speaking Charismatic prayer groups existed in the U.S. Canal Zone and spread to Spanish-speaking sections of Panama City, but it wasn't until the first Retreat in the Spirit that the movement would establish firmer roots in the country.

Father Alfonso Navarro Castellanos preached that first retreat in the archdiocese of Panama in September 1974. Navarro was one of the key figures in the Charismatic movement in Latin America, although he did not achieve the international recognition that MacNutt, Tardif, and García Herreros attained, for many reasons, including his single-minded espousal of SINE, a tightly packaged and controversial system of cateche-sis. When he introduced the renewal to Panamanian Catholics, Navarro had not fully worked out SINE and he was more focused on the renewal itself. His contribution to the movement in Panama was ignored by Fa-ther Teófilo Rodríguez, a significant figure in the Panamanian movement, when in 2006 Rodríguez preached the major commemorative sermon on the upcoming fortieth anniversary of the Catholic Charismatic Renewal worldwide and its presence in Panama.[22]

The support of the archbishop of Panama City was singularly neces-sary for the life of the movement. Archbishop Marcos McGrath, a native Panamanian, was one of the great architects of the Latin American Bish-ops Conference (CELAM) and of their landmark meeting in Medellín in 1968. His special strength was a profound grounding in theology. He had earned a doctorate in theology in Europe and had written highly admired position papers on the church in Latin America.[23] McGrath gave strong support to the movement and was prepared to do so especially because he had been a member of the Indiana Province of the Congregation of the Holy Cross and was strongly tied to the Theology Department and other branches of the University of Notre Dame. (Notre Dame, as mentioned before, became a major center for the Charismatic renewal in the 1960s and 1970s.)

An Augustinian friar, Fernando Valenzuela, served as an early advocate and chaplain for the movement, which quickly acquired Spanish-speaking and Panamanian roots and spread through the small country. Father Fa-miliar Cano led a number of young persons into the movement and he and Rodríguez were credited with enlisting a notable number of young Charismatics to enter the national seminary. The number of major semi-narians grew from 22 in 1972 to 166 in 2001, probably due in some degree to the Charismatic renewal. A number of key leaders arose among Pana-manians, including Monsignor Alejandro Vásquez Ponto and various lay leaders. In 2000 Barrett and Johnson estimated that about 9 percent of Panama's Catholics were Charismatics and only 1 percent of its priests.

Uruguay

Despite being between Brazil and Argentina, Uruguay's Catholic lay and clerical population did not catch the great waves of the Charismatic renewal. Typically the Uruguayan national church went its own way, emphasizing apologetics, that is the defense of the faith in the face of an onslaught of what it called "sects": Mormons, evangelical Protestants, and so forth. In this tiny country, lay Catholic movements had been very active for decades in countering the strongly secular cast to the culture of a country where many European immigrants came as agnostic and un-churched. The lively lay publication *Razón y Fé* (Reason and Faith) was indicative of the priorities of the church. Its editors and contributors concentrated on popular presentations of theological and biblical scholarship. One of the editors, Jorge Novoa, is a married deacon who has been active in the Charismatic renewal since 2002, but other editors and contributors did not acknowledge being influenced by the renewal.[24] In 2000, the national coordinating center for the renewal listed only 50 prayer groups that met weekly and almost no priests. Barrett and Johnson estimated some 208,000 members, about 8 percent of the Catholic population.[25]

A notable exception to the lack of clerical participation has been the tireless work of Father Julio C. Elizaga. On his fiftieth anniversary for the priesthood he was honored by the presence of various bishops and many priests and laypersons, as well as the papal nuncio for Uruguay. He was commended for his parish work and social outreach to the poor but no mention was made in the Catholic or secular press about his Charismatic work.[26] Among his many written works, he published *La renovación Carismática en la Iglesia Católica* (The Charismatic Renewal in the Catholic Church).

Uruguay is the only country in Latin America, aside from Cuba, to experience a decrease in clergy. From 1957 to 2008, the number of priests decreased by 30 percent.

Paraguay

As with Uruguay, Paraguay also shares borders with Brazil and Argentina but does not share in its Charismatic fervor. A Redemptorist missionary priest, Andrés Carr, brought the renewal to Paraguay relatively late in 1973. The first prayer groups held meetings in the parish of Perpetual Help in the capital city, Asunción. The movement then spread superficially to other parts of the country.

On the occasion of the fortieth anniversary of the movement in the world in 2007, the movement's coordinators made it clear that positive ecumenical steps taken by Charismatics in Argentina would probably not be welcomed in Paraguay. A Paraguayan Charismatic commemoration concluded with this declaration: "The Catholic Charismatic Renewal was born in the Church and [exists] for the Church and if it does not serve this role, it is worthless."[27]

Such a statement ignores the origins of the movement in Pentecostalism and Protestants who helped to initiate the Catholic branch of the movement in various countries. The Paraguayan church had only an estimated ninety-nine thousand Charismatic Catholics, about 2 percent of the Catholic population, and few Catholic priest participants. Thus Paraguay had the least Catholic participation in the renewal of any country in Latin America.[28] The attention of most Catholics seemed to be drawn to the landmark election in April 2008 of a former Catholic bishop, Fernando Lugo, as president of the country, ending the sixty-one-year hegemony of the Colorado Party. The change of government took place without bloodshed, also an unusual event in Paraguay.

Conclusion

That the movement spread to all of the countries of Latin America is remarkable since other strong revitalization movements—such as Catholic Action and the Cursillos de Cristiandad—tended to be planted unevenly in the region. Perhaps this indicates the more universal appeal of a spirit-filled religiosity to Latin Americans and other Christians in the global south where the larger Charismatic movement has 500 million followers. The movement, in Lamin Sanneh's terminology, has high translatability.[29]

While the movement spread widely, significant growth did not occur across Latin America. This was indicated by the percentage differences within Catholic populations of countries. These differences probably point to the wave quality of Charismaticism; like the sea it surges and retracts. To say that the countries described in this chapter showed lesser growth is no sure prediction for the future.

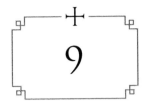

PUERTO RICO, CUBA, AND HAITI

Caribbean Exporters to the United States

In the surging sea of faith that the Catholic Charismatic Renewal (CCR) stimulated, the wave of enthusiastic faith spread first from the United States in the 1970s and began rebounding back to the United States a decade or two later. Small Caribbean countries under investigation here were part of this rebounding surge. These Caribbean Charismatics added to the revitalization of the church in the United States, joining Mexican and other Latin American immigrants, as already noted and as will be seen here and in the conclusion.

Puerto Rico

The Effect of Political and Cultural Turmoil on Religious Practice

The Catholic Charismatic Renewal arrived at a highly propitious time in Puerto Rico's history. Puerto Rico's Catholicism was most strongly tested by the series of events that followed the change of political regimes in 1898. The invasion by the United States and the abandonment of the island by the Spanish after four hundred years of rule and religious hegemony changed virtually everything for Puerto Ricans. Catholicism was no longer the state-sponsored religion. North Americans imposed a state education system administered by a Protestant pastor and aimed at converting Puerto Ricans away from Catholicism and toward North American Protestant values.[1] With the new regime, Protestant missionaries began actively proselytizing and challenging the Catholic Church's weak hold over the Puerto Rican faithful.[2]

Spanish clerical care in the Caribbean, especially in Puerto Rico and Cuba, had been highly deficient. (The Dominican Republic deserves separate attention.) There were not enough priests to give adequate pastoral care; religious education was sparse and shallow; and few Caribbean native-born persons joined the priesthood. By standards of local religious vitality, the Catholic Church was largely moribund in the rural areas of the Catholic Caribbean.[3]

At the time of the Spanish defeat in the Spanish-American War only 34 of the 137 priests were Puerto Rican.[4] The Puerto Rican Catholic Church was in terms of religious professionals a foreign church, a fact that was further emphasized when clergy and religious sisters from the United States gradually filled in for the departing Spanish bishop, priests, and sisters.[5] At a low point in this transition, of the 86 parishes on the island, only 34 were attended by clergy and of these some were barely taken care of.[6]

But there is a sense that at this lowest point in the history of Catholicism, Puerto Ricans began to take responsibility for their faith into their own hands and began a new era. A small number of convinced Catholic young laymen and women began to arise spontaneously as defenders of the Catholic faith in the remote mountain areas of Puerto Rico. They numbered several dozen and had an influence beyond their numbers. They were lay preachers, attempting to proclaim the main themes of the Catholic faith in confrontation with the Protestant preachers who had come in the wake of the American takeover. In many ways, they acted as precursors of the Charismatic renewal on the island.

The best-known lay preachers from this era were the Hermanos Cheos (Brothers Joe). They gained official approbation for their group from the North American hierarchy that took the place of the Spanish. The brothers went all over the island preaching Catholic orthodoxy and urging laypersons to seek the sacraments from parishes when parishes became staffed by the replacement priests from the United States. They built forty-six chapels as preaching points from which to evangelize as best they could through popular religion, especially using the principal Mysteries of the Faith (the so-called Joyful, Sorrowful, and Glorious Decades) contained in the rosary.

Samuel Silva Gotay, a major historian of religion in Puerto Rico and a Protestant, believed that the Cheos saved the Catholic faith of a majority of Puerto Ricans at the time.[7] But many Puerto Ricans joined historical Protestant denominations in the first decades of the twentieth century. This was just the first wave of direct challenge to Puerto Rican Catholics. Beginning in the 1940s, Juan Lugo, a Puerto Rican who had become a Pentecostal in California, returned to the island and set a religious fire going through Puerto Rico that was still blazing in the 1980s. Pentecostalism brought stagnation to historical Protestants as well as challenge to Catholics.

Catholics responded to religious challengers, among which was the African-based Santería, with a variety of responses.[8] Lay movements were the principal instruments of response through revitalization. Principal among them were the Cursillos de Cristiandad. These Short Courses in Christianity—a movement noted previously as a major precursor of the Charismatic renewal—were centered in four-day retreats for adult Christians. Since the Cursillos were largely led by lay preachers who emphasized the basic beliefs of the Catholic faith, these retreats were a natural evolution from previous efforts of the Hermanos Cheos and other lay preachers. In the early 1960s, Vatican Council II was an important influence in Puerto Rico[9] and set the stage for the Charismatic renewal, which seemed to embody the next step in spiritual growth for Catholic Puerto Ricans previously involved in other lay movements.[10]

In the 1950s and 1960s, the island and its diaspora were in political (and religious) turmoil. Puerto Ricans shot and wounded U.S. congressional representatives in Washington. Independence conspirators were picked up in Puerto Rico. And the Division Street Riot, involving Puerto Ricans, occurred in Chicago, among other critical events. The religious scene was turbulent for both Protestants and Catholics, with progressive reforms sought by leftist Protestants from Iglesia y Sociedad en América Latina (ISAL) and with radical criticisms of Catholic institutions by Monsignor Ivan Illich and other Catholic intellectuals in Puerto Rico, among other conflictual issues. The Charismatic movement arrived on the island in the early 1970s as this jumble of movements, causes, and personalities was reaching a stasis; that is, conflicts were diminishing and a search for spiritual growth was intensifying.

An ecumenical team came to Puerto Rico to conduct a Life in the Spirit retreat in November 1971. The team included Father James Burke, a missionary from Bolivia, and Father George DiPrizio, a missionary from Peru. They were joined by Rev. Joe Petree, a Methodist, and an unnamed

Protestant businessman from North Carolina. During the retreat, Father Tom Forrest, then working at Aguas Buenas, was baptized in the Spirit. This was "the event," the Charismatic scholar Peter Hocken wrote, "that loosed a flood of Charismatic blessing on the Island."[11] Forrest was made pastor of Aguas Buenas, near the city of Caguas. He and other Redemptorist priests built up Cristo Redentor, a retreat center that became famous throughout Latin America as a regional center for Catholic Charismatic Renewal, drawing many Catholics from the Caribbean and from Latin America.

Despite all of these efforts, further evangelization of Catholics in Puerto Rico was still needed. Archbishop Roberto González of San Juan brought new energy to the Puerto Rican church since taking over the see in 1999. One of his first acts was writing a blueprint for new evangelization in Puerto Rico.[12] Charismatics, who were numerous by this time, fit well into this activity. At the time of the Latin American Bishops Conference (CELAM) at Aparecida in 2007, Archbishop González reiterated that another wave of evangelization was needed for the island.[13] With a doctorate in sociology from Fordham University, he had a clear picture of the religious challenges facing the church.

The church's long-term response to challengers became more apparent when a sixth diocese was created within Puerto Rico in March 2008. After fifteen years of planning, the new diocese of Fajardo was carved out of parts of the San Juan and Caguas ecclesiastical jurisdictions, apparently to give greater focus to an area that was barely Catholic—15–20 percent—while the rest of the island was said by González to be 65–70 percent Catholic.[14] The Fajardo area was dominated by Protestant groups.

Thus, while Puerto Rican Catholicism was shaken to its roots by the change from Spanish to U.S. rule and cultural dominance, the open and free competition with other religions forced the Catholic Church to compete for the loyalty of its members, in part by offering spiritual goods that appealed to them—the sacraments, devotion to Mary and other saints, regard for the poor, and, more recently, physical and spiritual healing through the Holy Spirit. The new bishop of Fajardo appeared to be very much in that line of emphasis. His two master's theses were entitled "The Presence of Mary in the Popular Religion of Puerto Rico," and "Mary as a Sign of Hope and Liberation in Latin America."[15]

One should be clear that, despite the success of the Charismatic and previous lay movements, the spiritual renewal of the Puerto Rican church reached only a sector of the church. Many Puerto Ricans are similar to Judge Sonia Sotomayor of the U.S. Supreme Court, who was educated in Catholic schools but seldom attended Catholic Mass.

Unlike the Dominican Republic, where its great pioneering founder remained strongly based on the island, Puerto Rico's star, Father Tom Forrest, moved away from Puerto Rico and went on to larger transnational enterprises. Given Forrest's dynamism and organizational abilities, he went first to Brussels in 1978 and then to Rome to act as the director of the International Catholic Charismatic Renewal Office and chair of the International Council of the CCR. Among many other endeavors he coordinated a worldwide retreat for priests at the Vatican in 1984. Above all other enterprises, he promoted Lumen 2000, with hopes of raising millions of dollars so that five billion people would be reached by televised celebrations of the birthday of Jesus at the turn of the new millennium.

Despite Forrest's departure, Puerto Rico remained a hot spot for the movement. This was especially true at Aguas Buenas, where leaders from all over Latin America congregated from time to time. Indicating its early importance within the renewal within Latin America, Aguas Buenas was the site of the Third Latin American Encounter of the Charismatic Renewal (ECCLA III) in 1975. This was the first place outside of Bogotá to be chosen for the meeting. Leaders of the movement from that period recalled the meeting at Aguas Buenas as the reunion that consolidated the movement's growth and engendered a full regional cooperation beyond the Colombia-Bolivia axis and beyond Francis MacNutt's English-language mentorship.[16]

Latin Americans from other countries went on a regular basis to Aguas Buenas for inspiration and for a model of renewal they might replicate in their own countries. Among them was Father Jacinto Aguado, a priest from the remote area of El Petén, Guatemala. He learned of the movement at Aguas Buenas, which was then thought to be one of the movement's most active centers in the world. But with Forrest's attention on the larger picture, the center at Aguas Buenas lacked its wonderworker and, for a time, his level of dynamism. In other words, Puerto Rico had nothing comparable to Emiliano Tardif and his lasting heritage in the Dominican Republic, with his covenant communities and his religious-order brothers that Tardif had influenced to join in his work.

Nonetheless, several effects have remained as strong imprints of the movement upon Puerto Ricans. The first is healing. Two influential centers of spiritual formation on the island, Aguas Buenas[17] and Manresa, both included *sanación interior* (interior healing) as principal emphases of their centers.[18] Casa Cristo Redentor at Aguas Buenas offered Charismatic retreats for family healing and sent healing teams to families. Manresa offered not only courses on interior healing but psychotherapeutic resources as well.

Healing was already well embedded in Puerto Rican popular religion in the early part of the twentieth century. The Charismatic renewal added new weight through its emphasis on following early Christian beliefs in healing prayer and ceremonies. Most of all, the renewal conveyed what Michael Scanlon, the chancellor of Steubenville University, called "the testimony of hope of what the sacraments and ministries of the Church could be for people in desperate need of the healing power of Jesus Christ."[19]

Healing has been seen by investigators, such as Thomas Csordas, as especially important to Puerto Ricans. Csordas, who was trained at Harvard University in psychiatric anthropology, is a distinguished anthropologist at Case Western University. When Csordas interviewed Charismatic leaders in Boston they suggested to him that healing was "more liberating" for Puerto Ricans than for non–Puerto Ricans. This was in part because they reportedly experienced "deeper hurts" with respect to poor self-image as a result of colonial exploitation. They were also prone to what Csordas considered to be exaggerated guilt and remorse arising from intense moralism and from harboring deep emotional pain without expressing it. And they were subject to fear of the dark, of curses, and of spirits. These fears, Csordas believed, were often healed by Charismatic prayer.[20]

The second effect that has left a strong imprint on the Charismatic renewal in Puerto Rico and among Puerto Ricans on the mainland is the movement's strong emphasis on the family in ways that were not common among non-Hispanics. Many personal and family issues are treated as social issues. The Charismatic centers at Aguas Buenas and Manresa had healing teams among the lay auxiliaries that addressed individual problems but within a circle of family, friends, and neighbors. They carried out home visits by healing teams, in which friends and neighbors were included in the process.

Both centers include wide and active lay participation in retreat offerings. While Father Aurelio Adan Espinosa was the director of Manresa, dozens of lay associates had been working with priests for years to make

the retreats effective. The same is true at Aguas Buenas, where lay Charismatics act as worship leaders, prayer ministers, and members of healing
teams. Furthermore, regularly attended retreats throughout the island
continue to draw in people newly committed to spiritual renewal, the lay
apostolate, and older members.

Lay initiative is also evident in a singing and performing group called
New Pentecost, a Catholic Charismatic ministry of evangelization and
revival. The group specializes in Puerto Rican Christian *reguetón* music.
Again, as with other Charismatics (not older Pentecostals), they bring
their music and culture into the church. Wherever Puerto Ricans are celebrating religion, they seem to be having fun (or finding solace, at least).
Members of New Pentecost reach out to Catholics, going to virtually all
corners of Puerto Rico and to other countries as well, including Nicaragua and Venezuela.

More than forty years of the renewal produced a diffused Charismatic
influence upon the island's Catholics, with more than half a million, or
18 percent, identifying themselves as Charismatics in 2000. As seen, they
added yet another strong piece to the lay spiritual movements that have
been active in Puerto Rico and among the diaspora.

The Diaspora and the Renewal

It is not useful to discuss Puerto Rico and its Catholicism without also
discussing the Puerto Rican diaspora, since the two are intimately related. (Puerto Ricans have been citizens of the United States since 1917
and move to and from the mainland with ease.) Puerto Ricans perceive
a relatively equal split in their numbers, saying that there are about 8 million Puerto Ricans, 3.9 million who reside on the island and another 3.9
million who live mostly in the mainland United States.[21]

On the mainland they have been an important part of what Díaz-
Stevens and Stevens-Arroyo call the Latino resurgence of Catholicism.[22]
Díaz-Stevens, teaching and writing from Union Theological Seminary in
New York, was one among several scholars who called attention to the
Puerto Rican contribution to this resurgence;[23] that is, to the special contribution of Puerto Ricans employing popular religion and the Spanish
language within North American churches. The Charismatic renewal
came with Puerto Ricans to the mainland United States, as well. Thus,
a very rich mixture of Puerto Rican Catholicism with popular religion,

exuberant worship style, belief in healing, and other facets is part of the changing face of religion in Latin America and in the United States.

The importance of the Charismatic renewal in Puerto Rico carried over to Puerto Ricans resident on the mainland. A well-funded (and replicated) study by Pew found that a majority of Latino Catholics described themselves as either Charismatic or (Catholic) Pentecostal. In contrast, only 10 percent of non-Latino Catholics described themselves in that fashion. Of all the Latin American groups in the mainland United States, Puerto Rican Catholics identify as Charismatic at the highest rate, 62 percent. (The norm for Latino Catholics was 54 percent as Charismatic.) In general, Latino Catholics are four times as likely as non-Latino Catholics to identify with Charismaticism.[24]

However, Puerto Rican Charismatics are dispersed among Catholic parishioners on the mainland. They tend not to belong to Catholic Charismatic organizations. Thus, it would be easy to overlook them and believe, as some experts do, that the movement does not "amount to much" because they expect to see a formal Charismatic prayer or covenant group.

The character of Latino Catholic Charismaticism was focused upon by the Pew researchers in repeated studies because of its unique qualities. The researchers reached several conclusions: Contrary to past history, Latino Catholics currently are more likely to be Charismatic. Latino Charismatics place a strong emphasis on personal experience with God and on the role of the Holy Spirit. They do not place special emphasis on baptism in the Spirit as understood in Pentecostal circles but tend to emphasize the Catholic sacrament of baptism. One-third of Latino Charismatics participate in small prayer groups that include persons praying for miraculous healing or deliverance. They are familiar with such Pentecostal practices as receiving a word of knowledge or speaking in tongues, but they are far more likely to emphasize traditional Catholic practices. High percentages pray to Mary and believe in the Catholic Eucharist; half say the rosary once or twice a month and go to confession a few times a year. Latino Charismatic Catholics are comfortable with popular religion. This is a religiosity that adds on, rather than subtracts, and apparently fits in extremely well with the Latino religious resurgence that has been under way in the United States since the late 1980s and that is partly powered by traditional popular religion from Puerto Rico, Mexico, Cuba, Haiti, the Dominican Republic, and Central America.

Latino Charismatics are also an asset for Catholic pastors and their pastoral teams since they are more involved than most Catholics in parish activities, such as being a lector or a member of the parish council. They represent a break with the past tradition of being passive parishioners, being twice as likely as other Latino Catholics to serve in the parish. This surge represents a movement that has changed religion in Latin America and is having an effect in the United States.

Cuba

Growth amid Repression

Though not considered significant enough to merit much attention, the Charismatic renewal in Cuba bears observation because anything that manages to penetrate the obstacles placed on religion on the island and persevere for forty years is worth looking at. The Cuban government tightly controlled religion by controlling information and formation (education). That Catholics on the island were able in the 1970s to import religious innovations, such as the Charismatic movement, was remarkable since so few visitors were allowed into Cuba at that time. In fact, it wasn't until the 1990s that an opening to tourism took place. Certainly not many of the tourists in the 1990s came with the intention of bolstering religious belief and practice among Catholics. Rather, Cuban authorities granted some latitude for more public worship in the year before and the time during the visit of Pope John Paul II to the island in 1998.

The Catholic Church was so tightly controlled before the papal visit that individual Cuban Catholics found almost no opportunities for educational or occupational advancement in government, education, and the professions since openings to those positions were for Communist Party members. Christians were not allowed membership in the Communist Party in the first decades of the Cuban Revolution. Neighborhood Committees for the Defense of the Revolution also kept watchful eyes on who went to Sunday Mass or in other ways appeared to be a practicing Catholic, an undesirable trait in one aspiring to a position in society. These strictures worked both well and poorly. They helped to reduce the practice of attending Sunday Mass from about 4 percent of the population to about 2 percent. But the (largely bloodless) persecution reinforced and deepened the conviction of an important remnant that remained faithful to Catholicism.

Members of this group of a few hundred thousand persons found their own ways to renew and reinvigorate the national Catholic Church, which had been traditional and needing renewal at the time Castro took power in 1959 and then declared the revolution Marxist-Communist in 1961. In the 1960s and 1970s, the bishops and a few key laypersons were allowed to travel to church meetings outside of Cuba. Some Catholic publications and pamphlets from other countries found their way sub rosa to Cuban Catholics, so that they were, in a general way, able to keep up with what was going on in the church, especially the momentous changes of Vatican Council II in general and of the Latin American church in particular.

Mostly, though, the Cuban church received innovations through the reduced number of foreign priests and sisters allowed to work in the country after the revolution of 1959. Most U.S. missionaries departed in the early 1960s. Thus, the movement came to the island through one of its main sources: Canadian missionaries. In the archdiocese of Havana, Sister Eliette Gagnon, a missionary of the Immaculate Conception, started one of the first prayer groups in the country. Likewise did Father Iván Berguerón in the diocese of Matanzas. These foundings occurred in 1975, somewhat behind other countries and with a historical trajectory that stagnated quickly because of strong reaction "on the part of persons and Church circles, not knowing what they were doing, reacting against the movement." So wrote the anonymous historian for the movement as posted on the movement's Web site.[25] Only one group persevered at Havana. This lack of perseverance was attributed to the lack of knowledge about the movement, the relative isolation of Cubans from what was happening in the rest of the world and in the church, and the very tense relations between church and state. In other words, Cubans (maybe most people) need to see other people taking seriously unusual religious innovations before considering them seriously themselves.

For more than ten years one prayer group continued to meet in the parish of Corpus Christi in Havana, the only group that continued despite unspecified difficulties and criticisms.[26] The group did take in persons from other parishes for their formation as Catholic Charismatics, but it operated with extreme care not to "scandalize" Cuban seculars or Cuban

Catholics by the typical public manifestations associated with Charismatic religious practices, ones that would call attention to themselves.

Catholicism in Latin America, at least as practiced in Mexico and the greater Caribbean region, is a religion that takes to the streets especially processions, as during Holy Week. Cuban Catholics could not carry their religion to the streets and presumably turned down the volume of the loudspeakers and suppressed spontaneous jumping and dancing associated with Charismaticism. Hence, for lively Cuban Charismatics this repressed mode must have been a great sacrifice. Life in the Spirit seminars were conducted but not identified as such to avoid attention from the general public. A few participants in the seminars and the movement were said to have received baptism in the Spirit.

The movement continued in this subdued, largely subterranean manner for the better part of ten years until February 1986, when the monumental and defining meeting of the Cuban church took place: the Encuentro Nacional Eclesial Cubano (National Pastoral Encounter, ENEC).[27] It was the first national meeting of all ranks of the church since the revolution began in 1959 and it was preceded by months of preliminary meetings between clergy and laity to state clearly the position of the church within the context of a revolution that was not going away.

Without anyone planning it, so the official account goes, after the ENEC meeting Charismatic prayer groups began to multiply in the archdiocese of Havana.[28] Two months after the meeting six prayer groups had formed; six months after there were twenty groups. In April 1968 an archdiocesan Encuentro was held in the Havana archdiocese and shortly thereafter classes began for the persons responsible for the direction of the Charismatic groups. In August Charismatic leaders presented their report on the progress of the movement to the archbishop. Father Luis Entrialgo from the Archdiocesan Pastoral Council became the unofficial liaison between the archbishop and the movement. Two years later the archbishop made Father Entrialgo the official coordinator of the movement.

From these slow beginnings the movement spread in the 1990s from Havana to other regions of the island and included priests and laypeople. An estimate of the Charismatic movement in 2000 placed its population at 350,000 of about 4 million baptized Catholics. That amounts to about 8 percent of Cuban Catholics.

Two Founts of Charismaticism for Cuban Exiles

Cubans in the United States have two founts for becoming Charismatic. Some, especially later exiles—after 1985, say—carried Catholic Charismatic preferences with them from Cuba's renewal. But more likely Cuban Americans joined the movement in the United States. Several prominent Cuban Charismatics are typical of this sector. María Vadia, who was born in Havana, came to the United States when she was ten and remained a "Sunday Catholic," without interior devotion until entry into the Charismatic movement in 1987. This was the beginning of her extremely active pastoral life, while raising four children. She became an accomplished lay preacher, preaching around the world, including Indonesia and India. She authored three books. Locally, in Miami, she served as the leader of a prayer group for fifteen years and carried her ministry to women prisoners as well as the homeless. She was one of the main advisors to Magnificat International, a Catholic Charismatic fellowship of women with numerous chapters in the United States.

The change in style of religiosity was monumental not only for María Vadia but for many other Latinos and Latinas of that time. Faith moved from the "culturally conditioned, ritualistic faith into which most Hispanics are born," wrote Allan Figueroa Deck, "into a personal, relational faith experience that expressed itself in testimony and building community."[29] The Cursillos de Cristiandad and then the Charismatic movement especially promoted that sea change.

Thirty-nine Cuban exile men attended the first Cursillo in Miami in 1962, starting a spark of revitalization that led to a deepening of faith for dispirited refugees and which led them not only from the trauma of dislocation but to spiritual well-being through evangelization and pastoral care. This took place over decades. In general terms, there was a thick web of lay renewal organizations, with plentiful retreats that aided them. The Cursillos, the Movimiento Familiar, the Knights of Columbus, the Council of Our Lady of Cobre, and other movements were typical among Cuban Americans at that time. The intended goal was adjusting migrants to the American style of parish life, with its full panoply of parish institutions, such as parochial schools, religious education for students in public schools, adult Bible classes, communion breakfasts, and so forth.

The consequence of these movements, evident years later, was the increasingly active role assumed by the laity. In 1962 no Catholic laywoman from Miami, much less a Cuban American laywoman, was preaching all over the world, writing three books on spiritual growth, and visiting women prisoners in the city jail, as was María Vadia several decades later.

While she is exceptional in some regards, many other Hispanic and non-Hispanic lay Catholics have felt empowered to come forward for one or another ministry. A number of parishes in Florida were exemplary in the full range of organizations, ministries, and activities that were taking place. St. Agatha parish in western Miami had eight commissions of the Pastoral Council, forty-nine ministries, and twenty-five small base communities. The Hispanic pastor, Father Rolando García, supports a special group of Cubans who recently arrived in the United States to incorporate them in the church and U.S. society. This is not a passive experience. The newly arrived are asked to help one another and reflect together on their social dislocation and their faith in altered circumstances.

Dana Roberts, a professor of history at Boston University who has been studying and publishing on world Christianity for twenty-five years, believes that a different kind of Christian has been emerging from the organizations and processes described, especially when paired with the Charismatic movement. Cuban Catholics had been raised in a traditional church to receive, to have things (as sacraments) done to them. The active involvement—reflecting and acting on their own and with other laypersons—changed the process to empowerment. According to Roberts, "Not only a different kind of Christian, but a different kind of energy emerged."[30]

The Catholic Charismatic group at St. Agatha's, called the Disciples of Jesus, with its Friends of Jesus and Mary ministry for children, is but one of many movements and organizations at St. Agatha's. The incorporation of one or more Charismatic groups within parishes appeared to be typical of much of Florida. Rather than a movement sometimes previously found on the "fringe of real Catholic life," as one critic of the early movement told me, Charismatic groups are embedded in parish life. In the centrally located diocese of Orlando, twenty-eight parishes have Charismatic prayer groups as integral parts of the parish. In an ironic sense, Charismatics who were viewed as arising out of competition with Pentecostals find themselves in friendly competition with other Catholic organizations and movements.

St. Agatha's wide presence of lay movements was matched elsewhere. Chosen at random, St. Timothy's, the Catholic parish in Lady Lake, central Florida, had twenty-nine ministries, four clubs, and twenty-four spiritual movements, including small Christian communities and a Charismatic prayer group. Here again, Charismatics are one group among many others.

Raúl Angulo, a Cuban exile who was part of the Pedro Pan exodus of children from Cuba, became a priest through the movement. He had stayed away from attending church in the United States for many years until he participated in a Catholic businessmen's retreat in Conyers, Georgia, and thereafter joined a Charismatic prayer group at the Catholic Student Center at the University of Florida. After studying at university, he became a priest and served as the pastor of Mother of Christ, an extremely active parish in Miami.

Among Latino priests and laity in Florida, Colombia, and nearby countries in 2009 considerable mixing of Charismatic and non-Charismatic preachers at spiritual conferences and retreats seems to be occurring regularly. As Dana Roberts and other scholars, viewing the Charismatic movement globally, have pointed out, the Catholic Charismatic Renewal "pokes holes in categories of religion that are presumed to have high boundaries."[31]

The movement in Florida was grounded in parish prayer groups, but larger annual Charismatic conferences, diocesan and national, have been important for maintaining motivation and for incorporating new members into a wider world movement. Even the smaller diocese of Pensacola-Tallahassee had held twenty-seven annual conferences by 2009. In that year, four hundred participants met at the Edgewater Beach Resort at Panama City for four days. "All of us are in a different place in our journey," said one of the conference's organizers. "Some need spiritual renewal, some need guidance, and some need healing."[32]

The archdiocese in Miami was the bellwether for the movement in Florida and there, too, healing was emphasized. Healing meant a variety of things to the now thoroughly mixed group of Hispanics (Cubans and other Latinos) and non-Hispanics (Haitians and others). Healing the ills of uprooting and being delivered from spirits were foremost in the minds of some participants while the conference's organizers had in mind something more diffuse when they scheduled a ceremony of persons "in need of physical, spiritual, or mental healing."[33]

Another sector of Cuban Charismatics, especially in Florida and the Southeast, are lay Charismatic healers. These are mostly women from the movement who discern in themselves a special affinity for healing. The number of these healers is unknown. What little scholarly work on them has been done by Olivia Espín.[34]

Haiti

The very strong and public impact on Haitian Catholicism by the Charismatics was in contrast to the largely hidden effect of the Charismatic movement upon the national church in Cuba. Haiti became a major player in the Charismatic movement, with strong connections to its expatriates in the United States and Canada. Above all, the Charismatic renewal changed the practice of Catholicism in Haiti in important ways, reducing ties to liberation theology or to Vodou on the part of individual Catholics. The Charismatic renewal has shaken and re-formed Catholicism in Haiti and in the Haitian diaspora in the United States and Canada. (Canada is treated here only tangentially.)

The Charismatic renewal has gained a great following in Haiti. In doing so it is also replacing liberation theology as the dominant religious discourse (pro or con) of the clergy and of Catholic activists. The renewal came later and more quietly to Haiti than to much of Latin America. A Canadian nun began Charismatic prayer groups in 1972 among upper- and middle-class women in the capital, Port-au-Prince.[35] Because these meetings of the Charismatic groups were conducted mostly in French, lower-class Haitians who spoke only Creole were excluded. But after a few years, the movement spread beyond the enclaves of the capital and Creole became commonly used in Charismatic Masses and other services. With this change the movement began expanding with explosive force throughout the Haitian part of Hispaniola Island, matching the similar growth of its larger Spanish-speaking neighbor on the island, the Dominican Republic.

The renewal thus built bridges across the deeply embedded class divisions of Haitian society. In this social inclusion, the movement contrasted with the liberation theology for which Haitian Catholic activists were renowned but which largely attracted the poor that formed 80 percent of Haitian society at that time. The main carrier of liberation theology was Haiti's version of Christian base communities. These were called Ti legliz, Creole for "little church." The main person associated with liberation theology and the small communities was Jean-Bertrand Aristide, a former priest who became the president of Haiti (1991, 1994–96, 2001–4). Aristide was the more public face of liberation theology, but its wellsprings were deeply embedded for some time within the national Catholic seminary. There Father Gabriel Charles, one of the founders of the Ti legliz movement, was a longtime teacher and rector of the seminary. Aristide and the version of liberation theology he professed largely failed the hopes of the poor and were replaced by the attractiveness of the Catholic Charismatic Renewal. Aristide's failures as a political leader and his separation from the priesthood diminished younger priests' commitments to a liberation agenda but did not do away with their concern for social justice. Many younger priests were open to the influence of the renewal and so added both influences to their theological and pastoral kits.

The Great Challenge of Haitian Vodou

In addition to the positive qualities of the renewal shown in previous chapters and repeated in Haiti, the Renouveau Charismatique Catholique released practitioners from the considerable psychic and economic burdens of Vodou. Vodou is treated extensively here because it is a major force in Haiti while being virtually unknown to Catholics in the United States and Canada. When older North Americans hear "Vodou," they may be tuning in on Cole Porter's "Houdou, Vodou," but the image in their imaginations is more likely that of a zombie, as in *I Walked with a Zombie* (1943). Vodou became the native religion of Haiti and even recently was the living religion of a large number of Haitians, that is, four million persons.[36] Vodou was also commonly portrayed as touching the religious lives of Haitian Catholics in New York, Boston, Miami, and elsewhere. Such was the strength of Vodou in the 1980s that it gained adherents among even English-speaking persons who discovered it in the Vodou temples of New York.

The Vodou of New York was not the Vodou of Haiti, since Vodou absorbs local religious elements, adapting the religion to the area where it is practiced. If ever a religion was capable of showing its power of adaptation to social and economic conditions, of bringing meaning for many classes of people, it was Vodou. Through its ability to adapt it became a major religion in the Caribbean. But until recently Vodou was not well known, since through most of its long history it had to remain secretive. With the fall of the immediate family of Duvalier in 1986 (his political organization continued to a lesser degree), Vodou has been much more in the open.

Recent history thus allowed observers to view Vodou in ways not previously possible. What was hidden behind hedges or closed doors was practiced more in the open. After Baby Doc (Jean-Claude Duvalier) fled Haiti in 1986, Vodouisants were free to practice. This openness occurred not only because of Duvalier's self-exile but also from a long evolution of lifting the veil.

Historically, practitioners of Vodou had been secretive about its existence and its practices in part because the official religion was Catholicism and in part because Vodou was a hidden survival mechanism for slaves. The French and other upper-class overlords knew Vodou indirectly, often through rumors communicated in their social circles. What they saw, too, they sometimes feared: strange markers left at crossroads, ceremonies in cemeteries, and stories of bewitchment and poisoning. Antisuperstitious efforts were carried out at various periods, including campaigns by Haitian governments in 1896, 1913, and 1941. These campaigns reinforced the secretive quality of the religion and at times confirmed violent aspects of slave sects organized as rebellious.

As secrecy lifted, an increase in scholarly research on Vodou took place in the 1980s and 1990s, helping to bring forth works such as Leslie Desmangles's *The Faces of the Gods: Vodou and Roman Catholicism in Haiti*, which portrayed Vodou as a living religion and not as black magical mystery. While this was a fertile era for research, contemporary scholarly work was built on the long and solid work of predecessors, such as that of Alfred Métraux and Maya Deren.[37] Without them and the research of Bastide, Mintz, Hershovits, Price-Mars, Bastien, and others, the current work could not have been carried on.[38]

Vodou became a living religion for the masses of poor Haitians living in rural areas and also in towns and cities. Its relation to the upper classes has been more tentative. Perhaps no other Afro–Latin American religion gained the degree of hegemony of Vodou. Vodouisants accomplished this in large part because of a lengthy period of separation of Haiti from Rome and the Vatican from 1804 to 1860. During the period of revolution preceding the ascendancy of Jean-Jacques Dessalines, many missionaries were slaughtered and others departed in self-exile. When Dessalines and subsequent leaders gained control of the government, they made themselves the head of the church. The fifty-six years of separation from Rome allowed Vodou relatively free rein to develop into an amalgam of Christianity and African religion at the grass-roots level, away from the gaze of political leaders. The ruling black elites did not set the stage for this, for they too staged anti-superstition campaigns. Indirectly, the measure Dessalines and other leaders took in appointing largely uneducated ex-slaves as priests further weakened the church.

When the Catholic Church was allowed to return to the exercise of religion in 1861, it was "too late," as Desmangles says, for two generations of Haitians had lived without Catholic instruction and without personal experience of Catholic rituals.[39] Vodou was now firmly established as the religion of Haiti. Catholics, in Desmangles's view, had lost control, or, in a less severe judgment, would be playing catch-up for a long time.

After validly ordained priests and educated religious brothers and sisters from other countries took up residence as missionaries after 1861, the institutional church, typically with a small number of Catholic priests and sisters in cities and towns, pushed ahead with attempts to educate and evangelize. At times (1941 was the last), the church felt strong enough to seek alliance with the civil power to outlaw Vodou and to attempt to sweep it out of the country. In 1941 Opération Nettoyyage (Operation Clean-up) was carried out, in its latter stage with police help, destroying hundreds of ritual centers and paraphernalia.

That campaign marked the end of an era. Within twenty years the church would find itself the object of a cleansing "creolization" campaign. In 1960 François Duvalier expelled the European-born archbishop and three bishops, the Jesuits, many foreign priests and teachers, and closed the major seminary. Relations with the Vatican were cut off until 1966. Since then, foreign priests and teachers have returned, but leadership of the church has passed largely to Haitian bishops and priests who have practiced more tolerance of Vodou than foreigners. Then, with the death of the patriarch François Duvalier in 1971, Vodou priests and followers practiced more openly and denunciation of Vodou (as a religion, but not as an expensive way to rid oneself of evil spirits, often without results) by the government quieted. Ceremonial drums were heard again.

Unlike the plurality of African or Afro-based religions that grew in Brazil, Vodou achieved an underlying unity. As Desmangles describes it, Vodou is a "generic religion," one that embraces various tendencies, even "sects." Unlike Catholicism or Protestantism, Vodou has limited institutional structures: no central spokesperson, seminaries, formal schooling. Rather, it operates through informal recruitment and selection of *ougans* and *mambos* (priests and priestesses) and apprenticeship training.

Desmangles points to three factors giving Vodou its distinctive character. Out of the diverse religions of Africa, Vodou wove various patterns into a more unified fabric. Vodou continued African traditional religion with adaptations to fit the circumstances of its new land (slavery in Haiti instead of slavery or freedom in Africa). And it wove Christian and African elements into a distinctive religion, investing saints and African deities with new meanings. Not all was borrowed, however. Religious inventions were made in Haiti, including at least one important "sect" that advocated violence as part of its religious ideology when confronting the horrendous realities of slavery in eighteenth- and nineteenth-century Haiti.

What Vodou offered its practitioners was a remedy for ills, explanations for deeply felt questions, and hope that they would in some way survive death. In these basic quests Vodou did not differ greatly from some mainline religions. But Vodou shared features with borderline religions, such as the orgiastic cults of the Mediterranean, that made it seem more exotic to outsiders than it did to its practitioners: sanctuaries, dances followed by spirit possession, and initiation rites. As with many religions, Vodou demanded a sensitivity to the world of spirits, and ougans or mambos who cultivated a life of the spirit were especially useful in helping Vodouisants achieve direct access to the spirit world. Believers hoped that spirits would overtake and direct them as a rider does a horse at least once and, even better, several times in life, since frequency of spirit possession not only allowed one to "become god" but also increased religious commitment and authority within the community.

But Vodou also impoverished people who were already poor. Vodou ougans and mambos did not receive partial state support as did the Catholic Church for salaries or the upkeep of churches. Contributing to ougans was expensive and sometimes without the results that were hoped for. Thus, complaints about ougans were frequent.

The major contemporary step forward in the emancipation of Vodou was the Constitution of 1987, which granted religious freedom. But Catholicism was integral to many Vodouisants' lives. At least some practitioners believed they must be baptized Catholic in order to be Vodouisants.[40] From one point of view, as Desmangles described it, the rituals of Catholicism offered a means through which its communicants could participate in Haiti's official culture.

From another point of view, that of priests in Haiti, Vodou was part of

Haitian culture and was to be practiced when beneficial rather than be condemned. The easiest aspect of Vodou to deal with for many who were "singularly-minded" Catholics was healing. "There is no question but that *ougans* have remarkable knowledge of alternative medicine, especially with ailments of the tropics," said Father Gerald Fitzgerald, a priest who worked in Haiti and with Haitians in Boston. "I only regret that there are some charlatans charging plenty of money among the healers."[41]

Members of Haiti's elite class, which Desmangles estimated at 15 percent of the population in the 1980s, were traditionally ambivalent about Vodou. As bearers of high culture they had to show some distance from lower cultural expressions. Then, too, their knowledge of Vodou was indirect. They had to guess at what was taking place, hearing tales of werewolves and ceremonies of witchcraft. And at times in the last century members of the elite were killed by Vodou adherents, thus furthering the contemporary elite's negative impressions. Nonetheless, through contacts with trustworthy practitioners, upper-class members were drawn to the practice of Vodou.

Some upper-class Haitians, like middle- and working-class Haitians, practiced both religions without attempting to resolve contradictions and paradoxes. What, indeed, did Haitians have as the content of the intellectual side of their belief: that they were attempting to practice two religions, Catholicism and Vodou? Or, did they have only one faith, a Haitian belief in God? Desmangles presented a view that is more appropriate to academics, delineating the religions as two entities, as when he judges: "While there has been a Catholic influence, Vodou is more important in Haitian life."[42] This view has been eclipsed by later religious developments and research as will be seen.

In becoming president, Jean-Bertrand Aristide had to make peace with Vodou politically without doing so religiously. He had deal with the myth of the Haitian head of state as somehow connected to Vodou. The Haitian patriarch François Duvalier, who was the president from 1957 to 1971, wrapped himself in Vodou symbols: trekking on an arduous trip to a sacred mountain, receiving a spirit, maintaining a spirit room in the palace, and participating in religious ceremonies to control his enemies.[43]

Other religious forces were undercutting the hold of Vodou and its inclusion within the practice of Haitian Catholicism. Protestants, especially Pentecostals, grew from a small beginning in the country more than forty years ago to gain adherents among probably 30 percent of Haitians by 2008. These versions of Protestantism—there were more than one group—tended to emphasize Christianity as a refuge from evil spirits and freedom from the often considerable economic burdens of Vodou practice.[44]

In a word, Pentecostalism, including its Catholic variant form, the Catholic Charismatic Renewal, strongly resisted connections to evil spirits. Deliverance as previously noted is a recurrent important theme in Catholic Charismaticism. In relation to the bondage of Haitian Vodou, Métraux noted years ago that "Protestantism beckons as though it were a shelter, or more precisely a magic circle, where people cannot be got at by *lwa* or demons. . . . If you want the *lwa* to leave you in peace, become a Protestant."[45]

Since its inception in Haiti, the Charismatic renewal has offered the same magic circle to Catholics. The renewal offered a way to be Catholic, drop Vodou accretions to Haitian Catholicism, and turn one's back on the ancestral spirits that torment a person. Thus commonly in Charismatic healing services in Haiti participants give testimony to having been liberated from the *lwas*, the ancestors, and at times from zombification.[46]

Some scholars of Haitian religions have been slow to mark the changes in the growing lack of adherence and often outright denunciation of Vodou accretions to Haitian Catholicism brought on by the Charismatic renewal. Terry Rey, who has taught religious sociology both in Haiti and Florida, has challenged the perceived scholarly exaggerations about the degree to which diasporic Haitian Catholics practice Vodou.[47]

In observing the Charismatic renewal in Haiti and Miami, Rey has noted that in rural Haiti it became common for Catholic Charismatic missionaries to exorcize persons they judged to have been harmed by Vodou. Such exorcisms, Rey said, sometimes led to radical conversion experiences.

The Catholic Charismatic Renewal became a major and powerful break in the pattern of mixing religions or, as commonly called, syncretic religions. This break presumably opens the way to the practice of more orthodox Catholicism. It also lifts the economic and psychic burdens that following Vodou practices imposed. The renewal adds bounce and spirit to Masses and other religious services in Haiti and in Haitian churches in the United States and Canada.

Almost eight hundred thousand Catholics in Haiti are estimated to be deeply involved or leaning toward Charismatic practices. Some 9 percent of priests are reported by the movement to be Charismatic while 12 percent of the laity is so inclined. In the United States, the number of Haitian Charismatics is high enough that celebrations of the most important feast days for Haitian Catholics often have a dominant Charismatic tone and style in the larger gatherings, as at the Pierre Toussaint Haitian Catholic Center and Notre Dame d'Haiti Catholic Church in Miami.

Haitian Migrants and the Renewal

Few other migrants from Latin America took part in the renewal with the vibrancy and numerical strength of the Haitians. In part, this has to do with identity: Haitians affirm their identity as Haitian and Catholic through the renewal, which has given them reason to turn their backs on Vodou, enmeshed as it was with the practice of Catholicism in Haiti for generations. The renewal as practiced in Haiti and the United States also emphasized strong Catholic markers. Charismatics gathered in great numbers in both countries for the feasts of Mary, the Mother of Jesus, and they are at home in venerating the saints, in contrast to Protestant Pentecostals, who abhor both of these practices almost as much as they detest Vodou practices.

The vibrancy of Haitian Catholicism can be seen in Haitian Sunday Masses in Queens and Brooklyn, Boston, Washington, Miami, and other cities where the hundreds of thousands of Haitian expatriates live. More recently they have formed significant Catholic enclaves in Atlanta and other cities of the Deep South. Their lively practice of the faith is due in part to deeply held beliefs and is channeled through what they have learned of the renewal. The large percentage of Haitian adherents to Charismaticism can be seen in the crowds of Haitians who attend the national conference of Haitian Charismatics each year. Despite the relative poverty of many Haitian migrants, thirty thousand attended a recent national meeting and, on average, stayed at the meeting for several days.

Probably some one million Haitians reside in the United States. They began migrating in larger numbers in the late 1950s not only to escape the economic misery of the island but especially the political repression of the Duvaliers. The United States and Canada were seen as safe harbors.[48] Themes of liberation (theology) thus were especially appealing to them. Furthermore, moving to the United States meant separation from Vodou and the beliefs in evil spirits. Embracing the renewal became, as Terry Rey described it, "a welcome strategy to the Haitian diaspora, as immigrants may now maintain the familiarity of Catholic practice and still distance themselves from Vodou."[49] Whereas Haitians used to join Protestant churches to free themselves from Vodou beliefs in evil spirits, remaining Catholic (as a Charismatic) was the preferred option.

Remaining Catholic also meant the full embrace of Catholic feast days. In her dated account of Haitian celebrations of Catholic feast days in the Harlem section of New York City, Elizabeth McAlister described them as deeply infused with Vodou.[50] By contrast Karen Richman and Terry Rey have shown that Haitians in Florida tended to sever ties to Vodou.[51] Celebration of the Catholic feast days, especially those concerned with Marian devotions, became central to many Haitians in the United States and Canada. Of these celebrations none is more important than that of Our Lady of Perpetual Help, the patron saint of Haiti. In Miami the feast on July 27 has become a nine-day-long celebration (a novena). In attendance in 2002 were some fifteen hundred people for the three central days of the novena.

Haitian Americans stand out in their numbers in attendance and their organizational skill in the annual Haitian Charismatic Congress. The congress moves to various cities each year, piggybacking with the U.S. Charismatic Congress, sponsored by the National Catholic Charismatic Service Committee. Haitian Americans attend some sessions of the general congress but they come alive in their own congress. There they can use French or Haitian Creole. They ardently affirm their identity as Haitians and as Catholics, driven away from Vodou and from memories of authoritarian rule by the Duvaliers or their military successors.

In 2008 Haitian Americans held their seventeenth Haitian Charismatic Congress. Priests and lay leaders from Haiti have taken part in the annual congresses with their counterpart clerical and lay leaders from the United States. The congresses have been drawing large numbers from Canada, especially Quebec, where the Charismatic renewal has been enlivened by Haitians. The congresses have helped form a bond of cultural and religious identity and unity in a globalizing world. Haitians have been unusual in this regard. No other national group among Charismatics has matched their reach across international borders.

Haitian Charismaticism changed some of its characteristics in its relocation to the United States, with the inclusion of two aspects borrowed from North American black churches' preaching and affiliation. Priests ministering to the Haitian Catholic parishes, at least in South Florida, have adopted the call and response method of preaching familiar to those acquainted with Martin Luther King Jr. and a wide array of black preachers of the twentieth and twenty-first centuries. This style was reflected in the 1970s and 1980s in Haiti by Father Jean-Bertrand Aristide and other preachers of the Ti legliz movement. In this dynamic style preachers make key points by raising their voices and stopping at the syllables of a given word, allowing the congregation to call out the completion of the word. The other feature of contemporary U.S. parish life affecting Haitians is the free choice of parish. Instead of being constrained by the traditional views that one is bound to attend the church where one resides, Catholics have moved toward the selection of a parish based on the personal qualities of a priest who is assigned to a particular parish.

Often the choice of parish for Haitians is because Father X emphasizes healing or Father Y is especially adept at deliverance (or at talking about deliverance) from evil spirits. By 2007 several notable preachers appeared to have incorporated the twin strains of Haitian Catholicism—liberation theology and Charismatic theology—into an attractive version of Catholicism. On successive days for the major Haitian feast (and novena) of Our Lady of Perpetual Help, preachers took up as central themes Mary, the Voice of the Voiceless and Mary, the Mother of the Poor, themes closely associated with liberation theology, while adding devotion to Mary as a definite Catholic marker.

Conclusion

Puerto Rican, Cuban, and Haitian Catholics all went through severe challenges to their Catholic identities from hostile environments and from religious challengers. Catholics reinforced their commitment to the church through earlier lay movements, such as Catholic Action and Cursillos de Cristiandad, and later through the Catholic Charismatic Renewal. The renewal stimulated interest in spiritual growth and contributed to a spiritual reawakening in these countries.[52] Other religious groups, including Pentecostals, shared in this religious revival.

As strongly evident here, rational actor and subcultural identity theories help explain the processes of this growth. Within the supply side of religious goods, the Catholic Church through the Charismatic movement offered practitioners attractive ways to gain benefits from religion (healing, solace, deliverance) while emphasizing the sacraments and the popular religion that are hallmarks of Catholicism in the countries considered in this chapter.

For many persons, being Catholic is no longer a situation of having been born Catholic (inherited status) but of choosing deliberately and working to be Catholic (acquired status). The great church-state changes and increased competition eventually brought choices of religion and increased vitality resulting from personal ownership.

Large numbers of Puerto Ricans, Cubans, and Haitians also migrated to the mainland United States. While earlier Latino migrants from Latin America were somewhat hidden and subdued in parishes in the United States (having Spanish or Creole Masses in the basements of U.S. parish churches), later-arriving Latino Charismatics brought with them more open demands on parishes and a preference for Charismatic practices, such as expressive worship styles at Mass, more involved participation in parishes, and volunteering for leadership roles in parishes. Latino Charismatic Catholics added new life and numbers to U.S. Catholicism.

The journey also benefitted the migrants in ways that have yet to be analyzed fully. But clearly, belief in the deliverance and freedom from evil spirits promised by the Charismatic movement benefitted many from the Caribbean, especially Haitians, who believed in the influence of evil spirits. Catholicism in the Caribbean and mainland United States looks different in the twenty-first century and Charismaticism is part of the reason.

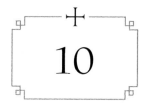

GUATEMALA

Evangelization and Mission

As a conclusion to the foregoing narrative of a surging sea of faith, Guatemala illustrates the inflows and ebbings of this sea, moved by various internal and external forces. Similar to the sea, its motions are endlessly fascinating to observe: turbulent on the surface while the main body shifts so imperceptibly that observers need to revisit often to record changes.

The Guatemalan Catholic Church was the prototype of a fading religious institution at the mid-twentieth century. It had few Guatemalan priests, had lost relatively more members to Pentecostals than any other national church in Latin America, was losing its influence among the majority of the indigenous population, and was soon to be assailed by internal war. Only a large influx of foreign missionaries and vigorous recruiting to lay revitalization movements pushed it back from further collapse.

Guatemala was the first Latin American country where the bishops approved the Charismatic movement. It is also the Latin American country with the highest percentage of Pentecostals (estimated at 25–30 percent of the national population). Furthermore, traditional religion has flourished in some sectors of its very large indigenous population.

In 1986 the bishops issued the "Guidelines for Charismatic Renewal" in which they noted the fruits of the action of the Holy Spirit in terms of deepened spiritual lives of laypersons and priests. They expressed the common fears on the part of church administrators that, without close watching on the part of authorized chaplains, "Charismatic groups easily go off the tracks" into such practices as peculiar kinds of prayers, exclusive attitudes (such as frowning on traditional Catholic forms of praying), and overemphasis on emotions. The approval came too late to hold on to perhaps the first Catholic Charismatics in the country. One of this group had participated in the Charismatic movement in the southern United States, formed a prayer group among family and friends, found no priest to act as chaplain, and turned to a Protestant pastor who reportedly used the group as the basis for forming one of the most important neo-Pentecostal groups in Guatemala City.[1]

A tentative start to the Catholic movement was made by three women religious and a respected lay leader who in 1971 and 1972 carried their enthusiasm for charismatic prayer to Guatemala after encountering the movement in other countries. They were part of the first group to take part in a Life in the Spirit retreat, the traditional entry point into the movement. This retreat was given in English by Francis MacNutt and his team at Casa Emaus in Guatemala City in September 1973.

However, the ultraconservative archbishop of that period, Cardinal Mario Casariego, who had heard of the movement through the archbishop of New Orleans, preferred to endorse the movement through inviting Father Harold Cohen, S.J., the coordinator of the movement in the archdiocese of New Orleans, to give a retreat in Guatemala City. Casariego convoked for December 1973 what he called the First Retreat in the Life of the Spirit. The movement dates itself from this time. Cohen preached his retreat in two sections, first to priests and brothers and then to religious sisters and laypersons.[2] The latter took place at the National College for Nurses. (The Guatemalan movement acquired an emphasis on health care that was extraordinary among national movements.) Casariego named one of his auxiliary bishops, José Ramiro Pellicer, his delegate to the movement.

Bishop Pellicer's appointment confirmed the archbishop's desire for strong organizational oversight and control. However, the movement flourished more through lay initiatives than hierarchical ones and followed the path of Cohen's own trajectory into mass communications.[3]

The movement expanded into other regions of the country, including the Petén, the northern deeply forested region bordering on Mexico that is the most remote section of Guatemala. The bishop there, Luis María Estrada, and Father Jacinto Aguado, a priest who knew of the movement from visiting one of its most active centers at Aguas Buenas in Puerto Rico, spread the movement quickly. When the bishop retired, his successor, a Salesian bishop, strongly supported lay movements, especially the Charismatic renewal and the Cursillos de Cristiandad.[4] The continued existence of the movement in the Petén indicated that the renewal was being actively promoted among Guatemala's indigenous Catholics. The indigenous had been largely overlooked in the initial stage of the movement in the country when it was fundamentally a European, white, and middle-class movement.

Vigorous activity by Catholic Charismatics brought great success in terms of recruitment into the movement. In 2006 the Pew Forum on Religion conducted a study of Pentecostals and Charismatics in Guatemala. The researchers found that about 60 percent of Guatemalan Catholics were Charismatic.[5] This may be the highest percentage in Latin America. In comparison with the other countries studied by Pew researchers, Charismatic Catholics are about 50 percent of the Catholic population in Brazil and about 25 percent in Chile.

The movement in Guatemala had several impulses toward outreach, unusual among Guatemala's previously introverted Catholics. One thrust was toward evangelization. This was believed by the archbishop and a number of other ecclesial leaders to be the principal goal of the movement. Lay members of the movement expanded the vision of the bishops to emphasize evangelization through mass communication, especially radio. By 1989 missionary work would also become a primary goal of a vibrant sector of the movement.

Catholic Charismatics in Guatemala were recruited from a very strong base of lay movements that took place in the country in the 1950s and 1960s. Catholic Action, largely imported by Spanish missionaries, was deeply rooted among indigenous populations in rural areas.[6] A similar lay movement, the Christian Family Movement,[7] took root in the cities, but in these urban areas Cursillos de Cristiandad was the main lay movement, drawing in some 50,000 laypersons, an extraordinary number in a country of 5.6 million inhabitants in 1973.[8] That the Cursillos were a stepping stone to the Charismatic movement has been noted in previous national histories. David Bundy, a religious scholar, considered the Cursillo movement "crucial for understanding the Catholic Charismatic Renewal."[9]

These older lay movements declined especially in urban areas after Vatican Council II (1962–65) because many clergy and laity believed that the new directions of Vatican Council II rendered them obsolescent.[10] The Cursillos especially were orphaned by the church.[11] However, the movements left several lasting effects. For one thing, lay members of these movements had grown accustomed to sacramental participation as part of their identity as Catholic to a degree that was uncommon in

Guatemala. For another, many laypersons had a desire for deeper spiritual lives. Lastly, lay members had grown accustomed to a high degree of lay leadership and initiative within the church through the movements. In the Cursillos they routinely preached during retreat conferences and during liturgical services. When the Charismatic movement arrived in Guatemala, it appeared to many laypersons to be the next step in their spiritual development.[12] For many laypersons, too, the Charismatic renewal would be a carrier of their apostolic zeal and of their desire to preach.

The Cursillos de Cristiandad were intense four-day retreats in which the essential beliefs of Christianity and personal conversion on the basis of those beliefs were stressed. Cursillistas who made the transition to becoming members of the Catholic Charismatic Renewal found evangelization and turning outward to others through mass communication (radio and television) a natural next step.

However, this type of public display of faith was not typical of Catholic believers of that era in Guatemala where Catholics did not attempt to share their beliefs with others. Catholics had also been greatly offended by aggressive public displays of religion first by historical Protestants from 1880[13] through the 1920s and 1930s when Protestant preachers took to the streets and second by the evangelistic rallies of the Central American Mission that filled stadiums. Then came a rush of North American Pentecostals and neo-Pentecostals into Guatemala following natural disasters and civil strife in the 1970s and 1980s.[14] More quietly, the Protestant groups that grew most in Guatemala, such as the classical Pentecostals associated with the Assemblies of God, began work in indigenous communities much earlier, in the 1930s.[15]

Beginning in the late nineteenth century, the Catholic Church in Guatemala fell on extremely hard times, weakened by anticlerical governments. The number of Catholic clergy was severely controlled and remained undermanned until the mid-1940s.[16] The arrival of Protestants, who had been personally invited by Guatemala's president, Rufino Barrios, in the 1880s, had evolved into a massive Pentecostal challenge to the Catholic Church by the 1970s.

The Indigenous and Catechists

Protestants were not historically the first major challenger to the Catholic Church. Rather, that challenger was indigenous religion. What was *not* widely understood about Latin American Catholicism was that the Catholic Church had largely lost control of native religious practices. Large areas of Latin America were priestless and had been for generations.[17] Beginning in the early 1800s, clergy left indigenous regions in large numbers. Spanish clergy, affected by the wars of independence, went to other regions of the world. Anticlerical governments in some regions, as in Central America, were determined to maintain a reduced influence of the church. Guatemala, the largest of the Central American countries, restricted the number of Catholic clergy to about 110 from the late 1870s to the 1940s.[18] As a result, indigenous areas had very few resident clergy, and visiting clergy typically came only for yearly celebrations of local fiestas.

These fiestas, central to the religious culture of the indigenous populations, came increasingly to be organized without priests by what anthropologists called the civil-religious hierarchy. This local organization saw that *la costumbre*, centered in yearly religious celebrations, was carried out. Thus the *cargo* religious system, with its economic burdens of sponsoring fiestas, passed from loose church control to native religious leadership. Under supervision of the civil-religious hierarchy, members of the local communities routinely assumed *cargos* (offices), sponsorship of fiestas. These responsibilities implied great economic hardship. Assuming the role of *patrón* for a fiesta meant that Indians exhausted their slim economic surpluses to maintain a traditional religious system.[19]

Thus, in the absence of priests, the native religious system rebuilt itself. It was this civil-religious hierarchy of native religion that offered opposition to the Catholic missionaries of the twentieth century. When Maryknoll missionaries from the United States turned to sending missionaries to Guatemala instead of China in the 1950s, they found no priests resident in the rural areas where most Indians resided. What they and many other missionaries encountered was passive-aggressive opposition to their presence by the civil-religious leaders who viewed the Catholic priests as usurpers.[20] Maryknoll missionaries expected to take over abandoned churches and other buildings left unused by Catholic priests for decades. Instead, native leaders, sacristans, and majordomos resisted turning over church keys, prized images of patron saints, and use of buildings.[21] Not only was the *cargo* system a religious enterprise, it was an economic microsystem as well, and it was seen as being challenged by the missionaries.

Thus the Catholic Church found itself in a deeply pitched struggle to regain the hearts and minds of hundreds of thousands of indigenous souls. (The notable struggle of Protestant churches with native practices took place alongside the Catholic Church's efforts. The Protestant effort deserves separate attention.)[22]

The struggle was titanic. The stakes were high in this religious competition. The church could have lost millions of indigenous peoples to the practice of native religion. Orthodox Catholicism, as understood by North American, Spanish, and other European missionaries, was pitched against the heterodox understandings of a Christianity thoroughly mixed with traditional religious practices that had returned or intensified in the absence of priests.

Thus this mid-twentieth-century battle meant that the Guatemalan church was faced with the challenge of indigenous religion.[23] The struggle was a fitting prelude to the challenge of Pentecostalism, which has intensified in the present century. In both cases catechists were central actors. The missionaries who took charge of the church in indigenous areas from the 1950s onward had to engage in a renewed evangelization of these peoples.[24] This they did through training indigenous evangelizers. More commonly called catechists, these persons not only had to teach their peoples in their native languages but they also were responsible for Catholic worship and other aspects of church life, such as care of the sick, in their communities. In the interaction of catechists and missionaries it became clear that the Christian faith had to be made understandable to the members of the culture being evangelized. In turn, the missionaries began their own theological valuing of the indigenous religious experience and of its cultural expressions. Cultural adaptation, commonly called enculturation in the Catholic Church, was taking place.[25]

The catechesis had a strongly biblical content reflective of the biblical renewal in the Catholic Church in the twentieth century. This gave it evangelical dynamism and the capacity to sustain a renewal. Furthermore, as John Gorski notes, the Latin American missionary resurgence (Latin Americans becoming missionaries) had its origins in the grass-roots challenges of the indigenous ministry.[26]

Two types of catechist may be noted here. Several hundred thousand worked in the special field of the indigenous church. For all of Latin America, I estimate their number as being in the four hundred thousand range.[27] They deserve the special title of catechist because they mainly deal with evangelization among peoples of non-Christian religions. The Vatican congregation dealing with this type of evangelization calls them catechist-leaders, implying a role and status in their community beyond that of mere teacher. Thousands of indigenous individuals became catechists in Guatemala during the 1960s and 1970s.

The other catechists—perhaps eight hundred thousand—were mostly working as adult religious educators among the 90 percent of the population of Latin America who are not indigenous. The majority of this sector of catechists became active in the 1980s in the new evangelization, described earlier. They tended to be roughly similar to teachers of adults' and children's Sunday schools, without necessarily implying community leadership. But in Latin America they did share in the missionary function of the church.

To begin a discussion of what catechists represent institutionally, I turn first to the role of the more traditional catechist, the one working among the indigenous peoples. A monumental task of the Latin American church in the last half of the twentieth century was creating an indigenous church. Guatemala, with 55 percent of its people being from Mayan backgrounds, was a major area of the indigenous church. For centuries the church attempted to assimilate its indigenous populations into a standardized Western mold. But a major shift in policy from integration to cultural diversity occurred at Vatican Council II: the church wanted to respect cultures other than European to the degree that the seeds of revelation were thought to be present in other cultures. At the very least Christians in contact with other cultures would have to look for expressions of the divine in those cultures.[28]

Furthermore, lacking a native clergy, the indigenous church could have catechists. Catechetical centers trained persons especially in understanding the Bible. These centers became something similar to indigenous seminaries. For at least fifty years the practice grew of having a native catechist in each rural settlement area.

Under the impact of the missionary presence religious life has changed in many areas of the Central American and Andean regions where most Indians reside. Missionaries and their catechist collaborators conducted intensive educational campaigns to re-evangelize the Indians. These modern efforts often included innovations such as rural Catholic Action with small cell-like study and prayer groups, and memberships in cooperatives and credit unions; that is, they comprised strategies that included political action or socioeconomic betterment. Kay Warren, Hans and Judith Buechler, and other anthropologists noted the effect of missionary work in the shift toward a more orthodox Catholicism.[29] They called this religion either folk Catholicism or reformed Catholicism, in contrast to *la costumbre*, the indigenous religion that centered its practice in fiesta sponsorship. The fiesta or *cargo* system had held a hegemonic grip on community life in much of Central America and the Andes for decades. The hold of fiesta sponsorship has diminished to a considerable degree. In some areas it is gone entirely.

Furthermore, Warren and others traced changes in Indians' consciousness that resulted from their new openness to acculturation and participation in development projects. The Catholic Action groups, called by Warren study groups, were small groups that acted as compensation for the lack of priests and decentralized the large territorial parishes and the settlements tied to parishes. Catechists were typically community leaders trained for evangelization and leadership within Catholic Action. These Catholic Action cells were in direct opposition to the civil-religious hierarchy that controlled the religious beliefs and central rituals of the Indian brotherhoods, the *cofradías*, that perpetuated unorthodox religious beliefs. Catholic Action was only one of the challenges to the power of the civil-religious hierarchy. Modernizing forces of various origins were taking their toll on traditional indigenous authority, especially twentieth-century-style political parties that made incursions into indigenous territories to organize electoral politics.

The contemporary history of the indigenous areas has been playing out in an entanglement of local and global forces.[30] Indigenous ethnic groups have been interacting with national political forces as well as international market penetration. Fundamentally, the situation touches upon personhood and identity, an interaction of religion, persons, community, nation, and the parts of the larger world that affect Central American and Andean agriculture, commerce, and economic lives. Viewed from the grass roots, catechists act as a major factor in the processes affecting changes in personhood among the indigenous that have been taking place in these areas.

Catechists are lay specialists, mostly volunteer actors in Quiché and other indigenous communities. Missionaries have been important in indigenous revitalization but catechists are equally important. Catechists recruit and lead. They act as intermediaries between missionaries and communities. They act as a new layer inserted between original layers of a religious organization, that is, between priest and congregation. They became increasingly important actors in the wide, intense, and influential discourse of ethnic identity that has been taking place in the indigenous resurgence occurring in Latin America.

Making persons catechists—that is, investing them with an official office in the church—creates a role, brings forth a commitment and recognition, and establishes responsibility. Official roles anchor an institution. Persons view themselves differently as do others who view them as having a new capacity. Furthermore, status within an institution matters within most societies, certainly within Latin American societies.

Status helps to ensure incorporation within an institution. A commitment to a duty or responsibility on the part of the layperson who becomes a catechist is required, increasing loyalty and decreasing the likelihood of being drawn off by competitors. Indeed, one of the chief characteristics of the Pentecostal and evangelical competitors to Latin American Catholicism has been the assumption of organizational duties. These competitors have a low threshold of entrance requirements and a regular progression of duties within the churches, from tidying up after worship services to public-worship reader to street apostle. In other words, most of the rapidly expanding churches in Latin America bestow increasing levels of responsibility upon new members. This, in turn, reinforces affiliation. Thus, one can trace a discernible conversion career pattern (here thinking of conversion as a deepening commitment), including increased responsibilities within the institution, as Henri Gooren and others have shown in *Conversion of a Continent*.[31]

The need for the office of catechist flows from the nature of modern organizations. Max Weber argued at the dawn of the last century that modern institutions accomplish their goals through making the goals the responsibility of designated, specialized officials. Catechists have come forward to become designated, specialized officials for informal education in the church. (Again, these are shared goals and responsibilities with priests and other officials.) Most catechists are unpaid but understand that they fulfill a vital function in the church. In the process of being catechists they acquire a sense of ownership. They are the ultimate fulfillment of that policy choice of *pastoral de conjunto* (clerical-lay shared leadership) made at the time of the bishops' return from Vatican Council II, as previously described.

Turbo-Charged Efforts

There is a strong sense of urgency in what many groups within the church are doing to employ laypersons in evangelization. Many of the persons becoming active in the third millennium of the church are, in fact, "turbo-charged"[32] by the need to the meet the Pentecostal challenge that took away millions of poorly educated Catholics.[33]

The second—and internal—impetus for recruiting men and women as catechists centered in the renewal efforts that swept through the Latin American church in the latter third of the twentieth century. Evangelization efforts in Latin America have produced the hundreds of thousands of lay catechists who work with the majority non-indigenous populations.

As a goal of the whole church (not just the ordained), evangelizing was clearly invoked by the Latin American church at the Latin American Bishops Conference (CELAM) at Puebla in 1979.[34] In the 1980s, persons in lay renewal movements in the Latin American church—movements already described—reached a level of maturity at which they wished to share their intensified faith and spirituality with other Catholics. Members of the Catholic Charismatic Renewal were in the forefront of this impetus.

One of the first great signs of this Charismatic thrust was Evangelization 2000, which was headed by Father Tom Forrest, a Redemptorist missionary who had achieved admirable results working in Aguas Buenas, Puerto Rico. Evangelization 2000 was started in 1986 as a very ambitious project promoting a decade of evangelization in anticipation of the great jubilee year 2000. By the following year, *Christianity Today* was reporting that the ten-year project hoped to raise one billion dollars and would culminate with a worldwide satellite telecast on Christmas Day in the year 2000 when the pope would speak to a potential audience of at least five billion people. The project, said Forrest, looked forward to giving Jesus Christ a two-thousandth birthday gift of a world more Christian than not.[35]

At the same time in the late 1980s, the Latin American church had its attention focused more immediately on two events that would occur in 1992, not 2000. The events overlapped: the fifth centenary of Columbus's arrival in Hispaniola (the present-day Dominican Republic and Haiti) and the Latin American Bishops Conference that would take place at Santo Domingo, the capital of the Dominican Republic, in October 1992. The juxtaposition of 1492 and 1992 suggested a contrast between the first evangelization, considered a providential but incomplete event, and the need for a new evangelization; that is, presenting the Christian message with greater intensity than was typical of Latin American Catholics and with attention to the evangelization of cultures. General conferences of the church in Latin America are preceded by months of preparation, including the preparation of conference documents by theologians and pastoral experts, consultation about these documents with laity and clergy, and discussions of the vetted documents among bishops at meetings within national bishops' conferences.[36] The results of these consultations were then passed on to participants of the CELAM in Santo Domingo. There as he presided over the meeting, Pope John Paul II further highlighted evangelization. The Santo Domingo document reflected this priority.[37]

General conference documents are taken seriously in Latin America. The national episcopal conferences use the general conference statements as the starting point in their strategic planning. Many conferences use formats such as three-year or five-year plans, readjusting their priorities and evaluating their progress against these plans.

John Paul II reinforced evangelization through his frequent and widely noticed visits to Latin America. In these visits he further elaborated his ideas to reinforce his strong concern that Catholics use modern technological media for their message (and not allow this field to be dominated by evangelical and Pentecostal competitors). He was especially emphatic about evangelization by mass communications in his pastoral visit to Guatemala in 1983.

Since evangelization, first as well as new, was the main topic on the table within the Latin American church, it became the theme that was hotly debated and eventually accepted as the Latin American church's first priority. The topic was contested because a number of progressives considered poverty and development more urgent than evangelization at that time.

The groups that stepped forward to take the lead in evangelization in Guatemala were from the Catholic Charismatic sector. These groups were diverse in their founding, the dates of entry into evangelization, and the means they used in evangelization.

Leading Edges of the Guatemalan Renewal

Guatemalan Charismatics went quickly through the stages shown in other countries: at the beginning, virtually everyone belonged to a prayer group and then some prayer groups evolved into covenant communities. The covenant communities typically had core groups whose members lived common lives, with shared prayer and shared income, and communities of alliances whose members supported the core groups especially through economic sharing. Core groups typically had well-defined ministries.

One of these core groups came to be called Eventos Católicos (Catholic Events, or Happenings). Its members described themselves as laypersons burning with the love of Christ.[38] The center of its activities was a radio station, Radio Eventos Católicos.[39] From this radio ministry a much larger enterprise sprang up in May 1994: Obras Sociales de Eventos Católicos. These social works were conceived by the core community to meet basic needs in the country and to give aid to persons in need without discrimination. Whatever their diffuse plans were in 1994, their helping others came to be focused on health and the distribution of used clothing and toys.

The community's grand event became the Catholic International Fair (Feria Católica Internacional) that ran for four days once a year. By 2008 the fair was being conducted in a large area of Guatemala City, la Parque de la Industria, and drew two hundred thousand people from twenty countries, making it the largest event of its kind in the Americas. Many people were drawn to the one hundred musical performances, but also on display was a full panoply of Catholic organizations from some six hundred parishes and from many other organizations, including religious communities, confraternities, Charismatic organizations, and youth groups. In later years free medical attention was added. Fifty thousand people received medical attention, food, and an estimated one million pieces of clothing in one recent year.

Much of Eventos Católicos's regular outreach became concentrated in health care. On a daily basis some three thousand people were treated in the group's clinics in various places in Guatemala City. Eventos Católicos also had mobile teams that traveled on invitation to various parts of the country for health clinic weekends. Similarly, it sponsored visits of foreign medical specialists to Guatemala for special medical interventions beyond the capacity of local doctors. A chain of pharmacies cooperates with Eventos Católicos in making a variety of medicines available. This emphasis on health flowed from the emphasis on healing that marked this Guatemalan movement, including its slogan that divine love in itself heals.[40]

The white-hot competition with Pentecostals increased a desire among many Charismatic Catholics to meet this competition head-on. One area where Catholics had clearly failed was mass communications, specifically radio and television. During his heyday in the 1980s, Jimmy Swaggert, the U.S. Pentecostal television evangelist, brought record crowds to his stadium appearances and home audiences to his television presentations during his regularly occurring visits to Guatemala. He also began pledging money to Pentecostal schools, called by locals Swaggert schools. (Swaggert later reneged because of financial problems and the schools were reported to be struggling.)

The more constant irritation for Catholics was the dominance of Pentecostals on radio, a medium enjoyed by all in poor countries. Catholics felt excluded by the constant evangelical messages on the radio in a country where Catholics had held a monopoly on religion for four hundred years. Some of the first messages of Catholic resistance were those posted in 2000 and 2001 on billboards in sections of Guatemala City, such as municipal zone 7 near the center of the city. On the billboards appeared pithy messages sponsored by Catholics, either attacking Pentecostals' alleged slandering of Catholicism or promoting private Catholic schools as alternatives to false doctrines taught elsewhere. But many cab drivers, housewives, and teenagers found the Pentecostal radio messages, music, and chat shows their constant companions.

Thus, Catholic Charismatics moved into radio ministry full blast without a grand plan but with plenty of entrepreneurial zeal. They put six stations on the air and supplied Charismatic programming for already existing stations. Eventos Católicos became one of the leading purveyors of Catholic messages, or evangelization, on AM radio. The group backed this up with radio programs available on the Internet.

Eventos Católicos was much more than a handful of believers trying their hand in radio. The community began in 1984 through the initiative of Orlando Coronado Juárez, who up to his conversion to Charismatic Catholicism had been a singer-songwriter working in various countries.

Coronado, his wife, Anabella, and other laypersons formed a covenant community to work full time in radio and similar activities emphasizing what they called *eventos* (events), such as retreats, concerts, congresses, and information communicated by radio. Coronado and his associates needed financial backing. They sought one thousand families through a project called Pesca to back them up through regular donations of the equivalent of U.S.$2.25.

The radio station celebrated twenty-five years in 2008. Eventos Católicos would count as its major activities the annual Catholic International Fair and its associated Festival de Canción Mariana (Marian Song Festival). Coronado saw these activities as the active making of peace in a country still in the grip of violence after years of internal war (1954–96).[41]

Two years after Eventos Católicos began its radio broadcasts, another Catholic station, Radio Estrella FM, came on the air with a strong Charismatic orientation as well. The station was controlled by laypersons and aired virtually all religious content, again aimed at evangelization. The station celebrated twenty-two years of broadcasting in 2008. As Byron Valdizón, the station's director, noted, it was no small achievement, given the lack of advertising and expensive news reporting, to keep listeners up to date on the church in the world and in Guatemala. The station aimed at *promoción humana* (social assistance) but seemed to steer away from issues of social justice.[42]

The Salesian religious congregation is among the largest and most influential religious group of men through most of Latin America and especially in Central America. Salesians were especially involved in spreading the Charismatic movement in Guatemala, including former students from their high school, María Auxiliadora, in the capital city. A group of these alumni, calling themselves Hombres Católicos en Acción (Catholic Men in Action), worked for twenty years at spreading the Charismatic movement through giving more than forty retreats, prayer luncheons, and ninety-minute radio program.[43]

None of that initiative would seem extraordinary among Pentecostals, but it was highly unusual among Catholics, especially those educated by conservative priests. Here were laypersons organizing closed retreats, preaching most of the conferences, and putting forward at length their ideas about the Catholic faith on the radio.

Central Personalities and New Ministries

Out of the considerable Catholic revival that began in Guatemala in the 1970s has come an unusual Catholic Charismatic: Josué David Cruz Urratia. He has become one of the great lay preachers in Latin America produced by the renewal. By 2008 he had preached at more than one thousand Charismatic retreats, drawing thousands of persons into the movement in various parts of the world and inspiring laypersons to take private vows (as he has) and devote themselves full time to religious work.

His own life, and that of many other Guatemalan Charismatic leaders, preachers, and entertainers, was clear evidence of the generational effect of earlier lay movements and the religious renewal that took place in Guatemala beginning in the 1960s. His parents spent some fifty years in the Cursillos de Cristiandad and in other apostolic movements. They became active in the Charismatic movement and Fernando Cruz, Josué's father, served as the president of the Cursillo movement. (Cruz's parents later joined in their son's Charismatic missionary endeavors.) One of Josué's earliest memories is of waking up and finding his father reading the Bible early in the morning. As a young person he felt, though, that he had not yet received his own special calling. That vocation became clearer when he participated in a long retreat while in high school. Josué had a spiritual experience leading to a radical conversion and months of spiritual ecstasy. His unusual behavior and temporary aloofness after this experience alienated his high school friends for a time, but Josué eventually won them over and some of his friends joined the prayer groups that he organized.

After high school, Cruz wanted to become a missionary (a dream shared by few Latin American laypersons at the time) and went to the archbishop to ask for counsel. Archbishop Próspero Penados del Barrio advised him to obtain a university degree and come back. Cruz graduated as an industrial engineer and returned. He consecrated himself to God as a layperson with private vows. His first goal was organizing a lay community called Dios Habla Hoy (God Speaks Today). He spent fifteen years fostering this community before taking the next step of creating the Charismatic community called the Misioneros Contemplativos del Sagrado Corazón (Contemplative Missionaries of the Sacred Heart) in 1989. The members of the community gave themselves full time to promoting and conducting Cruz's principal work, el Centro Misionero Católico Internacional (the International Catholic Missionary Center).

Basically an innovation of the Charismatic movement, this founding by laypersons of a missionary group sent and sustained laypersons as missionaries. For some centuries missionary activity involved in the globalization of the church, that is, the planting of the organization in China, India, and elsewhere, was conducted by religious orders of men and women. Lay missionary societies were more commonly found among Protestants. It appeared that missionary energy from Latin America—lacking for centuries—was now so strong that it flowed through new channels. What is clear is that there is a new age of the laity in the Latin American church.

Cruz and his associates began the mother institute, the Centro Misionero, in Guatemala City in 1989. In the next two decades they expanded into other countries; in 1999, they created a second center in Guatemala at the indigenous area of the Petén. To establish anything in the Petén three years after the peace accords took place and while chaos and violence flooded through the region required extraordinary faith (or imprudence).[44] Ten years later the Centro Misionero had a small group of followers at Santa Elena, Flores, in the Petén. They worked at moving from door to door, in visits similar to their evangelical brothers and sisters. They organized communal forms of prayer (including evening adoration of the Blessed Sacrament), and radio programs for Radio Tikal.

By 2008 missionary centers had been established in Costa Rica, El Salvador, Puerto Rico, Peru, and Chile. The most successful outpost was at Arequipa, Peru, where a longtime Guatemalan associate of Cruz, César Folgar, was gaining audiences on radio and television.[45]

Other notable laypersons came from Guatemala's Charismatic renewal. No accurate account of the number of covenant communities in the country has been made. Nonetheless one of the most flourishing was the Charismatic group called Jesús Resucitado in Guatemala City, whose sixteen branch communities had more than twenty years of nourishing their members.

The Jesús Resucitado community helped to put Giovanni Blanco, a singer, on stage and in the sanctuary. The liturgies and celebrations of Charismatic groups like Jesús Resucitado, often in parish settings, nurtured ministries of praise or song, which were new full-time ministries for Catholics.[46] Giovanni Blanco spent years coordinating prayer groups until, at the end of 2001, he assumed the role of minister of praise or minister of song at various Charismatic festivals and concerts in the United States,

Europe, Mexico, and throughout Latin America.[47] He also cut eight solo CDs and five with a group.

Also well known in Catholic popular music circles is Silvia Mertens from Guatemala City. She came into the renewal in 1982 and by 1985 decided to dedicate herself full time to the ministry of praise as a soloist and as a member of the group she founded, Buenas Nuevas. Through the years she has sung, preached, and entertained throughout Latin America, as well as the United States, Europe, and Israel.[48]

The Consequences of Religious Renewal

The Catholic Charismatic movement was not the only source of the generalized religious renewal that took place in Guatemala from, say, 1972 to the present. As noted, the Cursillos de Cristiandad, especially among Guatemalan Catholics of European ancestry, and Catholic Action among the indigenous contributed mightily to this renaissance. But those movements diminished and the Charismatic renewal took center stage. All of the movements emphasized *pastoral de conjunto*, bringing laypersons into the life of the church. The movements recruited and trained people to enter into this deeper affiliation. The net effect was the strengthening of families and individuals and the enlistment of these talents for the church and often, as well, for society.

Increases in vocations to the priesthood and religious life are strong indicators of the effects of this renewal. In Guatemala the number of priests increased 301 percent between 1956 (when the first surge of missionaries occurred) and 2006. This increase occurred despite the loss of eighteen priests who were murdered and attrition in the priesthood due to aging and to the loss of many foreign missionaries who returned home. In the 1960s the percentage of foreign priests was calculated as 81 percent of the Catholic clergy.[49] Now virtually all new priests are Guatemalan. The number of seminarians in Guatemala—signs of the future—increased 169 percent from 1972 to 2006. The numbers of seminarians had been dismal in Guatemala: 54 students attended the major seminary in 1956. The number in 2006 was 343.

Women in religious life in Guatemala grew from 1,018 in 1972 to 2,743 in 2006. In contrast with the decrease in the numbers of women religious in the United States and Europe, the women religious of Guatemala are thriving. They are also actively engaged in civic and religious organizations to rebuild the church and society.

Despite lay catechists being the targets of thousands of political murders in Guatemala from 1954 to 1993, by 2006 their number had increased phenomenally to 50,267. In many ways these lay ministers are comparable to Pentecostal pastors. While much of the growth of catechists took place before the end of the twentieth century, the number of catechists grew by 6,849 in 2000–2006. Virtually all catechists are dedicated to evangelization. Among them are a number of lay preachers who are also participants in the Catholic Charismatic Renewal. The church that was persecuted and lost thousands of members by death in the internal war has come alive with thousands of active lay ministers, evangelists, and communicators bent on spreading a Catholic evangelical message in ways that were not common before the years of internal war (1954–96).

Beyond the specialized offices of priest and catechist, rank-and-file Catholics were caught up in the religious renewal. After many decades of low church attendance, a major newspaper, *La Hora*, reported in 1990 that Catholic churches were filled on Sundays.[50]

The peace movement in the 1980s was strong at the grass roots of the Catholic Church in Guatemala, but the degree of Charismatic participation then is unknown. Charismatics have been involved evidently in more recent peacemaking. The effort at constructing peace had to continue after the peace accords went into effect in Guatemala at the end of 1996 because the conditions for a lasting peace had not been established. Members of the Charismatic movement have emphasized prayer as a means of bringing peace (often in ecumenical settings) and activity (such as a Guatemalan health clinic called the Peace Clinic, which is accessible to people of all faiths). The Charismatics' most public work for peace has been the staging of peace vigils with notable Charismatic performers. At the end of October 2006, the movement sponsored the Central American Vigil for Peace in Guatemala City. Some thirty thousand people attended, even though traveling within the city, especially in the evening, is dangerous because of violent crime.

In his pioneering work on the Charismatic movement in Latin America, Andrew Chesnut described the movement in Guatemala as being determinedly Catholic, shunning Protestant Pentecostal practices.[51] To the extent that this occurred, the move toward Catholic identity would be important for the competition between Catholics and Pentecostals.

As noted, Guatemala had the highest percentage of Pentecostals in Latin America. The country has also been showcased by many journalists and some historians as the most Protestant and Pentecostal country in Latin America.

The heavy hand of Archbishop Mario Casariego of Guatemala City at the beginning of the movement rather effectively marginalized Francis MacNutt's introduction of the movement to Guatemala. MacNutt typically conducted Life in the Spirit retreats, considered the sine qua non entry point in the movement, with Protestant members on his retreat team. Nonetheless, the pulling together of Catholics, Lutherans, and to a much lesser extent Pentecostals in the peace movement over many years made prayer in ecumenical settings a routine event.

What set Catholic Charismatics apart from their Protestant Pentecostal cousins were two elements, the sacraments (especially the Mass) and devotion to Mary. Probably more than most countries where the Catholic Charismatic Renewal has taken root, Guatemalan Charismatics have emphasized devotion to Mary. Orlando Coronado Juárez, the driving force behind Eventos Católicos, made a modern expression of Marian devotion into an international event. By 2008 the Marian Song Festival was in its twenty-fourth year.[52] The festival drew competitors from Spain and various countries of Latin America.

Through its radio station in Guatemala City, Eventos Católicos carried live the recitation of the rosary, the ancient Marian devotion, from the large Dominican downtown church. The connection of the rosary, a late medieval devotion, to the Charismatic movement, sometimes characterized as a postmodernist invention, was unusual but indicative of a determined effort at maintaining a Catholic identity.

Catholics: Winning or Losing Guatemala?

Commentators on the great Pentecostal challenge to Latin American Catholicism turned from Guatemala to Brazil as the principal test case as to whether the Catholic Church is winning or losing what journalists tended to call the battle for the hearts and minds of Latin American Catholics. They did this in 2007 because Pope Benedict visited Brazil for the first time as pope, because in that year the Latin American Bishops Conference met at Aparecida, Brazil, and because Brazil is the largest Catholic country in the world. Before 2007 Guatemala had been the main barometer since the percentage of Pentecostals was much higher there: some 25–30 percent of the population compared to 15 percent in Brazil. Guatemala deserves to be considered alongside Brazil in the competition for members.

A word first about statistics is in order: statistics estimating the distribution of religious denominations in Latin America are widely disputed because the numbers and percentages were collected by government, academic, and religious organizations using different methods and collecting for different purposes. Statistics about Guatemala have been especially contested. However, several sources indicated that in the 1990s Catholics were no longer losing members. The respected polling organization CID-Gallup, the World Christian Database at the Center for the Study of Global Christianity at Gordon-Cornwall Seminary, and Clifton Holland, a highly regarded Protestant poll watcher who is a resident in Central America, all reported lower percentages of Protestants in Guatemala and trend lines of Protestants holding steady without new growth.[53] Scholars of Guatemalan religions, such as Bruce Calder, a professor emeritus of Latin American history at the University of Illinois, Chicago, believed that Pentecostalism had reached the limits of its growth. Others have expressed similar judgments, that Pentecostalism at the end of the twentieth century had stopped growing in Guatemala.

Rather than the end of Pentecostal growth, however, the period of lack of growth may have been a temporary pause in an upward trend. Three things are clear: 1) Pentecostal growth slowed considerably as a national trend; 2) Catholics are enjoying a religious revival in Guatemala, so that it is fair to say that both Catholics and Pentecostals are doing well; and 3) Charismatics, being a large sector of the Catholic church, form the leading edge of this renewal. The long-standing perspective of journalists and Protestant scholars that portrayed the Pentecostal-Catholic situation as a battle in which Pentecostals were winning and Catholics losing ignores the logic and reality of another point of view: that both religious traditions are prospering. One may reasonably conclude that a religious renewal is going on in Guatemala in which Pentecostals and Catholics alike share.[54]

The root finding behind that conclusion is that competition has been good for the Catholic Church in Guatemala.[55] But those who argue that the Catholic Church in Latin America simply imitated its competitors ignore the evident pattern of influence. Charismatics in Guatemala rightly trace their beginning to the United States. Guatemalan Charismatics are not simply imitators of the market-driven success of Pentecostals. They are part of a global trend that has also spread to Africa and Asia.

Then, too, strong evidence exists for connecting Guatemalan Catholic growth to its lay movements. I tracked carefully the yearly growth in the workforce of the church in Guatemala—its priests, seminarians, sisters, catechists, and lay missionaries. The growth has been steady since the early 1970s and appears then to be the fruit of lay movements: first of Catholic Action, then the Cursillos, and lastly the Charismatic renewal.[56] All of these movements were the result of either global trends within the Catholic Church or imported innovations carried by foreign missionaries. The movements were also changed and shaped by Guatemalan Catholics, clerical and lay.

What the Charismatics especially added to competition with Pentecostals in Guatemala is what John Allen of the *National Catholic Reporter* has called "turbo-charged" efforts at evangelization. This education and nurturing in the Catholic faith was pushed and expanded by Charismatics to new levels. The intensity of their efforts, the public quality of Eventos Católicos's Catholic International Festival and other major events by Charismatics, and Catholic programming widely available on radio where little was previously to be found have subtly shifted the momentum of struggle to a more equal battle.

In describing Catholics who became Pentecostal, it is prudent to ask if the so-called loss is really a loss. The majority of Catholics who changed affiliation to Pentecostal and neo-Pentecostal groups were nominal Catholics who did not attend church. That they became churchgoers and practitioners of a form of Christianity like Pentecostalism hardly seems like a loss.[57]

Overall, the country can be described as being characterized by Pentecostalized religion. This refers both to certain religious beliefs (such as turning wholeheartedly to religion and to God through conversion) and to the experience of particular pneumatic religious practices (such as speaking in tongues and public praise of God).

Conversion plays a major role in the religious careers (that is, the longitudinal path of religious life over a lifetime) of Guatemalan Catholics. In 1993 Timothy Steigenga conducted a survey on the religion of Guatemalans in Guatemala City, Antigua, and surrounding rural villages in the Department of Sacatepéquez. The survey asked about personal conversion, and Steigenga considered the reports of conversion by Catholics to be extraordinarily high. Seventy-one percent of Catholics said they experienced a personal conversion. Steigenga presumed that a significant portion of these conversion experiences are related to the growth of Catholic Charismaticism, while others may involve individuals who converted to social Catholicism.[58]

Along with the conversion experience, a large portion of Guatemalan Catholics placed great faith in religious healing in one form or other. Slightly more than 70 percent of Catholics reported having experienced miraculous cures. As Steigenga noted in his survey, the importance of healing for understanding recruitment and conversion should not be underestimated.[59]

Conversion for Catholic Charismatics meant a new way of life, a commitment with new elements (such as healing) that are referred to as gifts of the Holy Spirit. This depiction as a way of life accords with Henri Gooren's characterization of conversion careers and his five-level typology of religious activity.[60] Within this framework, Charismatics, for the most part, are at the third and fourth levels of religious activity. They have gone through the ritual of affiliation/initiation, baptism, at an early age. Beyond mere affiliation, group membership now forms a central aspect of their lives and, indeed, of their identities. They have advanced from indifferent or lukewarm affiliation to deeper affiliation. Gooren has depicted this deeper level as confession (confession meaning here proclamation). Charismatics tend to practice a high level of participation inside their religious group and have a strong missionary attitude toward people outside their group.

Healing is central to many in the Charismatic movement, so the link between healing and conversion is crucial to the discussion here. Healing that is attributed to faith takes several forms. The first is conversion itself, which induces healing. The unconverted individual is diminished as a person by a disordered relationship with God and with other people. Conversion is believed to bring about the reordering of social and religious attitudes in line with what God wishes. The theologian Donald Gelpi believes this reordering heals the human heart at its deepest center.[61]

Given the Catholic view of the precarious quality of conversion, the community (such as a prayer group, a parish, or a covenant community) assumes a responsibility to nurture the newly initiated. The community does this through mentorship in prayer, in supporting the move away from bad habits, such as addictions of various forms, in helping new members assume new roles in the church, and through positive example. For their part, new members are expected to attend community meetings frequently, to have docility to spiritual elders, and to bring in new members. The main thrust of life after the initial intense religious experience, the stage of life called here second conversion, is *revisión de vida*, a change of life, avoiding what is considered evil and the occasions that will lead to slips and falls and attempting to be active and generous with others.

The Charismatic movement also appears to be an excellent exemplification of what David Smilde analyzed as networks and publics.[62] Catholic Charismaticism is not a movement that started from above. It spread from a middle level through various networks. At its inception, the Guatemalan hierarchy responded cautiously to the movement being promoted by three sisters and a lay leader and then attempted cooptation through controlled sponsorship. The bishops delayed more than a decade in granting approval to the movement. The movement began from the mid-level workforce and from the grass roots. Priests and laypersons accepted the themes and practices of Charismatics from the United States or from neighboring countries after importation from the states and communicated what they knew to small groups in Latin America whose members in turn recruited others.

The few researchers who have looked into the Charismatic movement have stressed problem solving as a central motivation for persons to join the movement. Sickness, addiction, suffering in various forms—this is almost a universal condition among the masses in Latin America—draw many into the movement. In an early work Andrew Chesnut described this as the pathogens of poverty.[63] The research issue then becomes one of determining which persons address those needs through religion. After all, many do not choose religion; they find other means to address their needs, continue suffering, or explain them away.

The attraction of Charismatic religion can be explained, in part, by combining the explanations of Henri Gooren and David Smilde. In doing so, one may note that crisis, often in the form of suffering that needs a solution, acts as a catalyst, moving some to the Charismatic movement and conversion because of the powerful attraction of a network. Others who suffer from the same problems but without the influence of a network do not choose this religious solution. For individual persons conversion

264 / The Rise of Charismatic Catholicism in Latin America

and confession frequently occur as solutions to crises. For the Catholic Church it means that persons become active in the church in an intense and participatory manner that revitalizes the institution.

Members of the Charismatic movement clearly overflow church structures into both private and public sites that serve as the grounds for network activity. They meet in one another's homes to pray and to discuss the practical problems in Christian living; in schools and church buildings for larger assemblies; and noteworthy among Guatemalan, Brazilian, and Colombian Charismatics, in public spaces through retreats, musical festivals, and fairs. Charismatics also carry their messages to the public at large through radio and sometimes television. The networks are primarily made up of laypersons, although priests and sisters often form part of the networks. Nonetheless, the Guatemalan church at least in its evangelizing and missionary work has become driven by laypersons, with their energy, money, and vision being the dominant elements.

Economics and the Renewal: Who Pays for Religion?

To the economic question of who pays for (Catholic) religion in Guatemala and Latin America, for centuries the response used to be largely the state and the wealthy. Then in the nineteenth and twentieth centuries, the response was foreign missions. Now one can say that increasingly many persons in the pews pay for religious service and that ordinary laity support radio and other evangelizing, missionary work, and an increasing measure of health care. When Orlando Coronado needed money for Eventos Católicos and Josué Cruz sought financial support for Centro Misionero, they did not embark on primary money-raising journeys to Europe or the United States. They raised the money locally. Guatemalans are paying for evangelization and missionary work in ways no one predicted. Furthermore, this is unusual because this activity has no immediate economic return for the givers or their families.

Latin Americans had been notoriously ungenerous in giving to the Catholic Church. According to J. Reginaldo Prandi, the noted Brazilian sociologist, Brazilian Catholics had never thought of themselves as responsible for providing the resources or financing of religion. No one paid a tithe or any systematic contribution.[64] He said Brazilians had grown accustomed to the state's providing churches as part of central cities or towns. Churches were always open, places where one went to meet friends, to watch others, and to be seen. Brazilians expected rich people to build chapels and put their names on them. In other words, any Catholic could pass his entire life without giving a cent to the church.[65]

The unshakable grip that this tradition has in Latin countries can be seen even in modernized countries such as France. French individuals give eight times less to philanthropy than Americans or Canadians. Charles Truehart, writing in the *International Herald Tribune*, says, "The people's historic faith in the state to take care of the dispossessed (and everyone else) have made the French far less inclined than their neighbors . . . to take care of matters of charity and philanthropy in their own hands."[66]

This dependent attitude has been the curse of the Latin American church. It has not fully recovered from this state-and-elite provisionist attitude, even after the separation of church and state took place in Latin America. In sum, until recently Latin American Catholics, by and large, were not generous in steady weekly support of their parishes and church enterprises. I interviewed many Latin Americans in Peruvian and Bolivian parishes during the late 1950s and early 1960s (before Vatican Council II). When asked if they could make steady contributions during the offertory of Sunday worship, they invariably responded, "No es nuestra costumbre" (It's not our custom).[67]

Pentecostalism in its various branches, including Catholic Charismaticism, brings to its participants a primitive Christian generosity similar to the early days of Christianity. Pentecostal Protestants have shown that ordinary lower- and middle-class Latin Americans can be persuaded to support the church. Their generosity is legendary. Being a Pentecostal is, in fact, relatively expensive. Many Pentecostal congregations expect members to contribute a *diezma*. (A tithe, 10 percent of income, is a biblical custom, one that continued for centuries by Christians.) The older Pentecostal groups were the most numerous in Latin America. Until recently they lived on the sidelines of society, unobserved by the media or sociologists. They quietly gave large portions of their incomes to support the church and its works, including missions.

The Pentecostal scholar Douglas Petersen estimated in 1993 that Assemblies of God Pentecostals in Central America had accumulated U.S.$150 million in physical assets.[68] This is but one of many Pentecostal groups in Central America. Since a greater range of assets exists further south, following the early twentieth-century foundations of Pentecostals in Brazil and Chile, one may presume that the overall size of Latin American Pentecostal assets is enormous.

In the 1970s, a new style of Pentecostalism came noisily to public attention. In some places its practitioners were called neo-Pentecostals in contrast to the traditional Pentecostals. Neo-Pentecostal practitioners believed that God delivered material wealth to them in response to their faithfulness. One of the most publicized neo-Pentecostal churches was the Showers of Grace church in Guatemala City, where members are asked, "Who here wants to own their own business?"[69] These churches drew in large contributions from parishioners who hoped to receive material benefits in exchange for generosity to the church. The appeal of neo-Pentecostals thus was health and wealth. Of Guatemala, Virginia Garrard-Burnett of the University of Texas says that Protestantism of all stripes is clearly associated with prosperity.[70] To the elite and the upwardly mobile, neo-Pentecostal churches offered both the means and the rationale for upward mobility in a society where it was otherwise unattainable.[71]

Catholic Charismatics did not repeat the blatant promises of the neo-Pentecostals, but in Guatemala, as elsewhere in Latin America, they have taken upon themselves a far greater financial support of the Catholic Church than has ever been demonstrated in the five hundred years of the church's existence in Latin America. This is a major achievement of the movement. It is also one that is not acknowledged by most scholars of religion.

Conclusion

Alongside the economic advances and other improvements made by the movement's members, another achievement should be noted. Catholics notably reinforced their identities as Catholics through the movement. Robert Wuthnow, a distinguished sociologist at Princeton University, considered religious identity a major theoretical and practical religious issue of the twenty-first century.[72]

As noted in this chapter, various challenges, especially the intense competition with evangelical Protestants, were posed to the Catholic Church in its role as reinforcing Catholic identity. From the point of view of the individual in Guatemalan society, the quest for identity was important and difficult in the turbulent times of civil war and changing cultural mores.

The Catholic Charismatic Renewal offered persons ways to be Catholic and Guatemalan. It was appropriately symbolic of this effort that Orlando Coronado Juárez and his fellow Charismatics named their radio station and other ministries Eventos Católicos (Catholic Events, or Happenings).

There is a further reason why the renewal has thrived in Guatemala. Charismatic groups used local preachers and generated enough commitment to the local prayer group, covenant community, or parish community that a kind of mutual aid society emerged among the members. Whereas the transnational Catholic Church was faced in the twenty-first century with diminished resources in supplying both foreign missionaries and finances from Europe or North America,[73] Guatemalan Charismatics supplied economic resources and personnel to assume religious roles in much increased numbers.

Guatemala's Catholic Church had been partially but effectively stifled by anticlerical governments. From the 1870s until the 1940s, national governments kept the number of priests in this, the most populous Central American country, to about 110 priests.[74] Beginning in the 1950s, foreign missionaries came to Guatemala and brought the number of priests to the 400 range. Foreigners amounted to 81 percent of the priestly workforce in 1965.[75] Missionaries began to die off (most by natural means, although more than twenty were murdered in the civil war) or move to assignments in other countries in the 1980s. Guatemalan priests simultaneously began to take their places. There were 864 priests in 1995, increasing to 1,000 in 2007, a respectable 14 percent increase in twelve years.

Seminarians, who were preparing to be ordained priests, increased from 69 in 1972 to 712 in 2007, a 488 percent increase. Religious sisters, many of whom acted as pastoral ministers in local congregations, grew from 1,018 in 1972 to 2,641 in 2007. Here, too, Guatemalans replaced foreign sisters, who comprised probably half or more of the sisters in the count of 1972.

Most of these increases are thought by veteran observers of Guatemala, myself included, to have been the fruit of the long succession of revitalization movements in Guatemalan Catholicism, most recently the Charismatic movement. The contemporary Guatemalan church has made itself into much more of an active ground for laypersons to preach, evangelize, and engage in missionary work than anyone predicted forty years ago. Then the church was a fading nineteenth-century Euro-baroque institution emphasizing hierarchical control. In 2008, almost sixty thousand lay catechists acted as community leaders and interpreters of Christianity and gave the church a very different and everyday vitality.

This volume began with the assertion that a religious revival is going on in Latin America in which the Catholic Church shares and that a major sector in this renewal is Catholic Charismaticism. Now, having seen the evidence, one may say that Charismaticism is the most important religious movement in Latin America.

NOTES

Preface

1. Jenkins, *The Next Christendom*, 2.

Introduction

1. John Allen selected Charismatics and Pentecostals as a major trend in his *The Future Church*.

2. Academics in the United States generally prefer the term "evangelical" for Protestants in Latin America.

3. Barrett and Johnson, "The Catholic Charismatic Renewal, 1959–2025," 118–31.

4. Estimate of World Christian Database, cited by the Pew Forum on Religion and Public Life's "Spirit and Power: A 10-Country Survey of Pentecostals," viewed at http://www.pewforum.org.

5. Considine, *A Call for Forty Thousand*.

6. Costello, *Mission to Latin America*; and Dries, *The Missionary Movement in American Church History*, especially chaps. 8 and 9.

7. This renewal has been examined recently by Cleary, *How Latin America Saved the Soul of the Catholic Church*.

8. Smilde, "Contradiction without Paradox," 75–102; and interview by phone Sept. 16, 2007.

9. Interview with Marta Lagos, the director of Latinobarómetro, New York, Nov. 6, 2009; see also Cleary, "Shopping Around," 50–54.

10. Bowen, *Evangelism and Apostasy*, passim.

11. Martin, *Pentecostalism*, 17.

12. Talavera and Beyers, "Retrato del movimiento evangélico a la luz de las encuestas de opinión pública," 67.

13. For a wide and authoritative view of Pentecostals and Charismatics, see Burgess, *The New International Dictionary of the Pentecostal and Charismatic Movements*. See also Anderson, *Vision of the Disinherited*.

14. Menzies, *Anointed to Serve*, 90.

15. Hunt, Hamilton, and Walter, *Charismatic Christianity*, 2.

16. See Burgess, "Neocharismatics," 928, in which he explained the change of usage for the Third Wave Pentecostals.

17. Hocken, "Charismatic Movement," 517.

18. Freston, "Charismatic Evangelicals in Latin America," 188.

19. Interview with Peter Hocken by phone, April 22, 1997.

20. Freston, "Charismatic Evangelicals in Latin America," 189.

21. See Cleary, *How Latin America Saved the Soul of the Catholic Church*, passim.

22. Sullivan, the Jesuit historian, includes no direct connection from the council to the Renewal Movement in his analysis, "Vatican II," 1171–74. See also Hocken, "Charismatic Movement," 481.

23. Prentiss, "John Paul II and the Catholic Charismatic Renewal," 811.

24. Martin, *Pentecostalism*, 20.

25. Ibid.

26. See, for example, Nolan, *The Ideology of the Sandinistas and the Nicaraguan Revolution*.

27. Interviews with Tom Walker, a scholar specializing in Nicaragua; Rev. Thomas Blau, formerly an employee of Domino's Pizza in Nicaragua; and other Nicaraguan informants, Dec. 1990. See also Mary Jo McConahay, "Latest Battle in Nicaragua Is in Schools," 9.

28. Freston, "Charismatic Evangelicals in Latin America," 188–201. See also Hocken, "Charismatic Movement," 477–519.

29. Burgess, *The New International Dictionary*, xix.

30. Other Catholics were brought into the movement (or "baptized in the Spirit"), notably Barbara Shlemon Ryan, before the event at Duquesne.

31. See Gelpi, *Charism and Sacrament*, 150–51.

32. Thigpen, "Catholic Charismatic Renewal," 461.

33. Ibid., 464.

34. Interviews by the author.

35. O'Connor, *Perspectives on Charismatic Renewal*; McDonnell, *Catholic Pentecostalism*; see especially various authors on sound recordings made at the Symposium of the Holy Spirit, Duquesne University Centennial, Oct. 16–20, 1978; and MacNutt, *Healing*.

36. MacNutt, *Healing*.

37. For a short history of relations with the Catholic hierarchy, see Thigpen, "Catholic Charismatic Renewal," 464–65.

38. See O'Connor, *Pope Paul and the Spirit*; and Prentiss, "John Paul II and the Catholic Charismatic Renewal," 810–11.

39. McDonnell, a Catholic Charismatic leader, was a longtime participant in the Catholic-Pentecostal dialogue. See his "The Death of Mythologies."

40. Hocken, "Charismatic Movement," 519.

41. "Charismaticism" is also used throughout Hunt, Hamilton, and Walter, *Charismatic Christianity*.

42. I have published historical accounts of church renewal, especially in *Crisis and Change*.

43. Camp published an exceptional but slightly dated sociopolitical analysis of the contemporary Mexican church in his *Crossing Swords*.

44. Brazilian Bishops Conference, "Basic Christian Communities (1982)," 44 (italics mine).

45. For a North American view, see Wuthnow, *I Came Away Stronger*.

46. Ibid., 2.

47. Sheppard, "Sociology of World Pentecostalism," 1084–85.

48. Iannaccone, "Religious Markets and the Economics of Religion," 123.

49. Ibid. For a recent discussion of demand and supply-side theories about religion in Latin America, see Steigenga and Cleary, *Conversion of a Continent*, 14–24.

50. The description of the book is from the publisher's statement on the back cover of the 1998 edition.

51. Finke and Stark, *The Churching of America, 1776–1990*; Stark, *The Rise of Christianity*; Iannaccone, "Religious Markets and the Economics of Religion"; and Bainbridge and Stark, *A Theory of Religion*.

52. http://www.providence.edu/las. A similar site also was posted at http://www.utexas.edu/lanic.

53. Gill, *Rendering Unto Caesar*, 11.

54. Chesnut, "Specialized Spirits," 77.

55. See Smilde's discussion of a theory of cultural agency in his *Reason to Believe*, 45–53.

56. C. Smith, *Moral Believing Animals*, 114.

57. Foweraker, *Theorizing Social Movements*, esp. 45–49.

58. Gooren, "Conversion Careers in Latin America," 52–71.

59. Smilde, "Relational Analysis of Religious Conversion and Social Change," 93–113.

60. Congar, *I Believe in the Holy Spirit*, 198.

61. Gelpi, "Conversion," 32.

62. John Paul II, *Ecclesia in America*.

63. The five distinctive features are given an expansion in Thigpen, "Catholic Charismatic Renewal," 465–66.

64. See, for example, Congar, *I Believe in the Holy Spirit*.

65. Gelpi, *Charism and Sacrament*, 90.

66. Barrett and Johnson, "The Catholic Charismatic Renewal, 1959–2025," 118.

Chapter 1. Bolivia: Learning While Doing

1. The countries and dates were given to me by Francis MacNutt.

2. MacNutt, *The Nearly Perfect Crime*, 150.

3. Ibid.

4. The innovation of small communities is treated by Cleary, *Crisis and Change*, 104–24.

5. Ruibal also was controversial for supporting the dictator General Banzer. See Rivière, "Bolivia," 17–18.

6. Pentecostalism came to Bolivia from the United States with few theological or pastoral adjustments needed at the beginning. The style of English-language religious services was reproduced in large part in the services held in Spanish. Charismatic branches of Pentecostalism seem not to have penetrated historical Protestant churches in Bolivia.

7. A selection of Geraets's reflections is contained in Roach and Sauto, *Cris y Daniel*, 223–42 and 363–420.

8. Both also understood the historical nature of Mass rituals, having witnessed the demise of the Dominican rites during the reforms of Vatican Council II.

9. Roach and Sauto, *Cris y Daniel*, 154.

10. Daniel Roach, interview by author, Santa Cruz, Bolivia, June 19, 1989.

11. When I interviewed a Dutch Dominican priest in July 2009, he recounted his strong negative reactions to the Charismatic Mass he attended at Santa Cruz. He considered heterodoxy to be taking place.

12. Not only lacking were professional speech and rhetoric training but also the time-honored method of apprenticeship of novice to master preacher.

13. Scholarship on the history of Latin American preaching is still a minor strain, but Perla Chincilla from the Universidad Iberamericana has made a notable start.

14. Three decades later one thousand Spanish-speaking Catholic Charismatics held a conference in Kansas City. By then non-Hispanic Catholic Charismatics were much less visible, said the *Catholic Key* ("The Dioceses of Kansas City," Nov. 11, 2007.)

15. Synan, *The Holiness-Pentecostal Tradition*, 260–61.

16. MacNutt organized the Christian Preaching Conference and edited its periodical, *Preaching*, from 1966–70.

17. Versènyi, *Theater in Latin America*, 152–91.

18. Samuel Escobar, a senior evangelical mission leader from Latin America, told me on several occasions that pastoral care offered by the Catholic Church, in his judgment, had been inadequate in modern times and was the cause of many Protestant conversions.

19. The biographies of Fathers Cris and Dan and their core teachings are included in Roach and Sauto, *Cris y Daniel*.

20. Ibid.

21. Literacy, gained in order to read the Bible, was a major factor in the economic development of Europe four centuries earlier.

22. Further information can be viewed at http://www.lamansion.org/.

23. Based on my visits to Pentecostal and evangelical seminaries in six countries, 1985–2005.

24. In 2006 the number of lay catechists in Latin America was 1.2 million, according to Vatican statistics. See the *Catholic Almanac, The Official Catholic Directory,* and a variety of Web sites and Vatican publications.

25. "Where the church, with or without ordination, not just for an individual case but professionally and officially hands to someone an aspect of this power that distinguishes clergy from laity it makes that person into a cleric" (Rahner, "Notes on the Lay Apostolate," 321).

26. See, for example, Prandi's seminal article on who pays for religion: "Religião paga, Coversão e Serviço," 60–86. Bishop Ramirez of Las Cruces, N. Mex., has made the same argument about Hispanic Catholics in the United States: "Stewardship Tradition in U.S. Hispanic Communities," 308–12.

27. Petersen, "The Formation of Popular, National, and Autonomous Pentecostal Churches in Central America," 23–48.

28. Chesnut, *Born Again in Brazil.*

29. Brouwer, "Nieuwe scheppingen in Christus," quoted by Gooren, "Conversion Careers in Latin America," 59.

30. Smilde, "Relational Analysis of Conversion and Social Change," 93–111.

31. Private communication with Father Michael Mascari, Dominican superior, Oct. 11, 2008.

32. My interviews, Bolivia, 1973–79 and 1994.

33. Article forthcoming in *Journal of Latin American Studies.*

34. My interviews with national seminary students in Cochabamba, 1987 and 1996.

35. Statistics for 2007 are from *Catholic Almanac* (2009); the figure for native clergy is from Fernández and García, *El clero en Bolivia,* 151.

36. Robertson, "The Globalization Paradigm," 211.

37. Barrett and Johnson, "The Catholic Charismatic Renewal, 1959–2025," 117–25.

Chapter 2. Colombia: Social Justice and Pneuma

1. The adjective Protestant is absent in official organizational histories of Minuto de Dios. Hocken identifies the visiting team leader as Harald Bredesen in his "Charismatic Movement," 498.

2. Samuel Ballesteros remained with his wife and children in Colombia from 1968 to 1974. He formed his first prayer group there in 1969.

3. Conflicting opinions about García-Herreros's views were given in interviews

274 / Notes to Pages 55–70

with participants of meetings of the Encuentros Carismáticos Católicos Latinoamericanos (ECCLA). I follow here Jaramillo, *Rafael García Herreros*, 196–203.

4. See, for example, Haddox, *Sociedad y religión en Colombia*, 167.

5. Both types of small communities were found in Protestant and Catholic churches in Latin America.

6. The project seemed to have spurred parallel housing schemes in the national government during the mid-1970s.

7. While pursuing theological studies in Rome, he was influenced by Felix Moreleon, the Belgian Dominican apostle of mass media.

8. Giraldo, "Biography of Father Rafael." See also Jaramillo, *Rafael García Herreros*.

9. Before the evening time slot was settled, García-Herreros had earlier in his career a morning time and an evening time. In each case the goal was to give a short message about God and his relationship with human life. These messages were, in effect, sermonettes.

10. Interview on Feb. 1, 2008 with Ralph Rogawski, O.P., a participant in the first ECCLA meeting in Bogotá.

11. Ibid.

12. Jaramillo was followed on the board by his colleague, Father Camilo Bernal Hadad, the president of Minuto de Dios University.

13. Uribe had already been giving retreats to factory workers in Medellín.

14. The importance of laity in the vitality of the church is the central argument of Cleary, *How Latin America Saved the Soul of the Catholic Church*.

15. Interviews, Medellín, June 1972, and Bogotá, June 1975.

16. Jaramillo, *Rafael García Herreros*, 203–4.

17. YouTube, viewed Jan. 30, 2008.

18. Montoya, "Encuentro Personal con El Señor."

19. "Emisora Minuto de Dios 1.230 A.M."

20. Linero, "Reflecciones sobre la música."

21. MacNutt, "First Latin American Charismatic Leadership Conference" (unpublished notes).

22. Ibid.

23. Ralph Rogawski recounting conversations with García-Herreros, phone interview by author, June 17, 1998.

24. Second General Conference of Latin American Bishops, "Conclusions," passim.

25. The greater tolerance of the Catholic Church and the lesser tolerance of the historical Protestant churches with regard to the Charismatic movement is noted by Lamin Sanneh, the authoritative scholar of world Christianity, in his *Disciples of All Nations*, 192. The theme is also treated later in this chapter.

26. Memories of participants concerning the date of the first meeting differ. I follow here MacNutt's notes from the time period.

27. In their places Father Rogawski and Sister Helen sent two laypersons from Bolivia.

28. Cleary, *Crisis and Change*.

29. Among many works, see McDonnell, *Charismatic Renewal and the Churches*; Gelpi, *Pentecostalism*; and Congar, *I Believe in the Holy Spirit*.

30. MacNutt's many works on healing include *Healing* and *The Nearly Perfect Crime*.

31. See, for example, Duffy, *The Stripping of the Altars* and *Marking the Hours*.

32. Members of the ECCLA said they sought another notable goal: Christian unity. But it was not clear how they might attain that unity.

33. The sequence of the meetings was irregular and became biannual on an even year basis in 1996.

34. Statistics are from Barrett and Johnson, "The Catholic Charismatic Renewal, 1959–2025," 117–25.

35. The World Council of Churches, a Protestant body, shows 1,270,980 Protestants in a Colombian population of 45,600,214 on its Web site, http://www.oikoumene. org.

36. Brooke, "Religious Issue Roils Colombia."

37. Martin, *Pentecostalism*, 20.

Chapter 3. The Dominican Republic: The Preacher and His Island

1. Interview, Emelio Betances, April 5, 2008, based on his research, much of it reported in his *The Catholic Church and Power Politics in Latin America*.

2. See Klaiber, *The Church, Dictatorship, and Democracy in Latin America*, passim; and Mainwaring and Wilde, *The Progressive Church in Latin America*, passim.

3. See Betances, *The Catholic Church and Power Politics in Latin America*, passim.

4. Interview with Bishop Giovanni Gravelli, Santo Domingo, May 15, 1982.

5. Costello, *Mission to Latin America*.

6. Fidel Castro has vivid remembrances of his priestless childhood in Betto, *Fidel and Religion*.

7. Catherine LeGrand of McGill University supplied extensive background material for this chapter.

8. See the search by MacKinnon's nephew into what happened at his death in MacKinnon, *Dead Man in Paradise*.

9. The Charismatic Renewal in Quebec was highlighted by Bourassa, "Canada's Charismatic Province," 27–31.

10. Tardif preferred to center healing prayers within Catholic rituals rather than a lecture-conference context.

11. Similar evangelizing covenant communities were formed in other countries in a much shorter time.

12. In the jargon of the community, there were nine houses and a "fraternal cell."

13. By 2008 Francis MacNutt had published ten books in English on various aspects of healing.

14. http://www.cscv.info.

15. The decline was noted by the Charismatic scholar Kilian McDonnell in his "Catholic Charismatic Renewal," 392.

16. Interviews, June 1981 and October 1992.

17. Sáez, *Los Jesuitas*, 2: 212.

18. Barrett and Johnson, "The Catholic Charismatic Renewal, 1959–2025," 117–28.

19. See my Web site, "Religion in Latin America," http://www.providence.edu/las, maintained through Providence College.

20. Interview, posted by http://www.panamundo.com.

21. E-mail letter I received, June 9, 2009.

22. Meunier and Warren, *Sortier de la Grande Noirceur*.

Chapter 4. Brazil: The Charismatic Giant

1. Chapter on Brazil in Pew Forum, "Spirit and Power."

2. Interview, Cecília Loreto Mariz, Rio de Janeiro, March 14, 2004.

3. Barrett and Johnson, "The Catholic Charismatic Renewal, 1959–2025, " 119.

4. Sonnichsen, *Pass of the North*.

5. Keller, "Father Harold Rahm Receives Award."

6. Araujo, "Padre Harold admite tendecia ao alcoolismo."

7. The book is out of print. See the video version: Ross and Curtis, *The Cross and the Switchblade*.

8. A Renovação Carismática Católica no Brasil, http://www.rccbrasil.org.br.

9. Chesnut, *Competitive Spirits*, 68, states that Dougherty had a free travel pass on Brazil's Varig Airlines.

10. Sales was one of the first leaders to write of the early days of the Brazilian movement in his *Renovacâo Carismático do Brasil*.

11. The spread of the movement was far from evenly dispersed at the beginning and parallel efforts to Dougherty's were crucial.

12. The date of founding is variously given by the Associação do Senhor Jesus and others as 1979 and 1980.

13. Sanneh, *Disciples of All Nations*, 129–30 and passim.

14. *Veja* carried articles on April 2, 1997 and April 8, 1998; *IstoE* on Dec. 24, 1998; and *Caros Amigos* in April 1998.

15. Pew Forum, "Spirit and Power," http://www.pewforum.org.

16. Interview, Rio de Janeiro, Jan. 2, 2004.

17. The lay leaders who were invited to Aparecida came from less popular movements.

18. Cleary, "Shopping Around," 50–54.

19. The inefficient deployment of missionaries/pastoral workers is discussed in Barrett, Crossing, and Johnson, "Missiometrics," 29.

20. Lima and Oyama, "Católicos en transe."

21. CBS, *Sixty Minutes*, aired on Oct. 14, 2007 and updated on Dec. 20, 2007.

22. "Joel Osteen Answers His Critics."

23. See, however, the different histories of Communist and Catholic cells in Cleary, *Crisis and Change*, 4.

24. "Desenvolvimento e outros desafios."

25. *Monsignor* typically means bishop in Latin America, but here it means an honorary title for a priest designated as part of the papal household.

26. The official and semi-official histories of Charismatic renewal in Brazil typically include Abib while other early accounts, such as Chesnut's *Competitive Spirits*, do not.

27. Interview with Professor Edward Sweet, Providence, R.I., April 15, 2006.

28. Lima and Oyama, "Católicos en transe."

29. A number of persons interviewed in the United States from 1970 to 1980 expressed criticisms of the guru-like posturing and authoritarian control of Charismatic leaders of that period.

30. The seating capacities were supplied by *Veja*, Dec. 8, 2004.

31. Janine Deckers, the Singing Nun, left the convent and died in 1985.

32. Mariz, *Coping with Poverty*, passim.

33. See the observation in Sanneh, *Disciples of All Nations*, 192.

34. Mariz, "Comunidades de vida no Espirito Santo."

35. The Jesus Movement in the United States also grew out of the spontaneous sharing of food and religion, as well as music.

36. Miranda, *Carisma, sociedade e política*.

37. O Globo's countermoves are detailed in Souza, *Igreja in Concert*, 24–25.

38. Among various accounts of the conflict over the acceptance of the Charismatic renewal in Brazil, see Carranza, *Renovação Carismática Católica*, 129–40.

39. Moreno, *Before Fidel*, 26.

40. Souza, *Igreja in Concert*, 22.

41. CBS *Early Show*, Oct. 19, 2007.

42. The growth in lay catechists is delineated in Cleary, *How Latin America Saved the Soul of the Catholic Church*.

43. Current statistics on lay catechists in the countries of the world are available in the *Catholic Almanac*, which is published yearly.

44. "CBS *Sixty Minutes*, Dec. 24, 2007.

45. M. Ramiriz, "Preacher Bringing Prosperity Gospel to Chicago."

46. Garrard-Burnett, "Stop Suffering," 220.

47. Ibid., 218–38.

48. Freston, "Charismatic Evangelicals in Latin America," *Evangelicals and Politics in Asia, Africa, and Latin America,* and *Protestant Political Parties.*

49. See details in Miranda, *Carisma, sociedade e política,* 97–120.

50. http://www.erosbiondini.com.br.

51. See Cleary, *How Latin America Saved the Soul of the Catholic Church,* chap. 10.

52. Marcelo, Reginaldo, Zezinho, and Zeca all had music videos on YouTube as viewed on Jan. 21, 2008. The latter two are discussed in the next chapter.

53. Cleary, *How Latin America Saved the Soul of the Catholic Church,* chap. 10.

54. The estimate is derived from interviews with Catholic missionary trainers at the Catholic Missiological Institute of the Facultad de Teología, Universidad Católica Boliviana at Cochabamba, Bolivia, June 11–16, 2003.

55. See, for example, Chesnut, *Competitive Spirits.*

56. Seminarians were 939 in 1972 and 9,369 in 2007, an increase of 898 percent. The figures are from the *National Catholic Almanac,* 1975 and 2009.

57. Martin, *Pentecostalism,* 48.

58. A. Smith, "Toward Global Culture?," 171–91.

Chapter 5. Brazil: Superstar and Competition with Pentecostals

1. Souza, *Igreja in Concert,* 68.

2. Not to be confused with other religious orders or congregations also bearing the designation "Sacred Heart."

3. Souza, *Igreja in Concert,* 67.

4. As a comparison, Charles Wesley, the great Protestant hymn writer, composed some six thousand songs.

5. The numbers were supplied by Larry Eskridge, Institute for the Study of Evangelicals, Wheaton College, Wheaton, Ill.

6. Phone interview on Jan. 17, 2008 with Larry Eskridge of the Institute for the Study of Evangelicals and the author of a forthcoming book on Christian music from Oxford University Press.

7. Archbishop Câmara was listed by the newsweekly *IstoE* as one of the ten most influential Brazilian religious figures of the twentieth century, a recognition denied him for many years by repressive military governments that kept his name out of the media.

8. http://www.christianguitar.org.

9. His legal name is José Luiz Jensen de Mello Neto.

10. Rio's beach communities have their own soccer and volleyball leagues and their own community newspapers.

11. A parish, Nossa Senhora de Loreto, created a nonprofit organization called Deus e Dez that was headed by Zeca and aimed at evangelization. In 2007 the organization was dormant and awaited Zeca's return from studies in Rome.

12. *Epoca* 25 (Dec. 25, 2000), 86–93.

13. *Jornal do Brasil* (Nov. 10, 2000).

14. Antoniazzi, "As transformaôes e o futuro da paroquia," 6–7. See also Benedetti, "O 'novo clero,'" 88–126.

15. One of the differences is that Abib's church has seating capacity for seventy thousand and another thirty thousand standing while the structural configuration for Rossi's church is the reverse: thirty thousand seated and seventy thousand standing.

16. See Dolan, *Catholic Revivalism*.

17. A comparable network of shared rides from São Paulo and Rio to Cochaceria Paulista was created for Padre Jonas and Comunidade Nova Cançào.

18. Brazil separated church from state in 1890 but the Catholic Church continued to receive government support for some years. See Serbin, "Brazil," 204–19.

19. Terra Cinema e DVD, http://www.cinema.terra.com.br.

20. *A Folha da São Paulo* (Nov. 20, 1998).

21. This argument has periodically broken out in the United States since the entry of evangelicals into politics in the 1980s.

22. C. Boff, "Carísmaticos e libertadores na Igreja," 36–53.

23. National Conference of Brazilian Bishops, *Orientações Pastorais sobre el RCC*.

24. Note also his profound reservations in L. Boff, *Etica da vida*, 168–69 and 184–89.

25. Oliveira, "O Catolicismo," 823–35.

26. Interview, Rio de Janeiro, May 29, 2004.

27. Weis, "O bem o a banal."

28. Calvin College, http://www.calvin.edu/summerinstitutes.

29. Gonzalez, "Música y religión."

30. Parker, *Popular Religion and Modernization in Latin America*, 128.

31. Richard Strasser has authored *Music Business*, among other publications.

32. Interview with Richard Strasser, Providence, R.I., Feb. 7, 2008.

33. Interview with Father Nicanor Austriaco, Providence, R.I., June 3, 2008.

Chapter 6. Mexico: Number One Exporter to the United States

1. The 2000 census showed that 3.52 percent of the population had no religious affiliation. Barrett and Johnson provided an estimate in their "The Catholic Charismatic Renewal, 1959–2025," 121.

2. Consult Mexican census figures over time. See also the descriptive and analytic analysis of the Protestant scholar Clifton Holland and his Programa de Estudios Socioreligiosos, especially *Prolades Encyclopedia of Religion in the Americas and the Iberian Peninsula*, posted at http://www.prolades.com.

3. Bowen, *Evangelism and Apostasy*, 71.

4. Nesvig, Introduction to *Religious Culture in Modern Mexico*, 2.

5. Ibid., 3.

6. Attendance at Mass in Mexico was relatively high: 49 percent of adults attending weekly in 2000 and through the last few decades. See data from *Comparative Study of Electoral Systems* and *World Values Survey*, http://www.cara.georgetown.edu.

7. Bryan Reising, private communication, Jan. 30, 2010.

8. Ibid.

9. Díaz de la Serna, *El movimiento de la Renovación Carismática*; and Cerdi, "El Dios," 107–22.

10. See, for example, Foweraker and Craig, *Popular Movements and Political Change in Mexico*.

11. See the section on Peru in chapter 7, "The Strong Middle Countries."

12. Volumes could be written about conflicts over strange and sometimes cruel practices of Mexican folk religion, such as actual crucifixion.

13. Hollander, "The Great Parade of Easter Devotion."

14. Lida, *First Stop in the New World*, 118–33.

15. Final Document, Fourth General Conference of Latin American Bishops, no. 368.

16. Froehle and Gautier, *Global Catholicism*.

17. Private communication, July 16, 2007, from Mary Gautier, the co-author of *Global Catholicism*.

18. See, for example, Cleary and Steigenga, *Resurgent Voices*, passim.

19. Gorski, "How the Catholic Church in Latin America Became Missionary," 60.

20. See, for example, Consejo Episcopal Latinoamericano, *De una pastoral indigenista a una pastoral indígena*.

21. Judd, "The Indigenous Theology Movement in Latin America," 210–30.

22. For a theological account of this encounter, see Sarmiento, *Caminos de la teología india*.

23. Sieder, *Multiculturalism in Latin America*, 1. Also see statistics from the World Bank, http://www.worldbank.org.

24. Gorski, "How the Catholic Church in Latin America Became Missionary," 60.

25. Froehle and Gautier, *Global Catholicism*, 222.

26. Legionnaires of Christ, http://www.legionairiesofchrist.org.

27. The numbers for Mexico are from Froehle and Gautier, *Global Catholicism*, 222; and for Brazil, *Catholic Almanac*, 324.

28. Froehle and Gautier, *Global Catholicism*, 80–81.

29. The figure (6,020) for 1957 is from Considine, *New Horizons in Latin America*, 322; the figure (12,218) for 2001 is from *Catholic Almanac*.

30. Interviews I conducted in New York, Washington, Chicago, and Los Angeles, 2000–2009.

31. The English translations of the final documents are contained in Eagleson and Scharper, *Puebla and Beyond*.

32. Escuelas de Evangelización San Andrés, "Proyecto Pastoral San Andrés 2006," 4.

33. Wilkes, *Excellent Catholic Parishes*, especially chap. 2; and Ernesto Elizando in Martin and Williamson, *John Paul II and the New Evangelization*, chap. 21.

34. Brunetta, "Response to Query."

35. Duffy, *Walking to Emmaus.*

36. Raycraft, *Fruit of Our Labor.*

37. Gómez, *Formación de predicadores.*

38. Comunidad Carismática de Alianza Santísima Trinidad, with branches in Buenos Aires and other cities.

39. http://www.evangelizacion.com/predicadores.

40. McDonnell, "Catholic Charismatic Renewal," 392; interviews with the Charismatic theologians Donald Gelpi, by phone, Aug. 14, 2002, and Giles Dimock, New Haven, Conn., May 14–20, 1994.

41. Barrett and Johnson, "The Catholic Charismatic Renewal, 1959–2025," 123.

42. "More Hispanics Losing Their Religion."

43. I follow here the customary designation of "Hispanic" by the U.S. federal government and the national Catholic Church, but, like many others, including the Pew Hispanic Center, I also use "Latino."

44. Marcelli and Cornelius, "The Changing Profile of Mexican Migrants to the United States," 105–11.

45. See both the Pew and Notre Dame surveys respectively: "Changing Faiths," 1; and Espinosa and Miranda, *Hispanic Churches in American Public Life*, 14.

46. Williams, Steigenga, and Vásquez, *A Place to Be*; and Lorentzen, *Religion at the Corner of Bliss and Nirvana.*

47. Williams, Steigenga, and Vásquez, *A Place to Be*, especially 52, 217.

48. "Changing Faiths," 1.

49. Ibid.

50. Bantjes, "Popular Religion and the Mexican Revolution."

51. Duffy, *The Stripping of the Altars*, 2–4.

52. Taylor, *Magistrates of the Sacred*, 73.

Chapter 7. The Strong Middle Countries

1. Barrett and Johnson, "The Catholic Charismatic Renewal, 1959–2025," 117–25.

2. Ibid.

3. This characterization is based on many interviews I conducted in Argentina over forty years; it was also made by a lay member of the Argentine national coordinating team in an interview with Abelardo Soneira, "El movimiento carismático en La Argentina," n.p., n.d., 49.

4. Pope Paul VI's addresses to the First and Second Conferences for International Leaders are contained in Pesare, *Then Peter Stood Up . . . ,*" 14–25.

5. Soneira, "Quiénes son los carismáticos?," 49.

6. See endnote 3. Also, Barrett and Johnson, "The Catholic Charismatic Renewal," 126.

7. Soneira, "Quiénes son los carismáticos," 50.

8. Mallimaci, "El catolicismo latinoamericano al fines del milenio," 170. The work quoted is Seguy, *Christianisme et societé.*

9. Soneira, "La Renovación Carismática Católica en la Argentina," 149–61.

10. See comments on itinerant preachers in chapter 8 in the section on Costa Rica.

11. Negative reactions by apparently Argentine Catholics (they remain anonymous) could be found in an extensive critique of Betancourt's written works at http://www.panodigital.com.

12. Soneira, "Quiénes son los carismáticos?," 48. See also his later work: *La Renovación Carísmatica Católica en la República Argentina.*

13. Osvaldo Cuadro Moreno was also the director of the periodical *Misión y Comunión.*

14. "Encuentro Ecuménico en Buenos Aires."

15. Rubín, "Encuentro religioso entre evangélicos y católicos carismáticos."

16. J. Norberto Saracco addressed the Plenary Session on Church Unity at the Ninth Assembly of the World Council of Churches, which took place at Porto Alegre, Brazil, Feb. 14–23, 2006.

17. Pastor Gerardo Oberman reported that mainline Protestants "had lost lots of members, while Pentecostals have been growing since the 1970s," at the 2008 Calvin College Institute of Christian Worship, Feb. 12, 2010, viewed at http://www.calvin.edu.

18. The statistics are from Barrett and Johnson, "The Catholic Charismatic Renewal, 1959–2025," 122.

19. "Renovación Carismática Católica de Venezuela," http://www.rccvenezuela.com.

20. Pulido, "32 Años de Historia de la Renovación Carismática Católica de Venezuela."

21. See Froehle, "The Catholic Church and Politics in Venezuela," 105–28.

22. Interviews with Catholic leaders in Caracas and other Venezuelan cities and towns, Jan. 2007.

23. Statistics are from the *Catholic Almanac.*

24. Gustavo Dudamel, one of the youngest directors of the world-class Los Angeles Symphony Orchestra, grew up at Barquisimeto.

25. Maney, *Basic Communities.*

26. Fé y Alegría was created forty years earlier than those initiatives and avoided many of their pitfalls and aggravations.

27. Barrett and Johnson, "The Catholic Charismatic Renewal, 1959–2025," 123.

28. Ibid., 117–18.

29. The account of the start of the Peruvian movement is based on interviews and on documents furnished by Francis MacNutt and others, as well as the master's thesis written by the Carmelite bishop Michael LaFay Bardi of Sicuani on the history of the Peruvian movement for the Faculty (Dept.) of Theology of the Pontifical Catholic University, Lima, 1972. Sections of this thesis were posted at http://www.rccperu.org.

30. Roger Wolcott, described by Bishop LaFay (above) only as a "Protestant minister," was scheduled to be the co-director of the first Charismatic retreat but was assigned at the last moment to Mexico.

31. Costello, *Mission to Latin America*, 53–55.

32. See, for example, O'Connor, *Perspectives on Charismatic Renewal*.

33. As noted elsewhere in this account, the events at Duquesne University were not the single source of the Catholic Charismatic movement, even though Charismatic movement centers often repeat this myth.

34. Interviews with lay and clerical leaders in Lima, especially at the Pontifical Catholic University, June 2003 and July 2004.

35. Hocken, "Charismatic Movement," 499.

36. *Censo Nacional de la RCC.*

37. For a relatively brief time the care of the diocese of Chimbote was entrusted to Dominicans of the Eastern Province of the United States, and one of their members, James Charles Burke (not to be confused with the Dominican Charismatic preacher James Colum Burke of Bolivia and Houston) was made bishop of Chimbote.

38. Geraets and Roach were from the Chicago Province of Dominicans, which was formed from the Eastern Province of the United States, of which Caprio was a member, in 1939. There were some largely minor differences in the educational programs of the provinces. The larger discrepancy was generational, the former two being educated before Vatican Council II and Caprio afterward.

39. The Peruvian Charismatic renewal is exceptionally well organized in terms of organizational charts, goals, and plans, giving the impression of corporate strength when, in fact, the number of adherents does not back up the appearance.

40. Barrett and Johnson, "The Catholic Charismatic Renewal, 1959–2025," 121.

41. The statistics are from ibid., 119.

42. Ibid., 120.

43. "Historia de la Comunidad 'Jesús es el Señor,'" http://www.jessquito.com.

44. He maintains http://www.padrecharlygarcia.blogspot.com for his client-fans.

45. Bishop Isern, among others, was a notable defender of the Mapuche Indians in Chile. See Obispos del Sur, *Por la dignificación del pueblo mapuche.*

46. The other percentage increases are Peru, 1,004; Chile, 898; and Ecuador, 634. Figures for 1957 are from Considine, *New Horizons in Latin America*, 327–68; and *Catholic Almanac*, passim.

Chapter 8. The Lesser Growth Countries

1. Panama is not strictly part of Central America since historically and culturally it was part of Colombia.

2. The percentages are derived from 1957, a point just before the main surge of foreign missionaries came to the region in the late 1950s, and then from 2008, by which time most missionaries had departed.

3. Lay movements, especially those centered in families, were credited with stimulating growth in the priesthood.

4. The Costa Rican scholar interviewed in Rome, May 12, 2006, did not wish to be identified.

5. The spelling of the priest's name varies from Pol to Poll in several accounts.

6. Córdova, *El movimiento cárismatico en Costa Rica*, 35.

7. Stoll, quoted by Holland, "Historia y cronología del movimiento de renovación carismática en América Latina."

8. Quoted in Holland, "Serie de Perfiles Socioreligiosos Nacionales sobre Nuevos Movimientos Religiosos: Costa Rica," 4.

9. Ibid.

10. In my review of research literature in the 1980s on short-term and long-term preaching, I found general consensus that six weeks was the minimum required for a new message to have an impact.

11. U.S. Dept. of State, "Report on Religion."

12. This is a commonplace finding in organizational psychology.

13. My colleagues and I will pursue this theme in a historical investigation of Catholicism without priests to be published by Paulist Press.

14. This account is based on interviews with Father Brian Pierce, O.P., a missionary to Honduras, over several years.

15. Peterson and Vásquez, "Upwards, Never Down," 191.

16. Their activities and ecclesiastical approbation were on display at http://www.centromisionero.org (accessed Oct. 13, 2008). The Web site notes that their Salvadoran spiritual advisor, Monseñor Fernando Rodríguez, is also the official exorcist for the Archdiocese of San Salvador. Deliverance from evil spirits is a common Charismatic concern, but it is often left unexplained. For one of several possible explanations, see MacNutt, *Deliverance from Evil Spirits*.

17. Wirpsa, "San Salvador Archbishop Ousts Jesuit Pastor of Barrio Parish."

18. Peterson and Vásquez, "Upwards, Never Down," 191.

19. Nolan, *The Ideology of the Sandinistas and the Nicaraguan Revolution*.

20. Hocken, "Ralph Martin," 861–62.

21. McConahay, "Latest Battlefield in Nicaragua Is Schools," 8.

22. Rodríguez, "Quarenta Años de Renovación Carismática."

23. See, for example, McGrath, "Signs of the Times in Latin America Today," 70–106.

24. Information obtained by interviews in Montevideo, June 2003, and from the Web site: http://www.feyrazon.org.

25. Barrett and Johnson, "The Catholic Charismatic Renewal, 1959–2025," 122.

26. Elizaga was also commended for his long priestly career by the Junta Departamental de Montevideo in Sept. 2008 but without mention of his ties to the Charismatic renewal.

27. "40 Años Sirviendo a la Iglesia Católica 1967–2007."

28. Barrett and Johnson, "The Catholic Charismatic Renewal, 1959–2025," 121.

29. See, for example, Sanneh, *Disciples of All Nations*, 178–81.

Chapter 9. Puerto Rico, Cuba, and Haiti: Caribbean Exporters to the United States

1. Gotay, *Catolicismo y política en Puerto Rico*, passim.

2. Ibid.

3. See, for example, Fidel Castro's recollections of his childhood without priests present in his region in Betto, *Fidel and Religion*, passim.

4. Gotay, *Catolicismo y política en Puerto Rico*, especially 313–22. (The reference here is from 240.) Gotay's works also reflected wide scholarship through his organization of a large working group called the Equipo Inter Universitario de Historia y Sociología del Protestantismo y Catolicismo en Puerto Rico.

5. Not all replacements were North American. Several Spanish groups remained or returned to the island. Dutch Dominicans supplied new leadership in place of the Spanish Dominicans.

6. Gotay, *Catolicismo y política en Puerto Rico*, 241.

7. Ibid., 317.

8. This includes the ecumenical efforts of Monsignor Ivan Illich and others from the Catholic University at Ponce.

9. One of the major figures in the follow-up to Vatican Council II was Monsignor Ivan Illich, the vice-rector of the Catholic University at Ponce.

10. Interviews with Dr. Guidoberto Mahecha, Universidad Bíblica Latinoamericana, San Jose, Costa Rica, June 7, 1996; and Pastor David George, Instituto Superior Evangélico de Estudios Teológicos, Buenos Aires, Jan. 14, 1997. Both were then administrators at the Protestant seminaries and followed church growth and decline. Published statistics were considered unreliable. Similar interviews were conducted with Dr. Pablo Sywulka, the secretary general of the Asociación Evangélica de Educación Teológica en América Latina, June 14, 1996; and Dr. Sergio Ojeda Cármano, the president of the Seminario Evangélico de Puerto Rico, June 10, 1996.

11. Hocken, "Charismatic Movement," 498.

12. González, *Caminos de la Nueva Evangelización en Puerto Rico*.

13. His homily on May 30, 2007 to the conference's participants stressed evangelization and cited the work of the blessed Carlos Manuel Rodríguez, a Puerto Rican lay minister at the Catholic University Student Center at the University of Puerto Rico, Rio Piedras, in the 1930s. Moreover, in interviews from the Latin American Bishops conference in Aparecida in 2007 Rodríguez emphasized evangelization as a priority for Puerto Rican Catholics.

14. Meléndez, "Católicos con nueva diócese y obispo."

15. Bishop Eusebio Ramos Morales wrote his first thesis at the Gregorian University in Rome and the second at St. Vincent de Paul Seminary in Florida.

16. Phone interviews with Ralph Rogawski, O.P. (1995–2009) and Patrick Rearden, O.P. (2005–9).

17. Casa Cristo Redentor at Aguas Buenas calls itself "A Center of Spiritual Healing and Personal Growth."

18. Calendars of activities for 2009 for both institutions include interior healing retreats.

19. Michael Scanlan, back cover testimonial to MacNutt's *Healing*. Scanlan himself is author of *Inner Healing*.

20. Csordas, *Language, Charisma, and Creativity*, 21.

21. Interview with staff at the Puerto Rican Tourist Office, San Juan, Jan. 7, 2009.

22. Díaz-Stevens and Stevens-Arroyo, *Recognizing the Latino Resurgence in U.S. Religion*.

23. Díaz-Stevens, *Ox-Cart Catholicism on Fifth Avenue*.

24. "The Renewalist Movement and Hispanic Christianity," 29–40.

25. http://www.rccuba.com.

26. This history largely follows that posted at http://www.rccuba.com during 2007.

27. Kirk, "Waiting for John Paul II," 147–66.

28. http://www.rccuba.com.

29. Deck, *The Second Wave*, 67–69.

30. Interview, New Haven, Conn., May 2, 2009.

31. Interviews, Roberts and other participants, Oxford Studies in World Christianity Workshop, New Haven, Conn., May 2, 2009.

32. Cuttita, "Spirits Lifted during 27th Annual Charismatic Conference."

33. "Spirit-filled Weekend Set."

34. Espín, *Latina Realities*.

35. The Canadian sister was unnamed in the history of the movement that was included in the diasporan history posted at http://www.crccho.org (accessed Nov. 23, 2008).

36. The estimate is based on my review of research on Haitian religions.

37. Interview by phone, Oct. 5, 1993.

38. See, for example, Bastide, *African Civilizations in the New World*; Mintz, Introduction to *Voodoo in Haiti*; Mintz, "Toward an Afro-American History," 317–32; Price-Mars, *Ainsi parle l'oncle*; Bastien, *La familia rural haitiana*.

39. Desmangles, *The Faces of the Gods*, 43, 56.

40. Interview with Father Gerald Fitzgerald by phone, Oct. 5, 1993.

41. Ibid.

42. Desmangles, *The Faces of the Gods*, 52.

43. See, especially, Abbott, *Haiti* and Trouillot.

44. Métraux, *Voodoo in Haiti*, 351–52.

45. Ibid.

46. Rey, "Marian Devotion at a Haitian Catholic Parish in Miami," 372, n. 5.

47. Ibid.

48. Many Haitian migrants were "boat people," similar to Cuban refugees but subject to different criteria for residency by the Immigration and Naturalization Service.

49. Rey, "Marian Devotion at a Haitian Catholic Parish in Miami," 355.

50. McAlister, "The Madonna of 115th Street Revisited."

51. Rey, "Marian Devotion at a Haitian Catholic Parish in Miami"; Richman, "Anchored in Haiti and Docked in Florida."

52. Among other indicators, the World Values Survey from the University of Michigan noted the high weekly church attendance among all Puerto Ricans, 52 percent, the sixth highest in the world. Survey results are posted at http://www.ns.umich.edu (accessed April 21, 2009).

Chapter 10. Guatemala: Evangelization and Mission

1. Interview with Dennis Smith, an expert on Guatemalan religion and a radio broadcaster, Guatemala City, June 1996.

2. The historical account here of the first years of the movement follows that given by Delgado, "Renovación Carísmatica en Guatemala."

3. Father Cohen started a radio and television ministry in 1981 called Closer Walk Ministries. He died in 2001, but his work was carried on by Father M. Jeffrey Bayhi.

4. Loarca, "Nombran Arzobispo de Los Altos."

5. In 2000, Barrett and Johnson provided a much lower estimate of 9 percent of the Catholic population, or a total of 854,000 Catholics, in their "The Catholic Charismatic Renewal, 1959–2025," 120 and passim. The discrepancy is probably due to differing definitions of affiliation and time period.

6. See, among many other sources, Warren, *The Symbolism of Subordination*.

7. The international Christian Family Movement, with headquarters in Chicago, grew out of the long experience of its founders in Catholic Action.

8. Interviews with apostolic movement leaders, Guatemala City, May 1997 and June 1999.

9. Bundy, "Cursillo Movement," 567–68.

10. Cleary, *Crisis and Change*, 8–26.

11. One symbol of that orphaning was Casa de Retiros Buen Camino, a large Cursillo center at Guatemala City that stood as an empty shell for some years.

12. Interviews with clergy and laity conducted in various regions of Guatemala, 1989–2003.

13. Often cited by Catholics who were interviewed in Guatemala was Protestant public preaching, as at the juncture of Cinco Calles in Guatemala City, and massive evangelism rallies by the Central American Mission.

14. Historical Protestants and Pentecostals have a varied history in Guatemala. See Garrard-Burnett, *Protestantism in Guatemala*; and Cleary, "Evangelicals and Competition in Guatemala," 167–96.

15. Wilson, "Identity, Community, and Status," 133–51.

16. Cleary, "Evangelicals and Competition in Guatemala," 170; Calder, "Interwoven Histories," 94–95.

17. For Guatemala, see Holleran, *Church and State in Guatemala*; for Mexico, see Martínez, *La Constitución de 1857*; and for Argentina, see Liebscher, "The Catholic Church in Argentine Society."

18. Estimate supplied by Professor Bruce Calder, Dept. of History, University of Illinois at Chicago.

19. Annis, *God and Production in a Guatemalan Town*, 140.

20. Interviews at Guatemala City and by phone with Maryknoll Missioners, 1981–91, especially David Kelley, Carroll Quinn, and Bishop Richard Ham.

21. Kelly, *History*, 5–6.

22. See, for example, Wilson, "Identity, Community, and Status," 131–51.

23. A similar battle also took place in other Latin American countries.

24. Some efforts at evangelization in rural areas before contemporary missionaries arrived were made by the Guatemalan priest Rafael González Estrada as early as 1934.

25. See especially Judd, "The Indigenous Theology Movement in Latin America," 210–30.

26. Gorski, "How the Catholic Church in Latin America Became Missionary," 60.

27. In the comparisons of the numbers of priests versus Pentecostal pastors, native catechists should enter into the comparison as well, since catechists are educated similarly to Pentecostal pastors and perform many of the same functions, including preaching.

28. See Vatican Council II's Declaration on the Relation of the Church to Non-Christian Religions.

29. Warren, *The Symbolism of Subordination*; Buechler, *The Masked Media*.

30. For an authoritative account of Mayan resurgence, see Calder, "Interwoven Histories," 93–24.

31. Steigenga and Cleary, *Conversion of a Continent*.

32. John Allen Jr. used this characterization in a phone interview, July 23, 2007.

33. Allen, *The Future Church*, 386–87.

34. The English translations of the final documents are contained in Eagleson and Scharper, *Puebla and Beyond*.

35. Duin, "Evangelization 2000"; Wang, "By the Year 2000."

36. General conferences are convened about every ten years; ordinary conferences of the Latin American bishops are held yearly.

37. The final document of the Santo Domingo conference is published in English in Hennelly, *Santo Domingo and Beyond*.

38. http://www.eventoscatolicos.net.

39. Its station, Radio 940AM, made itself available online through its Web address, http://www.eventoscatolicos.net.

40. http://www.eventoscatolicos.net.

41. Escobar, "Orlando Coronado Desde Los Ojos de la Fe."

42. Programming available at http://www.radioestrella.com.

43. http://www.hombrescatolicosenaccion.org.

44. See Manz, *Paradise in Ashes*.

45. César Folgar was available for viewing on YouTube.

46. Ministers of music have long been a part of many parishes. The term "Charismatic ministers of praise" refers more to individual performers.

47. http://www.giovanniblanco.com.

48. http://www.reddemusicacatolica.com.

49. PMV Special Note, 3.

50. *La Hora*, July 18, 1990.

51. Chesnut, *Competitive Spirits*, 68.

52. A smaller national festival of Marian song was entering its eighth year in Peru.

53. Interviews with Dr. Guidoberto Mahecha, and faculty members, Universidad Bíblica Latinoamericana, San Jose, Costa Rica, June 7, 1996.

54. In addition to high levels of religious practice, Guatemalans ranked high in world standings of the 2002 Pew Global Attitudes Project, in which 80 percent said that religion was very important to them.

55. A wider argument can be that competition has generally been good for religious groups. This argument has been made systematically by those political scientists who follow rational choice theory, as does Gill, *Rendering Unto Caesar*.

56. Interviews were also conducted at seminaries in Guatemala City and Quenaltenango.

57. For further discussion of losses, see Allen, *The Future Church*, 386–89.

58. Steigenga, "The Politics of Pentecostalized Religion," 259. Steigenga also recognized that a small number of Catholics surveyed may have been Protestants at one time.

59. Ibid., 260.

60. Gooren, "Conversion Careers in Latin America," 52–71.

61. Gelpi, *Charism and Sacrament*, 90.

62. Smilde, "Relational Analysis of Religious Conversion and Social Change."

63. Chesnut, *Born Again in Brazil*.

64. Prandi, "Religiâo paga, Conversâo e Serviço," 72.

65. Ibid.

66. Truehart, "French Lag in Charity, Giving."

67. Interviews, 1958–62.

68. Petersen, "The Formation of Popular, National, and Autonomous Churches in Central America," 3.

69. Llana, "Wealth Gospel Propels Poor Guatemalans."

70. Garrard-Burnett, *Protestantism in Guatemala*, 165.

71. Ibid.

72. Wuthnow, *Christianity in the Twenty-first Century*, 183–91.

73. The Vatican underwent severe financial shortages in the late twentieth century.

74. Calder, "Interwoven Histories," 93–94.

75. PMV Special Note, 3.

BIBLIOGRAPHY

"40 Años Sirviendo a la Iglesia Católica 1967–2007." *Renovación Carismática Católica.* http://www.rcca.org.py (accessed Nov. 14, 2008).

Abbott, Elizabeth. *Haiti: The Duvaliers and Their Legacy.* New York: McGraw-Hill, 1988.

Allen, John. *The Future Church.* New York: Doubleday, 2009.

Anderson, Robert Mapes. *Vision of the Disinherited.* New York: Oxford University Press, 1979.

Annis, Sheldon. *God and Production in a Guatemalan Town.* Austin: University of Texas Press, 1987.

Antoniazzi, Albert. "As transformaôes e o futuro da paroquia." *Jornal de Opináo* (March 19–25, 2001): 6–7.

Applebome, Peter. "Is Eloquence Over?" *New York Times,* Jan. 13, 2008, Week in Review section.

Araujo, Artur. "Padre Harold admite tendecia ao alcoolismo." *Diário del Povo* (Campinas), Sept. 2, 1996.

"A Renovaçâo Carismática Católica no Brasil." http://www.rccbrasil.org.br (accessed Dec. 16, 2007).

Bainbridge, William, and Rodney Stark. *A Theory of Religion.* New Brunswick, N.J.: Rutgers University Press, 1996.

Bantjes, Adrian. "Popular Religion and the Mexican Revolution: Towards a New Historiography." In *Religious Cultures in Modern Mexico,* ed. Martin Nesvig, 222–40. Lanham, Md.: Rowman and Littlefield, 2007.

Barrett, David, P. F. Crossing, and Todd Johnson. "Missiometrics." *International Bulletin of Missionary Research* 32, no. 1 (Jan. 2008): 29.

Barrett, David, and Todd Johnson. "The Catholic Charismatic Renewal, 1959–2025." In *Then Peter Stood Up . . . ,* ed. Oreste Pesare, 118–31. Vatican City: International Catholic Charismatic Renewal Services, 2000.

———. *World Christian Encyclopedia.* 2nd ed. New York: Oxford University Press, 2001.

Bastide, Roger. *African Civilizations in the New World.* New York: Harper and Row, 1971.

Bastien, R. *La familia rural haitiana.* Mexico City: Libra, 1951.

Benedetti, Luiz Roberto. "O 'novo clero': Arcaico ou moderno?" *Revista Eclesiástica Brasileira* 59, no. 2 (Jan. 1999): 88–126.

Betances, Emelio. *The Catholic Church and Power Politics in Latin America: The Dominican Case in Comparative Perspective.* Lanham, Md.: Rowman and Littlefield, 2007.

Betto, Frei. *Fidel and Religion: Castro Talks on Revolution and Religion with Frei Betto.* New York: Simon and Schuster, 1987.

Boff, Clovodis. "Carísmaticos e libertadores na Igreja." *Revista Eclesiástica Brasileira* 60, no. 237 (March 2000): 36–53.

Boff, Leonardo. *Etica da vida.* Brasília: Letraviva, 1999.

Bourassa, Louisa. "Canada's Charismatic Province." *New Covenant* (May 1976): 27–31.

Bowen, Kurt. *Evangelism and Apostasy: The Evolution and Impact of Evangelicals in Modern Mexico.* Montreal: McGill University Press, 1996.

Brazilian Bishops Conference. "Basic Christian Communities (1982)." In *The Path from Puebla: Significant Documents of the Latin American Bishops since 1979*, ed. Edward L. Cleary, 44. Washington, D.C.: National Conference of Catholic Bishops, 1988.

Bromley, David, ed. *New Developments in Theory and Research.* Greenwich, Conn.: JAI Press, 1991.

Brooke, James. "Religious Issue Roils Colombia." *New York Times*, June 19, 1994. http://www.nytimes.com (accessed March 20, 2009).

Brouwer, Janneke. "Nieuwe scheppingen in Christus." M.A. thesis, Utrecht University, 2000.

Buechler, Hans. *The Masked Media: Aymara Fiestas and Social Interaction in the Bolivian Highlands.* New York: Mouton, 1980.

Bundy, David D. "Cursillo Movement." In *The New International Dictionary of the Pentecostal and Charismatic Movements*, ed. Stanley Burgess, 567–68. Grand Rapids, Mich.: Zondervan, 2003.

Bunson, Matthew, ed. *Catholic Almanac.* Huntington, Ind.: Our Sunday Visitor Press, 2003.

Burgess, Stanley. "Neocharismatics." In *The New International Dictionary of the Pentecostal and Charismatic Movements*, ed. Stanley Burgess, 928. Grand Rapids, Mich.: Zondervan, 2003.

———, ed. *The New International Dictionary of the Pentecostal and Charismatic Movements.* Grand Rapids, Mich.: Zondervan, 2003.

Calder, Bruce. "Interwoven Histories." In *Resurgent Voices in Latin America: Indigenous Peoples, Political Mobilization, and Religious Change*, ed. Edward L. Cleary and Timothy J. Steigenga. New Brunswick, N.J.: Rutgers University Press, 2006.

Calvin College Summer Institutes. Calvin College. http://www.calvin.edu/summer-institutes (accessed Jan. 8, 2008).

Camp, Roderic A. *Crossing Swords: Politics and Religion in Mexico.* New York: Oxford, 1997.

Carranza, Brenda. *Renovaçào Carismática Católica: Origens, mudanças e tendências.* Aparecida: Editora Santuário, 2000.

CBS *Early Show*, Oct. 19, 2007.

CBS *Sixty Minutes*, aired on Oct. 14, 2007, updated on Dec. 20, 2007.

———, aired Dec. 24, 2007.

Censo Nacional de la RCC. http://www.rccperu.org (accessed July 26, 2005).

Center for Applied Research in the Apostolate. "Comparative Study of Electoral Systems." Georgetown University. cara.georgetown.edu (accessed April 11, 2009).

———. "World Values Survey." Georgetown University. cara.georgetown.edu (accessed April 11, 2009).

Cerdi, Elizabeth Juárez. "El Dios, que a todos otorgó la heredad, el reino, el sacerdocio, la santidad." *Relaciones: Estudios de Historia y Sociedad* 16, no. 65–66 (1996): 107–22.

"Changing Faiths: Latinos and the Transformation of American Religion." Washington, D.C.: Pew Hispanic Center, 2007. http://www.pewforum.org (accessed Aug. 16, 2008).

Chesnut, Andrew. *Born Again in Brazil: The Pentecostal Boom and the Pathogens of Poverty.* New Brunswick, N.J.: Rutgers University Press, 1997.

———. *Competitive Spirits: Latin America's New Religious Economy.* New York: Oxford University Press, 2003.

———. "Specialized Spirits: Conversion and the Products of Pneumacentric Religion in Latin America's Free Market of Faith." In *Conversion of a Continent: Contemporary Religious Change in Latin America*, ed. Timothy Steigenga and Edward Cleary, 72–92. New Brunswick, N.J.: Rutgers University Press, 2007.

Cleary, Edward L. *Crisis and Change: The Church in Latin America Today.* Maryknoll, N.Y.: Orbis, 1985.

———. "Evangelicals and Competition in Guatemala." In *Conflict and Competition: The Latin American Church in a Changing Environment*, ed. Edward L. Cleary and Hannah Stewart-Gambino. Boulder, Colo.: Lynne Rienner, 1992.

———. *How Latin America Saved the Soul of the Catholic Church.* Mahwah, N.J.: Paulist Press, 2009.

———. *Mobilizing for Human Rights in Latin America.* Bloomfield, Conn.: Kumarian Press, 2007.

———, ed. *The Path from Puebla: Significant Documents of the Latin American Bishops since 1979.* Washington, D.C.: National Conference of Catholic Bishops, 1988.

———. *Resurgent Voices in Latin America: Indigenous Peoples, Political Mobilization, and Religious Change.* New Brunswick, N.J.: Rutgers University Press, 2006.

———. "Shopping Around: Questions about Latin American Conversions." *International Bulletin of Missionary Research* 28, no. 2 (April 2004): 50–54.

———. "The Vitality of Religion in a Changing Context." In *Latin America and Carib-*

bean Contemporary Record, vol. 8, ed. James Malloy and Eduardo Gamarra. New York: Holmes and Meier, 1996.

Congar, Yves. *I Believe in the Holy Spirit.* Vol. 2. New York: Seabury, 1983.

Consejo Episcopal Latinoamericano. *De una pastoral indigenista a una pastoral indígena.* Bogotá: Consejo Episcopal Latinoamericano, 1987.

Considine, John. *A Call for Forty Thousand.* New York: Longmans, Green, 1946.

———. *New Horizons in Latin America.* New York: Dodd, Mead, 1957.

Córdova, Alberto Pozo. *El movimiento cárismatico en Costa Rica.* San José, Costa Rica: Universidad Nacional de Heredia, 1979.

Costello, Gerald. *Mission to Latin America: The Successes and Failures of a Twentieth-Century Crusade.* Maryknoll, N.Y.: Orbis, 1979.

Csordas, Thomas. *Language, Charisma, and Creativity: Ritual Life of a Religious Movement.* Berkeley: University of California Press, 1997.

Cuttita, Chrissy. "Spirits Lifted during 27th Annual Charismatic Conference." http://www.thefloridacatholic.org (accessed April 30, 2009).

Davis, Wade. *Passage of Darkness: The Ethnobiology of the Haitian Zombie.* Chapel Hill: University of North Carolina Press, 1988.

Deck, Allan Figueroa. *The Second Wave: Hispanic Ministry and the Evangelization of Cultures.* New York: Paulist Press, 1989.

Delgado, José María. "Renovación Carismática en Guatemala." *Estudios Teológicos* (July–Dec. 1975). http://www.ecclaguatemala.org (accessed May 24, 2008).

Deren, Maya. *The Divine Horsemen: The Voodoo Gods of Haiti.* New York: Delta Publishing, 1972.

"Desenvolvimento e outros desafios." Ministerio Universidades Renovadas. http://www.universidadesrenovadas.com (accessed Dec. 27, 2007).

Desmangles, Leslie. *The Faces of the Gods: Vodou and Roman Catholicism in Haiti.* Chapel Hill: University of North Carolina Press, 1992.

Díaz de la Serna, María Cristina. *El movimiento de la Renovación Carismática.* Mexico City: Universidad Autonoma Metropolitana—Iztapalapa, 1985.

Díaz-Stevens, Ana María. *Ox-Cart Catholicism on Fifth Avenue.* Notre Dame, Ind.: University of Notre Dame Press, 1993.

Díaz-Stevens, Ana María, and Antonio Stevens-Arroyo. *Recognizing the Latino Resurgence in U.S. Religion: The Emmaus Paradigm.* Boulder, Colo.: Westview, 1998.

"The Diocesis of Kansas City." *The Catholic Key,* Nov. 11, 2007. http://www.catholickey.org (accessed March 3, 2009).

DiPrizio, George. *Dios Mío, Necesito Algo.* 1987. http://www.carismaenmisiones.com (accessed Oct. 8, 2008).

Dolan, Jay P. *Catholic Revivalism: The American Experience, 1830–1900.* Notre Dame, Ind.: University of Notre Dame Press, 1978.

Dries, Angelyn. *The Missionary Movement in American Church History.* Maryknoll, N.Y.: Orbis, 1998.

Duffy, Eamon. *Marking the Hours: English People and Their Prayers 1240–1570*. New Haven, Conn.: Yale University Press, 2006.

———. *The Stripping of the Altars: Traditional Religion in England 1400–1580*. New Haven, Conn.: Yale University Press, 1992.

———. *Walking to Emmaus*. New York: Burns and Oates, 2006.

Duin, Julia. "Evangelization 2000." *Christianity Today*, Feb. 6, 1987. http://www.missionfrontiers.org (accessed April 30, 2008).

Eagleson, John, and Philip Scharper, eds., *Puebla and Beyond*. Maryknoll, N.Y.: Orbis, 1979.

Elizaga, Julio C. *La renovación Carismática en la Iglesia Católica*. Buenos Aires: Lumen, 2005.

"Emisora Minuto de Dios 1.230 A.M.: Su Portal de Internet." http://www.cristomania.com.

"Encuentro Ecuménico en Buenos Aires." http://www.cristianos.com.ar (accessed Nov. 2, 2008).

Encuentro Episcopal Latinoamericano. "La renovación carismática católica." La Ceja, 1987. http://www.rcc.cuba.cu (accessed Feb. 8, 2008).

Escobar, José Luis. "Orlando Coronado Desde Los Ojos de la Fe." *Siglo 21* (June 4, 2008). http://www.sigloxxi.com/ (accessed May 27, 2008).

Escuelas de Evangelización San Andrés. "Proyecto Pastoral San Andrés 2006." http://www.evangelizacion.com (accessed March 18, 2008).

———. http://www.evangelizacion.com/predicadores (accessed March 7, 2008).

Espín, Olivia. *Latina Realities: Essays on Healing, Sexuality, and Migration*. Boulder, Colo.: Westview, 1997.

Espinosa, Gastón, Virgilio Elizando, and Jesse Miranda. *Hispanic Churches in American Public Life: Summary of Findings*. http://www.latinostudie.nd.edu (accessed April 29, 2009).

Eventos Católicos. http://www.eventoscatolicos.org/ (accessed May 27, 2008).

Fernández, Oscar Uzín, and Jaime Ponce García. *El clero en Bolivia*. La Paz: Instituto Boliviano de Estudio y Acción Social, 1979.

Fe y Razon. http://www.feyrazon.org (accessed Nov. 14, 2008).

Finke, Roger, and Rodney Stark. *The Churching of America, 1776–1990: Winners and Losers in Our Religious Economy*. New Brunswick, N.J.: Rutgers University Press, 1992.

Foweraker, Joe. *Theorizing Social Movements*. Boulder, Colo.: Pluto Press, 1995.

Foweraker, Joe, and Ann Craig. *Popular Movements and Political Change in Mexico*. Boulder, Colo.: Lynne Rienner, 1990.

Freston, Paul. "Charismatic Evangelicals in Latin America: Mission and Politics on the Frontiers of Protestant Growth." In *Charismatic Christianity: Sociological Perspectives*, ed. Malcolm Hamilton, Stephen Hunt, and Tony Walter. New York: St. Martin's Press, 1997.

————. *Evangelicals and Politics in Asia, Africa, and Latin America.* New York: Cambridge University Press, 2001.

————. *Protestant Political Parties: A Global Survey.* Burlington, Vt.: Ashgate, 2004.

Froehle, Bryan. "The Catholic Church and Politics in Venezuela: Resource Limitations, Religious Competition, and Democracy." In *Conflict and Competition: The Latin American Church in a Changing Environment*, ed. Edward L. Cleary and Hannah Stewart-Gambino, 105–127. Boulder, Colo.: Lynne Rienner, 1992.

Froehle, Bryan, and Mary Gautier. *Global Catholicism: Portrait of a World Church.* Maryknoll, N.Y.: Orbis, 2003.

Garrard-Burnett, Virginia. *Protestantism in Guatemala: Living in the New Jerusalem.* Austin: University of Texas Press, 1998.

————. "Stop Suffering: The Iglesia Universal del Reino de Dios in the United States." In *Conversion of a Continent: Contemporary Religious Change in Latin America*, ed. Timothy J. Steigenga and Edward L. Cleary, 218–237.

Gelpi, Donald. *Charism and Sacrament: A Theology of Christian Conversion.* Mahwah, N.J.: Paulist Press, 1976.

————. "Conversion." *Dialog: Journal of Theology* 41, no. 1 (Spring 2002): 32.

————. *Pentecostalism: A Theological Viewpoint.* New York: Paulist Press, 1971.

Gill, Anthony. *Rendering Unto Caesar: The Catholic Church and State in Latin America.* Chicago: University of Chicago Press, 1998.

Giraldo, Juan David. "Biography of Father Rafael." In *La Biblioteca Luis Angel Arango.* http://www.lablaa.org (accessed Jan. 26, 2008).

Gómez, Salvador. *Formación de predicadores.* Mexico City: Publicaciones Kerygma, 2007.

Gonzalez, Elmer. "Música y religión." *Latin Beat*, Aug. 1, 1997; *High Beam Encyclopedia*, http://www.encyclopedia.com (accessed July 14, 2009).

González, Roberto. *Caminos de la Nueva Evangelización en Puerto Rico.* Bogotá: Lito Camargo, Ltda., 2001.

Gooren, Henri. "Conversion Careers in Latin America: Entering and Leaving Church Among Pentecostals, Catholics, and Mormons." In *Conversion of a Continent: Contemporary Religious Change in Latin America*, ed. Timothy J. Steigenga and Edward L. Cleary, 52–71. New Brunswick, N.J.: Rutgers University Press, 2007.

Gorski, John. "How the Catholic Church in Latin America Became Missionary." *International Bulletin of Missionary Research* 27, no. 2 (April 2003): 57–63.

Gotay, Samuel Silva. *Catolicismo y política en Puerto Rico: Bajo España y Estados Unidos; Siglos XIX y XX.* San Juan: Editorial de la Universidad de Puerto Rico, 2005.

Haddox, Benjamín. *Sociedad y religión en Colombia.* Bogotá: Tercer Mundo, 1965.

Hayford, Jack, and S. David Moore. *The Charismatic Century: The Enduring Impact of the Azuza Street Revival.* New York: Warner Books, 2006.

Hennelly, Alfred, ed. *Santo Domingo and Beyond.* Maryknoll, N.Y.: Orbis, 1993.

"Historia de la Comunidad Jesús es el Señor." http://www.jessquito.com (accessed Nov. 11, 2008).

Hocken, Peter. "Charismatic Movement." In *The New International Dictionary of the Pentecostal and Charismatic Movements*, ed. Stanley Burgess, 477–519. Grand Rapids, Mich.: Zondervan, 2003.

———. "Ralph Martin." In *The New International Dictionary of the Pentecostal and Charismatic Movements*, ed. Stanley Burgess, 861–62. Grand Rapids, Mich.: Zondervan, 2003.

Holland, Clifton. "Historia y cronología del movimiento de renovación carismática en América Latina." http://www.prolades.org.

———. "Serie de Perfiles Socioreligiosos Nacionales sobre Nuevos Movimientos Religiosos: Costa Rica." Programa Latinoamericano de Estudios Socioreligiosos, San Pedro, Costa Rica. http://www.prolades.com (accessed June 7, 2008).

Hollander, Kurt. "The Great Parade of Easter Devotion." *New York Times*, March 16, 2008, Travel section.

Holleran, Mary P. *Church and State in Guatemala*. New York: Columbia University Press, 1949.

Hunt, Stephen, Malcolm Hamilton, and Tony Walter, eds. *Charismatic Christianity: Sociological Perspectives*. New York: St. Martin's Press, 1997.

Iannaccone, Laurence. "Religious Markets and the Economics of Religion." *Social Compass* 39, no. 1 (1992): 123.

Jaramillo, Diego. *Rafael García Herreros: Una vida y una obra*. Bogotá: Editorial Minuto de Dios, 1984.

Jenkins, Philip. *The Next Christendom: The Coming of Global Christianity*. Oxford and New York: Oxford University Press, 2002.

"Joel Osteen Answers His Critics." *CBS News*, Dec. 23, 2007. http://www.cbsnews.com (accessed Jan. 20, 2007).

John Paul II. *Ecclesia in America. Caminos de Conversión* no. 28. Online at http://www.vatican.va (accessed Jan. 22, 1999).

Judd, Stephen. "The Indigenous Theology Movement in Latin America." In *Resurgent Voices in Latin America*, ed. Edward L. Cleary and Timothy J. Steigenga. New Brunswick, N.J.: Rutgers University Press, 2004.

Keller, John M. "Father Harold Rahm Receives Award." Drug Prevention Network of the Americas. http://www.dpna.org (accessed Dec. 18, 2007).

Kelly, David. *History: Guatemala–El Salvador Region, 1943–1969*. Guatemala City: Maryknoll Missioners, 1969.

Kepel, Gilles. *The Revenge of God: The Resurgence of Islam, Christianity, and Judaism in the Modern World*. University Park: Pennsylvania State University Press, 1994.

Kirk, John M. "Waiting for John Paul II: The Church in Cuba." In *Conflict and Competition: The Latin American Church in a Changing Environment*, ed. Edward L. Cleary and Hannah Stewart-Gambino, 147–66. Boulder, Colo.: Lynne Rienner, 1992.

Klaiber, Jeffrey. *The Church, Dictatorship, and Democracy in Latin America*. New York: Maryknoll, 1998.

"Legionnaires of Christ." http://www.legionairiesofchrist.org (accessed July 14, 2001).

Lemego, María, and Harold Rahm. *Sereis batizados no Espírito*. São Paulo: Edicôes Loyola, 1972.

Lida, David. *First Stop in the New World: Mexico City, the Capital of the 21st Century*. New York: Riverhead Books, 2008.

Liebscher, Arthur. "The Catholic Church in Argentine Society: Córdoba, 1883–1928." Master of Sacred Theology thesis, Jesuit School of Theology, Berkeley, 1986.

Lima, Samarone, and Thaís Oyama. "Católicos en transe." *Veja*, Aug. 4, 1998. http://www.veja.abril.co.br (accessed Dec. 21, 2007).

Linero, Alberto. "Reflecciones sobre la música." Mi Riohacha. http://www.miriohacha.com (accessed Jan. 30, 2008).

Llana, Sara Miller. "Wealth Gospel Propels Poor Guatemalans." *Christian Science Monitor*, Dec. 17, 2007. http://www.csmonitor.com (accessed June 5, 2008).

Loarca, Carlos. "Nombran Arzobispo de Los Altos." *Prensa Libre*, April 20, 2007. http://www.prensalibre.com (accessed May 26, 2008).

Lorentzen, Lois Ann. *Religion at the Corner of Bliss and Nirvana*. Durham, N.C.: Duke University Press, 2009.

MacKinnon, J. B. *Dead Man in Paradise*. New York: New Press, 2007.

MacNutt, Francis. *Deliverance from Evil Spirits: A Practical Guide*. Grand Rapids, Mich.: Baker Books, 1995.

———. "First Latin American Charismatic Leadership Conference." Unpublished notes.

———. *Healing*. Notre Dame, Ind.: Ave Maria Press, 1974.

———. *The Nearly Perfect Crime: How the Church Almost Killed the Ministry of Healing*. Grand Rapids, Mich.: Baker, 2005.

Mainwaring, Scott, and Alexander Wilde, eds. *The Progressive Church in Latin America*. Notre Dame, Ind.: University of Notre Dame Press, 1989.

Mallimaci, Fortunato. "El catolicismo latinoamericano al fines del milenio: Incertidumbre desde el Cono Sur." *Nueva Sociedad* 136 (March–April 1995): 170.

Maney, Thomas. *Basic Communities: A Practical Guide for Renewing Neighborhood Churches*. Minneapolis: Winston Press, 1984.

Manz, Beatriz. *Paradise in Ashes: A Guatemalan Journey of Courage, Terror, and Hope*. Berkeley: University of California Press, 2004.

Marcelli, Enrico, and Wayne Cornelius. "The Changing Profile of Mexican Migrants to the United States." *Latin American Research Review* 36, no. 3 (2001): 105–111.

Mariz, Cecília. "Comunidades de vida no Espirito Santo: Um modelo novo da familia?" Presented at 8th Congreso Luso-Afro Brasileiro, Coimbra, Portugal, Sept. 2004.

———. *Coping with Poverty*. Philadelphia: Temple University Press, 1994.

Martin, David. *Pentecostalism: The World Their Parish*. Oxford: Blackwell, 2002.

Martin, Ralph, and Peter Williamson. *John Paul II and the New Evangelization*. Cincinnati: St. Anthony Messenger Press, 2006.

Martínez, Albesa. *La Constitución de 1857: Catolicismo y liberalismo en México*. Mexico City: Porrúa, 2007.

McAlister, Elizabeth. "The Madonna of 115th Street Revisited: Vodou and Catholicism in an Age of Transnationalism." In *Gatherings in Diaspora: Religious Communities and the New Immigration*, ed. S. R. Warner and E. G. Wittner, 123–60. Philadelphia: Temple University Press, 1998.

McConahay, Mary Jo. "Latest Battle in Nicaragua Is in Schools: Where the Prize Is Minds and Hearts of Children." *National Catholic Reporter* 26 (Aug. 10, 1990).

McDonnell, Kilian. "Catholic Charismatic Renewal." In *New Catholic Encyclopedia*, 2nd ed., 392–93. Detroit: Thomson-Gale, 2002.

———. *Catholic Pentecostalism: Problems in Evaluation*. Pecos, N. Mex.: Dove Publications, 1970.

———. *Charismatic Renewal and the Churches*. New York: Seabury Press, 1976.

———. "The Death of Mythologies: The Classical Pentecostal/Roman Catholic Dialogue." *America* 172 (March 25, 1995).

McGrath, Marcos. "Signs of the Times in Latin America Today." In *The Church in the Present-Day Transformation of Latin America in the Light of the Council*, 1: 97–106. Bogotá: Conferencia Episcopal de América Latina, 1970.

Meléndez, Libni Sanjurjo. "Católicos con nueva diócese y obispo." *Primera Hora*, March 12, 2008. http://www.primerahora.com (accessed April 14, 2009).

Menzies, William. *Anointed to Serve*. Springfield, Mo.: Gospel Publishing House, 1971.

Métraux, Alfred. "Les rites d'initiation dans le Vodou häitien." *Tribus* (Linden Museum, Stuttgart), n.s. 4/5 (1954–55): 177–98.

———. *Voodoo in Haiti*. New York: Schocken, 1972.

Meunier, E. Martin, and Jean-Philippe Warren. *Sortier de la Grande Noirceur: L'horizon personnaliste de la revolution tranquille*. Sillery, Québec: Septentrion, 2002.

Ministerio de Hombres Católicos en Acción. http://www.hombrescatolicosenaccion.org/ (accessed May 27, 2008).

Mintz, Sidney. Introduction to *Voodoo in Haiti*, 2nd ed., by Alfred Métraux, 1–20. New York: Schocken, 1989.

———. "Toward an Afro-American History." *Cahier d'histoire mondiale* 13 (1971): 317–32.

Miranda, Julia. *Carisma, sociedade e política: Novas linguagens do religioso e do politico*. Rio de Janeiro: Relume Demará, 1999.

Montoya, Juan. "Encuentro Personal con El Señor." http://www.rcc-concepción.cl.

"More Hispanics Losing Their Religion." *USA Today*, Dec. 12, 2002. http://www.usa-today.com (accessed Sept. 24, 2004).

Moreno, Francisco José. *Before Fidel: The Cuba I Remember*. Austin: University of Texas Press, 2007.

National Conference of Brazilian Bishops. *Orientaçôes Pastorais sobre el RCC*. Brasília. Nov. 1994.

Nesvig, Martin Austin. Introduction to *Religious Culture in Modern Mexico*, ed. Martin Austin Nesvig, 1–17. Lanham, Md.: Rowman and Littlefield, 2007.

Nolan, David. *The Ideology of the Sandinistas and the Nicaraguan Revolution*. Coral Gables: Fl.: Institute of Interamerican Studies, University of Miami, 1984.

Obispos del Sur. *Por la dignificación del pueblo mapuche*. Temuco, Chile: Obispado de Temuco, 2001.

O'Connor, Edward D. *Perspectives on Charismatic Renewal*. Notre Dame, Ind.: University of Notre Dame Press, 1975.

———. *Pope Paul and the Spirit: Charisms and Church Renewal in the Teaching of Paul VI*. Notre Dame, Ind.: Ave Maria Press, 1978.

Oliveira, Pedro A. "O Catolicismo: De CEBs á Renovacâo Carismática." *Revista Brasileira Eclesiástica* 59 (1999): 823–35.

Panorama Católico Internacional. http://www.panodigital.com (accessed Nov. 2, 2008).

Parker, Cristián. *Popular Religion and Modernization in Latin America*. Maryknoll, N.Y.: Orbis, 1996.

Pesare, Oreste, ed. *Then Peter Stood Up....* Vatican City: International Catholic Charismatic Renewal Services, 2000.

Petersen, Douglas. "The Formation of Popular, National, and Autonomous Pentecostal Churches in Central America." *Pneuma* 16, no. 1 (1998): 23–48.

Peterson, Anna, and Manuel Vásquez. "Upwards, Never Down: The Catholic Charismatic Renewal in Transnational Perspective." In *Christianity, Social Change, and Globalization in the Americas*, ed. Anna Peterson, Manuel Vásquez, and Philip Williams, 185–209. New Brunswick, N.J.: Rutgers University Press, 2001.

Peterson, Anna, Manuel Vásquez, and Philip Williams, ed. *Christianity, Social Change, and Globalization in the Americas*. New Brunswick, N.J.: Rutgers University Press, 2001.

Pew Forum. "Spirit and Power: A 10-Country Survey of Pentecostals, October 2006." Pew Forum on Religion and Public Life. http://www.pewforum.org (accessed Jan. 21, 2008).

PMV Special Note 15 (Oct. 1970): 3. Published by the Pro Mundi Vita Institute in Brussels.

Prandi, J. Reginaldo. "Religiâo paga, Conversâo e Serviço." *Novos Estudos* 45 (July 1996): 72.

Prentiss, Craig. "John Paul II and the Catholic Charismatic Renewal." In *The New International Dictionary of the Pentecostal and Charismatic Movements*, ed. Stanley Burgess. Grand Rapids, Mich.: Zondervan, 2003.

Price-Mars, J. *Ainsi parle l'oncle*. Port-au-Prince: Imprimerie La Phlange, 1928.

Pulido, Erling. "32 Años de Historia de la Renovación Carismática Católica de Venezuela." http://www.rccvenezuela.com (accessed Oct. 30, 2008).

Rahner, Karl. "Notes on the Lay Apostolate." In *Theological Investigations* 2: 319–52. Baltimore: Helicon, 1963.

Ramirez, Margaret. "Preacher Bringing Prosperity Gospel to Chicago," *Chicago Tribune*, Aug. 16, 2007.

Ramirez, Ricardo. "Stewardship Tradition in U.S. Hispanic Communities." *Origins* 28, no. 18 (Oct. 1998).

Raycraft, Helen Marie. *Fruit of Our Labor: Experiences in Evangelization*. San Antonio: Centro de Comunicación, Misioneros Oblatos de María Inmaculada, 1980.

Red de Música Católica. "Música Católica." http://www.reddemusicacatolica.com/ (accessed May 20, 2008).

"The Renewalist Movement and Hispanic Christianity." In *Spirit and Power: A Ten-Country Study of Pentecostals*. Washington, D.C.: Pew Forum on Religion and Public Life, 2006. http://www.pewforum.org (accessed April 15, 2009).

Renovación Carismática Católica de Cuba. http://www.rccuba.com (accessed Dec. 16, 2007).

Renovación Carismática Católica de Peru. http://www.rccperu.org (accessed Oct. 2008).

Renovación Carismática Católica de Venezuela. http://www.rccvenezuela.com (accessed Nov. 5, 2008).

Rey, Terry. "Marian Devotion at a Haitian Catholic Parish in Miami: The Feast of Our Lady of Perpetual Help." *Journal of Contemporary Religion* 19, no. 3 (2004): 353–74.

Richman, Karen. "Anchored in Haiti and Docked in Miami." Unpublished paper for Social Science Group on Religion, Immigration, and Civic Life, December 20, 2001.

Rivière, Gilles. "Bolivia: El pentecostalismo en la sociedad aymara del Altiplano." *Nuevo Mundo*. http://www.nuevomundo.revues.org (accessed March 2, 2009).

Roach, Daniel, and Gugui Roda de Sauto. *Cris y Daniel: Los principios de la Mansión*. Santa Cruz de la Sierra: La Mansión, 2003.

Robertson, Roland. "The Globalization Paradigm: Thinking Globally." In *New Developments in Theory and Research*, ed. David Bromley. Greenwich, Conn.: JAI Press, 1991.

Rodríguez, Teófilo. "Quarenta Años de Renovación Carísmatica." http://www.panoramacatolico.com/ (accessed Oct. 12, 2008).

Ross, Dick, and Ken Curtis, producers. *The Cross and the Switchblade*. Worcester, Pa.: Vision Video, 2003.

Rubín, Sergio. "Encuentro religioso entre evangélicos y católicos carismáticos." *El Clarín*, Aug. 27, 2007.

Sáez, José Luis. *Los Jesuitas*. Santo Domingo: Museo Nacional de Historia y Geografía, n.d.

Sales, Joâo Batista Malagâes. *Renovacâo Carismático do Brasil*. Belo Horizonte: Loyola, 2006.

Sanneh, Lamin. *Disciples of All Nations: Pillars of World Christianity*. New York: Oxford University Press, 2007.

Sarmiento, Nicanor. *Caminos de la teología india*. Cochabamba: Editorial Verbo Divino, 2000.

Scanlon, Michael. *Inner Healing*. New York: Paulist, 1974.

Second General Conference of Latin American Bishops. "Conclusions." In *The Church in the Present-Day Transformation of Latin America in the Light of the Council*, 2: 55–268. Bogotá: General Secretariat of CELAM, 1970.

Seguy, Jean. *Christianisme et societé: Introduction a la sociologie de E. Troelstch*. Paris: Cerf, 1980.

Serbin, Kenneth. "Brazil." In *Religious Freedom and Evangelization in Latin America: The Challenge of Religious Pluralism*, ed. Paul Sigmund. Maryknoll, N.Y.: Orbis, 1999.

Sheppard, J. W. "Sociology of World Pentecostalism." In *The New International Dictionary of the Pentecostal and Charismatic Movements*, ed. Stanley Burgess. Grand Rapids, Mich.: Zondervan, 2003.

Sieder, Rachel. *Multiculturalism in Latin America: Indigenous Rights, Diversity, and Democracy*. New York: Palgrave Macmillan, 2002.

Smilde, David. "Contradiction without Paradox: Evangelical Political Culture in the 1998 Venezuelan Elections." *Latin American Politics and Society* 46 (Spring 2004): 75–102.

———. *Reason to Believe: Cultural Agency in Latin American Evangelicalism*. Berkeley, Calif.: University of California Press, 2007.

———. "Relational Analysis of Religious Conversion and Social Change: Networks and Publics in Latin American Evangelicalism." In *Conversion of a Continent: Contemporary Religious Change in Latin America*, ed. Timothy J. Steigenga and Edward Cleary, 93–114. New Brunswick, N.J.: Rutgers University Press, 2007.

Smith, Anthony D. "Toward Global Culture?" In *Global Culture: Nationalism, Globalization, and Modernity*, ed. Mike Featherstone. New York: Sage, 1990.

Smith, Christian. *Moral Believing Animals: Human Personhood and Culture*. Oxford: Oxford University Press, 2007.

Soneira, Abelardo. "La Renovación Carismática Católica en la Argentina: Religiosidad popular, comunidad emocional, o nuevo movimiento religioso?" *Scripta Ethnológica* 22 (2000): 149–61.

———. *La Renovación Carísmatica Católica en la República Argentina: Entre el carisma y la institución.* Buenos Aires: Educa, 2001.

———. "Quiénes son los carismáticos?" *Sociedad y Religión* (1999): 18, 41–54.

Sonnichsen, C. L. *Pass of the North: Four Centuries on the Rio Grande.* El Paso: Texas Western Press, 1980.

Souza, André Ricardo de. *Igreja in Concert: Padres Cantores, Mídia e Marketing.* São Paulo: Annablume, 2005.

"Spirit-filled Weekend Set." http://www.thefloridacatholic.org (accessed April 29, 2009).

Stark, Rodney. *The Rise of Christianity: How the Obscure, Marginal, Jesus Movement Became the Dominant Religious Force.* New York: HarperOne, 1997.

Steigenga, Timothy J. "The Politics of Pentecostalized Religion." In *Conversion of a Continent: Contemporary Religious Change in Latin America,* ed. Timothy J. Steigenga and Edward L. Cleary, 256–79. New Brunswick, N.J.: Rutgers University Press, 2007.

Steigenga, Timothy J., and Edward L. Cleary, eds. *Conversion of a Continent: Contemporary Religious Change in Latin America.* New Brunswick, N.J.: Rutgers University Press, 2007.

Stoll, David. "Historia y cronología del movimiento de renovación carismática en América Latina." The Religion-in-the Americas (RITA) Database. Revised Feb. 15, 2007. http://www.prolades.com (accessed Oct. 9, 2008).

Strasser, Richard. *Music Business: The Key Concepts.* New York: Routledge, 2010.

Sullivan, Francis. "Vatican II." In *The New International Dictionary of the Pentecostal and Charismatic Movements,* ed. Stanley Burgess. Grand Rapids, Mich.: Zondervan, 2003.

Synan, Vinson. *The Holiness-Pentecostal Tradition.* Grand Rapids, Mich.: Eerdmans, 2000.

Talavera, Arturo Fontaine, and Harald Beyers. "Retrato del movimiento evangélico a la luz de las encuestas de opinión pública." *Estudios Públicos* 44 (Spring 1991).

Taylor, William B. *Magistrates of the Sacred: Priests and Parishioners in Eighteenth-Century Mexico.* Stanford, Calif.: Stanford University Press, 1996.

Terra Networks Brasil. cinema.terra.com.br (accessed Jan. 9, 2008).

Thigpen, Paul. "Catholic Charismatic Renewal." In *The New International Dictionary of the Pentecostal and Charismatic Movements,* ed. Stanley Burgess, 460–67. Grand Rapids, Mich.: Zondervan, 2003.

Trouillot, Michel-Rolph. *Haiti: State against Nation; Origins and Legacy of Duvalierism.* New York: Monthly Review Press, 1990.

Truehart, Charles. "French Lag in Charity, Giving." *International Herald Tribune,* Nov. 27, 1998.

U.S. Department of State. "Report on Religion." http://www.state.gov (accessed Oct. 15, 2008).

Versènyi, Adam. *Theater in Latin America*. New York: Cambridge University Press, 1993.

Wang, Thomas. "By the Year 2000." *Mission Frontiers* (May 1987). http://www.missionfrontiers.org (accessed April 30, 2008).

Warren, Kay. *The Symbolism of Subordination: Indian Identity in a Guatemalan Town*. Austin: University of Texas Press, 1978.

Weis, Bruno. "O bem o a banal." *IstoE* 1579 (Jan. 5, 2000).

Wilkes, Paul. *Excellent Catholic Parishes*. New York: Paulist Press, 2001.

Williams, Philip J., Timothy Steigenga, and Manuel A. Vásquez, eds. *A Place to Be: Brazilian, Guatemalan, and Mexican Immigrants in Florida's New Destinations*. New Brunswick, N.J.: Rutgers University Press, 2009.

Wilson, Everett A. "Identity, Community, and Status: The Legacy of Central American Pentecostal Pioneers." In *Earthen Vessels: American Evangelicals and Foreign Missions*, ed. Joel Carpenter and Wilbert Shenk. Grand Rapids, Mich.: Eerdmans, 1990.

Wirpsa, Leslie. "San Salvador Archbishop Ousts Jesuit Pastor of Barrio Parish." *National Catholic Reporter* (Oct. 18, 1996). http://www.findarticles.com (accessed Oct. 13, 2008).

Wuthnow, Robert. *Christianity in the Twenty-first Century: Reflections on the Challenges Ahead*. New York: Oxford University Press, 1993.

———. *I Came Away Stronger: How Small Groups Are Shaping American Religion*. Grand Rapids, Mich.: Eerdmans, 1994.

INDEX

Edward L. Cleary, professor of political science at Providence College and Visiting Scholar in Latin American studies program at Stanford University, has authored or edited eleven books, most recently *Conversion of a Continent: Religious Change in Latin America.*